Innovation for Sustainable Integrated Development in Africa

Innovation for Sustainable Integrated Development in Africa

Editors
Angathevar Baskaran & Mammo Muchie

AFRICA WORLD PRESS
TRENTON | LONDON | CAPE TOWN | NAIROBI | ADDIS ABABA | ASMARA | IBADAN | NEW DELHI

AFRICA WORLD PRESS
541 West Ingham Avenue | Suite B
Trenton, New Jersey 08638

Book design: Dawid Kahts
Cover design: Ananthy Baskaran

Cataloging-in-Publication Data may be obtained from the Library of Congress.

ISBNs: 9781569027288 (HB)
9781569027295 (PB)

Contents

Acknowledgements

We would like to thank the DST/NRF SARChI (Innovation and Development) at the Tshwane University of Technology, Pretoria, South Africa for funding this research project.

We recognize and appreciate the support given by Dr Jideofor Adibe, Adonis & Abbey Publishers Ltd, London, United Kingdom, which enabled publication of this book.

We also would like to thank the African Journal of Science, Technology, Innovation and Development (AJSTID) and extend our fullest appreciation and thanks to all the contributing authors.

We thank Jan B. Mwesigwa (www.janmwesigwa.com) our layout artist and Ananthy Baskaran, the cover designer, for their hard work and dedication to our book project. Finally, we would like to thank Divyaasiny R. Rajaghantham for her meticulous work in preparing this manuscript.

Preface:
African Unity with Innovative, Smart and Sustainable Development

Angathevar Baskaran & Mammo Muchie

The biggest challenge Africa continues to face is the unending reality that Africans still have not succeeded to own Africa. The Organisation of African Unity (OAU) was established in 1963; but the African Union is still not accomplished. Talking about unity is easy, but achieving real unity has remained difficult. Africa still remains divided with Unity talk and talk. The innovation to unite Africa is much needed to remove the reality of division. Trust, collaboration and inter-African engagement must guide the political, social, economic and ecological spheres to create innovative, renascent and united Africa where the wellbeing of the people and nature are paramount.

Africa needs an innovative theory of social capital now to unite all African people more than at any other time. If Africa unites, renascent Africa will emerge with the well-being of the people becoming the priority to make rich Africa serve the people in Africa and not those that colonised Africa. It is time to engender an innovation of hope by uniting Africa and creating social technology, social innovation and social entrepreneurship. A new culture and trust anchored collaboration with innovative, renascent and united Africa is now moreessential and necessary than at any other time.

Africa must create a new smart, integrated, sustainable African innovation system to make Africans own Africa and prevent huge wealth from flowing out of Africa. France still takes hundreds of billions of dollars by retaining the colonial pact with the former still called francophone countries.

Africa has to unite by creating a system of innovation that can remove poverty, unemployment and inequality. Africa has to unite the innovation to own the rich resources that others take as primary resources exports and after manufacturing them outside Africa by adding value import them to Africa at a higher added price.

Africa must innovate the African sovereign wealth fund to make the people achieve and secure their wellbeing, health and livelihood.

This edited book has contributions from scholars that cover a variety of areas focusing on issues and problems in the agriculture, mineral, raw material, manufacturing and services sectors driven by the hope to create innovate, integrated, sustainably developed and renascent Africa.

1

Introduction

Building Science, Technology & Innovation Research Systems for Development in African Countries

Mammo Muchie[1] & Angathevar Baskaran[2]

Africa is now facing both opportunities and challenges in the fourth industrial revolution.If it can catch-up and leapfrog into the 4th industrial revolution, Africa will make significant positive gains. The negative side is for Africa not to achieve full success by facing risks and disasters in this digital explosive internet of things and artificial intelligence cyber time.

The dangers are robotics can increase youth unemployment if actions are not taken how to create jobs and how to manage job losses through digital automation. There is also now digital gangsters and cybercrime and social media awash with the unregulated explosion of all kinds of morally and emotionally not intelligent information. Africa has to be on the march to undertake transformative innovation to generate the social, educational, political, economic and ecological, unified, smart, renascent, green, integrat-

1 DST/NRF SARChI Professor (Innovation & Development), Tshwane University of Technology, South Africa; Technology and Management Centre for Development (TMCD), Oxford University, UK; Associate Faculty Professor, Sussex University, UK; Adama Science and Technology University (ASTU), Ethiopia. Email: MuchieM@tut.ac.za

2 Associate Professor, Department of Development Studies, Faculty of Economics and Administration, University of Malaya, Malaysia; Senior Research Associate of SARChI (Innovation & Development), Tshwane University of Technology, Pretoria, South Africa. Email: baskaran@um.edu.my & anga_bas@yahoo.co.uk

ed development highway. The book on Putting Africa First: The Making of African Innovation Systems (2003) highlighted the critique of the current development promoted by both national and international organisations. No imitation of national innovation for Africa. No imitation of development economics for Africa. Africa needs a contextually anchored new model and system that synthesise transformative innovation with an African integrated and sustainable development pattern and pathway.

The real challenge is to discover how can Africa build an integrated, networked and unified innovation system for sustainable development by dealing with and responding to the complexities of the current global value chain?

Africa needs to construct an integrated, networked and unified sustainable development innovation system pathway by coming together rather than by going alone facing the prisoners' dilemma being caught within the boundaries of each of the 55 states.What to produce and where to produce and how to add value to which minerals and what market in Africa can be created need to be addressed. A new innovative approach to handle the rich resources and how to create both production applying high technology and innovation and creating consumption by making the African production to consumption value chain need to be addressed now more than at any time as the global value chain is changing dramatically by the current 4th Industrial Revolution time the world is in today.

It is possible to generate several models trying to capture as realistically as possible the uneven and lopsided existence of the innovation landscapes in the different regions in Africa (e.g. Muchie *et al*, 2003). The rise of Africa is now on the development agenda. The question is what development trajectory is evolving with this rise. According to McKinsey Global Institute report (2010), *Lions on the move: The progress and potential of African economies*, by 2010, 40 per cent of African population lived in urban areas (comparable to China's urban population) which has been continuing to expand. It estimated the number of households with discretionary income to reach 128 million by 2020 and the combined spending power of top 18 cities to reach $1.3 trillion by 2030.It also found that various macroeconomic structural changes brought about productivity revolution among African companies, which has been increasing aby 2.7 per cent annually since 2000, which helped them to achieve greater economies of scale and competitiveness.

According to another report by McKinsey Global Institute (2016), between 2000 and 2008 Africa's overall GDP growth averaged 4.9 percent a year. Although this declined to 3.3. percent between 2010 and 2015 due to problems faced by oil exporting countries due to price decline and countries affected by the political turmoil of the Arab Spring,2 in the rest of Africa, growth actually accelerated to 4.4 percent in 2010 to 2015 from 4.1 percent in 2000 to 2010.The report further states: "Future growth is likely to be underpinned by factors including the most rapid urbanization rate in the world and, by 2034, a larger working-age population than either China or India. Accelerating technological change is helping to unlock new opportunities for consumers and businesses, and Africa still has abundant resources.

Despite these very hopeful developments, Africa remains an agricultural and mineral-based economy where much of the export is from the mines of African countries and farmland. It is at the primary stage of the global value chain. It needs to climb up by catching up along the global value chain or breaking through it by creating an integrated sustainable smart and innovative path.

At present agriculture-manufacturing-services are weakly integrated into nearly all current African States. Agriculture has remained the primary occupation for the majority African population, with manufacturing growing very unevenly and slowly and, services also growing in some states more than manufacturing such as South Africa. The informal and formal economies are bifurcated and not connected. The informal is very large, the formal is smaller; in most states. There is still a job to be done: to integrate agriculture, manufacturing and services to enter the global value chain that is going through a data revolution that is creating products with senses. Africa cannot remain an economy mainly and largely that exports primary resources: minerals and agriculture. The unified and networked innovation system is needed to make Africa catch up in the current global value chain. Time to bring about a new paradigm in creating transformative innovation and sustainable development is now and it is imperative to empower, enable, capacitate and anchor the wellbeing of the African people and nature without fail once and for all.

There is thus an urgent need for new African innovation and sustainable development system (AISDS) founded and anchored on the African context to eradicate poverty and inequality.Africa does not need any donors if the Africans can create an innovation and sustainable development road map to own Africa and its rich wealth by learning to collaborate and work together for the betterment of all the people.

Development economics in the African context has to become a unified educational, social, economic, political and environmental, innovative, integrated, green and renascent development. The National Innovation System (NSI) too has to be re-engineered as it emerged in the economics of innovation literature. It did not emerge in Africa or the developing world although a number of developing countries including South Africa continue every five years to produce a white paper on national system of innovation.

The NSI conceptual framing originated in the late 1980s. It is Friedrich List (1856) who coined first NSI as the National Political Economy of Production. There have now been different thinkers that have been applying and writing about the peculiarities and distinctions of the Japanese, the American, the British, German, the East Asian Tigers and other varieties of constructing system models and conceptual framings.

The innovation system concept has evolved over the years and its application has been evolving to different sets of problems and areas. Innovation system has been defined as" the network of institutions in the public and private sectors whose activities and interactions initiate, import, and diffuse technologies" (Freeman, 1987:1). There has been an accent and emphasis on organisations that support R&D and promote the creation and diffusion of knowledge as the main sources of innovation (Nelson and Rosenberg, 1993: 5). Some stress: "All important economic, social, political, organisational, institutional and other factors that influence the development, diffusion and use of innovations" (Edquist, 1997:14).

Friedrich List (1856) and his concept 'national production system' may be seen as the historical origin of the national system of innovation (Freeman, 1995).According to Bengt-Åke Lundvall, the modern version of the concept appeared first in an unpublished contribution to OECD by Freeman (1982) and some years later Lundvall (1988) used the concept in formulating the importance for innovation of the concept of producer-user interaction and feedback for learning. Freeman used the innovation system concept in 1987 when he analysed Japanese economic performance (Freeman, 1987). Subsequently, Lundvall (1992) and Richard Nelson (1993) edited two books on the system of innovation that has become standard references on the subject. Muchie *et al.* (2003) attempted to apply the concept for economies in the developing world in general including Africa in particular.

Since early 1980s the notion of 'technological capability' has been given importance in the development literature. Building technological capability requires deliberate effort and is neither automatic, effortless nor without cost (Bell and Pavitt, 1993: 201; Nelson, 1990: 77; Dosi *et al.*, 1988: 463). The experience of developed economies shows that technological accumulation depends not only on the technological innovations of firms, but also on institutional innovations, which are influenced by social, economic and political factors (Freeman, 1992: 170). This explains "why the national system of innovation has worked better in certain environments than in others" (Katz, 1994: 251).

That is, the rate and shape of technological accumulation varies across countries as they are influenced by the nature of innovation system in their particular country (Nelson and Rosenberg, 1993: 4). Also, it is argued that the development of technological capability is relative and area specific, that is, it can be more or less advanced in different sectors or technologies (Enos, 1991: 167). Therefore, the effort to build competence and technology accumulation in different countries is likely to be influenced by their respective national innovation systems.

The normative assumption is that those that succeeded in building economic strength relied on the science, engineering, technology capability that made them attain an innovation advantage to put them in world, national or regional economic leadership positions.

The application of innovation systems to economies that barely can boast of setting up any system to speak of, in the sense that what is normal is the interaction of system elements with incoherence rather than system of innovation coherence, is a challenging intellectual and research enterprise.

The challenge is to excavate and explore how system of innovation elements with their dynamics of interaction can show emergent properties that exhibit a degree of coherence that can meaningfully and sufficiently permit their characterisation as showing properties of system emergence.If it can be ascertained that from system incoherence or chaos, they can evolve into emergent system coherence, then the next logical step is to ask whether the emergent system can also move along the trajectory of innovation system take-off.If there is success in system of innovation take off, then, the opportunity for dynamic state of innovation system build up towards maturity will be open. This kind of linear thinking is prevalent in a world where the rule of the game is fierce competition among states, nations, firms, countries and economies with different degrees of system coherence and incoherence built into the logic that drives the pursuit of their self-interest.

The concept of National Systems of Innovation (NSI) has come under close scrutiny from researchers who have witnessed the overwhelming sweep of the globalisation and internationalisation of research and innovation. Questions are being raised on whether the NSI concept is nearing its sale-by date as international and regional networks of innovation overtake them in the production of knowledge. The 'hollowing out of NSI', though not adequately researched, is an ongoing trend that any proposed review of NSI in Africa and beyond would have to address. Research has barely begun on how to harness the positive outcomes of the internationalisation of innovation systems for national development and on the policy implications for maintaining NSI in the face of sweeping internationalisation of innovation networks.Therefore, it may be useful and interesting to pay more attention to Networked innovation systems with boundaries of various nature giving way to the facilitation and incentivisation of networks that are often self-organising and self-maintaining.However, national systems of innovation remain important as laws and policies are still framed with a national context and by national governments notwithstanding the high visibility of regional and supranational networks and systems of innovation. The national state despite the corrosion of sovereignty by globalisation, is still important as proved by the recent Covid-19 virus crisis and the governance and stewardship of networks of innovation rests largely on the national state or on the supra/international organisations where the role of the national state is decisive.

The interesting questions that have recently appeared are: Can systems of innovation for smart economic growth be developed? Can systems of innovation for inclusive growth be developed? Can systems of innovation for justice, fairness and equitable distribution of resources to enhance the welfare of people starting from the least advantaged be built? Can systems of innovation for poverty eradication be built? Can systems of innovation for sustainable development be built? Can systems of innovation that overcome irrational fragmentations and help construct a project identity be built? How about systems of innovation that can combine modern scientific knowledge with indigenous local knowledge? How about systems of innovation capability for knowledge exchange rather than for knowledge transfer from those with strong systems of innovation to those with very weak systems of innovation? What would work better promoting system of innovation based on broad based innovation or system of innovation with high tech content or combining them together to create new synergies and syntheses?

There are different approaches to the system of innovation building process. There is the linear traditional route, and there is also the co-evolution and institutional route.

A key challenge is how to create a dynamic economy where agriculture and industry and services are integrated. The integration also is accomplished by promoting science, technology, engineering and innovation so that transformation and dynamic change becomes a reality consequently. Can this be best promoted by developing a co-evolutionary dynamic of agriculture with manufacture and services or by taking the existing division of labour and hope emergence and take off will lead to transformation?

An emergent field of science, technology, innovation for development (STI4D) or what is simply rendered as Innovation and Development (I&D) has opened up opportunities to incorporate explicitly research, knowledge, invention, creativity and innovation in changing the economic condition of underdevelopment that many economies face in the world in general and in Africa in particular. The explicit appropriation and incorporation of knowledge, invention and innovation to revitalise and dynamise the development debate by adding new and fresh perspectives and directions is indeed timely and necessary.The creative combination of innovation and development will generate new insights and approaches in examining the unacceptable continuation of the state of underdevelopment that has been plaguing many low income economies in Africa and elsewhere.

One important constraint is that innovation theory has evolved without consideringexplicitly the development context and issues. It evolved mainly as part of evolutionary economic theory, which in turn came in opposition to neoclassical economic theory. The theoretical effort to link innovation theory with development economics may require that both innovation theory and theory of development economics are re-thought and reconfigured. Something like the development economics of innovation may need to be developed. The attempt to do this has begun both with the GLOBELICS[1] research network initiative and some of the works that are coming out like the *Handbook of Innovation Systems and Developing Countries: Building Domestic Capabilities in a Global Setting* (Lundvall *et al.*, 2009). What remains a puzzle is that combining innovation systems with development economics remains problematic and finding ways to make the synthesis that generates conceptual framings, insights, learning, theorems and workable policy directions remain a big challenge. Whilst the move to make the combination is inspiring, the actual theoretical synthesis and its impact remain to be realised. Unifying innovation theory with development theory going beyond neo-liberal econmics and innovating out of the narrow validation of novelty and usefulnessstill remains to be achieved.In the African context, the combination of innovation with development is a big challenge.It is not easy to do it. The main reason is that Africa's economic development has been constrained by the load it still suffers from the colonial legacy. France still controls the treasury of the former colonies. Economic colonisation is still alive. The states as they exist are divided and when they form regions, they still remain divided. There are claims that Africa's fortunes are changing and conflicts are decreasing. There are some economies that are growing above 7%. Democratisation is slowly and surely growing. Technologically mobile phone users are growing and the ICT revolution in Africa may help Africa to leapfrog and join as a player rather than a victim of the division of labour in the world economy. Whilst these optimistic scenarios are useful and may counter the pessimism of diagnosis and pessimism of prescription that Africa has faced for centuries, we need to appreciate that the key to Africa's development remain the ability for Africa to create and build Science, Technology & Innovation systems for Development (STI4D) and help evolve an African united economy. The existing states or the regions they suffer from a formidable deficit, that is, failure to 'Put Africa First' and failure to formulate a united policy and strategy to deal with the colonial legacy and the new and current challenges Africa is facing today. Research on African innovation and development is needed at various levels to demonstrate what would work most effectively in the specific African context.

There are undoubtedly many areas of inquiry missed by conventional scholars of innovation studies in Africa. In Africa, the question of innovation is usually linked to economic growth and development. This is not to affirm that this trajectory is wholly undesirable or in fact over-rehearsed. However, it is also necessary to think of new disciplinary combinations and parameters that bring other fields of expertise into the discipline.

For instance, filmmakers and producers in West Africa have been able to evolve practices that follow neither the Hollywood model of film production nor Bollywood movie values. Accordingly, we have what has been termed Nollywood which has had a tremendous impact on the economy, culture and society of many regions beyond West Africa alone. Nollywood reportedly employs almost a million persons with a wide range of secondary industries attached to it. However, the Nollywood creative industry is not studied as a model of innovation and is more often confined to the realm of culture alone even though it is having a global impact in terms of transnational economies and globalizing African representation. The point to consider is that are there other innovative cultural practices within the African continent that are changing the economies and lives of Africans? Undoubtedly there are many such developments that require serious research to unearth and excavate.

We need to include the research work of scholars that can potentially contribute to the emerging innovation and development field new paradigmatic combinations.

This edited volume presents contributions on building science, technology and innovation research systems for development (STI4D) in African countries.They focus on the following themes:

- Strengthening Africa's Innovative and Technological Capabilities: Policy as the Missing Link
- National Quality Infrastructure in the context of Emerging Innovation Systems
- Structure and Dynamics of Uganda's Technological Innovation Systems

- Innovative Climate-Smart Agricultural System
- Technological Evolution in the South African and Argentine Automotive Manufacturing Sectors
- Development and Strengthening of Research Capacities in Madagascar
- Relationship between knowledge-capital and firm's performance in the resource-based industry
- Foreign Direct Investment, Firm-Level Capability and Human Capital Development
- Connecting the Dots between Knowledge, Openness, Networking, Partnerships and Innovation within Clusters
- Perceived Important Attributes in Dissemination rates of Maize Inventory Credit Innovations in Ghana
- Design Science and Living Lab Research for Innovation and Development in South Africa
- Nigeria Assessing the National Economic Empowerment Development Strategy as a development Plan
- Agricultural and Economic Development in Nigeria: Politics of Fertilizer Subsidy Implementation and Governance Structure
- The Transformation of the Global System and its Implications for Africa
- Technology Innovation Agency (TIA): A public support mechanism for technological innovation in a developing country

Steve Onyeiwu (Chapter 2) explores the missing policies that need to be corrected in order to strengthen Africa's innovative and technological capabilities. While East Asian countries have successfully used knowledge and innovation to transform their economies and alleviate poverty, African countries have been unsuccessful in accomplishing the same feat. The past three decades have witnessed debates about the causes of Africa's weak innovative and technological capabilities. A major perspective has been the notion that external constraints, such as the exercise of market power by multinational corporations, are largely to blame for Africa's technological dilemmas. This paper departs from externalist perspectives by considering the role of ineffective macroeconomic, trade, and technology policies of

African countries. After identifying the major determinants of innovation and technology, the chapter considers how various policies implemented by African countries since independence have circumscribed the capacities of these countries to strengthen their technological capabilities. Drawing from the experiences of India and South Korea, the paper proposes policy measures that should be undertaken in order to promote technological development, spur growth, and alleviate poverty in Africa.

Jan Peuckert and Jorge Gonçalves (Chapter 3) discusses the National Quality Infrastructure in the context of emerging innovation systems. The development of national quality infrastructures is a strategic policy option to address typical weaknesses of emerging innovation systems. They argue that through investments in this often-neglected area of public concern, governments may promote inter-sectoral linkages, the building up of necessary interface units, and foster both STI and DUI modes of learning.

In Chapter 4, Ezekiel, Alan Ayinde; Ayinde, OpeyemiEyitayo; Angathevar Baskaran; Adewumi, Matthew Olaniyi & Olaoye, Ibukun James present an Innovative Climate-Smart Agricultural System, using the case of Nigeria. It develops a methodology for obtaining different types of data to build an evidence base on Climate Smart Agriculture (CSA) practices, including incentives / barriers to adoption, mitigation-adaptation-food security synergies and trade-offs of different practice options (based on identification of food security and adaptation benefits, climate change indicators, mitigation potential and least-cost-investment options). In Nigeria, this combined data has shown that some farmers face difficulties in adopting Climate Smart Agriculture (CSA) practices, which potentially have productivity, adaptation and mitigation benefits. In some holdings, crop residues are needed for animal feed instead of soil cover and some households are too poor to wait several seasons for the benefits to materialize. However, CSA appears to be used as an adaptation response in areas of pronounced climate variability. The findings also indicate entry points for agricultural policies to increase food security under climate change and for extension services. The mapping of agricultural and climate change policy instruments, stakeholders / institutions and policy formulation and implementation processes is also being carried out with a view to enable greater policy alignment and more coordinated institutional arrangements.

Julius Ecuru, Lena Trojer, Ziraba N. Yasin & Peter O. Latin (Chapter 5) discuss the structure and dynamics of Uganda's Technological Innovation System. They provide insights into Uganda's evolving innovation system. The framework used to gain this insight presents science, technology and innovation as a function of financing, governance, human capital and the strength of interactions within and across the functional spheres. From the framework, it appears universities and public research organizations are playing a major role in building Uganda's innovation system. Public research organizations should, however, collaborate more closely with universities, and be more pragmatic in technology dissemination. It seems that in Uganda the public sector will continue to play a leading role in fostering innovation in the foreseeable future as the private sector grows. A crucial element of the public sector support is to have in place stable merit-based system of science funding where competitive grants are awarded annually for research and innovation.

Michael Gastrow and Ariel Gordon (Chapter 6) traces the technological evolution in the South African and Argentine automotive manufacturing sectors, the policy responses and results. The comparative review explores the means by which technological upgrading and innovation in the South African and Argentine automotive manufacturing sectors evolved over time, and highlights how policy interventions shaped this evolution. Policies affecting export orientation in turn affected technological trajectories in each case. While South African policy oriented the sector towards global markets, Argentine policy supported regional integration, primarily with Brazil. This resulted in technological trajectories that aimed towards meeting the specifications of developed countries and developing countries respectively. Argentina experienced competition for knowledge-intensive activities in which Brazil had an advantage due to its larger scale, but South Africa does not face such regional competition. The key policy implication is that technological trajectories merit consideration in the context of trade policy, since the latter has a material impact on the technological requirements, knowledge-intensity, and future competitiveness of the home industry

In Chapter 7, Jacques Gaillard and Anne Marie Gaillard examine the development and strengthening of research capacities in Madagascar. They analyse the impact of the activities of the International Foundation for Science (IFS) in Madagascar. Between 1976 and 2008, 50 Malagasy scientists have received a total of 71 IFS grants. Before presenting the results of the impact study, it briefly reviews the development of science and technology in Madagascar as well as the present institutional framework and governance system. It also provides an estimate of S&T human and financial resources as well as an overview of Madagascar's scientific output measured in number of publications indexed in international databases.

Despite heterogeneous and sometimes unsatisfactory results, especially with regard to S&T outputs, it is concluded that the positive results obtained by IFS in many ways, e.g. academic advancement of the grantees, access to executive positions, avoiding the brain drain, stimulation, and high degree of satisfaction for the IFS granting programme and additional services indicate that IFS has, to a great extent, fulfilled its mission and that its strategy is sound. Madagascar needs IFS today even more than before.

Oluseye Oladayo Jegede, Angathevar Baskaran & Mammo Muchie (Chapter 8) discuss the relationship between knowledge-capital and firm's performance in the resource-based industry. They provide an empirical analysis of the effects of knowledge-capital on performance at the firm-level. Multiple Linear Regression (OLS) was used to check the effects of knowledge capital (stock and flow) on firms' financial performance (turnover) using 106 mining firms in Nigeria. The firms sampled include those into quarrying, construction, dredging, rock processing, small scale mining and mineral exploration. Data was collected January to June 2015 eliciting information for the 2013 financial year. The result showed that employee size, presence of expatriate in work, R&D expenditure and acquisition of machinery, hardware and software had significant positive impact on the performance of the mining firms for the reference period.

Based on the evidence from the Kenyan manufacturing industry, Geoffrey G. Gachino (Chapter 9) analyses the relationship between foreign direct investment, firm-level capability and human capital development. He uses firm-level survey data of Kenyan manufacturing industry to examine the significance of FDI and firm-level capabilities in human capital development. Similarly, the paper undertakes a detailed descriptive comparison of human capital and other firm-level capabilities generated by both foreign and locally owned firms. The analysis shows that foreign firms generally enjoyed high human capital development and firm-level capabilities than locally owned firms. Empirical evaluation of human capital determinants revealed a statistically significant role played by FDI in determining human capital development in all the firms. Other factors which demonstrated an equally significant role included specific firm level capabilities; process, product, marketing and export performance. Interestingly, basic infrastructure, systemic embeddedness, firm size, labour market conditions and role of government were not statistically significant implying their weak role in human capital stimulation.

In Chapter 10, Billy Adegbola Oluwale, Oluseye Oladayo Jegede, Blessing Funke Ajao & Emmanuel Makanjuola Ogunjeilua discuss the role of openness, networking and partnership on production and innovation within the Otigba ICT cluster in Nigeria. Results from the questionnaire survey data (two hundred (200) purposively selected owners/employees of informal ICT microenterprises in the cluster) showed that there were competition and co-operation within the cluster with means of 4.64 and 4.10 respectively. Modes of openness within the cluster were by exchanging information and sharing experience with other technicians with means of 3.45 and 3.20 respectively. Firms were majorly (70%) involved in process and marketing innovations (30%). Openness, networking and partnership played a very significant role on access to information, customers, new domestic market, tools/technology, suppliers of raw materials and inputs among the enterprises. Majority (95%) of the respondent enterprises which exhibited cluster attributes were involved in one form of innovation. The study concluded that openness, networking and partnership had engendered growth among the enterprises.

Mawuena Aggey, Nana K.T. Ghartey & Charles Kweku Brown (Chapter 11) discuss the perceived important attributes in dissemination rates of Maize Inventory Credit Innovations in Ghana.There are calls for re-thinking the concept of "dissemination" amid recent observations that classical diffusion and innovation theory is an evolving science of dissemination requiring greater theoretical precision. Drawing on classical centralized diffusion theory and dissemination communication model, this work differentiates between actively directed diffusion (dissemination) and passive (spontaneous) diffusion arguing that proactive change agents may muffle the influence of adopter perception of innovation attributes on dissemination rates more than on diffusion rates. Adoption rates of 26 maize business innovative practices and adopters' perceptions of 15 attributes of these practices in a promotion-agent-led dissemination phenomenon are subjected to correlation analyses. Simplicity and clarity of results show very weak positive linear correlation with dissemination rates, but correlation with compatibility and association with main business are moderately positive; not entirely consistent with strongly positive correlations expected in spontaneous diffusion. Subtle differences between innovation dissemination and diffusion phenomena in how rates associate with adopter perceptions of innovation attributes important in adoption action are highlighted, suggesting the influence of adopter perceptions of innovation attributes may not be entirely same for dissemination and diffusion phenomena within certain thresholds.Further work is recommended to clarify how estimates of ratio between vertical and horizontal communication in spread phenomena may define a thresh-hold to explain differences between the rates of diffusion and dissemination of innovation within the same social system with implications for over adoption, and discontinuance when promotion agent withdraws support.

Adele Botha, Marlien Herselman, Ronel Smith & Hendri Coetzee (Chapter 12) discuss design science and living lab research for innovation and development in South Africa.They provide an overview of design science research methodology as well as Living Labs and how these two methodologies compare, the uniqueness of both and how they can support each another within a specific context. An example is provided to indicate how design research has been applied within a Living Lab environment where an artefact (Digital Doorway) was designed and deployed in a South African rural community in the North West Province. This shows how innovation and development is supported within a specific context. The main objective is to indicate how design science was applied to support the deployment of an artifact (the solar panel digital doorway) in an open innovation environment (Living Labs) where users from the rural community of the North West Living Lab were involved in providing feedback on the design and development of the artifact. To effectively plan and manage a large-scale project like the Digital Doorway where a multidisciplinary team work collaboratively to co-create and co-design an artefact like the digital doorway, it becomes imperative to provide an overview of how each of these research designs can support the end deliverable or product. Feedback from users was applied to improve the product to suit their needs and context. The end result was that a more robust and applicable product can be provided to sup-port rural community development and to involve the community in the innovation life cycle through design science research and living lab processes.

In Chapter 13, Enwere Dike and Kanayo Ogujiuba provide a theoretical assessment of Nigeria's National Economic Empowerment Development Strategy (NEEDS) as a development plan. There are six prerequisites of a development plan: (i) an over-arching development vision or philosophy; (ii) clearly specified objectives or goals; (iii) policy instruments for achieving objectives; (iv) a time horizon; (v) alignment between objectives and strategies; and (vi) a time preference function for judging whether the potential future benefits of the plan justify the resources invested to achieve them. Whereas the NEEDS fulfil prerequisites (i) to (iv), it is, at best, weak in (v) and (vi). But the NEEDS is not supported by macroeconomic models of the economy to permit analysis of the interdependencies in the economy.

Ayinde, Opeyemi Eyitayo; Olaoye, Ibukun James; Mammo, Muchie & Oloyede, Adeola Oreoluwa (Chapter 14) discuss the agricultural and economic development in Nigeria, with specific focus on the politics of fertilizer subsidy implementation and governance structure.Fertilizer subsidy remain a key policy instrument used by Nigeria Government to boost productivity and small-scale farm holder household's income in ensuring pro poor growth and development. Despite, subsidy huge financial implication, government have been revitalizing and changing it policy approach to ensure greater impact and target. Yet, the actualization of the policy objective remains more or less a mirage. Against this backdrop, this paper reviews the politics of fertilizer subsidy implementation and governance structure towards agricultural development in Nigeria. Specifically, the paper sought to examine fertilizer subsidy in Nigeria. It then highlights the political situation of fertilizer policy implementation. Further, it presents a snapshot of the world governance indicators (WGI) and its implication on agricultural production in Nigeria. Lastly, the paper presents the development consequences in terms of agriculture contribution to GDP and the status of governance in Nigeria. The study finds that, first, fertilizer subsidy policy in Nigeria have been changing in volume, structure and approach over time as power changes in the seat of government. Second, unhealthy politics observed among fertilizer policy stakeholders, subsidized fertilizer distribution and marketing as well as in the target and unintended beneficiaries. Third governance structure in Nigeria is poor given that all her governance indicators were negative. However, the impact and effectiveness of a policy implementation depend more on the governance structure of the country rather than the quality and policy implementation strategies. Finally, it is concluded that, fertilizer subsidy implementation strategies with absence of unhealthy politics and in combination with good governance structure will drive sustainable agricultural development in Nigeria and any other Africa country that has similar characteristics. Thus, we suggest that Nigeria government should dissociate any economic policy from patrician politics practices and strengthens her governance structure to ensure proper monitoring and evaluation of her policy.

In Chapter 15, Dani W. Nabudere discusses the transformation of the global system and its implications for Africa.He argues that the global economy is in crises raising the profound question of how humanity is likely to relate to the future. These crises seem to be deeper than mere industrial and financial cyclical upswings and downswings that appear periodically in short term and long wave cycles. It appears they may also defy the swings between liberal and Keynesian recipes to provide anti-cyclical measures to address these systemic disruptive structural breakdowns in the global economy. It appears the so-called Arab Spring is an expression or manifestation of this underlying economic downturn. This raises profound questions related to how the future beyond the current crises can be addressed. It looks African humanism in the philosophy of Ubuntu can be advanced as a possible way to salvage the future that the crises are ruining. There is much in African Ubuntu humanism that can be applied as a means to create a future by making a world out of the current deep crises.

Lastly, Dhesigen Naidoo (Chapter 16) discusses the Technology Innovation Agency (TIA), South Africa and highlights the necessity of a public support mechanism for technological innovation in a developing country.South Africa has since the dawn of democracy progressively built the science and research support components of the National System of Innovation (SANSI) with consistency. At national government level, science and technology developed from being a branch in the Ministry of Arts, Culture, Science and Technology in 1994, to a fully-fledged Ministry ten years later. Investments were initially heavier in developing sustainable research support system with encouraging results. A more recent set of reviews of progress with the development of the SANSI, including a comprehensive OECD review, has catalysed the development of a public sector innovation support system, the core of which is a new agency – the Technology Innovation Agency (TIA). The TIA has been established through the Technology Innovation Agency Act, as a public entity that will function as a key structural intervention to support government in stimulating and intensifying technological innovation and thereby enhance the country's capacity for local innovation and lessen dependence on imported know-how.

The various chapters have reflected analytically and critically on specific cases, issues and problems from the emergence to take off on how innovation and development in Africa and the rest of the Global South has been evolving differently from its origin in the developed world and the East Asian Tiger economies.

Africa is now in the fourth industrial revolution and the national innovation system has to include the economic, social, education, political and ecological sectors. A new paradigm shift mind set is much needed to generate a system of innovation that unifies all the sectors and create a renascent, united, independent and free Africa from loans, debt, aid and corruption. Africa must not fail the 4th industrial revolution as it did the first, second and third industrial revolutions. A new transformative, renascent, sustainable and integrated development model/ system is much needed urgently in order to bring about a vibrant future for all the people of Africa.

Endnotes

[1] See: http://www.globelics.org

[2] These include essentially Algeria, Tunisia and Morocco.

References

Bell, M. and Pavitt, K. (1993), 'Technological accumulation and industrial growth: contrasts between developed and developing countries', *Industrial and Corporate Change*, 2(2):157-210.

Dosi, G., Freeman, C., Nelson, R. and Soete, L. (ed.) (1988), *Technical Change and Economic Theory*, London: Pinter Publishers.

Edquist, C. (ed.) (1997), *Systems of Innovation: Technologies, Institutions and Organisations*, London: Pinter.

Enos, J.L. (1991), *The Creation of Technological Capability in Developing Countries*, London: Pinter publishers.

Freeman, C. (1982), 'Technological infrastructure and international competitiveness, (Draft paper submitted to the OECD Ad hoc-group on Science, Technology and Competitiveness, August, mimeo).

Freeman, C. (1987), *Technology Policy and Economic Performance: Lessons from Japan*, London: Pinter.

Freeman, C. (1992), 'From scientific and technical institutions in the national system of innovation' in Lundvall, B. (ed), *National Systems of Innovation: Towards a Theory of Innovation and Interactive Learning*, London: Pinter Publishers.

Freeman, C. (1995), 'The National Innovation Systems in historical perspective,' in *Cambridge Journal of Economics*, 19 (1).

Katz, J.M. (1994), 'Technology, economics, and late industrialisation', in Salomon J. (ed), *The Uncertain Quest: Science, Technology and Development*, Tokyo: UN University Press.

McKinsey Global Institute (2010), 'What's driving Africa's growth', 1 June 2010. Available at: https://www.mckinsey.com/featured-insights/middle-east-and-africa/whats-driving-africas-growth

List, F. (1856), *National System of Political Economy*, Philadelphia: Lippincott.

Lundvall, B-Å. (1988), 'Innovations as in Interactive Process: From User- Producer Interaction to the National System of Innovation', in Dosi, G., *Technical Change and Economic Theory*, London: Printer.

Lundvall, B-Å. (ed.) (1992), National Systems of Innovation: *Towards a Theory of Innovation and Interactive Learning*, London: Pinter.

Lundvall, B-Å., Joseph, K.J., Chaminade, C. andVang, Y. (2009), *Handbook of Innovation Systems and Developing Countries: Building Domestic Capabilities in a Global Setting*, Cheltenham, UK, Northampton, MA, USA: Edward Elgar.

McKinsey Global Institute (2010), Lions on the Move: *The Progress and Potential of African Economies*, Available at: https://www.mckinsey.com/featured-insights/middle-east-and-africa/lions-on-the-move

McKinsey Global Institute (2016), *Lions on the Move II: Realizing the Potential of Africa's Economies*, Available at: https://www.mckinsey.com/featured-insights/middle-east-and-africa/lions-on-the-move-realizing-the-potential-of-africas-economies

Muchie, M., Gammeltoft, P. and Lundvall, B. A. (2003), *Putting Africa First: The Making of African Innovation Systems*, Aaalborg: Aaalborg University Press.

Nelson, R. R. (1990), 'On technological capabilities and their acquisition', in Evenson, R.E. Ranis, G. (ed), *Science and Technology: Lessons for Development Policy*, London: Intermediate Technology Publications.

Nelson, R. (1993), *National Innovation Systems: A Comparative Analysis*, New York and Oxford: Oxford University Press.

Nelson, R. and Rosenberg, N. (1993), 'Technical innovation and national systems', in Nelson, R. R. (ed), *National Innovation Systems*, New York: Oxford University Press.

2

Strengthening Africa's Innovative and Technological Capabilities: Policy as the Missing Link

Steve Onyeiwu[1]

1. Introduction

Despite investing in education and establishing several research institutes since independence, Africa continues to be known as a region with weak innovative and technological capabilities. Concerns are being expressed by analysts and policy makers that Africa might not be able to take advantage of opportunities in the knowledge-based global economy. Thus, there is a resurgence of debates and discussions about what African countries should do in order to strengthen their technological capabilities.

This paper discusses some of the major determinants of innovation and technology and investigates how they have affected the ability of African countries to develop technological capabilities. It can be stated upfront that the lack of good policies is a major factor mitigating against the technological development of African countries. Consequently, the paper offers a policy blueprint for how African countries could strengthen their innovative and

1 Department of Economics, Allegheny College, Meadville, Pennsylvania 16335, USA. Email: sonyeiwu@allegheny.edu

technological capacities in order to spur growth, reduce poverty and achieve the Millennium Development Goal (MDG).

No doubt, Africa's weak innovative and technological capabilities have affected the region's growth and poverty rates adversely.[1] Because economists don't usually model technological innovation formally, they often miss the organic link between technology, growth and poverty in Africa (Onyeiwu, 2009). But such a link can be discerned very easily. First, Africa's weak technological capability has made it difficult for the region to attract growth-inducing and poverty-alleviating Foreign Direct Investment (FDI). Foreign investors in high-tech sectors such as information technology, semi-conductors, pharmaceuticals, aerospace, and medical equipment prefer to locate in countries with a highly skilled workforce and strong technological capabilities. The Republic of Ireland, for instance, was able to achieve a remarkable growth rate and significant improvements in living standards in the 1990s because of its reputation as a bastion of high-tech firms (Paus, 2005).

Given Africa's weak technological capability, the region tends to attract foreign investors in low-skill and low-wage sectors such as tourism, agriculture, agro-processing, assembly-type manufacturing and retail trade. While employment in these sectors is important for sustaining the growth, momentum experienced by African countries within the past decade, wages and incomes in these sectors are not usually high enough to spur the growth rates needed for significantly reducing poverty. Apart from poverty alleviation, a stronger technological capability would enable African countries to compete effectively in the new global economy, which has become more knowledge and skill intensive.[2] While the current focus of African countries on macroeconomic stability is appropriate, they should complement macroeconomic reforms with explicit policies that strengthen their innovative and technological capabilities. Indeed, some macroeconomic policy reforms in Africa tend to inadvertently undermine the capacity of African countries to strengthen their technological capabilities.

What kinds of policies are needed to spur innovation in Africa? How are they different from the ones implemented by African countries since independence? How might the new policies be implemented effectively? What lessons might African countries learn from the Indian and South Korean experiences? These are some of the central issues explored in this paper. The paper is structured as follows. Following the introduction, Section 2 uses key indicators of innovation and technology to review the state of knowledge and technological development in Africa. Section 3 discusses some of the determinants of innovation and technology, while Section 4 considers the effects of inappropriate policies on the technological capabilities of African countries. Section 5 focuses on the policies used by India and South Korea to promote technological development, and their implications for Africa. Section 6 is the summary, conclusion and policy recommendations of the paper.

2. The state of knowledge and technological capabilities in Africa

It is highly inconceivable that one would comprehend the factors responsible for Africa's weak technological capability without first understanding the extent of that weakness. Given the amorphous nature of the concept of innovation and technology, it is not always clear what analysts mean when they discuss Africa's weak technological capability. Do they mean the continued use of antiquated machines/equipment and the lack of access to advanced technologies? Perhaps they mean Africa's specialization in the production and export of low-tech consumer products such as textiles, footwear, soft drinks, soaps, detergents, etc. Are they also referring to the dearth of a skilled workforce in the region?

The notion of technological innovation and its corresponding indicators are so controversial and opaque that I won't even attempt to address the issue in this paper, as this is beyond the scope of the paper.[3] The goal of this section is to use some stylized indicators of technology (some of them also controversial!) to offer insight into the extent of the technological weaknesses of African countries, relative to other developing regions.

Figure 1

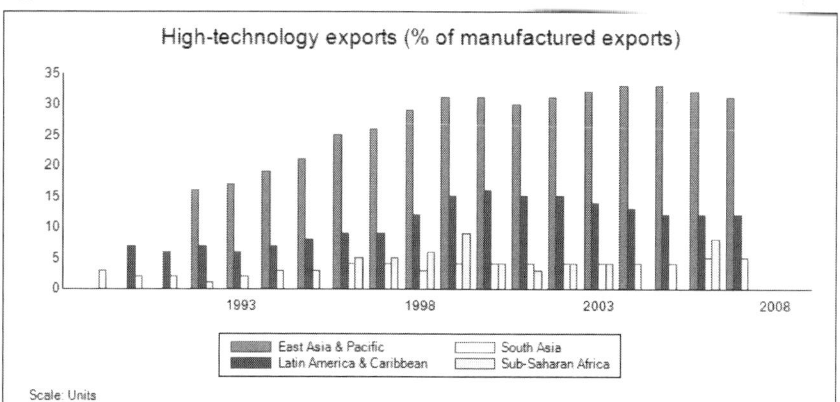

Source: World Development Indicators Database

Before presenting the statistics, it is worth pointing out that Africa and East Asia were almost at the same level of economic and technological development in the 1960s (Ackah and Kutsoati, 2008). But, look at what has now happened: Africa is nowhere close to East Asia in terms of several indicators of innovation and technology. Table 1 shows that Africa's Research and Development (R&D) intensity is one of the lowest in the developing world. For instance, North Africa's share of world expenditure on R&D was a paltry 0.2 per cent in 2001. Although that of Sub-Saharan Africa (SSA) was a bit higher at 0.5 per cent, it was far less than the 15.6 per cent for developing countries as a group; 27.9 per cent for Asia, and 3.1 per cent for Latin America and the Caribbean. Africa's expenditure on R&D as a percentage of GDP has not only been the lowest in the world, but has also been declining over time (UNESCO 2001).[4]

Table 1 also shows that SSA and North African countries spent an average of $7 and $6 per person respectively on R&D in 2001(the lowest in the world), compared to $20 for developing countries, $46 for Asia, and $34 for Latin America and the Caribbean. The table reveals that Africa accounted for less than 3 per cent of researchers in the world, again the lowest. The region's low investment in science and technology becomes more evident when the indicators are disaggregated into various countries as shown in Table 2. Most African countries spend less than 0.5 per cent of GDP on R&D, compared to 1.4 per cent in China, 2.6 per cent in Singapore, 3.2 per cent in South Korea, 1 per cent in Brazil, and 0.7 per cent in Chile.

Table 1: Regional Science and Technology Indicators

Regions/Countries	GERD as % World GERD*	GERD as % of GDP	GERD per Inhabitant (PPP $)	Researchers as a % of World Total	Researchers Per Million Inhabitants	GERD Per Researcher (thousands of PPP$)
Developing Countries	15.6	0.6	20	28.4	347	57.9
Developed Countries	84.4	2.2	377	71.6	3,033	124.2
Asia	27.9	1.3	46	34.5	537	85.1
Latin America & the Caribbean	3.1	0.5	34	6.7	715	48.2
SSA (excluding Arab States)	0.5	0.3	6	1.0	113	49.1
North Africa	0.2	0.2	7	1.5	489	14.9
Arab States (in Asia)	0.1	0.2	11	0.1	52	211.4
Arab States (All)	0.4	0.2	8	1.6	356	23.6
China	3.9	0.6	17	10.6	454	38.3
India	2.0	0.7	11	2.8	151	75.8

*GERD stands for Gross Domestic Expenditure on Research & Development

Source: Computed from UNESCO statistics published in *The State of Science and Technology in the World*, Paris, UNESCO Institute of Statistics, 2001, p. 7.

It should not be surprising; therefore, that Africa has the lowest volume of scientific and technical publications amongst the various regions of the world (see Table 3). Between 2000 and 2005, the number of scientific and technical publications in Africa grew by just 6 per cent, compared to 119 per cent for East Asia and the Pacific, 36 per cent for Latin America and the Caribbean, and 43 per cent for South Asia. According to UNESCO, Africa's share of world scientific publications was 1.4 per cent in 1990 and 2000, respectively, compared to 1.7 per cent for Latin America in 1990 and 3.2 per cent in 2000. Asia's researchers accounted for 14.5 per cent of world scientific publications in 1990 and 21.1 per cent in 2000.[5]

Because Africa has under-invested in innovation and technology, the region's technological output, as measured by the number of U.S. patents granted to African firms, lags behind those of other developing countries (see Table 4). Patent data show that, with the exception of South Africa, Kenya, Egypt and Nigeria, most African countries received virtually no patents between 2000-2008.[6] This is in stark contrast from countries like South Korea, China, India and Brazil that received thousands of patents within this period. Even when one controls for the relatively small size of African countries, their technological output has been grossly marginal.

Africa is a very heterogeneous region, and some countries have done better than others with regard to innovation and technical change. Top R&D spenders, according to Table 2, include Tunisia (1.0 per cent), South Africa (0.9 per cent), and Morocco (0.7 per cent). In terms of the number of researchers per million inhabitants, the leading countries are Tunisia (1,450), South Africa (361), Algeria (170), Seychelles (157), and Cape Verde (127). Tunisia and South Africa are thus the two leading countries in Africa, with regard to expenditure on R&D and the number of scientists. Notice, also, from Table 2 that these countries achieved respectable levels of economic growth during the 2005-2006 period, thereby providing anecdotal support for the notion that there is a correlation between technological capability and growth. South Africa, Kenya and Nigeria stand out amongst African countries with regard to the number of patents. Africa's low technological output is further manifested in Figure 1, which shows that high-tech exports constitute a very small proportion of the region's manufactured exports. In 2008, high-tech exports made up less than 10 percent of SSA's manufactured exports, whereas those of East Asia and Latin America were about 30 percent and 15 per cent, respectively.

Table 2: Technology Output, Absorptive Capacity and Economic Growth for Selected African Countries, 2005

Country	R&D as % of GDP*	Researchers per 1 million inhabitants*	Economic Growth in 2005 (%)**	Economic Growth in 2006 (%)**	Average Economic Growth (2005-2006) %***
Algeria	0.1	170	5	2	3.5
Botswana	0.4	-	5	3	4.0
Burkina Faso	0.2	22	6	6	6.0
Cameroon	-	26	2	3	2.5
Cape Verde	-	127	7	11	9.0
Dem. Republic of Congo	0.5	-	6	5	5.5
Cote d'Ivoire	-	68	1	1	1.0
Egypt	0.2	-	4	7	5.5
Ethiopia	0.2	20	12	11	11.5
Gambia	-	28	5	7	6.0
Lesotho	0.1	10	3	7	5.0
Madagascar	0.2	43	5	5	5.0
Mauritius	0.4	-	5	4	4.5
Morocco	0.7	-	3	8	5.5
Mozambique	0.5	-	8	9	8.5
Niger	-	8	7	5	6.0
Senegal	0.1	-	6	2	4.0
Seychelles	0.4	157	1	5	3.0
South Africa	0.9	361	5	5	5.0
Sudan	0.3	-	6	11	8.5
Tunisia	1.0	1,450	4	6	5.0
Uganda	0.2	-	6	11	8.5
Zambia	0.0	52	5	6	5.5
Argentina	0.5	980	8	7	7.5
Brazil	1.0	629	2	3	2.5
Chile	0.7	833	5	4	4.5
Costa Rica	0.4	122	4	7	5.5
China	1.4	926	10	12	11.0
Hong Kong	0.8	2,650	7	6	6.6
Indonesia	0.05	205	4	4	4.0
Malaysia	0.6	372	3	4	3.5

Singapore	2.6	6,088	5	5	5.0
South Korea	3.2	4,162	4	5	4.5

Sources: *UNESCO Statistical Database; **World Development Indicators
***Computed by Author

All of the above indicators have reinforced Africa's image as a region good only for safaris and humanitarian work, not as a destination for IBM, Nokia, Motorola, Intel, Microsoft and other high-tech firms. The bottom line is, one cannot expect sustainable growth, employment and poverty alleviation in Africa without strong science and technology capabilities. In the new global economy, what drives growth in many countries are small start-up, technology-driven firms that take advantage of new markets in telecommunications, energy, green technologies, pharmaceuticals, and electronics. Africa is missing out on these growth opportunities by virtue of its lack of technological capabilities.

Table 3: Regional Distribution of Number of Scientific and Technical Publications, 2000-2005

Region	2000	2001	2002	2003	2004	2005	Average 2000-2005	Growth Rate, 2000-2005 (%)
East Asia & Pacific	20,116	22,818	25,101	30,812	37,075	44,064	29,998	119
LAC	14,786	15,776	17,126	17,889	19,361	20,045	17,497	36
MENA	3,689	4,017	4,379	5,154	5,551	6,243	4839	69
South Asia	10,796	11,334	12,262	13,162	14,086	15,429	12,845	42
SSA	3,355	3,279	3,438	3,331	3,517	3,563	3,413	6
World	629,230	628,047	637,041	660,304	687,174	708,086	658,314	13

Source: World Development Indicators Database

Table 4: Number of U.S. Patents Granted to Selected African and Other Developing Countries (2000-2008)

Country	2000	2001	2002	2003	2004	2005	2006	2007	2008	Total
Benin	0	0	0	0	0	0	0	1	0	1
Cameroon	0	0	0	0	0	0	0	1	0	1
Cote d'Ivoire	0	0	0	0	1	0	0	0	0	1
Gabon	0	0	0	0	0	0	0	1	0	1
Ghana	0	0	0	0	0	0	0	1	0	1
Kenya	3	4	1	10	16	10	3	1	4	62
Mauritius	0	0	0	0	0	0	0	0	1	1
Namibia	1	0	0	0	0	0	0	0	1	2
Nigeria	2	1	4	4	1	0	0	1	1	14
South Africa	125	137	123	131	115	108	127	116	124	1106
Uganda	0	1	1	0	0	0	0	0	0	2
Costa Rica	8	12	8	10	10	13	26	17	13	117
Dominican Republic	5	0	1	0	0	2	2	2	3	15
India	131	180	267	356	376	403	506	578	672	3469
Indonesia	14	10	15	12	23	23	16	15	19	147
Brazil	113	125	112	180	161	98	148	118	133	1188
China (excl. Hong Kong)	161	265	390	424	597	565	970	1235	1874	6481
South Korea	3472	3763	4009	4132	4671	4591	6509	7264	8731	47142

Source: U.S. Patent Office Statistical Database, 2009.

Africa's weak technological capability is perplexing because the region has done better than some developing regions with regard to investment in education and establishment of research institutes. In fact, some African countries such as Botswana, Tunisia, Ghana, and South Africa spend more on education than high-growth Asian countries like China, Korea, and Singapore (Table 5). As of 1992, at least 186 research institutes were identified in 36 African countries (Abiodun, p.12).[7] Although many of these institutes have recorded significant successes, especially in the field of agricultural technology, their existence has not helped to change the perception of Africa as a technologically weak region.

So, what happened? Why have African countries failed to strengthen their technological capabilities like East Asian countries? To address this question, one needs to understand some of the determinants of innovation and technology.

Table 5: Indicators of Human Capital in Selected African, Latin American, and East Asian Countries

Country	Expenditure on Education, % of GDP*	Expenditure on Education, % of Govt. Expenditure*	Expenditure on Tertiary Education, % of Education Expenditure*	Adult Literacy Rate (%)*	GDP Growth (%)*	GDP Per Capita (PPP)**
Botswana	8.1	21	32	83	2.1	12,508
Cameroon	3.9	17	5	N/A	3.8	2,089
Egypt	3.7	12.6	N/A	66	6.8	4,953
Ghana	5.4	N/A	18	65	6.2	1,245
Malawi	4.2	25	N/A	72	7.4	700
Mauritius	3.9	12.7	11	87	3.5	10,571
Senegal	4.8	26	24	42	2.3	1,585
South Africa	5.3	17	13	88	5.0	9,087
Tunisia	7.1	21	22	78	5.2	6,859
Uganda	3.8	18.3	11	74	5.4	893
Argentina	4.5	14	18	98	8.5	11,985
Brazil	5.0	16	17	90	3.7	8,949
Chile	3.4	18	16	97	4.0	13,030
Costa Rica	4.7	23	N/A	96	8.2	9,564
China	1.9	13	21	93	10.7	4,644
Indonesia	3.5	18	N/A	92	5.4	3,454
Korea	4.2	15	15	N/A	5.0	22,988
Malaysia	4.7	25	36	92	5.9	12,536
Singapore	3.2	12	36	94	7.9	44,708
Thailand	4.0	21	20	94	5.0	7,599

* 2006 figures; ** 2007 figures

Source: UNESCO Statistical Database, 2010.

3. Determinants of innovation and technological capability

The field of science, technology, and knowledge transfer has been very controversial and subjective because there is no standard economic theory that proposes what a country should do in order to strengthen its innovative and technological capabilities. Despite the introduction of endogenous growth models about two decades ago, mainstream economists continue to marginalize the role of knowledge and innovation in the development process.[8] The non-inclusion of science and technology variables in growth econometrics has made it difficult for analysts to identify policy variables for promoting technological development in Africa. Consequently, knowledge about the driving forces behind innovation and technology has typically come from the experiences of the so-called "Asian Tigers," most notably South Korea, Taiwan, Hong Kong, and Singapore. Occasionally, too, analysts draw inferences from Japan's rapid technological development after the *Meiji Restoration*. India and China have also joined the ranks of successful innovators, whose experiences are often used as a basis for technology policy in Africa. The following determinants of innovation and technology are based on the experiences of countries that have succeeded in promoting technological innovation.

The Role of the State: Knowledge transfer and technological development often occur when the state supports the private sector. The experiences of East Asian countries suggest that a successful industrial policy is one in which the state partners with the private sector in areas such as R&D, technology transfer, training, and export promotion.

The ability of firms in a country to strengthen their technological capabilities depends substantially on the character of the state, particularly its ability to articulate and implement policies and programs that incentivize firms to strengthen their technological capabilities. As Brautigam (1997, p.1067) observes:

> The developmental state is a critical actor in establishing an "enabling environment" for industrialization. The developmental state enforces stability in important macroeconomic parameters, provides critical public goods: roads, power supply, security, and skills-based education, and possesses the policy instruments to channel private sector activity in accordance with national economic goals.

Apart from providing an enabling environment for investment in innovation, failures in the technology market may also justify state intervention. For instance, given appropriability problems and the public good nature of technology, firms are often reluctant to invest in knowledge and innovation (Coombs et al., 1987). While private returns to investment in innovation may not justify private costs, the social returns are usually substantial. In many cases, the marginal cost for providing innovation to the marginal user is zero. This provides a theoretical basis for the state to play an active role in the innovation process.

State support could come in various forms, including subsidies for undertaking innovative activities; tax credits, and direct collaborations with firms to develop specific technologies or train workers to acquire certain critical skills. In describing how the state helped develop the Brazilian telecommunications industry, Hobday (1985) notes that:

> ...none of Brazil's achievements could be described as "automatic or the result of market forces. On the contrary Brazil's successes were the result of the "visible hand" of government policy and strategy in translating a political will into an economic and technological reality. Without a sustained and innovative effort on the part of the government, there would not have been pressure on the private sector to transfer and develop the core technology needed to design and manufacture digital systems suited to Brazil.

As the leading facilitator of innovation and development, the state plays several roles, including the following:

Economic Policy: The goal of economic policy should not be conceived as simply the maintenance of full employment and macroeconomic stability. Economic policy can also be very instrumental in encouraging firms to undertake activities that expand the economy's knowledge base. Fiscal policy such as R&D tax credits for firms and government direct funding of R&D institutes can help strengthen a country's technological capability. So also is monetary policy that provides cheap credit for technology entrepreneurs and firms that invest in technology-related activities.

Trade Policy: The relationship between trade and technological capability is very complex. On the one hand, trade liberalization may spur firms to develop the technological capability to compete effectively in foreign markets (Krueger, 1997). However, exposing infant firms to foreign competition may have the latent effect of undermining their competitiveness. It is also true that a blanket protection of firms from foreign competition would encourage them to be complacent and therefore discourage them from investing in strengthening their technological capabilities. What, then, is the optimal trade policy that spurs innovation and technical change?

The experiences of East Asian countries have shown that an optimal policy is one that *gradually* exposes firms to foreign competition, while at the same time providing them with the support and incentives, they need to strengthen their innovative abilities. In a survey conducted by the Overseas Development Institute (ODI) to determine how a sample of 207 Korean firms responded to import liberalization, it was revealed that only 4.8% of the firms surveyed indicated that import liberalization resulted in lower technological development (Young, 1992) Thus, most of the firms surveyed responded to government incentives by upgrading both their technology and product quality after import liberalization. Young (1992) offers three explanations for why import liberalization was successful in spurring technological innovation in South Korea. First, many Korean firms were already internationally competitive before their exposure to foreign competition. In other words, these firms already had significant levels of technological capability before import liberalization. Second, the Korean government implemented import liberalization policies "gradually and cautiously," making sure they did not hurt domestic firms. Finally, the government provided support for small and medium-sized firms, especially through the flexible adjustments of the exchange rate, as well as the stabilization of wages and prices.

Science and Technology Policy: Economic and trade policies can be effective in promoting technological development only if they are juxtaposed with a well-articulated Science and Technology (S&T) policy. S&T policy can be defined as governmental actions *explicitly* designed to influence the intensity, nature, and direction of innovative activity. A well-articulated S&T policy is one that explicitly identifies a country's development objectives, and then incorporates scientific, technological and skill-intensive programs for the achievement of those objectives. In other words, a country's S&T policy must be mission and goal-oriented, rather than being abstract.

One example would help clarify the above proposition. Suppose a country's development objective is to alleviate poverty by enhancing the capacity of peasant farmers to process agricultural products for sale in both domestic and foreign markets. The country might than formulate an S&T policy that establishes research institutes that focus on agro-processing. Higher educational institutions would also be encouraged to establish programs that train agricultural students in food processing. Local equipment producers might be incentivized to produce cost-effective machines and equipment for agro-processing. Venture capital may also be mobilized to support entrepreneurs willing to invest in the marketing and export of processed agricultural products. The S&T policy may well include the establishment of a cluster of agro-processors within a region of the country. Producers in the cluster would then enjoy agglomeration economies, along with government subsidized infrastructures. The point being made here is that, when S&T policies are not tied to development goals, they become vacuous, incoherent and ambiguous.

Science and Technology Infrastructure: A country's S&T infrastructure consists of all the scientific, technological and educational resources that are available outside of industry, and which firms can use to strengthen their technological capabilities. Specifically, S&T infrastructure includes public research institutes, technology transfer agencies, science parks, business and technology incubators, professional and skills development centres, as well as higher educational institutions. Firms would have a higher propensity to innovate if they operate in a country with a well-developed S&T infrastructure. The level of development of a country's S&T infrastructure depends, to a large extent, on the nature of the state. A state that is genuinely committed to promoting technological development will have a higher propensity to develop a strong S&T infrastructure.

Techno-Economic Threats and Opportunities: Some random and unexpected events that threaten the survival of firms may occur in the economy. Sometimes, these exogenous shocks may spur firms into strengthening their technological capabilities. For instance, high energy costs and environmental concerns are encouraging firms to invest in energy-efficient methods of production. In the same token, the government may deliberatively create situations that threaten the survival of firms, or situations that challenge them to be more innovative. One example is the restriction of the importation of raw materials, spare parts, machinery and equipment. This restriction may have the effect of encouraging firms to develop in-house capabilities to modify and adapt their existing equipment or seek alternative raw materials and spare parts. During the Nigerian civil war (1967-1970), the secessionist Eastern region (otherwise known as "Biafra") was militarily blockaded by the Federal Government of Nigeria. With lack of access to many essential goods, the "Biafrans" were forced to develop the capacity to refine petroleum, produce spare parts for automobiles and other machines, manufacture military weaponry, and accomplished several scientific and technological feats. Some of those capabilities and technologies diffused within the Eastern region in the post-war era. For instance, Eastern cities such as Aba, Nnewi, and Onitsha have become bastions for indigenous technicians and engineers who have successfully developed the capacity to adapt and modify various imported technologies, particularly from Taiwan.[9] Brautigam (1997) discusses some of the technological feats accomplished by these indigenous innovators. The emergence of local innovators in the Eastern region of Nigeria suggests that, with the appropriate environment and motivating factors, Africans are capable of innovating.

Prior Accumulation of Scientific and Technological Knowledge: Technological capability has an exogenous dimension beyond the influence of firms, or even the state. The ability of firms to develop technological capability might depend on prior accumulation of scientific and technological knowledge in a country. Countries with a long history of industrialization are more likely to have firms with strong technological capability. Korean firms are believed to have developed technological capabilities partly because the country has a long history of industrialization dating back to the era of Japanese colonization (Amsden, 1989)

4. How ineffective policies have affected Africa's innovative and technological capabilities

As mentioned earlier on, African countries have the potential to innovate and strengthen their technological capabilities. In absolute terms, they have talented scientists and engineers, many of whom have emigrated to other regions in search of better opportunities. There is now a new generation of entrepreneurs in the region who are willing to invest venture capital in emerging technologies such as telecommunications, software development, etc. At the firm level, several African enterprises have shown potential to learn and adapt foreign technologies. In a study of the technological capabilities of Nigerian enterprises, Oyelaran-Oyeyinka (1996) observed that several small manufacturing firms succeeded in adapting imported machines to local conditions.

This section discusses some of the factors that undermine the ability of African countries to strengthen their innovative and technological capabilities. We start with the role of the state in Africa. Although many African governments have explicitly committed to promoting innovation and technology, they seem to have implemented the wrong policies. First, their concept of innovation as the mere acquisition of the latest machines, equipment, and software from abroad is outdated. Technology is much more than the mere acquisition of new vintages of equipment; it is more about developing the capacity to acquire, modify, adapt and improve on technology. Analysts have shown that, for developing countries, the ability to adapt and modify technology is more important for productivity growth than the generation of new technologies (Bell, 1987).

Because of their narrow and anachronistic conception of technology, African governments spend huge sums of money on the importation of machines and equipment, rather than focusing on policies that spur firms to invest in R&D, reverse engineering, and training their workers to acquire the skills needed to effectively use imported technologies. Technological knowledge is often embodied in people. It is people, working in firms and research laboratories that ultimately transform knowledge into new products, processes, and services. African countries should be investing *more* in enhancing the scientific, technical, and managerial skills of their people, and *less* in embodied technology.

The notion of technology as an embodied artifact has often led African countries to the choice of inappropriate technologies (in terms of costs and factor endowments). The African industrial landscape is replete with gigantic, costly and grossly inefficient projects that require massive state subsidies for their survival. One example of these projects is the Ajaokuta Steel Mill in Nigeria. Built by the Russians in 1979, the goal was to enable Nigeria to become self-sufficient in steel production. The mill was initially designed to produce about 1.3 million tons of cast steel annually, with possible expansion to 5.2 million tons in subsequent years. But little or no attempt was made to ensure that Nigerians acquired the capability to operate and manage the project after the departure of the Russians. The production targets set by the government were never achieved, and the project was eventually abandoned after a few years—with billions of dollars wasted in the process. To use a famous cliché, it became one of the several white elephant projects in Nigeria.

Another example is the National Fertilizer Company of Nigeria (NAFCON), Onne, Rivers State, which was built in the 1980s as the first and biggest modern nitrogenous fertilizer plant in SSA. The plant was constructed and managed by a consortium of American companies to help reduce Nigeria's dependence on the importation of fertilizers, by producing an annual output of about 1000 tons of ammonia and 1,500 tons of urea. Again, no explicit policy was put in place to promote local acquisition of the knowledge and capability to efficiently operate the fertilizer plant. NAFCON went out of business in 1999 due to technical and management problems. Similar stories can also be told of other African countries.

Another consequence of the narrow conception of technology by African governments is the nature of their economic policies, particularly fiscal and trade policies. African governments often grant accelerated depreciation of equipment to firms, which is evidence of the primacy they attach to production equipment. However, tax incentives are rarely granted to firms for training their workers in the use, modification, and adaptation of that equipment. The result is that, when this equipment break down, workers are unable to repair them, and engineers have to be flown in from abroad to fix the problems at considerable expense. When African firms are unable to pay for this expense, they go out of business, lay off workers and push many of these workers into abject poverty.

Regarding trade policies, African governments often make it easier for firms to import machines and equipment by setting lower tariff rates for capital goods. One of the latent consequences of this policy is the propensity for African firms to become complacent in developing the capacity to adapt, modify, and improve on technology. At the slightest sign of a technical problem, these firms rush to import new equipment, rather than focusing on how the equipment can be modified to reflect Africa's factor endowments, cost constraints, and local circumstances.

I next examine the nature of the S&T policies implemented by African governments since independence. Although these policies vary from country to country, they are marked by the establishment of several government R&D laboratories and research institutes. Herein lies one of the shortcomings of S&T policies in Africa: government R&D labs and research institutes have little or no relationship with the real sector of African economies. Quite often, the results from these research institutes are not used by enterprises within the economy (Vitta, 1993). Although there has been a phenomenal increase in the number of higher institutions of education in Africa, as well as the number of university graduates, their impact on the region's technological development has been marginal. In fact, there is an erroneous view in Africa that an expansion of the pool of educated people automatically leads to innovation and technical change. Increasing the number of graduates is counter-productive, unless efforts are correspondingly made to strengthen the technological capabilities of the country (Noland and Pack, 2007). Otherwise, the rate of graduate unemployment will rise, as is currently the case in many African countries

Regarding trade, African countries have implemented two extreme policies that have undermined their technological capabilities. In the post-independence era, they adopted Import-Substitution Industrialization (ISI) that provided blanket protection to local firms. The story of the effects of ISI, or what some analysts appropriately refer to as the "import-reproduction model," on Africa's industrial and technological development is well-known, and need not be regurgitated in this paper.[10] Following the failure of ISI, many African countries jettisoned ISI in the 1980s in favour of structural adjustment programs (SAP). A key component of SAP is the liberalization of trade, which has resulted in exposing local firms to international competition without giving them the opportunity (and support) to develop the capacity to compete effectively with well-established foreign firms. Rather than strengthening the technological capabilities of African firms, trade liberalization led to de-industrialization in many countries. Lall (1994) notes that "rapid liberalization, unaccompanied by supply-side measures to develop skills, capabilities and technical support, led to significant and costly deindustrialisation in Ghana." Adei (1990) also found that the failure of the Bonsa Tyre Company in Ghana to improve its performance after the implementation of SAP in the country was due to the firm's weak technological capability. In the same token, Pack (1993) argues that abrupt exposure of enterprises in developing countries to international competition, without first developing their technological capabilities, is not enough for productivity growth and international competitiveness.

The case of Nigerian textile firms, who were exposed to international competition after the implementation of SAP in 1986, also implies that structural adjustment can be counter-productive if not properly designed and implemented. Between 1991 and 2007, the number of firms in the industry plummeted from about 200 to 28, while the number of workers fell from 250,000 to 18,000 (NTMA, 2007, quoted in All Africa Global Media, December 7, 2007. Most of the surviving firms are fledgling, and more are expected to go out of business. According to the Secretary-General of the National Union of Textile, Garment, and Tailoring Workers of Nigeria, Issa Aremu, 15,000 jobs were lost in the industry in 2009 alone (Daily Champion, 2008).A recent survey showed that the cumulative market share of local textile firms in the Nigerian market is now 20 per cent, down from over 90 percent prior to SAP."[11] Preliminary evidence, therefore, suggests that SAP has been ineffective in promoting technological development in the Nigerian textile industry.

But, adjustment policies need not be inimical to innovation and technology. Both can be complementary, if designed the right way as East Asian countries did. Some Asian and Latin American countries have been able to promote technological development within the context of economic reforms (Lall, 1996). In the next section, I discuss how two of these countries –India and South Korea –successfully used various economic, trade and technology policies to strengthen their innovative capabilities.

5. Learning from the policy experiences of India and South Korea

India and South Korea are two Southern countries that have succeeded in strengthening their technological capabilities through effective policies. Their experiences suggest that technological capability cannot be developed overnight; it is a process that takes a very long time to yield dividends. For India, that process began in 1948 when the country introduced the *Industrial Policy Resolution.* Under the Resolution, various complementary policy measures were implemented that, overtime, enhanced India's technological capacities. In the following paragraphs, I summarize some of the major components of the *Resolution* and highlight their implications for Africa.

Trade Policy: India's trade policy, unlike that of many African countries, was explicitly designed to promote self-reliance in industrial production (Lall, 1987). To accomplish this objective, India pursued *both* ISI and export promotion simultaneously. Local producers were protected from foreign competition through the use of quantitative restrictions on imports. To promote the competitiveness of these producers, local firms were allowed to import intermediate inputs and spare parts *if* they were not available locally or if the firms intended to export the end-products. After 1978, however, the importation of intermediate goods became more liberalized, and imports were classified into two categories: a "restricted list" and an "Open General License (OGL)," i.e. importable without a specific license. Imports under the OGL were subject to heavy tariffs.

While many African countries focus on the development of the capability to produce consumer goods, India emphasized the development of the capital goods sector. Capital goods are the foundations of technology and industrial development; without them, industrialization cannot be sustainable (Alcorta, 2000). Consequently, Indian local manufacturers of capital goods were protected by means of complete quantitative restrictions. The Indian government simultaneously promoted exports using the following policies:

- Exemption from excise taxes and import duties on inputs used by exporters
- Import replenishment licenses for exporters, and these licenses could be sold at a premium in the domestic market
- Easier access to imported technology, equipment and foreign capital
- Exemption from capacity restrictions, and
- Establishment of an Export-Import bank to finance exports

Science and Technology Policy: One distinctive feature of India's trade policy is that it was complemented by explicit efforts to develop the country's S&T infrastructure. Since the 1950s, India had established a massive S&T infrastructure that provides scientific knowledge and commercial technologies to manufacturing, mining, agricultural and defence-related enterprises. Within this infrastructure are the 33 government-owned national laboratories of the Council of Scientific and Industrial Research (CSIR). The technologies developed by the CSIR network are often commercialized by the National Research Development Corporation (NRDC).

Incentives for In-house R&D: These include the provision of fiscal incentives by the Department of Science and Technology to firms with R&D

units. These firms received 125 percent of their R&D spending as fiscal concession, in addition to being granted accelerated depreciation of R&D equipment and customs duty exemption on their imports. Firms that used technologies developed locally were granted special investment allowances and licensing privileges. Royalties received by Indian firms from the sale of their technologies abroad were also exempted from income tax, while royalties earned within the country attracted a 40 per cent tax rebate.

The Indian Educational System: India places a lot of emphasis on technical, scientific and engineering skills, and less on the liberal arts. This emphasis has placed India as having one the world's largest number of scientists, engineers and technicians. Indian firms thus have access to abundant supply of skilled labour and at lower costs. The abundance of engineering and technical skills in India explains why the country is a locational choice for high-tech multinational corporations.

Selective Importation of Foreign Technologies: In the past, prospective importers of technology were required to obtain permission from the government. Requests to import technology were screened by the ministries of industry, finance, technology, as well as the CSIR. Applications could be rejected based on the cost of the technology, its appropriateness, the availability of local substitutes, and the ability of the technology to generate indigenous R&D capabilities.

The Technology Evaluation Committee (TEC) was established to evaluate the technological implications of joint-venture and licensing agreements entered into by Indian firms. The government also monitored licensing agreements, and capped royalties on imported technologies at 3-5 per cent of sales, in addition to subjecting those payments to a 40 per cent tax. Unlike some African countries that allow open-ended contracts between local firms and foreign suppliers of technology, India placed a maximum of five years for such contracts, making exceptions only for export-oriented industries.

The Indian government also outlawed technology contracts with "tie-in" clauses and export restrictions. The use of foreign brand names in the domestic market was discouraged, and Indian firms were allowed to sub-license foreign technologies to other local users -- an unusual practice in Africa. To deepen indigenous capabilities in engineering/consultancy, foreign consulting firms were restricted from playing the role of sole consultants in local projects.

I next turn to South Korea, a country known to have used technological innovation to spur growth, structural change and poverty alleviation (Stiglitz, 2001). Korea used two main strategies for promoting innovation and technological change: the "Apprenticeship Strategy" and the "Imitator Strategy" (Westphal and Pack, 1985). Many aspects of these strategies can be replicated in Africa. Under the "apprenticeship strategy," for instance, the Korean government made it mandatory for foreign firms to allow Koreans to participate in industrial projects undertaken by foreign investors in the country. Active participation of Koreans in foreign projects enabled them to acquire production, design, and investment capabilities. They were thus able to replicate those projects across the economy. Another strategy adopted by Korea was the "imitator strategy," in which Korean firms deliberately copied imported technologies and adapted them to local conditions. Information obtained from sales catalogues and visits to foreign manufacturers were also used to build up local technological capabilities.

These strategies were complemented by Korean government's policy of selective intervention in the economy. Korean industries were divided into two categories: the well-established, internationally competitive industries and infant industries. Infant industries were protected through import quotas and licenses, as well tax concessions and access to cheap credit. A major rationale for Korea's policy of selected intervention was to maintain the country's competitiveness in sectors in which it already enjoyed a comparative advantage, and to develop the capacity to compete in industries where its comparative advantage was low.

Contrary to the practice in Africa, the Korean government withdrew protection and other concessions as soon as an infant firm achieved international competitiveness. Where a protected firm remained perpetually inefficient, as is often the case in Africa, the government took over control of the firm and reorganized it. Quite often, these reorganized firms were initially run by private-public sector partnerships, but they subsequently reverted to complete ownership after they had been turned around. This policy applied to industries that were deemed to be strategically important for the country's entry into international markets. Korea's policy of selective intervention was thus accompanied by a monitoring system in which the progress of infant industries was carefully and continuously monitored.

6. Summary, conclusion, and policy recommendations

The global economy has become more knowledge-based, and Africa cannot compete in the new economy without developing technological capabilities. In the past, African countries have sought to promote industrial development by giving firms blanket protections from foreign competition and provided them with subsidies and other privileges. This approach to structural transformation was a complete failure in Africa and undermined the capacity of African manufacturers to compete internationally. But African countries need to do what India and East Asian countries did before they embarked on an export-oriented strategy. And that is to strengthen their innovative and technological capacities. With African's low wage advantage, the region has the potential to attract growth-inducing and employment-generating FDI. But this will only happen if African countries invest in innovation, technological change and skills. The state needs to play a more active and productive role in designing macroeconomic, trade and technology policies that spur technological development in Africa. Some of those policies have been discussed in this paper.

After strengthening their technological capabilities, African countries should use those capabilities to enter new markets. African countries often enter markets when the lifecycle of a given product is at the end stage. While this strategy may seem to be more realistic, given their skill levels and technological capabilities, it also limits their opportunity to achieve high-growth and employment rates. By the time they jump into the fray, markets are smaller and prices lower.

There are several growth opportunities available to African countries in the global economy, but they need to make the right choices. Africa missed the opportunity to tap into the market for information technology (IT), either as a producer of IT hardware or provider of IT support services. This is largely due to their weak technological capabilities. History has shown that fast-growing countries are usually those that succeed in taking advantage of new markets or a new wave of technology. African countries usually jump into a new market when the product lifecycle is at the end stage, at which time its growth-generating, and poverty-reducing capabilities are very limited. African countries need to be proactive, and not reactive, in their approach to acquiring knowledge, and using that knowledge to leverage growth opportunities, especially in green and energy-efficient products.

Efforts should also be made by African countries to create an enabling environment for technological entrepreneurship -- an area that has not been promoted adequately in Africa. Small, start-up enterprises established by technological entrepreneurs have become key drivers of innovation and technology economies across the world. Promoting innovation and technology in Africa would require the emergence of entrepreneurs willing to risk their capital in new ventures. Contrary to conventional wisdom, Africa does not lack entrepreneurs, defined broadly as risk-taking individuals motivated by the prospects of a high rate of return on their activities. The problem with

Africa is that the region lacks a critical mass of Schumpeterian entrepreneurs willing to take risks by investing in new technologies, new markets, discovering new sources of raw materials, new products and processes. Rather than invest in technological innovation and other high value-added activities, many African entrepreneurs depend on patronages from the government. Their "entrepreneurial spirits" are focused, not on creativity and innovation, but on how to secure government contracts. While entrepreneurs in East Asia and some Latin American countries are making waves by pioneering new products and technologies, African entrepreneurs stand along the corridors of power waiting for handouts from the political elites. This mentality has to change if Africa is to join the league of innovative countries. The future, however, is promising.

In recent times, for instance, Africa has seen the emergence of a few Schumpeterian entrepreneurs. They include Mo Ibrahim (Sudanese), who was a major force in the modernization of the telecommunication industry on the continent; Mike Adenuga (Nigerian), also a pace-setter in telecommunications and banking; Mashudu Ramano (South African), a pioneer in the African media and movie industry, and Aliko Dangote (Nigerian), a leading entrepreneur and investor in manufacturing. These entrepreneurs have made remarkable contributions to growth and employment in Africa, and more of them are certainly needed in the region. This can only happen if there is a fundamental shift in macroeconomic, trade, and technology policies in Africa.

Endnotes

1 East Asian countries have successfully used knowledge and innovation to transform their economies and significantly reduce poverty rates (see Figure 1). On the other hand, poverty rates remain very high in Africa, partly because of the region's lack of success with structural transformation.

2 According to Mytelka (1987, p.43): "If we include in knowledge not only research and development (R&D) but also design, engineering, advertising, marketing and management, then present trend suggests that knowledge inputs may be displacing capital, land, and labour as the primary defining feature of the production process in advanced industrial capitalism."

3 For an excellent discussion of the concepts of innovation and technological change, see (Bell, 1984).

4 Recent data on R&D expenditures and other technological indicators are not available.

5 See UNESCO's statistical database at the organization's website.

6 Based on patent data available at the U.S. Patent Office, about 95 per cent of African countries received less than 10 patents each during the past 30 years or so.

7 Recent data on the number of research institutes are not available.

8 For a representative discussion of the endogenous growth theory, see Romer (1986).

9 For more information on indigenous technological capabilities in Eastern Nigeria, see

Brautigam (1997)

10 Import-Substitution Industrialization (ISI) is predicated on a deliberate effort to develop the technological capabilities of local firms, while import-reproduction merely seeks to produce within the local economy, hitherto imported goods. The latter pays scant attention to technology, skills, and management.

11 Nigeria: How Nigerian Textile Failed to Tap Into the $31bn US Booming Garment Market, *Vanguard Newspapers* (Nigeria), April 14, 2008.

References

Abiodun, A.A. (2008), 'Human and institutional capacity building and utilization in science and technology in Africa: an appraisal of Africa's performance to-date and the way forward", in *African Development Review,* 10(1): 10-51.

Ackah, C. and Kutsoati, E. (2008), 'Towards an economic transformation in Ghana: strategic learning from high-growth nations" *Working Paper,* African Center for Economic Transformation, Accra, Ghana.

Adei, S. (1990), 'Technological capacity and aborted industrialization in Ghana: the case of Bonsa Tyre Company', in *World Development,* 18(11): 1501-1511.

Alcorta, L. (2000), 'New economic policies and the diffusion of machine tools in Latin America', in *World Development,* 28(9):1657-1672.

Amsden, A. (1989), *Next Giant: South Korea and Late Industrialization,* New York: Oxford University Press.

Bell, M. (1987), "Learning and the Accumulation of Industrial Technological Capacity in Developing Countries," in Martin Fransman and Kenneth King (eds.), *Technological Capability in the Third World,* London: Macmillan Press, pp.187-209.

Brautigam, D. (1970), 'Substituting for the State: institutions and industrial Development in Eastern Nigeria', in *World Development,* 25(7):1063-1080.

Coombs, R., Saviotti, P. and Walsh V. (1987), *Economics and Technological Change,* Totowa, NJ: Rowman and Littlefield.

Hobday, M. (1985), 'The impact of microelectronics on developing countries: the case of Brazilian telecommunications', in *Development and Change,* 16(2): 313-340.

ILO (2009), *Global Employment Trends,* Geneva: International Labour Organization.

Krueger, A.O. (1997), 'Trade policy and economic development: how we learn', in *American Economic Review,* 87(1): 1-15.

Lall, S. (1987), 'India's technological capacity: effects of trade, industrial science and technology policies," in Martin Fransman and Kenneth King (eds.), *Technological Capability in the Third World,* London: Macmillan Press, pp.225-243.

Lall, S., G.B. Navaretti, S. Teitel and G. Wignaraja (1994), *Technology and Enterprise Development: Ghana under Structural Adjustment,* London: Macmillan.

Lall, S. (1996), 'Structural adjustment and African industry," in Lall, S. (ed.), *Learning from the Asian Tigers,* New York: St. Martins Press, pp.124-147.

Mytelka, L.K (1987), 'Knowledge-intensive production and the changing international strategies of multinational firms', in Caporaso, J. (ed), *A Changing International Division of Labor,* London: Frances Pinter.

Noland, M. and Pack, H. (2007), *The Arab Economies in a Changing World,* Washington, DC: Peterson Institute for International Economics.

Onyeiwu, S. (2009), 'Does the lack of innovation and technology retard economic growth in Africa?' *Paper Presented* at the UNU-WIDER Project Conference on Africa Development: Myths and Realities, Accra, Ghana: 10-11, December, 2009.

Oyelaran-Oyeyinka, B. (1996), 'Industrial innovation in sub-Saharan Africa: the manufacturing sector in Nigeria', *Research Policy*, 25(7): 1081-1096.

Pack, H. (1993), 'Productivity and Industrial Development in Sub-Saharan Africa', in *World Development,* 21(1): 1-6.

Paus, E. (2005), 'Foreign Investment, Development, and Globalization', New York: Palgrave Macmillan.

Stiglitz, J.E. (2001), 'From Miracle to Crisis to Recovery: Lessons from Four Decades of East Asian Experience', in Stiglitz, J. E. and Yusuf, S. (eds), *Rethinking the East Asia Miracle*, New York: Oxford University Press.

UNESCO (2001), *The State of Science and Technology in the World,* Paris: UNESCO Institute of Statistics.

UNESCO (2010), *A Global Perspective on Science and Technology,* UNESCO: Paris.

Vitta, P.B. (1993), 'Short of target: why, in Africa, research rarely reaches use', in *Canadian Journal of Development Studies,* 12(2): 245-260.

Westphal, L.E. and Pack, H. (1985), 'Reflections on Korea's acquisition of technological capability', in Rosenberg, N. and Frischtak, C. (eds.), *International Technology Transfer: Concepts, Measures, and Comparisons,* New York: Praeger.

Young, S-G. (1992), 'Import Liberalization and Industrial Adjustment', in Corbo, V. and Suh, S-M. (eds.), *Structural Adjustment in a Newly Industrialized Country,* Baltimore: The Johns Hopkins University Press, 171-203.

3

National Quality Infrastructure in the Context of Emerging Innovation Systems

Jan Peuckert[1] *& Jorge Gonçalves*[2]

1. Introduction

The building-up of innovation capabilities in developing economies is vital for achieving the sustainability of their development processes, since it affects the technological upgrading, be it through the acquisition and diffusion of foreign technologies or through indigenous R&D. Improving the functioning of emerging innovation systems yet demands completely different measures than the usual policies of support for environments with intense interactive learning found in well-functioning mature innovation systems. Emerging innovation systems differ significantly from mature innovation systems concerning their incompleteness and lack of structure. Their relative inability to produce innovations can be traced back to weak linkages between and among different types of organizations (as firms, research institutes, laboratories, universities), as well as low competences of agents.

1 Department of Innovation Economics of the Berlin Institute of Technology. Email: jan.peuckert@tu-berlin.de

2 Department of Innovation Economics of the Berlin Institute of Technology. E jorgedbg@gmail.com

According to the innovation system theory, which has gained much influence for the understanding of the innovative activity of organizations (Lundvall, 1992; Nelson, 1993; OECD, 1997), the innovation performance of a single organization is dependent on the functioning of the whole network of actors and institutions that is called the innovation system, and particularly on the interaction and the mutual tuning of its system elements. Various attempts have been made to list the most important activities and basic functions of innovation systems. Bergek et al. (2008) identified the following essential system functions: (1) Knowledge development, (2) Knowledge diffusion through networks, (3) Resource mobilization, (4) Entrepreneurial experimentation, (5) Market formation, (6) Creation of legitimacy, and (7) Guidance of search. In order to investigate how to design policies that support the graduation of an emerging innovation system into a mature one, it is necessary to understand the systemic failures of emerging innovation systems.

According to Chaminade et al. (2009), the existing systemic problems of emerging innovation systems can be classified into two main categories: problems related with the components of the system (e.g. lack of competences and capabilities of organizations, weak institutional frameworks, and network problems), and problems related to the dynamics of the system (transition problems, i.e. the inability to cope with new technological problems, path shifts or radical innovations). Both issues imply the "inability of the system to support the creation, absorption, retention, use and dissemination of economically useful knowledge through the interactive learning or in-house R&D investments". As these authors further argue, in emerging innovation systems, the systemic failures result from one or some of the following weaknesses:limited inter-sectoral linkages, absence of interface units, a weakly-developed Science, Technology and Innovation (STI) mode of learning and low competences of users and a lack of trust between agents, a severely restricted Doing, Using and Interacting (DUI) mode of learning.

In this paper, we shall examine the building-up of national institutions and competences within the field of quality infrastructure as a policy instrument to address the above-mentioned weaknesses of emerging innovation systems faced by many developing countries. The remainder is organized as follows. In the next section, the concept of quality infrastructure and its main societal functions are briefly introduced. In the second section, we elaborate on how its constitutive elements contribute to the functioning of innovation systems in general, before we in the third section discuss its value in addressing the specific weaknesses of emerging innovation systems. The fourth section serves as a conclusion and discussion of further research questions.

2. The concept of a quality infrastructure

Quality, the congruence of the actual properties of a good or service with the expected characteristics, is the result of the integration and coordination of several interrelated institutions. Following the definition of the German Federal Ministry of Economic Cooperation and Development (2004), quality infrastructure specifically refers "to all aspects of metrology, standardization, testing, quality management, certification and accreditation that have a bearing on conformity assessment", including "both public and private institutions and the regulatory framework within which they operate".

This institutional complex is considered an infrastructure, as it is underlying many economic activities and transactions. But more than just facilitating micro-economic business transactions, quality infrastructure services play an important role in a much broader socio-economic context, contributing to the innovation capability of the whole economy. Its main societal function is to facilitate economic and social interactions by ensuring:

- Confidence: Products and services are traded conforming to the characteristics settled in the contracts.
- Reliability: Each enterprise can trust on its partners within the value chain regarding, for instance, the measurements units and procedures that are used, the materials or methods that are employed.
- Comparability: It is possible to compare different products and services in terms of their properties in the market and across countries or regions.

But, for quality infrastructure successfully achieving these aims, the involved institutions have to adhere to the following principles:

- Traceability: There exists an uninterrupted chain of comparisons of measurement instruments with increasingly higher accuracy instruments, starting at the instrument used in industry up to the national measurement standard.
- Competence: The different institutions (either private or public) within the quality infrastructure are technically able to perform the tasks that are assigned to them.
- Transparency: Practices and procedures of institutions involved in quality infrastructure activities are accessible and auditable by the civil society.
- Impartiality: Institutions performing quality infrastructure services are protected from political influence and regulatory capture in the fulfillment of their technical contribution.

- Furthermore, defining a strategy for a national quality infrastructure requires from the responsible decision-makers to take the complementarities between the different elements of the quality infrastructure into account.

3. The elements of the national quality infrastructure

Racine (2011) defines a national quality infrastructure as "the public or private institutional framework required to establish and implement standardization, conformity assessment, metrology and accreditation". In the following, we will analyse the effects of the four domains on the functioning of innovation systems separately, although it must be born in mind that these services are highly interrelated.

To serve as an illustration for their interdependence, it is not possible to formulate a standard regarding the properties of a product, unless the respective measurement units have been defined. A standard is only made effective when producers really comply with it, which is more likely if there are incentives to do so. A market incentive may exist when compliance can be credibly signalled to potential consumers through a certification scheme. The impacts of certification depend on the credibility of the certification body, which augments when the required competences of the certifier, as for instance its adequately calibrated measurement instruments, have been accredited by an independent institution.

Standardization

Standardization is the process of developing and agreeing upon technical specifications that formalize the requirements by the users or other stakeholder groups regarding the properties or production procedures of a certain good or service. Generally, we can distinguish between mandatory and voluntary standards, as well as between formal and informal standardization processes. Formal standard development organizations offer platforms to interested companies, users and other interested groups to develop voluntary standards, according to the principles of transparency, openness and consensus. By referring to these standards in technical regulations, governmental authorities may give them mandatory status.

References to minimum quality or safety standards in technical regulations are frequently used by governmental bodies to safeguard social and environmental interests or to dynamically regulate technological change. As with any regulation, there is the need to balance social benefits and compliance costs. Especially in emerging innovation systems, characterized by a large sector of financially strapped small and medium enterprises, too strict standards may suffocate the economy or induce enforcement problems. A strategy to avoid these problems is to ensure a broad participation of all stakeholders in the standardization process.

Since resources are almost always limited, it is important that, when various technological options exist, specific foci are chosen for further investment (Alkemade et al., 2007). Variety-reducing standards are such a selection instrument that, if used correctly, can boost specific technological innovation, providing necessary coordination and guidance to the actors of the innovation system. If new technologies can be coupled to a standard, this has most probably significant consequences for their diffusion, and sometimes may even be the only way of making their application economically viable by allowing for the exploitation of economies of scale or network effects. Moreover, compatibility and interface standards by providing a codified technical basis can also open up new markets for technologies that draw on the standardized technologies, thereby spurring complementary follow-up innovations.

Furthermore, as an act of codification of shared knowledge that facilitates the exchange of information among interested parties, formal standardization helps innovative actors to align their interests and build advocacy coalitions in favor of new technologies. The multi-level perspective literature on socio-technical transitions (Geels, 2002; 2004) considers the processes of de-alignment and realignment as fundamental in the struggle of technological niches to eventually become a dominant regime. Formal standardization, by assembling many stakeholders of a technology to agree on common definitions and specifications, is a forum for sector communication and coordination. To promote the much-needed diffusion of knowledge within emerging innovation systems this may provide an important instrument.

According to Blind (2004), governmental regulations or voluntary formal standards released by standard development organizations are confronted with an increasing tendency towards informal standardization: small consortia of companies, as well as consumer or other civil society organizations set their own standards and try to reach acceptance or even dominance through the market. By specifying market requirements, this standardization supports demand articulation on the one side while on the other giving producers orientation regarding further needs for research and technological development and reducing their uncertainty concerning market preferences and (possibly upcoming) legal provisions.

Conformity Assessment

Conformity assessment has to identify those goods and services that conform to a standard and may label them in order to differentiate them from those that (likely) do not. This element of quality infrastructure comprises the activities of testing and inspection, which are the examination procedures to verify whether a product or service complies with a technical regulation or a standard, and certification, which is the formal substantiation that it conforms. The important economic function is to reduce the asymmetric information inherent to many economic transactions, by increasing the information available to the buyer of a product or service. It establishes a "visible link between standards and the market" (DTI, 2007), thereby creating incentives for producers to upgrade their production processes.

A conformity assessment mechanism reduces the risk concerning the true value of a product faced by the potential buyer. Since the adoption of decisions for technological novelties are typically subject to very high uncertainties, risk reduction through conformity assessment can have an important impact on the actual formation of markets for innovative products.

This effect is even more fundamental in what concerns the so called credence goods: as some (production-related) characteristics are not observable to the buyer of a product even after its purchase, but may add an ideal subjective value to it, for which the buyer would be willing to pay a premium if he was convinced of its factuality. Such values could be for instance related to labor conditions, fair trade aspects, as well as to animal or environmental protection concerns. Innovators with superior performance regarding those quality aspects would not be able to capitalize on this fact without a credible conformity assessment scheme. The existence of conformity assessment services is thus fundamental for the creation of legitimacy and the formation of a market for this kind of innovations.

Metrology

Metrology can be subdivided into scientific metrology, which refers to research activities and the development of the highest level of measurement standards and measurement instruments, legal metrology, which assures the accuracy of measurements where these have an influence on the transparency of economic transactions, health and safety, and industrial metrology, which is concerned with the satisfactory functioning of measurement instruments in industry, production and testing.

The ability to bring quality into new domains of social, economic and environmental realities and of benefiting from a better correspondence between the actual characteristics of products and the formalized expectations depends on the functioning of metrology. The effectiveness of standards depends on the creation of measurement instruments, on the better accuracy of the existing tools and procedures, on the dissemination of the measurement knowledge and access to measurement technology.

Metrology, as the science of measurement, most directly serves the innovation system function of knowledge development. "To measure is to know" and "if you cannot measure it, you cannot improve it", are words attributed to Lord Kelvin, a 19th-century mathematical physicist. The provision of accurate information about product or process characteristics is an important input to R&D. Reliable feedback information about the consequences of small technical changes are precondition for technological experimenting and learning, hence supporting the creation and improvement of new technologies in general. An empirical study by Temple and Williams (2002) has demonstrated the high spillover effects from measurement technology into the wider economy of the UK, estimating an impact equivalent to around 2% of GDP.

The limits of measurement may pose a restriction on the government's ability to enforce the protection of public interests or guide technological change in a certain direction. Technical regulations are only feasible, when their enforcement can be credibly based on reliable control instruments. The quality of the legal metrology infrastructure therefore enables governments to better apply innovation policy instruments.

For companies, it can be hard to enter into (international) quality competition, if there is no adequate metrological infrastructure locally available that allows them to control quality characteristics at a reasonable price. Even voluntary standard requirements then may pose a market entry barrier to those companies that have difficult access to the necessary measurement instruments. Consequently, companies in countries with a weakly developed quality infrastructure often have to face fierce price competition at international markets instead of being able to differentiate their products through qualitative innovations.

Accreditation

The main role of accreditation is to evaluate and attest the competence of organizations or individuals to correctly perform conformity assessment services. It has to provide an independent assessment in order to effectively fulfill its main function, fostering the trust of users on the quality of the goods or services that they are acquiring.

Accreditation is supposed to lend credibility to the whole system of national quality infrastructure, by securing the adherence of the accredited institutions to the principles of transparency, objectivity and impartiality. Furthermore, it assures their integration within the international quality system by securing traceability of measurements to international standards and promoting the world-wide acceptance of their service activities.

Accreditation thus contributes to the innovation system functions of knowledge diffusion by establishing and fortifying international linkages and of market formation by enhancing the trust in the use value of national innovative products, particularly within foreign markets. It can yet be argued that it indirectly amplifies all the contributions of the other quality infrastructure elements to the innovation system.

4. The Role of Quality Infrastructure for Emerging Innovation Systems

As was demonstrated, quality infrastructure services contribute importantly to the functioning of innovation systems. The adequate design of a national quality infrastructure will always depend on its context. Considering the very limited resources of governments in developing countries, quality infrastructure investment decisions should envisage the specific problems faced by their national innovation systems.

According to Racine (2011), national quality infrastructures in many countries have followed common development paths and there are no countries where a functioning quality infrastructure has developed without governmental support. In most countries, metrology, accreditation, and standardization institutes are government owned, and although conformity assessment services are typically provided by private entities, the success of their market depends crucially on public support for the other quality infrastructure elements. The importance of a public intervention towards the establishment of a functioning national quality infrastructure in order to address the most common weaknesses of emerging innovation systems shall be discussed in the following.

Typically, the foundations of national quality infrastructures have been already laid long time ago with the establishment of legal metrologies. Yet, in many developing countries the existence of a functioning legal metrology cannot be taken for granted. For instance, Argentina re-introduced a legal metrology not until 2003, with immediate positive effects at various levels, including on technological upgrading of small and medium enterprises, as an impact study of the national metrology institute INTI indicates (Saavedra, 2011).

The main purpose of legal metrology is to facilitate economic transactions by creating trust between market participants. As there is no way consumers can verify the reliability of each measurement, this responsibility to ensure accuracy is given to public authorities. The lack of trust between actors of emerging innovation systems, which is considered one of the fundamental weaknesses hampering interactive learning, may also be due to a malfunction of this quality infrastructure element.

In general, one of the most relevant functions for innovation of the national quality infrastructure is to leverage the trust between actors. Besides the restriction of fraud through legal metrology, this also happens through the exchange of expectations and the creation of a common understanding between users and producers, between market competitors, and between private firms, regulators and other stakeholders in the process of standard formulation, and by securing through instruments of conformity assessment that products and production processes correspond to the expected characteristics. In this sense, quality infrastructure institutions work very much as interface units, potentially linking actors of an emerging innovation system and supporting particularly the DUI mode of learning, which usually dominates over STI learning in developing economies.

Furthermore, most innovation activity in developing countries is related to the absorption of technology rather than the creation of new-to-the-world innovations. The national quality infrastructure can thereby play a central role in bridging national and foreign economic actors. Integrating local producers in global value chains represents an opportunity to foster the technological upgrading and to participate in regional and global innovation systems, yet it is often a difficult task for developing countries whose productive systems lack credibility with foreign producers, or whose measurement units, procedures or product standards substantially differ from their economic partners.

Linkages between firms of different sectors, which are typically underdeveloped in emerging innovation systems, may not only be weak due to the absence of interfaces or communication platforms, but because there is a general lack of local industry sector diversity. In many developing economies, technological interconnectivity between sectors may therefore not so much be an issue for the strengthening of inter-sectoral linkages than it is the opening to international knowledge exchange and cooperation with foreign actors.

The local existence of credible conformity assessment services may be important to demonstrate to potential foreign partners that local companies are able to provide reliable goods and services. For instance, an empirical study by the metrology institute LATU (Santo and Ferreira, 2011) assessing the impacts of a long-term and comprehensive sector strategy for quality improvement in the Uruguayan milk industry, including the introduction and monitoring of milk quality standards, demonstrates that a significant diversification of foreign trading partners could be achieved in consequence.

To achieve international recognition, it might be necessary to harmonize local measurement procedures and units with international standards and provide national producers with the adequate metrological technologies, testing laboratories, and calibration services. The establishment of independent and transparent accreditation institutes and their integration in regional accreditation organizations is another effective way of gaining the trust of foreign actors in local quality infrastructure competences.

With the establishment of a functioning national quality infrastructure, attracting foreign direct investment (FDI) also becomes easier. This is often an objective of policy makers in developing countries because it is supposed to increase financial resources and accelerate the transfer of technological equipment and technical knowledge that may trigger virtuous development processes.

In order to attract FDI, the national productive system has to provide conditions that facilitate foreign technologies to be adapted and applied locally and assure that the goods that shall be produced will meet the requirements of foreign markets. The more prepared a national production system is to receive foreign technologies, to cope with foreign regulation, and to demonstrate to the foreign trading partners the reliability of its products and services, the more attractive will be this economy to foreign investors.

In order to increase the absorption capacity of indigenous firms, activities are required for the development and dissemination of metrological knowledge and tools necessary to cope with new technologies. Capacitating local producers to apply foreign technologies or processes in the local context creates an opportunity for innovation. At last, quality infrastructure shall be concerned not only in capacitating firms but also universities and research institutes, which will progressively take up their roles within the STI mode of learning.

5. Conclusion

As we have argued, quality infrastructure enhances the innovation capability of an economy and also contributes importantly to the improvement of emerging innovation systems, both by increasing the competences and capabilities of institutions and by supporting networks and the development of linkages between organizations. In an initial stage, the proactive intervention of public institutions is even more important to promote the emergence of networks, to deepen the ties between institutions, and to invest in fields of public concern.

The necessary regulatory framework can only be developed and effectively enforced by actors with legislative power. Moreover, there is a public interest in ensuring that quality infrastructure institutions adhere to certain principles, as for instance transparency, openness and consensus in the process of standardization, else it may be subject to private attempts of strategically raising barriers to competitors by regulatory capture or de facto industry standardization, which in consequence may seriously limit competition and hinder innovation.

There are high fixed costs associated with research in metrology and small marginal costs for the spreading of the developed knowledge, suggesting proactive public intervention and funding in this field. But, as this kind of investments may be very high for developing countries, the development of a national quality infrastructure should be gradual and start by those sectors that are strategically important for a country's economy while requiring high connectivity between institutions and sectors of activity.

Public authorities are also required for the integration of the national quality infrastructure in the international quality infrastructure - a vital step for the reduction of technical barriers to trade, and thereby to improve the access of local companies to global markets and value chains.

The impact of quality infrastructure policies on emerging innovation systems requires further investigation. The realization of empirical case studies would be particularly useful to further develop the theory here proposed and provide a solid basis for policy recommendations.

References

Alkemade, F., Kleinschmidt, C., Hekkert, M. (2007), Analysing emerging innovation systems: a function approach to foresight', in *Int. Journal of Foresight and Innovation Policy*, 3(2):139-168.

Bergek, A., Jacobsson, S., Carlsson, B., Lindmark, S. and Rickne, A. (2008), 'Analyzing the functional dynamics of technological innovation systems: A scheme of analysis', in *Research Policy*, 3793): 407-429.

Blind, K. (2004), *The Economics of Standards: Theory, Evidence, Policy*, Cheltenham, UK: Edward Elgar.

Chaminade, C., Lundvall, B-A., Vang, J. and Joseph, K. (2009), 'Innovation Policies for Development: Towards a Systemic Experimentation based Approach',

Paper presented at 7th Globelics Conference, Senegal, 2009. Available at: www.globelics.org.

DTI (2007), *Conformity Assessment Policy in the United Kingdom*, URN 07/594, UK Department of Trade and Industry.

Geels, F.W. (2002), 'Technological transitions as evolutionary reconfiguration processes: a multilevel perspective and a case-study', in *Research Policy*, 31(8-9): 1257-1274.

Geels, F.W. (2004), 'From sectoral systems of innovation to socio-technical systems: insights about dynamics and change from sociology and institutional theory', in *Research Policy*, 33(6-7): 897-920.

German Federal Ministry of Economic Cooperation and Development (2004), *Quality Infrastructure, Conformity Assessment - Metrology, Standardization, Testing, Quality Management (MSTQ)*, Bonn, Germany. Available at: https://www.ptb.de/lac/.../BMZ__2004__Quality_Infraestructure_.pdf

Lundvall, B.-A. (1992), *National Systems of Innovation: Towards a Theory of Innovation and Interactive Learning*, London: Pinter.

Nelson, R. (ed.) (1993), *National Innovation Systems: A Comparative Analysis*, Oxford: Oxford University Press.

OECD (1997*), National Innovation Systems*, Paris: OECD.

Racine, J. (2011), *Harnessing Quality for Global Competitiveness in Eastern Europe and Central Asia*, Washington D.C.: The World Bank.

Saavedra, M. (2011), Estudio del impacto económico del INTI en la Metrología Legal. In: Impacto de la Infraestrutura de la calidad en América Latina: instituciones, prácticas y desafíos para las políticas públicas, Eds.: Göthner, K.-C.; Rovira, S., Comisión Económica para América Latina y el Caribe (CEPAL), Naciones Unidas.

Santo, C. and Ferreira, E. (2011), Impacto de la Infraestructura de la Calidad en la Cadena Láctea en Uruguay. In: Impacto de la Infraestrutura de la calidad en América Latina: instituciones, prácticas y desafíos para las políticas públicas, Eds.: Göthner, K.-C.; Rovira, S., Comisión Económica para América Latina y el Caribe (CEPAL), Naciones Unidas.

Temple, P. and Williams, G. (2002), 'Infra-technology and economic performance: evidence from the United Kingdom measurement infrastructure', in *Information Economics and Policy*, 14(4): 435–452.

4

Innovative Climate-Smart Agricultural System:
The Case of Nigeria

Ezekiel, Alan Ayinde[1]*; Ayinde, Opeyemi Eyitayo*[2]*; Angathevar Baskaran*[3]*; Adewumi, Matthew Olaniyi*[4] *& Olaoye, Ibukun James*[5]

1. Introduction

Climate-Smart Agriculture (CSA) aims to increase agricultural productivity, profits, improve farmers' resilience, reduce farm produce waste, minimize agriculture greenhouse gas emissions and enhance carbon sequestration. It fortifies food security and ushers environmental benefits. CSA advocates agricultural best practices such as crop management, conservation agrarian practices, intercropping, improved

1 Department of Agricultural Economics, Ladoke Akintola University of Technology, P.M.B. 4000, Ogbomoso, Oyo State, Nigeria. Email: aaezekiel@lautech.edu.ng

2 Department of Agricultural Economics and Farm Management, University of Ilorin, Ilorin, Nigeria. Department of Agricultural Environmental, Development and Economics, Ohio State University, Columbus, Ohio, USA. Email: opeayinde@yahoo.com & opeyemiayinde@gmail.com

3 Associate Professor, Department of Development Studies, Faculty of Economics and Administration, University of Malaya, Malaysia; Senior Research Associate of SARChI (Innovation & Development), Tshwane University of Technology, Pretoria, South Africa. Email: baskaran@um.edu.my; anga_bas@yahoo.co.uk

4 Department of Agricultural Economics and Farm Management, University of Ilorin, Nigeria. Email: matolade@yahoo.co.uk

5 Department of Agricultural Economics and Farm Management, University of Ilorin, Ilorin, Nigeria. Email: olaoyeibikunjames@gmail.com

seeds, livestock management, management of grazing land, fertilizer management, agroforestry, as well as supporting growth investment in agricultural research. It is broader than adaptation, it calls for innovation and changing the farming methods to adapt to and mitigate climate change and sustainably increase productivity. CSA involves the transformation of agricultural policies and systems to increase food productivity and augment food and nutrition security, thereby encouraging the preservation of the environment and ensuring resilience to climate changes.

CSA gives the opportunity to tackle threats of climate change on global food security, and to reduce emissions from food systems, to help meet the target set out in the Paris climate agreement. For a better understanding of the conditions for agricultural innovation and adoption, the CGIAR Research Program on Climate Change, Agriculture and Food Security (CCAFS) depicts CSA as "a key approach to driving transformational change".In recent years, the international community has increasingly emphasized the need to accelerate the transformation agenda by scaling CSA. Different methods for scaling CSA practices are now being developed based on research and innovation. For example, the system of Rice Intensification and Alternate Wetting and Drying, with triple benefits of adaptation, mitigation, and increased productivity, has seen rapid, large-scale uptake. However, smallholders with more diverse land use require more interventions in the sense of biophysical suitability and market opportunities. There is an argument that the slow uptake is due to CSA being perceived as technology- and knowledge-intensive. One of the specific CSA-practices that frequently meets such criticism is agroforestry. Despite complex livelihood, adaptation and mitigation benefits, low adoption of agroforestry was attributed by farmers (who prioritized food security) to long period for return-on-investment, markets uncertainty and short-term loan offering by the banks.Therefore, in this chapter, the following questions are investigated: What is the climate-smart agriculture system (practices and technologies)? What are their potentials in increasing agricultural productivity? What are the key aspects, through which CSA can enhance both the policies and practices in the context of developing countries like Nigeria?

Thus, this chapter assesses the perspectives towards Climate-Smart Agricultural System and sustainable agricultural productivity.Specifically, it discusses the climate-smart agriculture system practices and highlights the CSA potentials in increasing agricultural productivity. It also identifies key changes required in policies and practices that can enhance the adoption of CSA to build a sustainable food system.

2. Theoretical and Conceptual Framework

Simelton et al. (2015) argued for a gradual transition towards promoting integrated systems to avoid loss through the application of modern technology. They suggested focusing either on the adoption of innovative crops or the management rather than changing both at the same time. They identified the problems and distinguished between 'generic' and complex CSA interventions such as agroforestry. They have divided the practices into *technologies* - how things are grown, and *components* – what is grown? Agroforestry/contour planting can be practiced anywhere; trees and crops in the system would depend on soil fertility. At this level, there is a need to consider a framework that focuses on participatory solutions at the field to landscape scale. " Simelton et al. (2015) didn't consider factors that enabled or limited scalability at districts or regions, such as policy backing, market prospective or risk for market saturation. The farmers might have been practicing climate-smart system, and the innovative factor may be making stakeholders know how farming practices can be improved to embrace climate or economic changes. In 2014, four climate-smart agriculture systems were selected in Ogbomoso and its environment: home garden, livestock, agriculture intensification, and forestry. Hence, this study categorizes common practices and purposive steps towards CSA interventions and identifies the opportunities for scaling-out climate-smart agriculture practices in Northern and South-Western Nigeria. The aim is to apply a pragmatic, hands-on methodology which farmers might use and scale-out their potential beyond the scoping area itself.Agriculture has been known as one of the biggest drivers of environmental change.Agricultural land occupies about 50 to 60% of the land surface (Smith et al., 2008). It is estimated that agriculture is responsible for about three-quarters of tropical deforestation (Wollenberg et al., 2012). It also accounts for about 10% to 12% of the total global anthropogenic emissions of greenhouse gases (GHGs). Smith et al. (2008) argued that the world needs more food than ever before to sustain the people living in extreme poverty, especially in Africa where about 70% of the people are engaged in some sort of agricultural activity.

Lessons from the findings will aid the future adoption of climate-smart agriculture in the study area and serve as practical guidance for the implementation of agricultural emissions reduction initiatives based on the knowledge and best practices. The ultimate purpose is to accelerate efforts towards mitigating agriculture-based climate change while at the same time enhancing livelihoods and food security (Adam et al., 1997)

About 75% of farmers in Nigeria are using animal manure (Crops Residue Manure) for crop and vegetable fertility while 25% of them use a combination of animal manure and inorganic fertilizer. There are about 300,000,000 cattle in Nigeria with a human population of about 160,000,000 which implies a ratio of about 3:1. Other farmers apply goat manure on high-value crops such as vegetables. Some of the advantages of using organic manure are the addition of natural nutrients to the soil which helps to improve the soil fertility and pH as well as the sequestration of carbon dioxide, thus reducing its adverse effects on global warming. Large quantities of crops residual manure are needed in the soil to yield fertility of the soil. The poverty level of farmers has not allowed them to have enough animals that can supply the quantity of manure needed to yield soil fertility. Also, the lack of transport of manure to fields which are not close to homesteads is another factor (Below et al., 2010).

Measures to Increase Agricultural Productivity

Transport Facilities: Good roads should link to market to facilitate the production of new farm inputs and to enable farmers to sell their products in the markets. This might raise their income which in turn would encourage the farmers to adopt better farm technology. Thus, it leads to more investment in improving the land.

Irrigation Facilities: Both the quality of input and irrigation facilities determine crop productivity. Therefore, canals and tube wells should be constructed to provide sufficient irrigation facilities for the crops. The devastation by the flood can be curtailed through extensive flood control measures.

Institutional Credit: Adequate credit facilities should be made available at reasonable and cheap interest rates in rural areas. The mortgage banks and co-operative credit societies should be strengthened to provide loans to the cultivators. Moreover, there must be an implementation of an integrated scheme of rural credit.

Proper Marketing Facilities: Marketing infrastructure should be broadened and strengthened to help farmers sell their products at better prices. There should be appropriate arrangements for unloading products in the markets. Also, price support policies must be adopted which would ensure minimum price for the produce of the small-scale farmers.

Supply of Quality Inputs: Adequate and quality inputs should be provided to farmers at controlled prices. To prevent middlemen from exploiting the farmers, steps need to be taken to check the sales of adulterated fertilizers to farmers.

Consolidation of Holdings: Consolidation of holdings is not satisfactory in some areas. Therefore, efforts should be made towards completing the consolidation work in a specific period. Reclamation of abandoned farmlands can be done to make them fit for cultivation.

Agricultural Education: In a bid to train farmers on new technological activities, agricultural education and extension services should be provided. It would enable farmers to take proper crop-care and thus lead to an increase in crop productivity.

Reduction of Population Pressure on Land: The majority of the population depends on agriculture to survive. This increases the population pressure on land which further leads to land fragmentation. Therefore, a proper climatic condition should be generated to encourage the farmers to be employed in subsidiary employment. This will also reduce the population pressure on land. Surplus labour will then be withdrawn from the agricultural sector and be absorbed in the non-agricultural sector.

Provision of Better Manure Seeds: The farmers should have access to chemical fertilizer which could be made available to them through co-operative societies.

Land Reforms: Efforts should be made to plug the loopholes in existing land legislation so that excess land may be shared among the small and borderline agriculturalists.

Co-operative Farming: To mitigate the effects of the fragmentation of holdings, co-operative farming should be launched. Such farming would result in the adoption of modern technology which would be effective on large farms. In this way, agriculture will become a profitable occupation through achieving economies of scale.

Development of Cottage and Small Scale Productions: In rural areas, cottage and small scale industries should be set up to raise the income of the peasants and keep them busy during the off-season.

What is climate-smart agriculture?

CSA is defined as a method of transmuting and reorientating farmers on agricultural innovation under the new realities of climate change (Lipper et al., 2014). The commonly used definition is given by the Food and Agricultural Organization (FAO), the United Nations.FAO defines CSA as food production that is sustainable, which increases productivity, enhances resilience (adaptation), reduces/removes GHGs and enables the realization of national food security and development goals. In this definition, the main essence of CSA comprises of food security and development (FAO, 2013a; Lipper et al., 2014); while productivity, adaptation, and mitigation are identified as the three interlinked pillars necessary for achieving this goal.

The three mainstays of CSA

- *Productivity:* CSA aims to sustainably improve agricultural productivity and proceeds from crops, livestock and fish, without having a damaging impact on the environment. This, in turn, will increase food and nutrition security.
- *Adaptation:* One of the aims of CSA is to reduce farmers' exposure to short-term risks and reinforce their resilience by building their capability to adjust and prosper in the face of shocks and longer-term pressures. Attention is given to ecosystem protectionprovided to the farmers, which is vital for maintaining efficiency and adaptation to climate changes.
- According to the World Bank, agriculture contributes about half of the global emissions of two of the most potent non-CO_2 GHGs: nitrous oxide (N_2O) and methane (CH_4). These non-carbon dioxide GHGs have powerful greenhouse effects and greater longevity than CO_2 (see Table 1).

Table 1: An overview of agricultural greenhouse gases with the trends as currently predicted (adapted from IPCC, 2009).

	CO_2	CH_4	N_2O
Atmosphere life time (year)	120	14.5	120
Direct GWP (Global Warming Potential)	1	24.5	320
Pre-industrial concentration	280ppmv	0.8ppmv	288ppbv
Current annual increase (%)	0.5	0.9	0.25
Major Agricultural Source	Deforestation	Ruminants	Synthetic N fertilizers
		Wetland rice	Animal Excreta
		Biomass burning	Biological N fixation
Percentage of global source stemming from agriculture	30	40	25
Predicted change 1990-2020	-	+	+

Features of Climate-Smart Agriculture

- *CSA reports climate change:* Climate change is incorporated into sustainable agriculture through CSA. This helps the planning and growth of sustainable agricultural systems. Also, this is in contrast to conventional agricultural expansion(Lipper et al., 2014).
- *CSA integrates goals multiplication and management of trade-offs:* Ideally, CSA produces triple outcomes: productivity increase, enhanced resilience, and reduction of emissions. Frequently, when it comes time to implement CSA, compromises must be made. This requires a synergy in weighing the costs and benefits of different options based on stakeholder objectives identified through participatory approaches.
- *CSA maintains ecosystems services:* Ecosystems provide farmers with essential services, including clean air, water, food and materials. It is imperative that CSA interventions do not contribute to their degradation. Thus, CSA adopts a landscape approach that builds upon the principles of sustainable agriculture. It goes beyond the narrow sectoral approaches, which results in uncoordinated and competing land use and adopts integrated planning and management (FAO, 2012b; FAO, 2013a).
- *CSA has multiple entry points at several levels:* CSA has multiple entry points which range from technological development and practices to climate change models and scenarios, insurance schemes, information technologies, value chains and the strengthening of institutional and political enabling environments. As such, it goes beyond single technologies at the farm level and includes the integration of multiple interventions at the food system, landscape, and policy level.
- *CSA is context-specific:* Climate-smart is contextual as its meaning in one place may not be same in another. Interventions must take into account the interaction of different elements at the landscape level. This should be considered among ecosystems and as a part of different institutional activities and political realities. The fact that CSA often strives to reach multiple objectives at the system level makes it particularly challenging to transfer experiences.
- *CSA engages women and marginalized groups:* To achieve the goal of food security and resilience, CSA approaches are needed. They should involve the deprived and most defenseless groups. These clusters often live on marginal lands which are most susceptible to climate challenges like drought and floods. Gender is another central aspect of CSA. Women typically have limited access and legal rights to the land which they farm on, or to other productive and economic resources which could help build their adaptive capacity to cope with events like droughts and floods

(Huyer et al., 2015). CSA strives to involve national, local and regional shareholders in decision-making. Only by doing so, it is possible to identify the most appropriate interventions and form partnerships and alliances needed to enable sustainable development.

3. Material and Methods

Reports on the daily rainfall, minimum and maximum temperatures for the period 1980-2015 were obtained from the Meteorological Department. These data were tested for conventional trend and variability analysis was done usingStata 12 to obtain the projection of rainfall and temperature trends and to assess the potential risk to the cropping system in Nigeria. We used climate change scenario RCP8.5 for Northern Region for the period 2003-2020. The meteorological department is located in the state secretariat of each study area. The climate change scenarios were updated and some specific details were also updated for temperature (increase projection) and rainfall (higher variability).

4. Results and Discussion

It was estimated that 75% of the landed property in Nigeria belongs to the Northern region of the country (Terdoo & Adekola, 2014). This region lies between latitudes 06° 27I N to 14° 00I N and between longitudes 02° 44I E and 14° 42I E, mostly occupied by farmers who are engaged in arable crops farming and cattle rearing. This serves as a means of livelihood for the majority of the people. The people of this region are generally regarded to be poor, financially and in educational terms, compared to other parts of the country (Omonona, 2009). The three types of climate in northern Nigeria are Guinea Savannah, Sudan Savannah and Sahel Savannah. Rainfall and temperatures vary from January to December (Akor, 2012). According to the Nigerian Meteorology Agency (NIMET)(2009), the northern region used to experience lower rainfall but progressively became wetter than the normal levels in the year 2011. The annual rainfall in the region ranges from 400 to 1000 mm. Further evidence suggested that climate change is more complex in this area. A comparison of average temperatures of previous years from 1941 to 2002 showed evidence that the long-term temperature increased across the country, according to the Nigerian Meteorology Agency (NIMET, 2009). The most significant increase recorded was in the North with the average temperature rising by 1.4 to 1.9°C. Comparison of rainfall from 1972 to 2001, by taking the record of a combination of the late-onset and early experience of rainfall shows that the length of the rainfall is shortened in most parts of the country (Building Nigeria's Response to Climate Change (BNRCC), 2011).This study discovered that between 1942 and 2001, the annual rainfall in most parts of Nigeria decreased by 3 to 9 mm. The dry season almost lasts for ten months, while rainfall only occurs seasonally but is often intensive, making it necessary for farmers to practice soil moisture conservation methods. Dutsin-Ma Local Government Area (LGA) in Katsina State, Northern Nigeria was considered in the Northern Region for this study. The majority of the inhabitants there are poor, living below the 500 Naira per person per day threshold. The Local Government Area has a population of 169,829 in about 18,800 households with ecological zones. Generally speaking, the mean monthly maximum temperature varies between 28 and 40°C. In the semi-arid zones comprising of Sudan and Sahel, the maximum temperature could be as high as 40°C between March and May while at the lower end the minimum temperature could be about28°C between December and January.

Assessment of Climate-Smart Agriculture Sustainability (ACSAS)

Descriptive statistics which include frequency, percentage distribution, mean and the standard deviation were used to assess the level of sustainability of CSA in Nigeria. The assessment of modern technologies gave a better understanding of the CSA framework. It was judged from the literature review, personal knowledge and observations from the field. Though it was not tested systematically to ascertain information presented in the available sources, weobtained robust results based on data from different sources (see Table 2).Five major steps were followed to achieve sustainability under securing mankind's existence; they are (1) human health protection; (2) satisfaction of basic human needs; (3) encouraging self-support; (4) sharing of opportunities for the use of natural resources; (5) and the appreciation of differences in income and wealth. The CSA provides knowledge of risk management; it ensures maximum protection against dangers and unacceptable risks for human health due to polluted environmental factors.

Table 2: Sustainability Assessment in Northern and South-Western Nigeria.

Aims	Steps	Standardized as a sustainable strategy	Comments	Predicates in the African context
Securing mankind's existence	Health protection	xxx	Raised alongside ecosystem health	It can help reduce risk from misapplication of fertilizers
	Securing the satisfaction of basic needs	xx	Emphasis on food with little mention of shelter and clothing	Ensures food security and reduces the risk of sickness from inadequate clothing and shelter
	Autonomous self-support	x	Little emphasis on preparation for old age in the face of the rapid flow of youths in urban areas	Prepares support for farmers in their old age
	Just distribution of opportunities for using natural resources	xx	Raised on benefit and cost-sharing, but less on access to resources	There are changes needed to formal laws to reduce usurpation of farmlands for other uses
	Appreciation of extreme differences in income and wealth	x	Emphasis on payment for ecosystem services and little or no mention of compensation for income differentials	Decrease exploitation among farmers
	Sustainable use of renewable resources	xxx	Emphasizes efficiency of available energy, as well as increasing the proportion of renewable energy	Can help create a good balance between increasing emphasis on fertilizers and organic manure through mixed farming
	Sustainable use of non-renewable resources	xx	Advocates reducing reliance on non-renewable external inputs	Attempts to stem the tide of a possible move from renewable to non-renewable resources

Upholding society's productive potential	Sustainable use of the environment	xxx	Emphasizes role of the aquatic ecosystem, forests and tree planting as environmental sinks	Can aid conservation of wetlands, which are often cleared in many African societies. Also serves as a good platform to encourage tree planting
	Avoidance of unacceptable technical risks	xx	Emphasis centers on concerns with potential long-term impacts of biotechnology	With the rapid uptake of biotechnology, directs emphasis to negative impacts
	Sustainable development of real, human and knowledge capital	xxx	Integrate systems that incorporate scientific and local knowledge sources	Promote indigenous knowledge
Keeping options for development and action open	Equal access to education, information and occupation	xxx	Emphasizes social protection including access to social services for education, health, nutrition	Helps enhance societal organization through the reduction of disparity between rich and poor in society
	Participation in societal decision-making processes	xxx	Emphasizes the need to broaden stakeholder participation with due consideration to cross-sectorial negotiations and planning processes	Ensures local people have a say in their development
	Conservation of nature's cultural functions	x	Less emphasis placed on cultural factors	May lead to a situation where culture is seen as entirely 'good' or completely 'bad'
	Conservation of 'social resources	x	Emphasizes the interactions between sectors.	Need to encourage inter-personal interactions especially among farmers.

Agricultural Practice and Environmental Change in Nigeria

The commonly practiced agricultural system in Northern and South-Western Nigeria has been a traditional farming system, such as crop rotation, farm rotation, bush fallowing and crop residual cultivation (Adams & Mortimore, 1997). The practices involved the cultivation of land, usually from one (1) to three (3) years and then, abandoning it for a period of years to fallow for fertility. The increase in population growth has resulted in land shortages, which has drastically reduced the amount of arable land available to farmers and reducing fallow periods. Farmers are engaged in cutting down the vegetation on plots and setting fire to the remaining foliage, the ashes are used to provide nutrients to the soil for planting food crops.

5. Conclusion and Recommendation

We have argued that introducing noble approaches like giving orders to a subordinate is not what is needed for sustainable development in Africa. There is a need to ensure that the approach is apt and has potential for success. In this line of thought, we have argued in favour of the sustainability of Climate-Smart Agriculture for adaptation in Northern Nigeria. Climate-Smart Agriculture has been proposed as an approach that can combat climate change and desertification comprehensively by emphasizing the adaptation to climate change. Having assessed the approach through the prism of the SAET framework, we found that, broadly speaking, it fits with what can be termed as a sustainable technology. Admittedly, there are many aspects, such as the emphasis on cultural functions that will need to be addressed. CSA in societies like Nigeria where the poor are often cheated out from programmes should integrate all the needs of the disadvantaged into the policy before its final adoption. Such a review has become necessary because the approach, as currently conceived, does not do enough justice to some of the critical issues in the agricultural sector in Nigeria. There is a need for an all-inclusive approach that would not only enhance environmental protection for the country but also respect social values. The outcomes of some of the current practices adopted to manage adverse environmental impacts were found to provide coping strategies that fit within the concept of CSA. However, these are still not very widespread. Therefore, we recommend the adoption of farm management and technology practices such as the use of cover crops, crop rotation, inter-cropping, improved seed varieties, tillage systems, water harvesting and management systems, improved pasture management systems and agroforestry. It is expected that, if consciously adopted by farmers in the region, the adverse impacts of climate change and desertification on the people shall be greatly mitigated. Furthermore, CSA shall enable farmers in the region to adapt effectively to the adverse impacts of climate change and desertification and, hence, improve the wellbeing of rural farm households (which constitute the majority population) and help Northern Nigeria attain food security and sustainable development.

References

AMAF (2015), *ASEAN Regional Guidelines for Promoting Climate Smart Agriculture (CSA) Practices* 2015, ASEAN Meeting on Agriculture and Forestry 7: Philippines.

Adams, W.M. and Mortimore, M.J. (1997), 'Agricultural Intensification and Flexibility in the Nigerian Sahel', *The Geographical Journal,* 163(2): 150-

160, Environmental Transformations in Developing Countries (July, 1997). Available online at: http://dx.doi.org/10.2307/3060178.

Below, T., Artner, A., Siebert, R. and Sieber, S. (2010), 'Micro-level practices to adapt to climate change for African small-scale farmers: A review of selected literature', *IFPRI Discussion Paper 00953*, Environment and Production Technology Division, International Food Policy Research Institute, Washington D.C.

Building Nigeria's Response to Climate Change [BNRCC] Project (2011), Available at: https://www.devex.com/organizations/building-nigeria-s-response-to-climate -change-bnrcc-31411.

Terdoo, F. and Adekola, O. (2014), 'Assessing the role of climate-smart agriculture in combating climate change, desertification and improving rural livelihood in Northern Nigeria', *African Journal of Agricultural Research*, 9(15):1180-1191.

FAO (2013), *Climate – Smart Agriculture: Sourcebook*, Rome: Food and Agricultural Organization, United Nations.

Lipper, T. P., Campell, B.M. and Torquebieu, E.F. (2014), 'Climate Smart Agriculture for food security', *Nature Climate Change*, 4: 1068 – 1072.

Omonona, B. T. (2009), 'Quantitative Analysis of Rural Poverty in Nigeria', *Nigeria Strategy Support Programme (NSSP) Background Paper 9*, International Food Policy Research Institute, Washington D.C.

Simelton, E., Dam, B.V. and Catacutan, D. (2015), 'Trees and agroforestry for coping with extreme weather events - experiences from Northern and Central Viet Nam', *Agroforestry Systems*, 89(6): 1065-1082.

Smith, P., Martino, D., Cai, Z., Gwary, D., Janzen, H., Kumar, P., McCarl, B., Ogle S., O'Mara, F.,Rice, C., Scholes, B., Sirotenko, O., Howden ,M., McAllister, T., Pan, G., Romanenkov, V., Schneider, U.,Towprayoon, S., Wattenbach, M., and Smith, J. (2008), 'Greenhouse gas mitigation in agriculture',*Philosophical Transactions of the Royal Society of London*, Series B: Biological sciences, 363 (1492): 789–813.

Wollenberg, E., Higman, S., Seeberg-Elverfeldt, C., Neely, C., Tapio-Biström, M.L., and Neufeldt,H. (2012), 'Helping Smallholder Farmers Mitigate Climate Change', *CCAFS Policy Brief 5: 1-6*. CGIAR Research Program on Climate Change, Agriculture and Food Security (CCAFS), Copenhagen, Denmark. Available online at: ccafs.cgiar.org/resources/reports-and-policy-briefs.

5

Structure and Dynamics of Uganda's Technological Innovation System

Julius Ecuru[1], Lena Trojer[2], Ziraba N. Yasin[3] & Peter O. Lating[4]

1. Introduction

In 2009 Uganda passed a national science, technology and innovation policy. The policy provides a broad framework for investment and capacity building in science and technology as well as regulation of scientific conduct. It lays out strategies intended to enable Uganda meet its aspiration for a science, technology and innovation-led growth and development. To this end, science, technology and innovation was for the first time designated in Uganda's National Development Plan for the period 2010-2015 as a sector that provides institutional and infrastructural support to the production of goods and services (MFPED, 2010; MFPED, 2009). A specific science, technology and innovation plan has been prepared.

These recent policy developments show that Uganda is making some effort to build its innovation system. Many countries around the world are

1 Blekinge Institute of Technology, Sweden and Makerere University, Uganda. Email: Julius.ecuru@gmail.com; Julius.ecuru@bth.se.

2 Professor, Blekinge Institute of Technology, Sweden. Email: lenatrojer@gmail.com.

3 Senior Lecturer, Makerere University, Kampala, Uganda. Email: ynziraba@tech.mak.ac.ug.

4 Senior Lecturer, Makerere University, Uganda. Email: plating@tech.mak.ac.ug.

building their innovation systems as a development and competitiveness strategy. The European Union, for example, wants to transform into an "innovation union" (European Commission, 2011). Finland in 2009 re-evaluated its innovation system to prepare it for future growth challenges, and South Africa has a ten-year innovation strategy (2008-2018) as its pathway to a knowledge-based economy. Following these examples, Uganda, indeed like other countries in the region such as Ethiopia, Kenya, Mozambique, Tanzania, and Zambia, to mention a few, has made "innovation" an integral part of its traditional science and technology policy (MFPED, 2009; UNESCO, 2009). Although this is a welcome move, it is not enough to foster innovation. Understanding how key organizations and firms in the innovation process interact and learn from each other, and the factors which influence such interactions, will be crucial for effective implementation of the science, technology and innovation policies.

Therefore, the aim of this study is to provide insight into Uganda's evolving innovation system. The study is limited to a discussion of the structure and functional elements of Uganda's innovation system. Key actors are identified and their relationship in the pursuit of science, technology and innovation is described. For purposes of this study, science, technology and innovation are taken together to mean a dynamic process involving discovery and generation of new knowledge and the application of knowledge to develop new and/or improve goods and services. In this sense, science, technology and innovation is the means by which new products and new processes are developed and deployed to use.

The study is organized as follows: A review of the relevant literature is in Section 2. Section 3 introduces a framework used to discuss the structure and functional elements of Uganda's evolving innovation system. This is followed by results and discussions of the functional elements in Section 4. Section 5 is concluding remarks.

2. Innovation System, What is it?

Innovation system is a concept first introduced in the 1980s and 1990s by Christopher Freeman, Bengt-Ake Lundvall and Richard Nelson (Lundvall *et al.*, 2009; Godin, 2009; Lundvall, 2007; Archibugi *et al.*, 1999). It refers essentially to interactions among diverse groups of actors involved in the production, diffusion and use of new and economically useful knowledge (Lundvall, 2010; Fischer, 2001).Lundvall recently described an innovation system as an 'open, evolving and complex system that encompasses relationships within and between organisations, institutions and socio-economic structures, which determine the rate and direction of innovation and competence building emanating from processes of science-based and experienced-based learning' (Lundvall *et al.*, 2009). For Lundvall learning is crucial in the innovation process. Such learning may be through formal educational and scientific organizations such as universities and research organizations; or it can be learning by doing, using and interacting such as is common in the workplace. Edquist & Johnson (1997) elaborate further that an innovation system has two components: organizations and institutions. Organizations are the actors or players, e.g. universities, research organizations or firms. Institutions are the common habits, rules, laws, and customs that influence the way the organizations relate. The patent law is an example of an 'institution'. It gives inventors the right to exclude others from exploiting their inventions over a prescribed period of time. Another example of an 'institution' could be the requirement to obtain informed consent from human participants in clinical trials. Institutions evolve with new values and organizations transform as a result. Therefore, innovation systems are dynamic; with people learning as they interact (Lundvall, 2010).

Innovation systems, however, differ across countries and communities. For example, the innovation system of South Africa may differ from that of Uganda. Countries structure and build their innovation systems differently according to their unique customs and traditions, political and socio-economic conditions. But regardless of the differences there might be, innovation systems usually have the same goal, which is, to 'support the development, diffusion and use of innovations' (Chaminade and Edquist, 2006; Edquist, 2001). Here "innovations" refer to new ideas or practices or new or improved goods and services introduced in society (Lundvall, 2007;Rogers, 2003; Witt, 2002). These could be products, i.e. new or better goods and services, or processes, i.e. new ways of production which may be technological or changes in management style (Chaminade and Edquist, 2006). Innovations may be radically new, for example, when a new malaria vaccine is introduced; or they could be existing technology that finds new application elsewhere, for example, when a local bank introduces internet banking services which is already in use somewhere else.

Building blocks of an Innovation System

As of now, there is no single way of describing the structure of an innovation system. Of recent, however, a number of scholars have opted to study innovation systems in terms of their functions or building blocks.These scholars argue that besides identifying organizations (actors) and what they do, knowledge about the system's structure and the way it functions is important to foster innovation (Liu and White, 2001; Edquist, 2001). Consequently, many variants of functions or building blocks of an innovation system have been put forward.Chaminade & Edquist (2006) as well as Hekkert *et al.* (2007) did an extensive review of functions of innovation systems. Table 1 is adapted with modifications from (Chaminade and Edquist, 2006). It is a summary of some of the functions of innovation systems suggested in literature.

Describing an innovation system in terms of its functions has attracted interest of many scholars. It is a subject of ongoing discussions (See Table 1). This paper contributes to the ongoing discourse by introducing another dimension of functions (or in this case, a framework) which could be used in deliberations on innovation systems particularly in low income countries. The framework is used to provide insight into Uganda's evolving innovation system. It uniquely recognizes the distributed and heavily decentralized way knowledge is currently produced and used in Uganda.

Table 1: Activities (functions) in Innovation Systems

Author(s)	Definition of function or activity	Main criteria for classification	Breakdown of functions, activities or building blocks
Edquist (2005)	Factors that influence the development and diffusion of innovation	Determinants of the innovation process	1. Knowledge inputs to the innovation process 2. Demand-side factors 3. Provision of constituents in system of innovation 4. Support services for innovating firms
Furman, Porter and Stern, (2002)	Building blocks required to produce and commercialize a flow of technologies new to the world over the long term	Determinants of national innovative capacity	1. Strong innovation infrastructure 2. Strong innovation environments (incl. input conditions, demand conditions, related and supporting industries and context for firm strategy and rivalry) 3. Linkages between 1 and 2.

Galli & Teubal, (1997)	Factors affecting the production and diffusion of innovations	Activities according to type of organization (hard or soft)	*Hard functions* 1. R&D 2. Supply of scientific and technical services to third parties *Soft functions* 3. Diffusion of information, knowledge and technology to bridging organizations. 4. Policy making by government offices 5. Design and implementation of institutions 6. Diffusion/divulgation of scientific cultures 7. Professional coordination through academies, professional associations.
Johnson & Jacobsson (2003)	Factors that affect the knowledge production processes	Knowledge production processes that can be influenced by public policy	1. Creation of new knowledge 1. Guidance of the research process 2. Provision of resources 3. Generation of knowledge economies 4. Dissemination of market information
Xielin Liu and Steven White (2001)	Fundamental activities of innovation systems	Performance implications of a system's structure and dynamics	1.Education 2.R&D 3.Implementation (or manufacturing), 4.End-use (i.e. customers of the product) and 5. Linkage

OECD (2002)	Core blocks in the system of innovation to be considered in a comprehensive innovation policy	Innovation policy	1.Enhancing firm innovative capacities 2. Exploiting power of markets 3.Securing investment in knowledge 4.Promoting commercialization of publicly funded research 5. Promoting cluster development 6. Promoting internationally open networks
Fischer (2001)	Building blocks of an innovation system	Elements encompassing the innovation process	1. Manufacturing sector (manufacturing firms & their R&D labs) 2. Scientific sector(education & training; universities & research organizations) 3. Sector of producer services (support to industrial firms) 4. Institutional sector (regulations, financing, rules)
M Hekkert, Suurs, Negro, Kuhlmann and Smits (2007)	Functions of *technological* innovation systems	Processes which take place in an innovation systems	1. Entrepreneurial activities 2. Knowledge development 3. Knowledge diffusion through networks 4. Guidance of the search (i.e. long term goals set by gov't) 5. Market formation 6. Resources mobilization 7. Creation of legitimacy

M Hekkert, Suurs, Negro, Kuhlmann and Smits (2007); Bergek, Jacobsson, Carlsson, Lindmark andRickne, (2008); Bergek, Marko Hekkert and Jacobsson, (2008)	Functions of *technological* innovation systems	Processes which take place in an innovation systems	1. Knowledge development and diffusion 2. Influence on the direction of search 3. Entrepreneurial experimentation 4. Market formation 5. Resource mobilization 6. Legitimation 7.Development of positive externalities or "free utilities"
Lundvall (2010)	Elements of a national system of innovation	Differences in structure of production systems and institutional set up of nation states	1. Internal organization of firms 2. Inter-firm relationships 3. Role of the public sector 4. Institutional set up of the financial sector 5. R&D-intensity and R&D-organization

Source: Adapted -with Modifications- from Chaminade and Edquist (2006).

3. The Framework

The framework consists of four functional elements. These are: Science, technology and innovation (Sti), Financing (F), Governance (G), and Human Capital (Hc) (see Figure 1). Assuming that the primary goal of any innovation system is to "support the development, diffusion and use of innovations" (Chaminade and Edquist, 2006), then:

$\text{Sti} = f(\text{F}, \text{G}, \text{Hc}, r)$,

Where '*r*' denotes the strength and intensity of the interactions (and learning) both within and across the functional elements or spheres. Science, technology and innovation (Sti) in this case represents dynamic processes, such as discoveries, inventions, knowledge generation, product development, dissemination and diffusion of innovations. Governance (G) includes policies and plans, laws and regulations, standards and guidelines which directly or indirectly guide the Sti process. Financing (F) includes funding for Sti activities, e.g. grants for research and innovation, venture capital (e.g. the Youth Entrepreneurship Venture Capital Fund announced in Uganda's 2011/12 national budget speech), direct support from government treasury or private sector and development partners. Human capital (Hc) involves educational and training activities aimed at imparting knowledge and skills necessary for Sti. It also includes knowledge tacitly acquired in the course of work or through experience. Universities, firms and other organizations engaged in local skills development, as well as schools and business, technical and vocational education and training colleges are the primary actors that supply the necessary human capital.

Within each functional sphere (Sti, F, G and Hc) actors operate on a continuum oscillating between sole role (sr) player, e.g. a full-time researcher, and dual role (dr) player e.g. a professor involved in both teaching and conducting research. Across functions an actor may perform multiple roles (mr), e.g. a professor who lectures at a university, does research, but also serves as a board member of a governmental agency. An actor may be an individual or an organization or a firm. Actors performing the same function may interact and learn from each other at specific times and situations within that functional sphere; but they may also interact and learn across functions (Figure 1).

4. Results and Discussion

Using the Framework: The Case of Uganda

The information used in the following section to illustrate the various functional elements of Uganda's innovation system were obtained by reviewing key science and technology related policy documents. These documents included the national science, technology and innovation and related policies, institutional reports, workshop proceedings, reports of scientific meetings, comprehensive national development frameworks, laws and regulations, research databases in Uganda, journal articles, papers and related work on innovation systems.These documents were read; key points were noted and summarized.Additional information was gleaned from science and technology policy dialogues, meetings and events both within Uganda and abroad.

Science, Technology and Innovation

Science, technology and innovation in Uganda can be traced back to the pre-industrial iron ore discoveries around Lake Turkana in Kenya, and carbon steel industry around the shores of Lake Victoria (Teng-Zeng, 2006). But later during the colonial era (1894-1962), science, technology and innovation was predominantly in health and agriculture; specifically, research on tropical diseases (malaria and sleeping sickness), cash crops (cotton, coffee, and tea) and fisheries (Teng-Zeng, 2006; EAC, 2000). Tsetse control and fisheries research were conducted in eastern Uganda (i.e. National Livestock Resources Research Institute), while tropical diseases research was done in central Uganda (i.e. Uganda Virus Research Institute at Entebbe). Interest in studying the African way of life led to the establishment of an East African Institute of Social Research at Makerere in 1948 (now Makerere Institute of Social Research). To date humanities, health, agriculture and natural sciences continue to dominate the fields of research in Uganda. In 2008, for example, social sciences and humanities accounted for 36 per cent of the research conducted in Uganda followed by health (31 per cent), natural sciences (21 per cent), and agriculture (ten per cent) and engineering and technology two per cent (Ecuru *et al.*, 2008). Uganda needs to do more to promote research and innovation in the engineering and physical sciences fields as well as the foundation for value addition and manufacturing. Also, latent potential of the informal sector engaged in metal fabrication, wood works, food and farm produce and herbal medicines is largely untapped.

Public universities and research organizations account for the bulk of scientific and technological activities in the country. Unlike in South Africa, where private companies account for almost half of the research and innovation investment, the contribution from private companies in Uganda is still very small.If Uganda is to achieve its goal of becoming a middle-income country as soon as possible, public universities and research organizations have to be more proactive in translating their research products into commercial ventures and enterprises.

Human Capital

Human capital constitutes the pool of knowledgeable and skilled people capable of generating new ideas and transforming ideas into socially valuable and economically viable goods and services. In Uganda this pool is still small. Human capital potential is shaped by the educational system of a country and by the learning environment in firms and other organizations.

Uganda's education system comprises two to three years of pre-primary schooling, seven years of primary, four years of lower secondary, two years of upper secondary, and three to five years of undergraduate study. Technical and vocational colleges offer one to three-year diploma and certificate courses providing technical skills in a variety of scientific and technological fields. Sustained efforts are needed to attract students into science and engineering career programmes, especially at universities. At the moment less than 25% of students enrolled in universities are for science and engineering programmes, which are about half the international average (Barugahara and Lutalo, 2011).

For a long time, Uganda had only one university, i.e. Makerere University, which started as a technical college in 1922 and was accorded a university status in 1949. Higher education reforms which took place in the early 1990s paved way for emergence of private universities. By the end of 2011 there were five recognized public universities and over 22 private ones. The Universities and Tertiary Education Act of 2005 further gave autonomy to universities and created the National Council for Higher Education to ensure good standards (high quality) in higher education.

Most of the reforms taking place in Uganda's education sector are geared towards supply of the much-needed scientific workforce. Since 1996, every child of school going age (i.e. six to 12 years) must attend primary school free of charge under the universal primary education program. Starting 2006 government further adopted a phased introduction of universal secondary education. The study of science subjects is compulsory in lower secondary education; and since 2005, 75 per cent of all government sponsorship (currently 4,000 students annually) for undergraduate student enrolment in public universities is towards science-based courses. As a government policy, all public universities established after Makerere University are supposed to emphasize science disciplines. However, they often end up with more humanities and arts students. By recruiting more students into humanities and arts courses, public universities can generate income internally to meet shortfalls in government funding.

Unless government intervenes with more sustained funding to the higher education sector, public universities may fail to achieve the policy goal of producing more science and engineering graduates. A continuing challenge cutting across the entire education sector in Uganda is ensuring higher quality of learning at all levels and reforming curricula to meet the changing skills demand in the economy.

Figure 1: Actors and Functions in Uganda's Innovation System

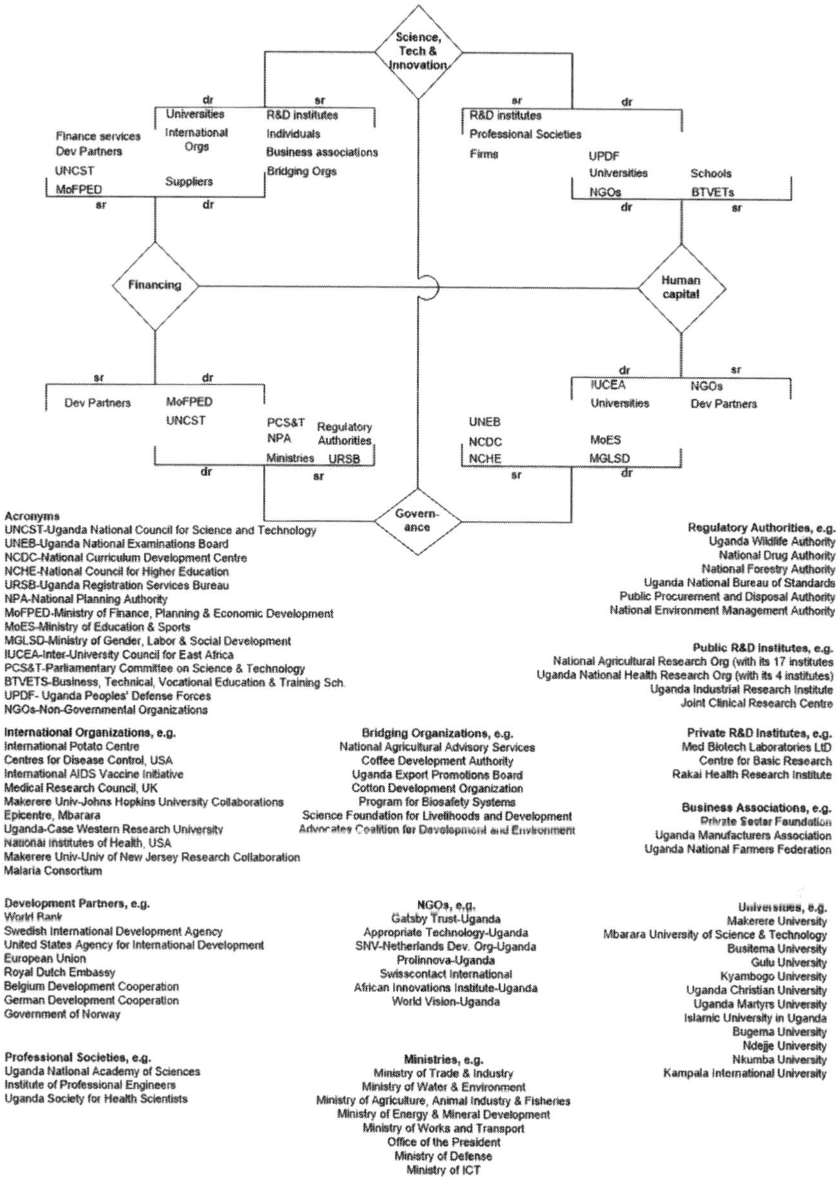

Capacity for postgraduate training at Ugandan universities, other than Makerere University is still very low. Owing to the limited facilities, a significant number of Ugandan students seek graduate studies abroad. Over the years, Makerere University has built considerable capacity to offer science-based postgraduate (PhD and MSc) training. Makerere University could, therefore, take advantage of its unique position and capabilities to expand its graduate school. This opportunity is somewhat identified in the University's strategic plan for the period 2008/09-2018/19 which aims to transform the university into a research-led university, essentially producing Master's and PhDs for other universities. To achieve this goal, however, would require the university to substantially reduce enrolment for undergraduate students. It would also mean losing revenue from undergraduate private students. Therefore, realizing the goal of a research-led university may take some time.

Governance

From independence in 1962 until the early 1990s policy for science, technology and innovation was such that research and technology dissemination were carried out within government's line ministries and departments. In 1970 a National Research Council was created by a Cabinet decision to guide and coordinate research in Uganda. This body became the Uganda National Council for Science and Technology (UNCST) duly established by Act of Parliament (Chapter 209) in 1990. Public Sector Reforms in the 1990s detached research from government ministries and line departments and created autonomous research organizations such as the National Agricultural Research Organization (established in 1992 but restructured in 2005 by the National Agricultural Research System Act of 2005). Granting autonomy to research organizations was aimed at reducing red tape, improving accountability and overall efficiency. However, it tended to alienate government from research and academia and vice versa. Interactions between research organizations and universities and government and industry became more difficult to achieve in practice.

Earlier on in 1990 need was felt for an explicit national policy on all fields of science and technology, hoping that it would provide a coordinated framework for science and technology development in the country. The first attempt to formulate this policy was at a National Workshop held toward the end of 1991. A draft of the national science and technology policy was prepared in 1993. The draft policy underwent several revisions until it was finally passed by government in August 2009. The goal of the policy is to strengthen Uganda's capability to generate, transfer and apply technologies, ensuring sustainable utilization of natural resources for development. Besides this framework policy, sectoral science and technology policies also exist including, for example, the National Agricultural Research Policy 2005 and the National Biotechnology and Biosafety Policy 2008.

Uganda has no standalone ministry for science and technology unlike its neighbours Kenya and Tanzania or South Africa for that matter. The Ministry responsible for science and technology is that of Finance, Planning and Economic Development, which is also the parent ministry to which UNCST belongs.Coordination of science and technology matters is, therefore, the responsibility of the UNCST. The UNCST was established in 1990 to advise on and coordinate the formulation of an explicit national policy on all fields of science and technology; and also to coordinate research and development, and facilitate science and technology integration into all sectors of the economy, among other functions. Over the years, UNCST has grown tremendously and evolved into an organization with three major clusters of roles. First, it functions as a national research and innovation funding agency. In some countries separate organizations are created and dedicated to play this role. In South Africa, for example, such a role is played by the National Research Foundation and other Research Councils. Second, UNCST plays the role of a science and technology policy think tank and advisory body to government. Such a function entails guiding the direction, setting goals and determining priorities for strategic investments in science, technology and innovation. Juma (2011) argues that such a function should be positioned at the highest possible level in government such as at presidential or cabinet level. Third, UNCST acts as a regulatory body in some situations e.g. for biosafety, human subjects research and access to genetic resources. Because these are crosscutting themes and sometimes involve new and emerging technologies, it is difficult to place them in any one single organization, other than the UNCST.

The challenge, however, is that the three major clusters of roles currently played by the UNCST are huge mandates in themselves and may with time overwhelm the capacity of UNCST as an organization. This is probably why a dedicated ministry for science and technology has been proposed (MFPED, 2010). The other challenge is that as the trends of research and innovation keep rising and knowledge production becomes increasingly diversified and distributed, the three clusters of roles could potentially conflict under one roof. If these clusters of roles are to be played more effectively in future, then having them executed in separate houses might be a prudent strategy as long as the resource envelope is able to sustain them as such.

As for legislation, there are different pieces of it which regulate various aspects of scientific conduct. For example, the National Environment Management Authority Act 1995 provides for environmental impact assessment of major scientific projects. The National Drug Authority Act of 1993 regulates clinical trials. The Uganda Wildlife Authority Act of 1996 regulates research in wildlife protected areas. There are other laws, regulations and guidelines, e.g. for quality of commercial and consumer products, intellectual property protection, plant quarantine, human research protection, biosafety, and radiation safety.

Therefore, it appears Uganda is not short of the basic policies, laws and regulations to guide science, technology and innovation. The key issue is the extent to which these policies and laws are harmonized to promoteresearch and innovation in the country. Although new policies and laws may be justifiable in some situations, more effort should be devoted to implementing, reviewing and consolidating the existing ones. Responsible agencies should have the means to quickly adjust their policy and legal regimes to accommodate significantly new and emerging areas of science, technology and innovation.

Financing

Financing for science, technology and innovation in Uganda is predominantly by government and development partners. In 2007/08 financial year, government's share of expenditure on research and development was about 42 per cent, development partners 51 per cent and other sources seven per cent. Government support was mainly for administrative costs such as utilities, maintenance and personnel. Contribution from private sector was miniscule. In middle income countries, private sector usually spends more on research and development.For example, in 2004/05 the business sector in South Africa financed 45% of research and development and performed 58% of total research and development, while international sources amounted to only 15% (OECD, 2007).Scientists in Uganda rely on grants from abroad, which are very competitive to win, and which sometimes may not be properly aligned to the country's development needs. For many Ugandan scientists, having good grants proposal writing skills is paramount and forging links with other scientists abroad is absolutely essential. In addition, having a supportive local research environment, e.g. efficient administrative processes, less cumbersome regulatory systems for research and less burdensome tax regimes for scientific equipment, would be necessary to attract more foreign research investment.

Between 2003/04 and 2007/08, total annual national expenditure on R&D as percentage of GDP averaged 0.3 per cent (Ecuru *et al.*, 2008). This is very low compared to South Africa, which spent between 0.8 per cent and one per cent of its GDP on research and development during the same period (OECD, 2007). Uganda should work towards spending at least one per cent of its GDP per annum on research and development in the medium term as recommended by the African Union Summit of 2007 in Addis Ababa, Ethiopia.

A key missing link in the financing of science, technology and innovation in Uganda is the absence of a stable merit-based competitive funding scheme coupled with weak contribution from the private sector. The Uganda Millennium Science Initiative (MSI) launched in February 2007 by President Y.K Museveni was the closest to having a national competitive/merit-based system for science funding. The MSI was a project worth US$ 33.35 million over 5 years co-financed by the government of Uganda (US$ 3.35 million) and the World Bank (US$ 30 million), and implemented by the UNCST. By the end of 2009 UNCST had awarded competitively a total of 39 grants each ranging between US$ 0.25 million to US$ 1.25 million for three to four years. Impressive results have so far been reported, including strengthening tertiary science and engineering curricula, potentially commercializable research products, outreach events, more skilled science and engineering graduates, etc. Building on the MSI model of financing research and innovation could be one way the Uganda government would operationalize the National Science and Technology Fund established in 1990 under Section 20 (3) of the UNCST Act 1990 (Chapter 209). The MSI project in Uganda appears to have been a step towards building a merit-based system for science funding in the country.

A merit-based system for research and innovation funding is desirable for harnessing ideas and knowledge and nurturing local talent. It would also encourage creativity and a culture of innovation in Ugandan universities, research organizations and firms. However, developing and sustaining such a system might also depend on the extent to which it is consistent with and supported by the current national budgeting regime.

Uganda's annual national budget is arrived at through a consultative process involving Sector Working Groups (SWGs). A SWG is a forum for negotiation, policy dialogue and agreement on priority plans as well as budget allocations within the sector. Presently designated SWGs are: Agriculture; Lands, Housing and Urban Development; Energy and Mineral Development; Works and Transport; Information and Communication Technology; Tourism, Trade and Industry; Education; Health; Water and Environment; Social Development; Security; Justice, Law and Order; Public Sector Management; Accountability; Legislature; and Public Administration (MFPED, 2011). Ideally, any government ministry or agency should fit in one of these SWGs. Universities, for example, belong to the Education SWG, the National Agricultural Research Organization is in the Agriculture SWG, and UNCST belongs to the Accountability SWG, where its parent Ministry of

Finance, Planning and Economic Development falls. In principle, therefore, each agency with significant science, technology and innovation activities should vie for financial resources within their respective SWGs. Since science, technology and innovation cuts across all the SWGs, it seems logical and plausible to have it rationalized within each SWG. However, this approach may not be welcomed by some members of the scientific community who strongly believe that science, technology and innovation deserve a sector status and, therefore, should also be designated a SWG. The SWGs, notwithstanding, it is important that agencies with significant science, technology and innovation activities have opportunities for joint cooperation in research and innovation with universities, research organizations and firms. This would be possible if government encouraged dual funding systems for research and innovation which, on the one hand, involves direct funding to universities and research organizations, and on the other, having in place a stable merit-based system where grants are competitively awarded annually to individuals and research groups. Countries with remarkable progress in research and innovation use multiple streams of merit-based as well as direct funding support to research organizations and universities. South Africa, for example, runs a merit-based system for funding scientific projects through the National Research Foundation, Technology Innovation Agency, Medical Research Council, among others.Uganda needs to do the same to bolster its innovation system.

5. Conclusion

In trying to understand the structure and dynamics of Uganda's innovation system, universities appear to be playing a more active role (Figure 1). They are active in human capital development and are the centre for most scientific and technological activities in the country. Universities in Uganda participate quite significantly in policy making processes (governance). University staff are often hired as consultants or are appointed to serve as members of advisory boards and technical committees of government agencies. Some public universities have started engaging in business enterprise development. Makerere University, for example, has an upcoming business incubator for innovations in foods and beverages, and is also active in creating and supporting business clusters. In Uganda, where the private sector is still weak, universities can play an important role in creating new enterprises or enhancing the competitiveness of the existing ones. Ugandan universities can harness their intellectual property assets in a pragmatic way to encourage private sector growth. Public research and development organizations can also do the same, particularly if they overcome rigid institutional boundaries which appear to confine them to research only.

Using the four functional spheres Sti, G, Hc, and F, therefore, may be an alternative way of understanding the structure and dynamics of an innovation system, particularly in a low-income country like Uganda. The framework, with its inherent limitations, recognizes the diversity of actors and their contribution to building Uganda's innovation system. However, to foster innovation, it is absolutely essential to create conditions for the actors to cooperate, collaborate and interact more intensely across each of the functional spheres. Further work is needed to assess the framework in other settings and to understand how it can be used to create enabling conditions for interaction both within firms and organizations and among different actors in the innovation process.

References

Archibugi, D., Howells, J. and Michie, J. (1999), 'Innovation systems in a global economy', in *Technology Analysis and Strategic Management*, 11(4): 527-539.

Barugahara, I. and Lutalo, B.R. (2011), *Science, Technology and Innovation in Uganda: Status Report 2009/2010*, Kampala.

Bergek, A., Hekkert, Marko, and Jacobsson, S. (2008), 'Functions in innovation systems: a framework for analysing energy system dynamics and identifying goals for system-building activities by entrepreneurs and policy makers', *Policy*, Chalmers.

Bergek, A., Jacobsson, S., Carlsson, B., Lindmark, S., and Rickne, A. (2008), 'Analyzing the functional dynamics of technological innovation systems: A scheme of analysis', in *Research Policy*, 37: 407-429.

Chaminade, C. and Edquist, C. (2006), 'From theory to practice: the use of the systems of innovation approach in innovation policy', In Hage, J. and Meeus, M. T. H. (eds.), *Innovation, Science and Institutional Change*, New York: Oxford University Press.

East African Community (2000), *Science and Technology Policy in East Africa*. Arusha: East African Community Secretariat in Conjunction with GTZ.

Ecuru, J., Nawegulo, L., Lutalo, B. R., Kasule, D., Tujunirwe, E. and Akampurira, I. (2008), *Research in Uganda: Status and Implications for Public Policy*, Kampala.

Edquist, C. (2001), 'The Systems of Innovation Approach and Innovation Policy: An account of the state of the art', *Growth (Lakeland)*, 1-24.

Edquist, C. (2005), 'Systems of Innovation: Perspectives and Challenges', In Fargerberg, J., Mowery, D. C.& Nelson, R. R. (eds.), *The Oxford Handbook of Innovation*, New York: Oxford University Press.

Edquist, C. and Johnson, B. (1997), 'Institutions and organizations in systems of innovation', In Edquist, C. (ed.), *Systems of Innovation: Technologies, Institutions and Organizations*, London: Routledge.

European Commission (2011), 'European Commission: Innovation Union', Available at:http://ec.europa.eu/research/innovation-union/index_en.cfm?pg=intro.

Fischer, M.M. (2001), 'Innovation, knowledge creation and systems of innovation', in *The Annals of Regional Science*, *35*(2): 199-216.

Furman, J. L., Porter, M.E. and Stern, S. (2002), 'The determinants of national innovation capacity', in *Research Policy*, 31: 899-933.

Galli, R. and Teubal, M. (1997), 'Paradigmatic Shifts in National Innovation Systems', In Edquist, C. (ed.), *Systems of Innovation: Technologies, Institutions and Organizations*, London: Printer.

Godin, B. (2009), 'National Innovation System: The System Approach in Historical Perspective', in *Science, Technology and Human Values*, 34(4): 476-501.

Hekkert, M, Suurs, R., Negro, S., Kuhlmann, S. and Smits, R. (2007), 'Functions of innovation systems: a new approach for analysing technological change', in *Technological Forecasting and Social Change*, 74(4): 413-432.

Johnson, B. and Jacobsson, S. (2003), 'The emergence of a growth industry: a comparative analysis of the German, Dutch and Swedish wind turbine industries', In Metcalfe, S. & Canter, U. (eds.), *Transformation and Development: Schumpeterian Perspectives*, Sprinter.

Juma, C. (ed.) (2011), *The New Harvest: Agricultural Innovation in Africa*, New York: Oxford University Press.

Liu, X. and White, S. (2001), 'Comparing innovation systems: a framework and application to China's transitional context', in *Research Policy*, 30(7): 1091-1114.

Lundvall, B.Å. (2007), 'National innovation systems - analytical concept and development tool', in *Industry and Innovation*, 14(1): 95-119.

Lundvall, B.Å. (2010), *National Innovation Systems: Toward a Theory of Innovation and Interactive Learning* (B.-Å. Lundvall, ed.), London: ANTHEM Press.

Lundvall, B.-Å., Joseph, K. J., Chaminade, C., & Vang, J. (eds.) (2009), *Handbook of innovation systems and developing countries: Building domestic capabilities in a global setting,* Cheltenham, UK: Edward Elgar, Northampton, MA, USA.

Ministry of Finance Planning and Economic Development (2009), *National Science, Technology and Innovation Policy*, Kampala.

Ministry of Finance Planning and Economic Development (2010), *National Development Plan 2010/11-2014/15, Development*, Kampala.

Ministry of Finance Planning and Economic Development (2011), *The Background to the Budget 2011/12 Fiscal Year Development*, Kampala.

Organization for Economic Cooperation and Development (2002), *Dynamising National Innovation Systems*, Paris.

Organization for Economic Cooperation and Development (2007), *OECD Reviews of Innovation Policy: South Africa*, Paris.

Rogers, E.M. (2003), *Diffusion of innovation*, 5th edition, New York: Free Press.

Teng-Zeng, F.K. (2006), 'Science, Technology and Institutional Co-operation in Africa: From Pre-Colonial to Colonial Science', in *Eastern Africa Social Science Research Review*, 22(1): 1-37.

United Nations Educational Scientific and Cultural Organization (2009), 'African Science, Technology and Innovation Policy Initiative', Available at: http://www.unesco.org/new/en/natural-sciences/science-technology/sti-policy/african-sti-policy/launch-of-the-african-science-technology-and-innovation-policy-initiative/ (Accessed: 16 May 2011)

Witt, U. (2002), 'How evolutionary is Schumpeter's theory of economic development?' in *Industry and Innovation*, 9: 7-22.

6

Technological Evolution in the South African and Argentine Automotive Manufacturing Sectors:
Policy Responses and Results

Michael Gastrow[1] *& Ariel Gordon*[2]

1. Introduction[1]

How do technological upgrading and innovation in developing countries evolve over time? And how do policy interventions shape this evolution? This study aims to contribute towards addressing the first question by undertaking a comparative review of technological upgrading and innovation in the automotive manufacturing sectors in two developing countries and aims to contribute towards addressing the second question by comparing the effects of diverging policy responses to common challenges in each sector. The automotive sectors in South Africa and Argentina are particularly suitable for such a comparative case study. The automotive sector is critical to the industrial development of many middle-income countries and plays a prominent role in both the South African

1 Research Specialist, Education, Science and Skills Development Research Programme, Human Sciences Research Council, Cape Town, South Africa. Email: mgastrow@hsrc.ac.za

2 Research Professor, Centro Redes and Universidad, Nacional de Quilmes, Argentina. Mansilla 2698 2º piso, C1425BDP Buenos Aires. E-mail: agordon@unq.edu.ar

and Argentine industrial sectors.Three key reasons for the importance of the automotive sector in industrial development are: Firstly, automobile production generates both direct employment and indirect employment through value chain linkages. Secondly, the sector has the potential to be a source of knowledge spillovers to the rest of the manufacturing sector. Thirdly, domestic production of motor vehicles reduces pressure on the country's balance of payments. There is a broad literature addressing these advantages (for example Arza and López, 2008; Black, 2002; Blömstrom and Kokko, 1998; Lorentzen and Barnes 2004). Argentina has a long-standing tradition of automotive manufacturing, being one of the first developing countries to receive investment from multinational corporations (MNCs) leading to the establishment of production facilities. South Africa has also a long-standing tradition of automotive industry, originating in the 1920's.

There is also value in comparing innovation and technological upgrading in middle-income economies from Latin America and Africa: the two continents face some similar development challenges, but language barriers have prevented an extensive comparative literature from developing, particularly in the field of innovation studies. There have, however, been some comparative studies in this area, for example Rasia (2004), but these have all used Brazil as the Latin American comparator – none have compared South Africa and Argentina. Argentina is arguably a useful comparator to South Africa since there is similarity in size, production output, GDP, and population. There are also structural similarities between the two countries' automotive manufacturing sectors that allow for comparisons that can throw clearer light on those variables that are markedly different, for example policy responses,trade composition, and innovation indicators. In both countries automotive manufacturing is a key industrial sector, has extensive value chain linkages, and has a well-documented economic history. These sectors also have similar levels of overall size and production output, they both experienced an expansion of production, exports and imports in the decade following 1995, they face similar issues regarding logistical challenges in global trade, and they both face the dominant influence of a similar set of MNCs in their technology and innovation processes (see Table 1).

For the current study, perhaps the most critical of these dimensions is the simultaneous and rapid expansion of exports, both absolutely and as a proportion of total production: in South Africa exports increased from approximately 16,000 units, or 4% of total production in 1995, to 284,000 units, or 50.5% of total production, in 2008. Over the same period, production for exports in Argentina increased from approximately 53,000 units, or 19% of production, to 351,000 units, or 60% of production (NAAMSA, 2010;

ADEFA, 2009). Thus, the time-scale of this comparative study focuses on a period in which both countries were gearing up for global markets. It is this gearing-up process that offers the greatest potential in terms of understanding the role of government policy and multinational firms in processes of innovation and technological upgrading.

The automotive manufacturing sectors in the two respective countries also have some remarkable parallels in their economic and technological histories. The fact that major changes occurred at approximately the same time allows us to examine the similarities and differences in the causes and consequences of those changes, including the policy responses of the respective countries and the results of these policies.Both Argentina and South Africa were heavily protected from world markets until the 1990's, in Argentina through Import Substitution Industrialization (ISI) and in South Africa through high trade barriers and a history of trade and investment isolation due to political factors. Both sectors had to respond to rapid exposure to world markets during the 1990's, and to a variety of related challenges: increased competition from imports, supply chain restructuring, global follow sourcing and follow design, more challenging requirements from customers, and increased FDI crowding out domestic ownership of production assets and value chains, amongst others.

However, the policy responses to these challenges differed: Argentina pursued regional economic integration, while South Africa pursued import-export complementation schemes and other financial incentives directed at stimulating exports to distant global markets, including Europe, the USA, Africa and the Middle East. Using available empirical data we explore how these differing policy responses impacted on the ongoing evolution of the two sectoral innovation systems. Since other factors (for example the challenges and dynamics of opening up to global markets in the 1990s) are relatively constant across both cases, we can more easily isolate and compare the effects of these different policies.

Table 1: Globalization of the automotive sectors in South Africa and Argentina

	Argentina	South Africa
Production 1995 (units)	277,707	389,392
Production 2000	322,043	356,800
Production 2005	324,863	525,227
Production 2008	562,965	589,557
Exports 1995 (units)	52,746	15,764
Exports 2000	135,760	68,031
Exports 2005	181,581	139,912
Exports 2008	351,092	284,211
Exports 1995 (as a % of production)	19.0%	4.0%
Exports 2000	42.2%	19.1%
Exports 2005	55.9%	26.6%
Exports 2008	59.6%	50.5%
OEMs	VW, Ford, GM, Fiat, Toyota, Mercedes-Benz, Renault, PSA Peugeot-Citröen, Honda (forthcoming)	VW, Ford, Nissan, GM, Fiat, Renault, BMW, Mercedes, Toyota

Sources: NAAMSA (2010), ADEFA (2009)

2. Methodology

This comparative case study focuses on two broad areas: firstly, we examined how exposure to world markets in the 1990's impacted on technological upgrading and innovation in the automotive manufacturing sectors in each country. Secondly, we examine the strategies developed in each country to respond to the challenges of globalization and look at how new industrial and trade policies shaped the technological trajectories of these sectors up until the world financial crisis that began in late 2008. These inter-related enquiries bring together existing literatures in both South Africa and Argentina, with a focus on the effects of policy changes on the technological trajectory of the sector. We therefore begin with a review and synthesis of this literature in South Africa, followed by a similar review and synthesis of the Argentine literature. The latter is almost exclusively available in Spanish; we therefore bring this knowledge into the English language and highlight relevant comparisons to the South African case. This comparison is followed by a discussion focused on the key variables of public policy, export orientation, and innovation indicators.

The arguments are supported by data that assist in describing technological trajectories. The National Association of Automobile Manufacturers of South Africa supplies data related to automobile production, trade, capital expenditure, and investment in engineering and R&D. Similar data for the components supply base is available from the National Association of Components and Allied Manufacturers of South Africa. The South African Automotive Benchmarking Club collects operational performance data from major components manufacturers, including innovation expenditure data. The South African R&D Survey and the South African Innovation Survey provide data about R&D expenditure and innovation intensity in the sector. Secondary data drawn from the literature review include indicators of the use of local technology among components manufacturers (Barnes, 2000), and foreign ownership of South African automotive firms (Lorentzen and Barnes, 2004).

For the Argentine case, the ADEFA (Asociación de Fabricantes de Automotores or the Argentine Automotive Manufacturers Association) provided data describing automotive production and trade. The Centre for Production Studies provided data on investment and exports. R&D Survey data specific to the Argentine automotive sector is not available, but relevant information about R&D intensity is available from the Argentine Innovation Survey. The US Bureau of Economic Analysis provided data on US automotive investment in both Argentina and South Africa.

3. Technological upgrading in the South African automotive manufacturing sector

There is an extensive literature describing the economic history of the automotive sector in South Africa. Here we present a synthetic overview, highlighting the sector's technological trajectory and the impact of policy choices on this trajectory. Our review is based on the key texts of Barnes (2000); Barnes and Morris (2000, 2008); Black (1994, 2001, 2002, 2009); Flatters (2005); Gastrow (2007); and Lorentzen and Barnes (2004); against a backdrop of literature describing trends in the global industry, including Humphrey and Oeter (2000); Humphrey and Memedovic (2003); Rutherford and Holmes (2008); Sturgeon and Van Biesebroeck (2010); Sturgeon, Van Biesebroeck, and Gereffi (2008, 2009); and Wad (2010).

As in many developing countries, including Argentina, South Africa's automotive manufacturing sector developed under the protection of high trade barriers. The first production facilities in South Africa were established in the 1920s (Black, 1994; Duncan, 1997). Domestic economic growth and high tariff barriers incentivized more assemblers (Original Equipment Manufacturers or OEM's) to invest in assembly plants. An industry of component manufacturers developed to support this; however, this industry was skewed in favour of local content due to local content programmes, which were introduced primarily to save on foreign exchange. The industry grew substantially: by 1960 it had reached an output of 87,000 units, more than any other developing country at the time, and sales increased tenfold from the 1950s to the 1980s (Black, 2001). However, production remained entirely for the domestic market, and South African producers remained isolated from global production networks (Black, 2001).

By the mid-1970's South Africa had an automotive sector of substantial size and scope that was weakly integrated into global production networks and which used the Fordist mass-production processes predominant at the time. The Soweto riots and the related political upheaval of 1976 were to effectively freeze this situation. Many MNCs, including those in the automotive sector, divested from South Africa. From this point the technological trajectory of the South African sector began to diverge from the global industry: the flow of technological and process improvements from international parent companies was greatly reduced, and sanctions made it more difficult to access these independently. At the same time, a heavily protected market allowed South African manufacturers to continue to operate at static technological levels without losing market share. South Africa missed the lean manufacturing revolution that originated in Toyota in the late 1970's; while the rest of the world scrambled to catch up to Toyota, South Africa remained locked in a Fordist mode of production that fell further and further behind the international frontier.

The 1980's was a period of 'stagnant volatility' characterized by low growth, political instability, and increasing international isolation (Black, 1994, 2001). However, by the 1990s political changes set in motion economic changes. After the 1994 election, policymakers recognised that sustained economic growth and a reduction of market distortions would require market liberalization. At the same time, it was acknowledged that this would present challenges for those sectors that had developed a large competitiveness gap during the period of isolation. It was therefore decided to link the market liberalization of the automotive sector to a suite of supportive policies that would help the sector move towards the global technological frontier while it integrated with global markets. In 1995, this suite of policies was brought together under the Motor Industry Development Plan (MIDP), which was scheduled to support the sector until 2012. This included a phased reduction in import duties, an import-export complementation scheme, special rebates and allowances on imports, a fixed capital investment incentive, and the abolition of local content requirements.

Despite these support mechanisms, the industry was placed under huge pressure, particularly the components manufacturers that supplied the recently globalised assemblers. These OEMs were no longer forced to source from domestic suppliers, which meant that for the first-time components manufacturers had to compete in an open market. This coincided with the rise of China as a manufacturing superpower, and many components manufacturers were simply priced out of business. There were also suddenly vulnerable to exchange rate fluctuations, such as the strong appreciation of the Rand in 2002, which disrupted their pricing strategies and made investment difficult.

The result was that local components suppliers experienced turnover and employment losses during the mid-1990's (Black, 2002). However, this period also saw the onset of major restructuring and competitiveness improvements in the sector. Components manufacturers either shut down or used benchmarking and the importation of skills from multinationals to raise their competitiveness in almost all the key operational performance areas (Barnes, 2000). At the same time there was an overhaul of the sector which rationalised production and gained increased economies of scale and specialisation (NAAMSA, 2010). By the end of the nineties, at the beginning of a period of sustained economic growth, the industry was leaner, more competitive and more globally integrated, and those firms that had survived market integration were more ready for the global economy. However, the sector continued to lag behind international competitors – highlighting the extent of the competitiveness gap that had evolved during South Africa's isolation (Barnes, 2000).

The MIDP was one of several factors that led to a transfer of ownership among both assemblers and components manufacturers after 1995; other factors included an increasingly stable political climate, a growing local market, and reduced trading barriers (Barnes, 2000). Foreign purchases transferred of the majority share of all South African assembly operations into multinational hands. As a result, components suppliers were now expected to meet more stringent international performance requirements.These changes also lead to new sourcing agreements which tied OEMs to component-producing MNCs. This incentivised component manufacturers from abroad to start up Greenfield operations or establish joint ventures in South Africa.Between

1997 and 2003 sourcing from domestic multinational subsidiaries increased from 26% to 37.5% of the supply base, while the use of local firms with local technologies declined from 25.8% to only 10% (Lorentzen and Barnes, 2004).

South African technology and South African R&D were therefore squeezed from the local automotive industry. However, this was part of a broader global trend towards the concentration of R&D in the automotive sector – see Humphrey and Memedovic (2003), Rutherford and Holmes (2008), Sturgeon and Van Biesebroeck (2010), and Sturgeon, Van Biesebroeck, and Gereffi (2007, 2008, 2009). The sum effect of these global dynamics on innovation in the South African automotive sector was to support inward flows of technology through MNCs, but simultaneously to reduce the demand for locally developed technologies, and hence local R&D. Interviews conducted in the late 1990s found that there had indeed been a long term decline in the use of locally adapted technology (Barnes, 2000).However, more recent data from the National R&D Survey indicates that R&D activity continues and is moreover relatively stable over the medium term (see Figure 1).This suggests that, until the financial crisis of 2008, there remained niche areas in which local firms had retained or even improved their R&D capacities – a finding supported by a series of interviews with OEM executives conducted in 2005 and 2006 (Gastrow, 2007).

The initial period of structural adjustment and re-integration into the global economy were difficult years for South African automotive manufacturers. As indicated in Figure 1, between 1996 and 1998 domestic production dropped by 20% while imports increased by 40%. This corresponds to the period in which components manufacturers and assemblers were still catching up to the global competitiveness frontier through MNC investment-driven upgrading and benchmarking activities. By 1999 the sector had become more competitive and was more integrated into global value chains; these factors led to increased output for export to global markets, which drove a 69% increase in overall production between 1999 and 2005. A buoyant domestic economy also stimulated production for the domestic market by 30% between 1999 and 2005, despite the high rate and level of import penetration.

Figure 1: South African Automotive Trade and Production (units) 1995 – 2005

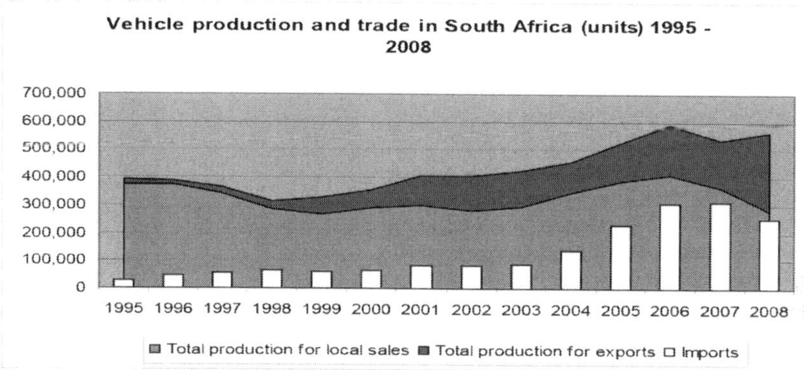

Source: NAAMSA, 2010.

The MIDP might be considered a success in terms of stimulating technological upgrading, insertion into global value chains, and increased domestic production. However, one key weakness has been the persistent and growing balance of payments deficit for the sector because of high levels of import penetration. This deficit grew from R7.9 billion in 2000, to R31.8 billion in 2006 (NAAMSA, 2010). There is an extended literature addressing the causes and dynamics of the overall growth in production (Barnes and Morris, 2000; Black, 2002) as well as whether the cost of the MIDP is outweighed by the benefits (Flatters, 2005). This literature identifies the incentives provided by the MIDP as a key driver of investment and production growth, along with domestic economic growth, the importation of skills from multinationals, improved processes and practices through benchmarking and upgrading towards World Class Manufacturing and increased domestic political security.

Technological upgrading and competitiveness improvements in the sector, combined with the incentives of the MIDP, drew in increasingly large investments in engineering and R&D (see Table2).Between 1997 and 2008 over R32 billion was invested in the automotive assembler industry, of which over R2.5 billion was dedicated to engineering and R&D fixed investment.

Table 2:SA Assembler capital expenditure (R Millions)

	R&D/Engineering	Total
1997	112	1266
1998	139	1343
1999	115	1511
2000	141	1562
2001	245	2078
2002	262	2726
2003	194	2325
2004	274	2220
2005	259	3576
2006	399	6215
2007	254	3096
2008	153	3290

Source: NAAMSA, 2010.

4. Technological upgrading in the Argentine automotive manufacturing sector

The literature related to the economic history of the Argentine automotive sector is substantial, but largely restricted to Spanish language publications. Our literature review in this area brings these publications into the English language through a synthetic overview, which again highlights the sector's technological trajectory and the impact of policy choices on this trajectory. Our review is based on the key texts of Albornoz, Milesi and Yoguel (2005); Albornoz and Yoguel (2004); Arza, and López, (2008); Bastos Tigre et al. (1999); CENDA (2008); Chudnovsky and López (2002); Miozzo (2000); Katz (1983); Kosacoff(2007); Kosacoff and Ramos (2001); Kosakoff,Todesca and Vispo (1991); Moralez and Katz (1995); Motta (2006); Novick et al. (2003); and Porta, Guidicatti and Vismara, (2004).

The technological evolution of the automotive sector in Argentina is dominated by the policy of Import Substitution Industrialization (ISI) (Kosacoff and Ramos, 2001. Automotive manufacturing prior to World War II consisted of local assembly of cars from imported parts. Industrialization accelerated in the early 1950's, with the opening of production facilities for Mercedes-Benz and Fiat. In 1959 the first Argentine Automotive Regime was established, which included tax and tariff reductions, as well as a prohibition on the import of finished units. Protected from global markets, the sector expanded during the 1960's and early 1970's. During this time the ISI strategy was expanded to create even more highly protected markets and incentivize MNCs to establish production capacity to serve the domestic market.MNCs in turn provided access to essential technologies and capital goods (Kosacoff and Ramos, 2001).

By the 1970s, local content requirements had increased to 90%, even higher than the 66% requirement then in place in South Africa. Under this policy, production reached almost 300,000 units in 1973, mostly for the domestic market, with exports only reaching 15,000 units in 1974 (ADEFA, 2008). The technologies and knowledge required for this growth were acquired through the import of capital equipment, manuals, blueprints, and patents (Miozzi, 2000). Industrial R&D efforts at the time were focused on the adaptation of imported technologies to local scales, local material input conditions, and local demand conditions (Kosakoff et al., 1991; Moralez and Katz, 1995).

However, local content requirements meant that the sector missed out on the economies of scale that were evolving elsewhere in the world, and production was characterized by a large variety of models produced at low runs at a low level of quality (Katz, 1983; Kosacoff and Ramos, 2001). The sector was also characterized by a high level of vertical integration and Fordist manufacturing practices, which resulted in a low level of supplier development and a shortage of specialized subcontractors (Kosacoff and Ramos, 2001). These factors contributed towards technological stagnation and relatively low productivity compared to the international frontier. All these characteristics were also found in the South African industry (Black, 2001; Barnes 2000).

The late 1970's saw a general economic stagnation in Argentina, characterized by high inflation rates, productivity losses, and balance of payments deficit. This led to a questioning of the ISI economic strategy. In 1976, while South Africa was experiencing political violence and the onset of international economic and political isolation, Argentina's armed forces performed a coup d'état. In both countries, these political changes brought about economic changes. Argentina's new military government established a market liberalization programme, with the intention of modernizing the economy and increasing efficiency. In the automotive sector, trade barriers to vehicle imports were eased, and local content requirements were abolished. MNCs initiated mergers or exited the country: General Motors left in 1978, Citroen in 1979, and Fiat and Peugeot in 1981 (this was mirrored in South Africa, which was also experiencing mass disinvestment from the sector).

At a macroeconomic level, Argentina also faced an explosion in external debt, leading to the 1982 financial crisis. The 1980's came to be called the "lost decade" in Latin America. This was largely a decade of economic contraction and technological stagnation, similar to the 'volatile stagnation' experienced in South Africa. The government elected in 1983 reinstated protectionist industrial policies. In the context of macroeconomic turbulence during the whole decade, industrial production dropped. Automotive average annual production fell from 242,277 units during the 1970s to 170,694 units in the 1980s (ADEFA, 2008).

These contextual factors allow for a comparison with the situation in South Africa. In both countries, 1976 precipitated a mass exit of MNCs, a continuation of protectionist policies, and a decade of stagnating production and technology. In Argentina this was due to a coup d'état, market liberalization and a macroeconomic crisis; the return of inward-oriented protectionist policies in the 1980s failed to return production to the level of the early 1970s because of the persistent macroeconomic crisis. In both countries, the 1990s were to bring about policy responses to these problems: in Argentina the focus was on administered trade liberalization and regional economic integration, while in South Africa the focus was on administered trade liberalization and financial incentives for export-oriented MNCs. Each of these policy responses brought about changes in the technological dynamics of the sector that unfolded throughout the 1990s and beyond.

In 1989 a newly elected government introduced neo-liberal structural reforms, with a focus on trade liberalisation. Shortly thereafter, in 1991, the MERCOSUR (Common Market of the South) created a common market between Argentina, Brazil, Uruguay and Paraguay. This was particularly significant to Argentina's automotive sector, where it consolidated the integration of the Argentine and Brazilian automotive sectors. The opportunities associated with the new enlarged market promoted the arrival of a new wave of FDI in the automotive sector (Chudnovsky and López, 2002).

During the early 1990s a series of policy instruments were implemented in Argentina that would influence the transformation of the automotive sector. These were the establishment of the Argentine Automobile Regime in 1991 and its compatibility with Brazilian automotive policy in the framework of industrial integration under MERCOSUR (Porta et al., 2005). The Argentine Automotive Regime was an exception in the context of national trade liberalization policies. Disregarding WTO regulations, the new regime protected assemblers from foreign competition by establishing import quotas, limits to the content of imported parts, obligations to incorporate local parts, and restrictions to foreign trade (CENDA, 2008). The regime included an industrial policy that required a commitment by assemblers to increase investment that would technologically upgrade their facilities. Trade policy also incentivized upgrading with a view towards exporting by introducing an import-export complementation scheme. This new framework was a key contributor to the sector's upgrading and expansion in the 1990s.

The compatibility with Brazilian automotive policy under MERCOSUR was the result of a bilateral protocol between Argentina and Brazil that aimed to integrate the two markets. This scheme was based on high tariffs for the import of automobiles and components from outside the trading bloc, and intra-zone administrated commerce in the form of compensated exchanges and an increase in trade quotas (Motta et al, 2006). As in South Africa, this new policy environment incentivized an increase in MNC investments, which in turn brought about higher levels of technology transfer, skills transfer, and integration into global value chains. Moreover, in both countries these factors stimulated an overall expansion in the sector that lasted until the financial crisis began in 2008.

Figure 2: Automotive production and trade in Argentina (units) (1995-2008)

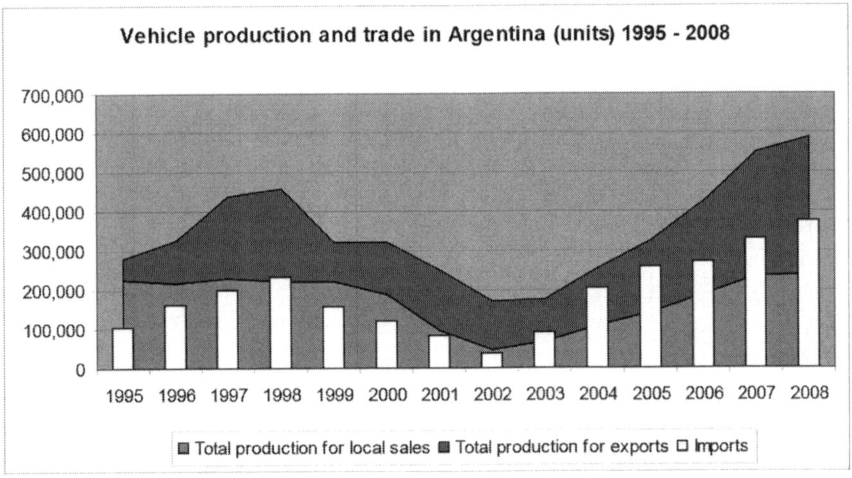

Source: ADEFA, 2010.

The initial response to the new policy and trade context was an increase in production for export markets. While production for the domestic market remained static from 1995 to 1998, overall production was substantially boosted by export growth (mostly to Brazil), from approximately 277 thousand units in 1995, to about 460 thousand in 1998. There were two contractions after 1995, coinciding with the Brazilian currency devaluation in 1999, the macroeconomic crisis of 2001, and the currency devaluation of 2002. After 2002 the (newly) competitive currency, idle productive capacity, and strong growth of both Brazilian and local demand, led to sustained growth in domestic demand and production (See Figure 2). However, as in South Africa, there continued to be a balance of trade deficit for the sector, as import penetration resulting from market liberalization and economic growth outpaced export growth (Centre for Production Studies, 2010).

These changes affected the evolving technological base of the sector, including the means by which technologies were developed or imported. Favourable policy conditions and the MERCOSUR trade agreement prompted MNCs to set up local subsidiaries rather than grant licences, as they did during the 1980s. The 1990s saw production facilities established or upgraded for Volkswagen, Ford, Renault, Toyota, Mercedes-Benz, Fiat, and Peugeot-Citroën. The arrival of MNC assemblers changed the landscape in the component sector in a manner strikingly similar to the South African case. Integration into global production networks meant that components suppliers were now expected to meet more stringent international performance requirements and many domestic components producers were bought by components MNCs. For example, 45% of components suppliers to Volkswagen Argentina and Toyota Argentina experienced a change of ownership during the 1990s (Novick et al., 2003), a trend with a strong parallel in South Africa.

New investments by MNCs utilised newer technologies and, as in South Africa, moved away from Fordist manufacturing practices towards World Class Manufacturing (Miozzi, 2000). Plants gaining from new investment updated and extended their usage of automation, computerised control of production, quality improvements, and higher environmental standards. However, like the South African case, there were limited spillovers into local firms, resulting in advancing technology among foreign supplier firms but often stagnating technology or even weakening capabilities among domestic firms. Also, as in South Africa, domestic components suppliers were left exposed. The rise of China as a manufacturing superpower left many domestic manufacturers unable to compete on a price basis, and supply-chain re-structuring left many local firms excluded. However, in the case of Argentina, domestic components manufacturers also faced competition from Brazilian suppliers, who benefited from larger economies of scale and FDI promotion schemes that led to the establishment of many components MNCs in Brazil to supply the whole MERCOSUR bloc.

Technological progress in the sector was set back by the Argentine macroeconomic crisis of 2001, but began to recover again after the currency devaluation of 2002 (this crisis is further explored in Motta et al., 2007). Thereafter, the sector experienced a boom in the years leading up to 2008. This was due in part to idle capacity created by investments during the 1990's, which amounted to over USD5000 million, and which also spurred technological upgrading and productivity increases (Porta et al., 2005). After 2002, investment recovered; although it did not match the levels achieved during the 1990s (see Figure 3). By comparison, investments in South Africa in 2007 were higher than those achieved in Argentina ($1.2 billion; NAAMSA).

Figure 3: Investments in Argentina's Motor Industry (Assemblers and Components)

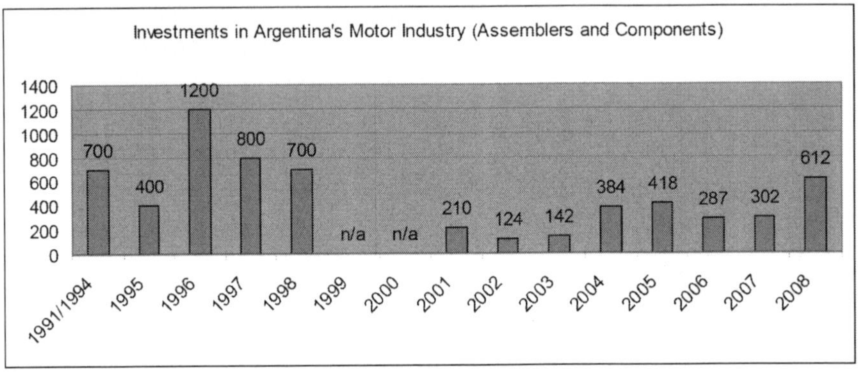

Sources: Booz Allen ADEFA until 1998, INDEC for 2001 and CEP-Investments Database for 2002 onwards. Unit: millions of current USD. Note: includes Greenfield investments and extensions.

5. Policy, export orientation, and innovation indicators

While the overall trajectories of foreign investment and technological upgrading share many similarities across the two comparators, three aspects stand out as distinctly different: their trade policies, export profiles, and profiles of R&D and innovation activity. Drawing on the above literature reviews, comparative analyses, and data, these key differences are further explored below, posing the question of how policy impacted on trade, and in turn how trade impacted on R&D and innovation.

Table 3: South Africa Automotive Exports (ZAR millions) 2006

European Union	25,802,688	45.60%
North-East Asia	8,269,076	14.60%
Nafta	6,117,330	10.80%
Pacific_Continent	6,063,139	10.70%
Sadc	2,781,142	4.90%
Central Europe	1,440,796	2.50%
Middle East	1,409,133	2.50%
North Africa	1,043,015	1.80%
Chinas	949,419	1.70%
West Africa	821,141	1.50%
N-East Africa	478,950	0.90%
Asean	477,249	0.80%
MERCOSUR	234,485	0.40%
Other	727,225	1.30%

Source: NAAMSA

Table 4: Argentina's Automotive Exports (USD millions) 2008

Brazil	250,683	71.40%
Mexico	39,662	11.30%
Europe	18,794	5.40%
Chile	12,959	3.70%
Venezuela	5,931	1.70%
Uruguay	5,723	1.60%
Rest of America	3,320	0.90%
Asia	2,897	0.80%
South Africa	2,102	0.60%
Australia & New Zealand	1,899	0.50%
Peru	1,821	0.50%
Colombia	1,688	0.50%
Central America	1,683	0.50%
Rest of Africa	1,310	0.40%

Source: Centre for Production Studies (2010)

The trade profiles of the comparators differ as a direct result of differing policy responses to globalisation, which in Argentina focused on regional integration with MERCOSUR, and in South Africa had a global scope with a focus on large markets in developed countries. These policy responses were partially motivated by geographical factors. Argentina's proximity to and integration with a large neighbouring market (Brazil) motivated its policy of regional integration. South Africa is geographically distant from all the major markets, and there is therefore less reason to distinguish one particular market through policy support.

Data describing the sectors' export profiles are illustrative. Brazil received 71.4% of Argentinean automotive exports in 2008, followed by Mexico (11.3%) and Europe (5.4%). By comparison, South Africa's export market has been far more diverse, with significant proportions of exports directed to the EU, Asia, North America, and the Pacific (see Tables 3 and 4).

A recent econometric study (Arza, 2008) asked whether MERCOSUR has indeed functioned as an export platform for the Argentine automotive industry. This study showed that intra-bloc trade significantly increased after 1994, and that it was not achieved at the expense of trade diversion. However, MERCOSUR did not seem to have an effect on market diversification. Brazilian automotive exports are, and have always been, more diversified than Argentinean exports, but not because of MERCOSUR. Therefore, Arza concludes that MERCOSUR as a bloc has not yet become an export platform of extra-bloc trade, but rather a facilitator of internal trade within the bloc.

This market focus influenced the technologies employed in production, as Argentina has focused on cars for developing markets, while South Africa has focused its production for global markets, largely in developed countries. South Africa has therefore had to develop or import technologies that allowed it to produce vehicles that met European or American specifications, while Argentina has had more latitude to follow a different technological trajectory. Where production was directed at developing countries (such as Brazil, its dominant trade partner), lower technical and technological standards were imposed. In the case of older models continuing production (such as the Gol, a vehicle similar to the Citi Golf in South Africa), assemblers were incentivized to bleed production assets and delay the expense of upgrading and technological change.

The presence of a large neighbouring market also appears to have had an influence on R&D and innovation activities. South Africa does not have a large neighbour to compete with for knowledge-intensive activities in the sector, and thus captures any R&D or innovation activities or niches for which the region has a comparative advantage. However, regional integration with Brazil has affected Argentina's technological upgrading and innovation patterns. Arza and López (2008) showed that innovation activities are far more developed in the Brazilian automotive industry than in Argentina and suggest that R&D in developing economies is more likely to be concentrated in the larger developing economies where economies of scale and more developed capabilities provide advantages. This pattern is strongly reflected in the literature on global trends in the automotive industry (Sturgeon et al., 2008, 2009, 2010).

Brazilian subsidiaries of MNCs have an active role in product design, particularly in the design of vehicles for developing country markets and in ethanol and flex-fuel engines. In comparison, Argentina has a less developed sectoral innovation system. Arza and López (2008) showed that Argentine subsidiaries of MNCs assemblers do not usually have an independent R&D department, and that product design, as well as adaptations are performed abroad.

The characteristics of R&D in the South African comparator were explored in a series of interviews with assemblers undertaken in 2006 (Gastrow, 2007). These included: BMW, Ford, Volkswagen, General Motors, and DaimlerChrysler.These firms reported two key differences from their Argentine counterparts: they did not report any pressure on R&D as a result from competition from neighbouring countries, and as a result of their export profile they conducted a higher proportion of their knowledge-intensive activities in support of producing cars for developed countries, rather than world cars. Within this context, niche areas remained where domestic R&D continued, particularly adaptive engineering, testing engineering, and cases where OEM subsidiaries had been designated lead engineers for certain models, both for developed and developing markets. A significant proportion of R&D was focussed on older models that remained in production, thus providing a consistent demand for development in the form of incremental upgrading. A key issue for comparison with Argentina remains the difference in technological standards for vehicles built for developed countries and those built for developing countries, often using previous generation capital equipment and technologies. This mode of production played a small part in creating demand for R&D in South Africa but is currently being phased out. However, this practice is more prevalent in Argentina, and provides a marked difference in the drivers of R&D in the two respective sectors.

Quantifying R&D and innovation considering the above findings must be done in the context of limited data. Argentine R&D data is not available for the automotive sector specifically, and proxy measures must be used. However, there is some R&D Survey data available for the South African sector for the period 2005 to 2008. Together with data gathered from the South African Automotive Benchmarking Club[2] for the years 2003 to 2006, these are reflected in Figure 4. Despite the pressure placed on local automotive R&D by insertion into global value chains, follow sourcing, follow design, and related dynamics, a significant amount of R&D remained.

Figure 4: Automotive Research and Development expenditure in South Africa (2003-2008)

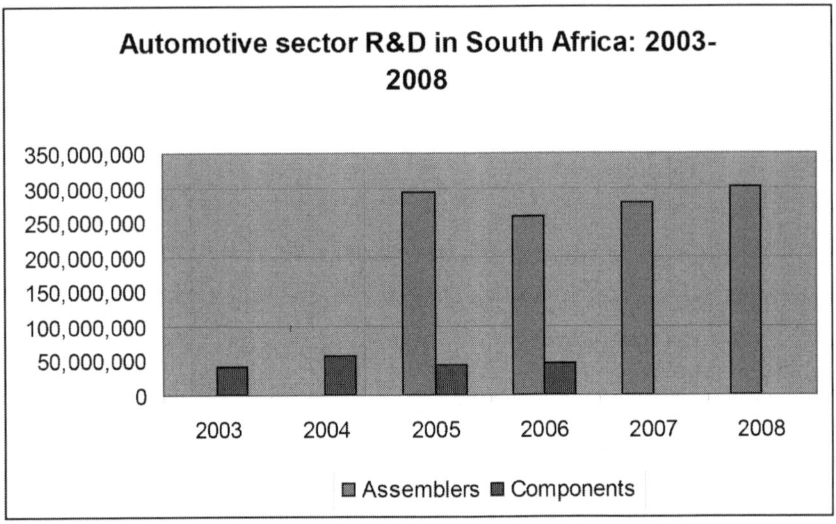

Sources: South African R&D Survey (assemblers, 2005-2008); B&M Analysts (components, 2003-2006)

There is currently no directly comparable data for the Argentine comparator. However, we have sourced all the available data from both countries in order to enable the best comparison possible. Innovation Survey data make it possible to compare R&D intensity in each case (see Table 5). In both cases, R&D intensity is declining over time. As is evidenced by turnover and R&D data sourced from the South African R&D survey, this does not reflect an absolute decline in R&D activity – rather it reflects the growth in turnover during this time in both sectors. However, it is clear that neither comparator has been positioned to increase its R&D activity at the same pace that production output has increased. The R&D intensity of both comparators is low compared to the proportion of sales invested in R&D by MNCs at the global level: 4.7% for Ford Motor Corp., 4.2% for Daimler-Chrysler, 4.2% for Toyota Motor Company,3.1% for General Motors, 3.3% for Volkswagen and 5.5% for Honda Motor (Source: National Science Foundation (USA) quoted in CENDA, 2008), highlighting that both countries operate on the margins of much larger systems.

The properties of the data make direct comparison between South Africa and Argentina difficult. In the only directly comparable year (2004), the South African sector had reported a higher R&D intensity. However, this is a comparison of R&D Survey data (in South Africa) with Innovation Survey data (in Argentina). These two surveys have very different methodologies, with the R&D Survey following the Frascati manual and using a purposive methodology that seeks to cover all the R&D in the country. The Innovation Survey follows the Oslo manual, which uses a random stratified sample and weighted distribution. Given the small number of players in the automotive sector, and the high concentration of R&D in a small number of firms, the R&D Survey may be capturing a higher proportion of automotive R&D. If we compare Innovation Survey data from Argentina (in 2004) with Innovation Survey data in South Africa (2005), we find that, contrary to the comparison with 2004 R&D Survey data, Argentina reports a higher R&D intensity. To reach an accurate conclusion, more research may be necessary.

One directly comparable source of data about R&D expenditure and intensity in the two countries is the Bureau of Economic Analysis of the Department of Commerce of the United States. Indicators of US foreign investment in the transport equipment industry (both assemblers and components producers) in Argentina and South Africa are limited but useful illustrations of global spending on R&D (See Table 6).

Table 5: R&D intensity in the South African and Argentine Automotive sectors

Country	Year	%
Argentina	2002	0.74
Argentina	2004	0.45
South Africa	2004	0.50
South Africa	2005	0.31
South Africa	2006	0.28

Sources: South African National Survey of Research and Experimental development (Department of Science and Technology, 2010), South African Innovation Survey (Department of Science and Technology, 2010). Argentine National Innovation Survey data sourced from Instituto Nacional De Estadística E Censos (INDEC).

Table 3: US sales, assets, and foreign investment in R&D the automotive sector, 1999 – 2007 (USD millions)

		1999	2000	2001	2002	2003	2004	2005	2006	2007
Argentina	R&D spending	1	4	4	2	5	7	1	6	10
	Total Sales	2294	1997	1788	1193	1445	2330	2768	3180	4182
	Assets	2164	1975	1422	911	999	1118	1272	1538	1936
South Africa	R&D spending	<0.5	<0.5	6	8	9	7	7	NA	NA
	Total Sales	504	1616	1783	1735	2439	4128	5352	5848	5627
	Assets	227	734	794	908	1228	2319	2080	2237	3665

Source: Bureau of Economic Analysis (BEA), Department of Commerce of the United States

In terms of the total capital stock invested, there were major reversals of the roles of South Africa and Argentina. In 1999 investment South Africa amounted to only 10% of the stock of capital invested in Argentina. By 2007, capital investment in South Africa was 89% higher than in Argentina. In Argentina, patterns of R&D spending were erratic. R&D expenditure South Africa was higher and more stable, with an increase in 2001 that levelled off after 2004.In Argentina the annual mean of R&D spending as a proportion of sales was 0.18% for the 1999-2007 period, whereas in South Africa it was 0.27% for the 1999-2005 period. This provides a valuable comparison to the R&D Survey and Innovation Survey data, as it indicates that the South African firms (with US ownership) indeed had a higher innovation intensity that their Argentine counterparts.

However, R&D spending by US firms was marginal in both countries compared to R&D investment over sales ratios by US firms in Brazil (1.97% in 2007), and lower than other middle-income countries such as Thailand 0.50% (2007), Turkey 0.58% (2005), Poland 0.35% (2007) or Mexico 0.48% (2007). R&D intensity is even more marginal compared to corporate spending at the global level. These figures indicate that have local subsidiaries of US Automotive MNCs been able to attract significant R&D activities in neither Argentina nor South Africa - which is a good proxy indicator of the situation in the whole sector. The data suggest that only a few developing countries have been able to integrate at a higher level in the global R&D networks of the automotive industry, and these countries have a leading role in these networks in product design for developing countries. Brazil seems to have been able to integrate at a higher level, concentrating R&D facilities and operations for product design aimed at developing countries. In the case of Argentina, proximity and integration with Brazil have meant that R&D

operations are mostly performed in the neighbouring country. By contrast, South Africa has not had to compete with a larger neighbour with economies of scale in R&D, but has also not had the opportunity to contribute to the development of vehicles for a large emerging economy.

6. Conclusions and directions for further research

A comparative analysis can take as a starting point the similarities and differences in historical trajectories of the automotive sector in each country, with a focus on their respective technological evolutionary paths. In both countries the automotive industry started in the early twentieth century in the context of "stand-alone" subsidiaries of MNCs in a protected market. After 1976, in both countries, there was a mass exit of MNCs because of political factors. In both cases this situation led to the 1980s being a decade of technological and production stagnation.

In the 1990s the automotive industry at the global level underwent major transformations. Global value chains were consolidated, thus transforming the conditions under which local subsidiaries of MNCs in middle-income economies operated. Stand-alone subsidiaries were no longer feasible, and local subsidiaries of MNCs in developing countries encountered a new operating environment in the context of the globalization and regionalization of production, global follow sourcing and follow design. At the same time, elections in Argentina (1989) and South Africa (1994) resulted in new governments favouring trade liberalization over protectionism. Thus, in both countries the 1990s saw the introduction of policies intending to partially liberalize the sector, and thereby technologically upgrade the production base, stimulate exports, and attain economies of scale. In Argentina the key policies were the Argentine Automotive Regime (in 1991), the establishment of Mercusur (in 1994) and various bilateral trade agreements with Brazil. In South Africa the key set of policies came together under the MIDP (1995). However, in both countries this liberalization was partial and was complemented with administrated trade schemes intended to protect domestic industry and promote a smooth catching up process to world class standards.

Prior to trade liberalization, inward-facing sectors used Fordist production methods and fostered inefficiency, low quality, low productivity, and low rates of technological upgrading. Trade liberalisation policies and industry support policies in each country strongly influenced technological trajectories. At first the components sectors in each country were left exposed and had to restructure and upgrade in order to compete internationally. Integration into global value chains, particularly follow-sourcing agreements and competition from China (and in the case of Argentina, also from Brazil), meant that domestic components producers had to rapidly become more competitive. Another result was that the use of domestically developed technology was reduced in favour of intellectual property belonging to parent MNCs. However, trade liberalization and policy support also encouraged export-driven growth from the mid-1990s until 2008 (except for 2000-2003 in Argentina). Integration into global value chains, along with policy incentives, domestic growth, and other factors, incentivized MNCs to set up local subsidiaries, whether through JVs, Greenfield operations, or purchasing of domestic firms.

As a result, MNC-driven technological upgrading characterized assemblers and MNC-owned/JV components suppliers. New investments from MNCs utilised newer technologies, and subsidiaries had greater access to the intellectual property of their parent firms. In addition to technological upgrading, the presence of MNCs, whether through ownership or competition, forced domestic firms to make the difficult move away from Fordist manufacturing principles towards World Class Manufacturing. Integration into global value chains also increased economies of scale in both countries by reducing the number of models produced but producing higher quantities. However, both Argentine and South African automotive producers integrated at a lower level than producers in other developing countries, as indicated by higher levels of R&D spending by subsidiaries of US MNCs in countries such as Brazil, Mexico, Poland, Turkey and Thailand.

The similarities between the two comparators are striking. However, it is in the differences between these comparators that further research questions originate. For example, South Africa pursued a policy of incentivizing production for export to global demand centres such as the EU and USA, and to a lesser extent African and the Middle East. The world class requirements of these markets meant that South African products needed to be at world class standards, and MNCs imported or developed locally the technologies necessary to meet these requirements. By contrast Argentina pursued a policy of regional economic integration, most intensively with Brazil. As a result its exports were almost only to neighbouring countries. This meant that Argentine producers more often developed cars specifically for developing economies, with lower costs and technologies that were further from the frontier.

It is also interesting that, in the context of administered trade liberalization, global follow-sourcing, and follow-design strategies, South Africa appears to have retained higher levels of R&D intensity than Argentina, although more data would be required to confirm this. The technological evolution of the automotive sector in Argentina was strongly influenced by the presence of a larger neighbour, Brazil, where greater economies of scale allowed it to retain R&D activities for product development for Latin America and other developing countries. The literature suggests that this effectively captured knowledge-intensive activity for the region, thus reducing demand for R&D and innovation in Argentina. Further research could shed light on this finding by seeking empirical evidence of this process. Another avenue for further research could be directed at the question of whether this is a global problem regarding the role of medium-sized developing economies in the global networks of MNCs, where central locations (or at least larger developing countries such as Brazil, India and China) retain most R&D activities.

Ultimately research in this direction would aim at answering the critical question of whether there is a place for R&D in the global strategies of MNCs for countries like South Africa and Argentina, or whether it will always be concentrated in developed countries and larger developing countries. The key policy implication of these findings is that the effect on technological trajectories merits strong consideration in the context of trade policy. Policies supporting integration with regional or international markets have a material impact on the technological requirements made of the sector, and thus on the knowledge-intensity and future competitiveness of the home industry.

Endnotes

1 This paper was written with the support of the South Africa – Argentina Science and Technology Bilateral Agreement. The authors thank Neo Molotja for assisting with R&D Survey and Innovation Survey data extractions. Thank you to Fernando Peirano, Carlos Bianco, Valeria Arza, Jo Lorentzen, and Glenda Kruss for their comments and advice. The usual disclaimer applies.

2 The Benchmarking Club consists of approximately 70 of South Africa's major components manufacturers and gather data annually from each of the member firms. This includes data related to innovation expenditure and R&D expenditure.

References

ADEFA (Asociación de Fabricantes de Automotores) [Automotive Manufacturers Association] (2008), *Yearbook Automotive Industry Basic Data*, Buenos Aires. Available at: http://www.adefa.com.ar/v2/index.php?lang=en

Albornoz, F., Milesi, D. and Yoguel, G. (2005), 'Knowledge circulation in vertically integrated production networks: cases of the argentine automotive and iron and steel industries,' in *Innovation: management, policy and practice*, 7(2-3): 200-221.

Albornoz, F. and Yoguel, G. (2004), 'Competitiveness and production networks: the case of the Argentine automotive sector,' in *Industrial and Corporate Change*, 13(4): 619-641.

Arza, V. and López, A. (2008), El Caso Argentino, en: La industria automotriz en el MERCOSUR [The Argentine case, in: The automotive industry in MERCOSUR] MERCOSUR Network, Buenos Aires. Available at: http://www.redmercosur.net/la-industria-automotriz-en-el-mercosur/publicacion/79/es/tem_17/

Barnes, J.(2000), 'Domestic Market pressures facing the South African Automotive Components Industry',*Research report No. 33, Industrial Restructuring Project*, School of Development Studies, University of Natal, South Africa.

Barnes, J. and Morris, M.(2000), 'An analysis of the endogenous and exogenous factors impacting on the success of the Motor Industry Development Programme,' *CSDS Working Paper No. 27, School of Development Studies*, University of Natal.

Barnes, J. and Morris, M. (2008), 'Staying alive in the global automotive industry: what can developing economies learn from South Africa about linking into global automotive value chains?', in *The European Journal of Development Research,* 20(1): 31-55.

Bastos Tigre, P., Laplane, M., Lugones, G.,Porta, F., y Sarti, F. (1999): ′Impacto del Mercosur en la dinámicadel sector automotor′, in: Garay L. and Taccone J. (eds.) Impactosectorial de la integración en el Mercosur, BID-INTAL, Buenos Aires,Rio de Janeiro y Washington.

Black, A. (1994), *An industrial strategy for the motor vehicle and component sector*,' Cape Town, South Africa: University of Cape Town Press.

Black, A. (2001), 'Globalization and restructuring in the South African automotive industry,' in *Journal of International Development*, 13(6): 779-796.

Black, A.(2002), 'The export success of the motor industry development programme and the implications for trade and industrial policy,' *Paper presented at the Trade and Industrial Policy Strategies 2002 Annual Forum*, Glenburn Lodge, Muldersdrift.

Blomström, M. andKokko, A.(1998), 'Multinational corporations and spillovers,' in *Journal of Economic Surveys*, 12(2): 1-31.

Bureau of Economic Analysis (BEA) (2010), *US Economic Accounts Data*, Department of Commerce. Available at: http://www.bea.gov/

CENDA (Centro de Estudios para el Desarrollo Argentino) [Research Center for Argentine Development], (2008), 'El complejo automotriz argentino: las terminales a la promoción y el desarrollo industrial al descenso' *["The Argentine automotive industry: the assemblers to the bottom of the table and industrial development to the second division"] in: Notas de la economía argentina [Notes on Argentina's economy], Ed.* 05, August 2008, Buenos Aires.

Centre for Production Studies, (2010), [*Centro de Estudios y Publicaciones (CEP)*].

Chudnovsky y López. (2002), *Integración regional e inversión extranjera directa. El caso del MERCOSUR*, [Regional integration and foreign direct investment. The case of MERCOSUR] Serie REDINT, INTAL, Inter-American Development Bank.

Department of Science and Technology, (2010), *South African National Survey of Research and Experimental Development*. Pretoria: Government of South Africa.

Department of Science and Technology, (2010), *South African National Innovation Survey*. Pretoria: Government of South Africa.

Duncan, D. (1997), *We are motor men,* Caithness, Scotland: Whittles Publishing.

Flatters, F.(2005), 'The economics of the MIDP and the South African Motor Industry,'*Paper prepared for TIPS/NEDLAC South Africa Trade and Poverty Programme (SATPP) Policy Dialogue Workshop,* Johannesburg, November 1-18.

Gastrow, M. (2007), 'An overview of research and development activities in the South African automotive industry,' in*Journal for New Generation Sciences*, 6(1): 1-15.

Humphrey, J. and Memedovic, O. (2003), *The global automotive industry value chain: what prospects for upgrading by developing countries?* UNIDO Sectoral Studies Series paper, Vienna.

Humphrey, J. and Oeter, A. (2000), 'Motor industry policies in emerging markets: globalisation and the promotion of domestic industry', in Humphrey, J.,Lecler, Y. and Salerno, M.S., *Global strategies and local realities: The auto industry in emerging markets*, London: Macmillan.

Instituto Nacional De Estadística E Censos (INDEC) (2010), Segunda encuesta nacional de innovación y conducta tecnológica de las empresas argentinas, Buenos Aires.

Lorentzen, J. and Barnes, J.(2004), 'Learning, upgrading and innovation in the South African Automotive Industry,' in *The European Journal of Development Research*, 16(3): 465-498.

Miozzo, M. (2000), 'Transnational corporations, industrial policy and the 'war of incentives': the case of the Argentina automobile industry,' in *Development and Change*, 31(3): 651-680.

Katz, J. (1983), 'Estrategia industrial y ventajas comparativas dinamicas,' [Industrial Strategy and dynamic comparative advantages], in: *Cuadernos de la Fundacion Eugenio A. Blanco [Eugenio A. Blanco Foundation Handbook]*, 1(1): 8-22

Kosacoff, B. (2007), 'Hacia un nuevo modelo industrial. Idas y vueltas del desarrollo argentino' [Towards a new industrial model. Comings and goings of Argentine development], *Capital Intelectual*, Buenos Aires.

Kosacoff, B. and Ramos, A. (2001), 'Cambios contemporáneos en la estructura industrial argentina (1975-2000)' [Contemporary changes in Argentine industrial structure (1975-2000)]. Universitary Handbooks, Num. 2, Quilmes National University, Bernal.

Kosakoff, B., Todesca, J. and Vispo, A. (1991), 'The Transformation of the Argentine automotive industry in its integration with Brazil', LC/BUE/L.122, Buenos Aires: CEPAL/ECLAC.

Moralez, R. and Katz, J. (1995), 'Industrial responses to liberalization and increased competitiveness in the Latin American automobile industry,' *Paper presented at the ECLAC/IDRC-UNU/INTECH Conference,* Marbella, Chile, 28-30 August.

Miozzo, M. (2000), 'Transnational corporations, industrial policy and the 'war of incentives': the case of the Argentina automobile industry,' in *Development and Change*, 31: 651-680.

Motta, J. (2006), 'The structure of the automotive components sector at the global level', in: *Actualidad Económica [Economic news]*, año XVI, num. 58, January-April, Argentina, pp. 27-32.

National Association of Automotive Component and Allied Manufacturers (NAACAM) (2010), *Key information on the South African Automotive Industry*. Available at: http://www.naacam.co.za/

National Association of Automobile Manufacturers South Africa (NAAMSA) (2010), *Industry data*. Available at: http://www.naamsa.co.za/extracts/

Novick, M., Yoguel G., Catalano A. and Albornoz F. (2003), 'New configurations in the Argentine automotive sector: The tension between production and marketing strategies', in Cuadernos del CENDES [CENDES handbooks], Nª 49, Caracas, Venezuela.

Porta, Guidicatti y Vismara, (2004), Microeconomic changes and wage evolution in Argentina's automotive industry, *Working Paper*, Centro REDES, Buenos Aires.

Rasiah, R. (2004), *Foreign Firms, Technological Capabilities and Economic Performance: Evidence from Africa, Asia and Latin America*, Cheltenham: Edward Elgar.

Rutherford, T. and Holmes, J. (2008), "The flea on the tail of the dog': power in global production networks and the restructuring of Canadian automotive clusters', in *Journal of Economic Geography*,8(4): 519-544.

Sturgeon, T. and Van Biesebroeck, J. (2010), *Effects of the crisis on the automotive industry in developing countries: a global value chain perspective. Policy Research Working Paper 5330*, The World Bank, Washington, D.C.

Sturgeon, T., Van Biesebroeck, J. and Gereffi, G. (2008), 'Value chains, networks and clusters: reframing the global automotive industry', in *Journal of Economic Geography*, 8(3): 297-321.

Sturgeon, T.J., Memedovic, O., Van Biesebroeck, J. and Gereffi, G. (2009), 'Globalisation of the automotive industry: main features and trends', in *International journal of Technological Learning, Innovation and Development*, 2(1/2): 7-24.

Wad, P. (2010), 'Impact of the global economic and financial crisis over the automotive industry in developing countries', *Working Paper 16/2009*, United Nations Industrial Development Organisation (UNIDO), Vienna.

7

Development and Strengthening of Research Capacities in Madagascar:

An impact study of IFS activities (1976-2008)

Jacques Gaillard[1] *& Anne Marie Gaillard*[2]

1. Introduction

Since the mid-1970s, the International Foundation for Science (IFS) supports young scientists in developing countries in Africa, Asia and the Pacific, as well as Latin America and the Caribbean. It includes individual research grants and capacity enhancing activities. Between 1974 and 2008, IFS supported close to 5000 research scientists in some 100 developing countries; over one-third were in Africa. The first research grants in Madagascar date back to 1976. By December 2008, 50 Malagasy researchers had received a total of 71 IFS grants, making Madagascar 13th among the 40 countries of Sub-Saharan Africa where IFS awarded grants (Nigeria, Kenya and Cameroon being the top recipient countries). Among the 50 Malagasy recipients, three have died and four have retired. Several are still professionally active although they have reached retirement age. By early 2009, 27 young scientists were still being supported by IFS, including

1 Senior scientist at the Institut de Recherche pour le Développement (IRD), UMR 201 Development and Societies (University Paris 1 Panthéon-Sorbonne/IRD), member of the « Institut Francilien Recherche, Innovation et Société » and Labex « Sciences, Innovations, et Techniques en Société » (SITES), France. Email: jacques.gaillard@ird.fr

2 Consultant (Social Anthropologist). Email: anmagaill@gmail.com

five new grantees from the December 2008 session. The grants, excluding travel and training subsidies, totalled some US$720,000.

To assess the effects of IFS support on the grantees' academic and professional careers, the IFS Secretariat has adopted an impact assessment methodology called MESIA (Monitoring and Evaluation System for Impact Assessment) which includes interviews, questionnaire surveys, bibliometric studies of grantees' scientific publications, and national impact studies, such as this one for Madagascar. The impact studies are carried out within a defined conceptual framework and follow guidelines to meet the requirements of international comparisons (Gaillard, 2000: http://www.ifs.se/Publications/Mesia/mesia.asp). In so far as is possible, they involve the IFS staff and affiliated organisations.

The MESIA study in Madagascar combine seven complementary approaches:

i. a historical, institutional, political and sociological study of the national research system;

ii. a retrospective analysis (1976-2008) of grant applications, candidates, grantees, and results;

iii. a bibliometric study of science in Madagascar (1987-2006);

iv. a desk analysis of IFS grantees' files at the IFS Secretariat;

v. a tracking study of grantees' personnel and professional life;

vi. a questionnaire survey sent to IFS grantees in Madagascar and

vii. in-depth interviews of 11 grantees.

The desk and field studies, as well as the interviews were carried out between May and December 2008. The impact study covers 45 scientists who received IFS support during the period between 1976 (when the first grants were awarded to Malagasy scientists) and August 2008. The present article summarizes some of the main findings (for greater details see Gaillard and Gaillard, 2010).

2. The context: a brief overview of science and scientific institutions in Madagascar

A brief history of science and technology in Madagascar

"Western" science was introduced into Madagascar before the colonial period[1]. The discovery of the island's wealth (wildlife and flora) in the 16th century attracted scientific expeditions, mainly interested in assessing resources preliminary to studies on conditions for establishing colonisation. The 19th century, prior to the French occupation, saw the arrival of numerous adventurers, naturalists and missionaries who contributed to the emergence of several fields of research that marked the origins of most of the country's preferred disciplines of contemporary science: inventories of natural resources, the sciences of nature, medicine, marine environments, anthropology, historic linguistics, cartography and geography (Rasoamampianina, 2010). Between 1896 and 1960, the colonial administration laid the grounds for the first scientific institutions, including the Institut Pasteur de Madagascar, the Académie Malgache and several agricultural research institutes. But it wasn't until the last years of the colonial period that Madagascar got its first institution of higher education, the Institut français des hautes études. This was the institutional situation in 1960 when the newly born Malagasy Republic founded the Université d'Antananarivo.

Despite independence, research remained "French" until 1972, the year when authority was transferred from the former colonial power to Madagascar and the year when institutions were nationalised, and the institutional landscape was redesigned. Today, Madagascar has six public universities, with a combined enrolment of 40,000 students. Over half (60%) attend the Université d'Antananarivo. Private institutes of higher education have become very popular in the last few years. Some 50 private higher education institutions were created since 1992. Most of these private institutions essentially offer curricula that prepare students for professional life and invest very little in academia per se. In the public universities, the teacher/student ratio has reached a critical level as a result of insufficient recruitment of teachers over the last 20+ years and a 100% increase in the student body over the last 6 years. Aging of teachers-researchers (with an average age of 56 years in 2008 reported by the University of Antananarivo) is another great cause for concern. Seven of the ten national research centres (Centres Nationaux de Recherche, CNR), are very small (between 5 and 17 researchers) and combine teaching, support services and expertise. There are three exceptions: The National Research Center for Rural Development (FOFIFA) and, to a lesser extent the National Research Center for Industrial and Technological Research (CNRIT) and The National Research Center for Environment (CNRE).

Table 1: Main Research Centers and Institutes in Madagascar (public and private)

Public Research Centers
Centre National de Recherche Appliquée au Développement Rural (FOFIFA)
Centre National d'Application de la Recherche Pharmaceutique (CNARP)
Centre National de Recherche Océanographique (CNRO)
Centre National de Recherche Industrielle et Technologique (CNRIT)
Centre National de Recherche sur l'Environnement (CNRE)
Parc Botanique et Zoologique de Tsimbasaza (PBZT)
Institut National des Sciences et Techniques Nucléaires (INSTN)
Institut Malgache des Vaccins Vétérinaires (IMVAVET)
Private Research Centers
Institut Pasteur de Madagascar (IPM)
Institut Malgache de Recherches Appliquées (IMRA)

Madagascar also has several private research centres. The Institut Pasteur de Madagascar (IPM) and the Institut Malgache de Recherches Appliquées (IMRA) rank among the most dynamic private centers and produce a tangible share of Madagascar scientific publications. Other research centres include institutes under the ministries of health, water resources, mines, economic affairs, finance, etc. and the Non-Governmental Organisations (NGOs). The growing importance of the NGOs including WWF, WCS, but also the Bibikely Biodiversity Center, Magasikara Voakajy and Vahatra, of most recent origin, is tangible in the institutional landscape. The latter group focuses essentially on environmental issues and biodiversity protection. Most of the IFS grantees work in the Université d'Antananarivo, the CNRs (FOFIFA, CNRE, CNRP, INSTN) and at IMRA. Two Malagasy researchers who work for the NGO Magasikara Voakajy have also received support from IFS over the last few years.

Research policy and governance

The research governance system has evolved using various models, whose history and chronology are described elsewhere in greater details (Gaillard and Gaillard, 2010; Randimbimahenina, 2010). A look at the ministerial reform of April 2008 shows an unprecedented situation that caused anxiety among Madagascar's scientists and supporters of scientific activities interviewed for this study: the words "research", "science" and "scientific" were totally missing from the ministerial titles. The only "survivor" was the term "higher education" but it has been demoted to the level of a "vice ministry" within the Ministry of National Education. The researchers, the teachers-scientists and the institution directors interviewed for this study were very worried. The most pessimistic ones said that, at best, the national research centres would be attached to the university, and, at worst, they would be closed down. The organisational chart of the Vice Ministry in charge of Higher Education, Technical and Professional Training, within the Ministry of National Education confirmed the role of the Department of Research in formulating and implementing the ministry's research policy.

Since the early 2009, Madagascar went through a new political crisis leading to the creation of a government of transition (Haute Autorité de Transition -HAT). One of the first decisions of this government was to create a Ministry of Higher Education and Research (MESUPRES). However, one short-term drawback is that some of the main donors and funding institutions (including the World Bank and the European Union), decided to stop funding ongoing projects. It includes projects supporting research and higher education activities. Consequently, research activities within universities and public research institutes stand often idle.

Human and financial resources

The number of teaching staff in Higher Education public institutions has remained unchanged over the last ten years (slightly more than 1,000), while the number of students doubled. Due to structural adjustment programmes, no recruitments took place between 1996 and 2006 leading to a critical ageing of the teaching staff population (4/5 are 50 years old or more than 50 years old; less than 4% of them are less than 40 years). Very few contribute to research activities on a regular basis (approximately 10%). The number of researchers in public research institutes has slightly decreased over the last ten years (today slightly less than 1,000). Staff ageing is even more critical for them. The youngest one was 38 years old and he the only one in the category below 40 years old.

The Malagasy budget for scientific and technical activities (national research budget, including wages) is in the lower range of research budgets in Sub-Saharan Africa. It has decreased from a high 0.9% in 1970 to 0.26% in 1986 (MRST, 1988). In 2007, it was estimated to be 0.14%. Research activities are seriously underfunded. This is causing the Malagasy national research system to depend heavily on foreign funding and research. Nearly no research is taking place today in Madagascar without foreign funding. In addition, the Malagasy scientific community is dispersed and often isolated, with numerous small and scattered research units that all too often duplicate each other's work.

Madagascar scientific outputs

Madagascar's scientific output measured in number of publications indexed in international databases, despite its biases and limitations, is useful for positioning national science (in relation to the rest of Africa and the world) and identifying fields of specialisation, institutions and leading authors. Madagascar, with its modest but increasing scientific production (see Figure 1), has a halfway position in Africa (20th in Africa as a whole, 16th in Sub-Saharan Africa in 2006), immediately followed by countries such as Burkina Faso, Côte d'Ivoire and Zambia, and just ahead of The Gambia, Sudan and Mali.

Figure 1: Evolution of the number of publications in Madagascar (1987-2006) in three databases (PASCAL, SCI and SCI extended)

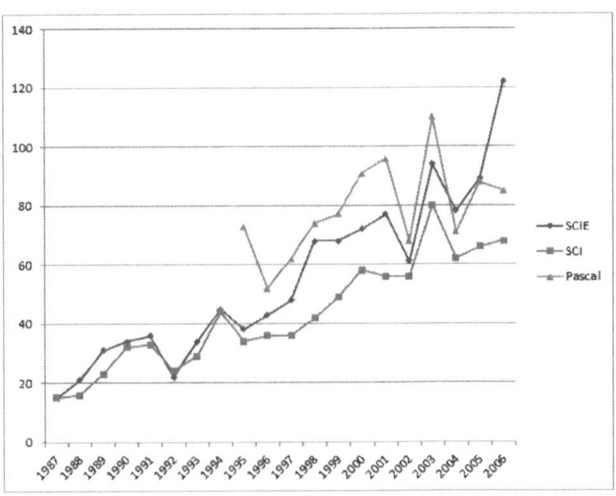

Two institutions are in the forefront and have produced half of the publications between 1995 and 2006 (see Figure 2): the Université d'Antananarivo and the Institut Pasteur de Madagascar (IPM). Actually, over half (56%) when adding the output of the Antananarivo CHU (university hospital). The Université d'Antananarivo has gained considerable standing during the last few years, mainly because of the increased number of publications co-authored with foreign scientists working for NGOs, increasingly in fields related to environment and biodiversity preservation. Mention should also be made of the relative importance of IRD (French public research institute working with Malagasy research institutions) and IMRA. A small number of publications (average under two per year) are produced sporadically in two universities in the provinces (Tuléar et Mahajanga). This is also the case for four public research institutes (CNARP, PBZT, CNRE and FOFIFA).

Figure 2: Evolution of production of the most visible institutions (1995-2006, WOS)

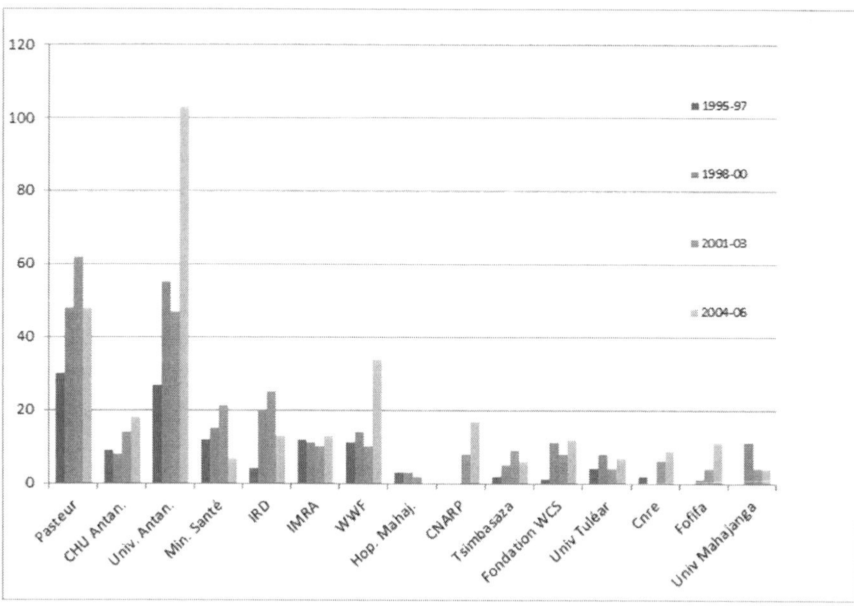

A look at fields of specialisation shows the overriding prevalence of medical sciences (60-70%) and the relative weakness of agricultural sciences (about 10%). Biology (which includes biological resources, more specifically zoology, ecology, etc.) is the only field that is gaining ground (from 12% in

1996-67 to over 30% in 2004-06). Attention must be given to the very great weakness of the exact sciences (mathematics, physics and chemistry) and the Land-Ocean-Atmosphere (LOA) sciences that used to be a preferred area of research in Madagascar (Figure 3).

Figure 3: Relative importance of the main research areas over four periods

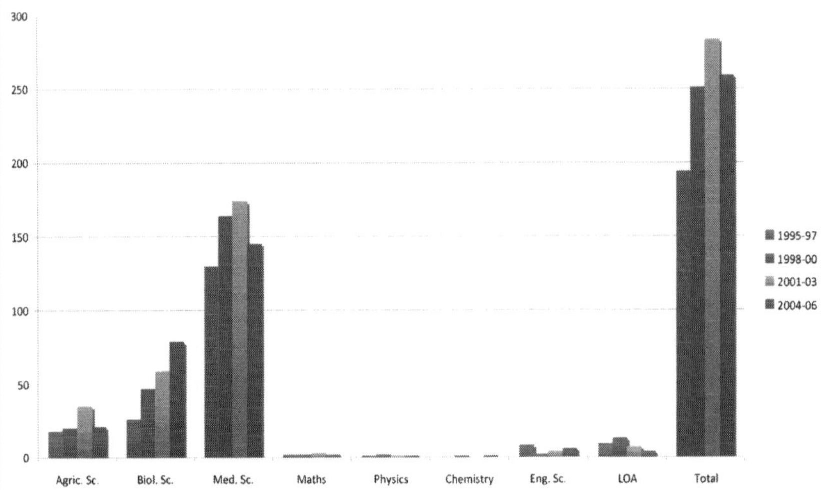

Source : base Pascal/Inist. Data computing : P.L. Rossi/IRD

Of the ten most reputed and prolific authors in international databases, two have received IFS grants. One is working at CNARP and the other one at IMRA. If we expand the selection to include authors who have published at least one publication per year between 2003 and 2007, there is another IFS grantee, now employed at IMRA (with seven publications indexed in five years). All three work on Natural Products. This is a positive outcome for IFS if we consider that more than half of the other scientists in the list of top publishing scientists are foreign scientists and/or scientists working at IPM, thereby not eligible for IFS grants.

International collaboration, measured through international co-publications, i.e. publications signed jointly with foreign authors, are very important, even excessively so. This phenomenon is not new, but they now account for 90% of all publications. The importance of collaboration with USA authors has grown since the end of the 1980s and, since 2005, has outweighed collaboration with Europe. As co-authored publications with USA rose, co-authoring with French scientists dropped proportionately. At the end of the 1980s, 60% of co-authored publications were with French scientists; in 2008 the level had dropped to 20%.

3. Results of the impact study of IFS activities

In an average year, IFS receives about ten applications for grants from Malagasy scientists of which two or so are eliminated at pre-screening, eight or so are scrutinised by the IFS scientific advisors and two or three are successful. It is noteworthy that an increase in IFS visibility through meetings, workshops, repeated visits by members of the IFS Secretariat, etc. usually leads to an increase in the number of applications. Since 2000, the average annual acceptance rate has been 24% of all applications received, which is well above the average for the African continent (18%) and the average for the countries of Sub-Saharan Africa (19%) during those same years. It is also above the average for Asia (19.5%) and for the world (21.5%) but slightly lower than the average for Latin America (28.6%). An analysis of the relative success rate for the last nine years shows major variations from one field to the next. Besides the quality of the project and of the candidate, very decisive factors are related to the relative development level of a research tradition and infrastructure and the quality of supervision they receive at their home institutes. Applications from young scientists working for institutions outside Antananarivo with little or no research traditions have nearly all been rejected.

IFS grantees' profiles

The largest number of grantees works in chemistry of Natural Products (16 scientists, 25 grants awarded) followed by Forestry and Agro-Forestry (10 scientists, 11 grants) and Crop Science (7 scientists, 11 grants). Natural Products is an old research topic in Madagascar, understandably so since the country is rich in endemic biodiversity and has discovered many drugs derived from plants. It has attracted a goodly number of national teams working in both public and private Malagasy institutions (CNARP, IMRA, CNRE, FOFIFA), universities, (mainly the Université d'Antananarivo), NGOs and the international pharmaceutical industry. Certain fields such as aquaculture (Aquatic Resources), and Food Science, even Animal Production have received very few grants, especially during the last few years. Yet, these fields are of high priority for Madagascar's development. Water Resources and Social Science are relatively new to the IFS granting programme, which may explain the relatively low number of research grants awarded in these two fields to Malagasy scientists. Recent efforts have been made to encourage grant applications in both.

On average, first-time IFS grant applicants are less than 34 years of age. Applicants and awardees over the last few years include scientists in the very early 30s and even some applicants under the age of 30. This may seem surprising since the average researcher in Madagascar is considerably older but can be traced to the fact that a growing number of IFS grantees selected during the last ten years are actually PhD students without permanent employment. Many of them are hired on contract and/or have short-term teaching jobs, which allow them to survive, and/or work for NGOs. In Madagascar, 38% of the grantees are women. This is less than parity but is high in comparison with the percentage of female IFS grantees in Sub-Saharan Africa (15.6%) and the world (25%). It is about the same as the ratio in Latin America (37%), the continent with the highest percentage of female grantees. For the period as a whole, around half (51%) of the awardees have more or less the equivalent of a PhD (3rd cycle thesis, doctoral thesis in Engineering, PhD thesis or Doctorat d'Etat). This is equivalent to what was found in the MESIA study in Cameroon (52%) and higher than in Tanzania (35%). Most of them (close to 75%) were trained in Madagascar and 20% studied in France (mainly doctoral studies). Two of them have studied and one is studying in the USA, as part of a sandwich programme.

Research as a profession

On the question of salaries, the results of the survey are almost unanimous: 28 out of 30 respondents said that their salary is not enough to cover their needs and the needs of their family. Eight went, as far as to say that, considering the cost of living, the salary was "far too low", even after adding bonuses. Besides their "main employment", all these scientists (30 out of 30) had other jobs, such as overtime teaching in their home institutions or other public or private institutions, consultancies and private business (2/3rds of them), to which they devote a considerable amount of their time (more than half spend over 40 hours a month on their second jobs). These activities generate added revenue, sometimes enough to double or more their basic salary.

Despite these "other jobs", the respondents said they spent more time on research in their home institutions than on teaching. The tendency to spend more time on research is even more pronounced among the current, younger batch of IFS grantees. This is a positive outcome for IFS in the Malagasy context where, especially in the university teacher-researchers population, only a small number of professionals do research, and the pace is very irregular.

IFS Malagasy grantees were also asked to give their opinion on the relative advantages versus disadvantages of a number of characteristics related to their professions. Responses reveal a rather mixed picture (Table 2). Salary scale is clearly identified as a disadvantage whereas job security, career development and promotion opportunities are perceived as an advantage of the profession. Opinions are more divided concerning retirement and social benefits

Table 2: Advantages and disadvantages of various professional characteristics

Professional characteristics	Positive	Negative	Neutral
Promotion opportunities	14	7	9
Salary scale	4	17	9
Career development	21	2	7
Job security	19	7	4
Retirement benefit	10	5	15
Social benefit	8	9	13
Total	76	47	57

Except for one scientist who said his 2008 research budget (excluding salaries) was US$37,000 the vast majority have budgets of between US $2,000 and US$13,000. These are relatively small budgets, especially for two of them whose budgets, they said, were under US$250. Yet, most of these reported budgets are much higher than the average (or median) individual research budget in Madagascar. As with all of the Malagasy research scientists, IFS research grantees, both past and present, are very dependent on foreign funding. Two-thirds of them claim to be totally dependent on funds provided through bilateral technical assistance, international organisations and private foundations. The amount of foreign funding varies enormously, ranging from a few thousand US dollars to US$430,000 for a project recently funded by IDRC (International Development Research Centre, Canada). Only 14 grantees have provided detailed information on foreign funding. For the IFS grantees all told, the magnitude of total foreign funding for research (excluding IFS and national funding) can be estimated to an amount approximately ten times bigger than the IFS investment during the same period. Besides international funding by the International Atomic Energy Agency (IAEA), the European Union (EU), the Agence Universitaire de la Francophonie (AUF) and the World Bank, especially through the FADES programme, there is also bilateral funding, led far and away by French technical assistance and French research institutes (mainly CIRAD and IRD) that provide support tools and programmes for research in partnership with French scientists.

Research practice, communication and perception of research

Concerning scientific interaction and contacts, the IFS grantees said both were close with their immediate colleagues but relatively weak with Malagasy colleagues in other institutions, thus evidencing the fragmentation and compartmentalisation of the Malagasy scientific community. There are also more opportunities to work with European colleagues than with colleagues from other African countries. Although IFS contributed to establish or promote several research networks in the region involving Malagasy scientists (e.g. the Natural Products Research Network for Eastern and Central Africa – NAPRECA), there is a need to further promote these regional and/or south-south networking activities.

The main limitations to their research are, in descending order: lack of equipment, materials and consumable items, (reported 18 times), lack or shortage of funding (16 times), difficulty in obtaining documentation (11 times), lack of knowledge (9 times), lack of time (7 times), scientific isolation (7 times), lack of science policy (6 times), administrative red tape (3 times), and lastly, lack of adequate financial incentive (3 times). When asked to rank certain recurrent problems, the scientists once again pointed most emphatically to "the procurement, access to and maintenance of research equipment" and "access to source documents". These results are very comparable to the two other impact studies carried out in Africa to date i.e. Tanzania and Cameroon (Gaillard et al., 2002; Gaillard and Zink (2003).

Overall, IFS grantees did participate actively in national and international conferences, most of them taking place in Madagascar and Europe. Since the beginning of their careers, the 30 IFS grantees who responded to the questionnaire-survey attended 485 conferences, of which more than one-third (37.5%) were held in Madagascar, over one quarter (28.8%) in Europe, less than one-fifth (17.7%) in other African countries and one-tenth (9.7%) in Asia. Relatively few of the scientists attended conferences in North America (26 conferences) and even fewer went to Latin America (4 conferences). IFS provided financial support for grantees to attend 57 of the 485 conferences, slightly over one conference out of ten (11.7%), mainly in Madagascar (23) and the rest of Africa (21), but also, to a lesser extent, in Europe (6), Asia (6) and North America (1). Most funding (58%) for participation in conferences abroad came from foreign sources (IFS + other foreign sources). In recent years (last 5 years), one quarter of the respondents did not participate in any conferences abroad, and one-third attended only one. A small minority (5 of the 25 scientists who answered this question) participated in at least five conferences abroad during the last five years, i.e. at least one conference per year. This latter group are all part of an earlier cohort of IFS grantees, but their grants were terminated at least ten years ago.

Research outputs and outcomes

Concerning scientific publications, 27 scientists (out of the 30 who participated in the survey) responded to this question. The group was extremely heterogeneous, concerning both the number and types of publications and the publication strategy. The most prolific (ex IFS grantee) scientist produced close to half of all works published in international journals and presented at conferences. At the other end of the spectrum, one grantee reported 95 written works in the "grey literature"[2] category, 8 in international journals, and even fewer presentations at conferences. There were many scientists between these two extremes; they published rather little. The most frequent mode of publication is articles in international scientific journals, conference presentations and conference proceedings. And then there was the grey literature, which by definition is not published, but which nonetheless was in third position, well before articles published in local journals. Following the grey literatures was chapters in books, films and documentaries and, finally, whole books (Figure 4).

Figure 4: Relative importance of scientific outputs

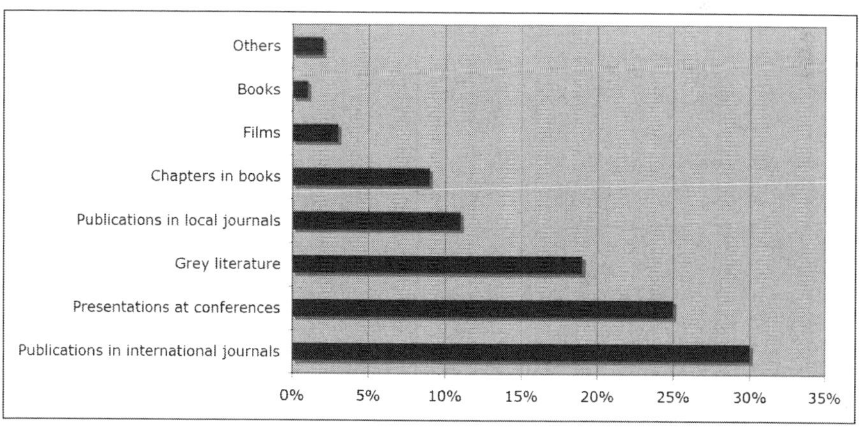

The relatively low number of articles published in local journals can be explained by the small number of local journals that exist in Madagascar and the fact that they are not published regularly. The relative share of publications that can be traced directly to IFS-supported work is 15%. It is slightly lower than in Cameroon and higher than in Tanzania. The number of publications per scientist, for each channel of publication, obviously depends on the scientist's relative seniority. Scientists working on Natural Products, publish the most in international journals (16.8 publications on average per scientist throughout his/her career), make the most presentations at seminars and conferences (12.2) and write the most book chapters (5.1). It is noteworthy that papers in international journals are nearly all co-authored with foreign authors.

Besides publications, the IFS grantees in Madagascar also transmit their research findings by teaching in establishments of higher education and by training and supervising students working toward master's and doctoral thesis. Several participate actively in NGOs, producer associations and community organisations to help optimise and transmit their research. Out of the 30 respondents to the questionnaire, 7 said that their research had led to at least one patent, commercial application or innovation. One-fifth of 32 patents, applications and innovations identified through the survey came from IFS-supported research. As for publications, we can recognise a concentration factor: two grantees produced 20 out of 32 (i.e. close to two-thirds) of what we have called "other research products". Furthermore, one of the two filed for 10 of the 14 patents listed. This grantee works on Natural Products and is also the grantee who published most in international scientific journals.

After having completed an IFS supported research project, and submitted a project report, grantees may apply for renewal grants. In total, a researcher is eligible to receive today[3] three research grants from IFS. Among the 23 Malagasy scientists whose IFS grants have ended, 14 obtained one grant, three obtained two, four obtained three, and two (belonging to the first generation of IFS grantees in Madagascar and working in the field of Natural Products) received four. Natural Products enjoyed the highest grant renewal rate, followed by Crop Sciences. The four grantees working in Animal Production received one grant each. The timeframe of an IFS research project or period should normally be 1-3 years. The average research period for the grants awarded to the 23 Malagasy scientists whose grants have ended, is 6.8 years[4], i.e. double the normal maximum length of an IFS research period (3 years). It however varies from 2 years up to 11 years. Scientists who enjoyed more than one grant tended to shorten their research periods (5.3 years) while the research period for one-time grantees was longer (8 years). Delays (and, to a certain extent, non-renewals) were caused by difficulties reported back to the IFS Secretariat, and during visits by experts and interviews on site. The main reasons were delays in purchasing and installing research equipment, administrative problems, difficulties in getting to the field, professional reassignments, unforeseen obstacles in conducting the research, personal crises and socio-political conflicts that caused the universities and research institutes to be closed for several months or even a whole year.

To date, out of the 23 Malagasy scientists no longer supported by IFS 8 grantees (about one-third) have submitted a final report to IFS. The cumulative figure for final reports and partial reports sent to IFS i.e. 15 (nearly two-thirds) can be considered as rather satisfactory. In 6 cases, IFS did not receive any partial or final reports by the time the grant files had been closed. All six were grantees were scientists who received one- grant only. On average, the number of grantees' files closed without reports in Madagascar is lower compared to Tanzania (Gaillard, Zink and Tullberg, 2002) but higher compared to Cameroon (Gaillard and Zink, 2003). For the 15 who submitted partial and/or final reports, the quality of the reports was very varied. Six were considered poor or unsatisfactory, five satisfactory, and four, good or excellent. These results concerning the quality of the reports were on average comparable to findings in Tanzania but less good than in Cameroon where most of the reports (88%) were judged to be "satisfactory" or better than satisfactory.

Advancement and mobility

Madagascar's IFS grantees made notable academic progress. In most cases, they were able to defend their doctoral thesis thanks to research projects carried out with IFS funding (3rd cycle thesis or doctorat d'Etat[5]). By 2008, 24 out of the 30 scientists (80%) had reached a level equivalent to PhD or above, at the least, while only 14 (less than half) had reached that level when the first grants were awarded. Since obtaining IFS support, several Malagasy scientists have been recruited to leading positions in research institutes and at the Université d'Antananarivo, or as advisors to ministers.

As in other IFS country impact studies carried out to date (Cameroon, Mexico, Tanzania and Vietnam) Malagasy scientists supported by IFS, remain in Madagascar throughout their research career, i.e. long after the IFS support was discontinued. Despite their high international mobility, they have all been committed to working in their home countries and strengthening local science capacity from the inside. Thus, to get a higher education degree, 20 of the 30 scientists who responded to the questionnaire survey had studied abroad for a period of between 1 and 10 years, the average being 4.1 years. The total number of years spent abroad (for studies and other reasons) is longer, since 21 of them spent between 1 and 30 years outside their country, the average being 5.7 years. The scientist who spent the most time abroad (30 years) is the only one among the 45 who moved abroad permanently for retirement after having worked for 13 years in Madagascar, and 6 years in Côte d'Ivoire and Tunisia.

The grantee tracer study carried out as part of this impact study showed that there were no confirmed cases of the "brain drain" among the Malagasy grantees. The case mentioned above reflects "inter-African circulation" rather than a typical case of South-North brain drain. We also saw a certain number of inter-institutional movements at the national level, but nearly all the Malagasy IFS grantees continued to work actively in their national scientific community. Many of them, as we saw above, work in research or higher education institutions, but as a side-line undertake expert studies or work as consultants. Only one scientist, up to now, went as far as to resign from his institution (CNRE) to become a full-time consultant to a mining firm, thus ending his IFS-sponsored project. Lastly, a teacher-scientist at the École Supérieure Polytechnique of the Université d'Antananarivo, who also worked as an expert in renewable domestic and industrial energy (mainly for the World Bank) created a company called Energie Technologie of which he is the manager and majority shareholder. This means that he combines teaching at the university, and working as an expert, a developer and a businessman.

An assessment of IFS support

Although most of the respondents said that lack of funding was the main constraint to their research, only 3 (out of the 27 who answered the question) said that they would not have been able to continue their project without the IFS grant. In contrast to their peers in other African countries, not many Malagasy scientists say that their research would not have been possible without the support of IFS. The fact that only 8 said that they could have continued their work without more financial support from IFS suggests that the majority of them were prepared to seek (and, according to what they said, obtain) support from other funding sources and/or eventually redesign (or even downsize) their project.

But there is a contradiction here: IFS has played a role in enhancing capacity for accessing other sources of funding and for obtaining support for the research activities. Out of the 25 grantees who answered the related question in the questionnaire survey, 19 said that the IFS grant helped them obtain other international funding, 16 said they received funds from their home institutions and 12 obtained national (public or private) funding. Receiving the grant allowed 15 of them to obtain better scientific and technical assistance from their institution and in 21 out of 23 cases to start new partnerships which lasted after the grant ended. So, on the one hand, some grantees are saying that they could have continued their project without the IFS grant but at the same time assert that the IFS grant was indeed very useful, if not pivotal, for their project/career.

The IFS Malagasy scientists were also asked to rate the quality of a number of services provided by IFS, even if some of them have been discontinued. Overall, they have a positive or very positive opinion of IFS services. The services that ranked highest were grant administration, purchase of research equipment, selection process, scientific workshops and contacts with the IFS Secretariat. The services which most grantees considered generally "satisfactory" but which received the highest number of "bad" and "very bad" ratings were: networking activities, publication assistance for research findings, follow-up activities after project completion, and research equipment maintenance, the only service for which negative opinions outnumbered the "good" and "excellent" ratings. Research equipment maintenance is typically a service that is no longer provided by IFS. The same applies to publication assistance of research findings that has never been a core activity of the IFS granting programme. For IFS, this is an indication of services that may be important to (re-) consider in the future in particular when IFS wants to focus its support to the scientifically weakest countries.

Science, society and scientists' career goals

The answers to the questions related to the role of science in society were confirmed by opinions conveyed during the interviews: IFS' Malagasy grantees support the traditional values of national public science. All of them feel that science contributes to development; nearly all feel that science is a public good, that scientific knowledge is universal and that the main goal of science is the production of knowledge. These values are enhanced by values related to loyalty to one's institution and one's country (most of the grantees feel that it is normal for the scientific institutions to select the research topics and the government to define the scientific priorities). Similarly, values linked to economic development and markets are, by the vast majority, considered to be positive; most of the grantees feel that science should first and foremost contribute to practical innovations, and that scientists should have business and managerial skills and should produce goods for a competitive market. Career choices also reflect the grantees' attachment to scientific professions and national ethics. Only three of the grantees would like to work for foreign or international institutions; the great majority would like to continue to work for national public research and/or development institutions.

4. Conclusion

Science was introduced into Madagascar before the colonial period and the colonial administration laid the grounds for the first scientific institutions between 1896 and 1960. Yet, the development and the institutionalization of the Malagasy science and technology system is of recent origin. The first University (Université d'Antananarivo) was founded in 1960 at the same time as the newly born Malagasy Republic. Research institutions were nationalized, and the institutional landscape was redesigned from 1972. Today, Madagascar has six public universities (the main one being in Antoananarivo in the capital city), ten national research centers, some 50 private higher education institutions created over the last twenty years and several private research centres (e.g. The Institut Pasteur de Madagascar (IPM) and the Institut Malgache de Recherches Appliquées (IMRA) ranking among the most dynamic private centres).

Since early 2009, Madagascar went through a long-lasting political crisis which outcome is difficult to predict. This led to a sharp cut in foreign funded activities and to a slowing down in research activities. Political crises are recurring in Madagascar and they are, in part, responsible for the difficulties regularly invoked by the recipients of IFS to explain the delays and constraints in their work. Malagasy researchers eventually adapt the best they can taking maximum advantage of the limited resources they have. But relying on one's own resources has its limits in a context of declining institutions. The universities are weakened, endangered by asphyxiation due to the massive increase in student numbers and face the "off-shoring" of research that is done increasingly outside its walls[6]. Several provincial universities and national research institutes are nothing more than empty shells, or in the process of becoming empty shells. The "de-institutionalization" of science is accompanied by a "de-professionalization" of research.

The deteriorating purchasing power and working conditions have resulted in the emigration of scientists even though many Malagasy scientists stayed at home (this is the case of IFS grantees), surviving by supplementing their meagre wages from various additional activities. The decline of institutions and the deterioration in the exercise of the profession of researcher have intensified due to the withdrawal of state, which was further increased in recent years. The former political power never truly trusted Malagasy researchers that it considered "mediocre" and not contributing to national development. The stated goal for 2010 by the "Madagascar Action Plan (MAP) to devote 0.1% of Gross National Product (GNP) to the national research budget (GERD) also confirms the lack of ambition of the deposed government to strengthen its national research capacity[7].In the absence of a national research strategy, policies are often reduced to laissez-faire. It is therefore hoped that a new democratically elected government will soon restart the process of developing a dynamic and ambitious national research policy to allow a real strengthening of research capacity in Madagascar.

The foregoing put the performance and outcomes of IFS grantees into context and perspective. It stresses the difficulty of developing and strengthening science in countries having weak institutions and weak scientific capacities. In such a context, there is a necessary tension between activities such as building a new road, which can generate increased production and development, thereby reducing poverty, versus improving the learning and working conditions of an increasing number of graduates and researchers, who will take a longer period of time before they contribute to development, and even then often indirectly, to poverty reduction.

The above-described context explains, at least partly, some of the main results of the impact study presented in this article, including the heterogeneous and sometimes unsatisfactory results of the research projects and outputs, especially with regard to reports submitted, publications, conference presentations, patents, commercial applications and innovations. This said, the positive results obtained by IFS in many ways, e.g. academic advancement of the grantees, access to executive positions, avoiding the brain drain, stimulation, and high degree of satisfaction for the IFS granting programme and additional services indicate that IFS has, to a great extent, fulfilled its mission and that its strategy is sound. Madagascar needs IFS today even more than before, but considering the growing uncertainty of the employment market, IFS, even more than in the past, must look more carefully that the future grantees will be able to devote enough time to research, and that their home institutions and laboratories can offer them good-quality and long-term on-the-job training and supervision. It means, among other things, carefully selecting not only the individual young scientists based on his/her own merits but also the research team and the institution where he or she works.

At a time when the International Foundation for Science has embarked on a process of reflection and review on the future direction of its support to young scientists in the developing world, the results of this impact study should be rather timely[8].

Endnotes

1 This does not preclude the existence of traditional knowledge and various forms of ethno sciences in Madagascar prior to the introduction of Western science. These ethno sciences no doubt contributed to transforming and shaping Western science being introduced to Madagascar (see e.g. Harding, 1996). On the spread of Western science in non-Western societies see Basalla (1967).

2 The term « grey literature » (or « gray literature ») is often, but not exclusively, used for scientific research. Examples of « grey literature » may include scientific or technical reports (e.g. IFS nonpublished progress or final reports), working papers from research groups or committees, white papers, or preprints. The identification and acquisition of grey literature poses difficulties for librarians and other information professionals for several reasons. Generally, grey literature lacks strict bibliographic control, meaning that basic information such as author, publication date or publishing body may not be easily discerned. Similarly, non-professional layouts and formats and low print runs of grey literature make the organized collection of such publications challenging compared to more traditional published media such as scientific journals and books.

3 Note that since the inception of the IFS granting programme and until 1994, a researcher was eligible to receive up to four grants from IFS.

4 The definition of a research period may differ and be controversial particularly for the last research grants awarded by IFS depending on the ending date taken in consideration: date of submission of final report or date of closure of a grantee's file. The definition used in this report is the time between a grant is awarded by IFS and the date when IFS officially terminates its support. Research periods average duration would be slightly shorter when using report submission as an ending date.

5 Inherited from the French system, these two diplomas are replaced today by a unique "doctorat" as part of the LMD reform (LMD = Licence, Master, Docorat or BSc, Master and PhD). The duration of a 3rd cycle thesis or 3rd cycle doctorat was normally three years, the first year being devoted to courses and the submission of a research report for the delivery of a DEA and the two last following years for conducting a research project. The delivery of the doctorat d'Etat is a much longer-term enterprise: up to seven years and sometimes more for the basic and experimental sciences and even more for the social sciences (10-15 years). The later degree recognizes a higher level of original research than the PhD. It was mainly used in the universities to become professor.

6 The success of the IMRA and the strengthening of research activities of several NGOs including at the outskirts of the University of Antananarivo confirm this trend that is common to many Sub-Saharan African countries (Waast, 2001).

7 The average country in sub-Saharan Africa (excluding Malawi, Uganda and South Africa) is about 0.3%.

8 As a consequence of these envisioning activities, the research grant process has been temporarily suspended. The IFS research grant application process is now re-opened. There will be two time-bound research grant application sessions before a new three programme strategy is adopted in 2012.

References

Basalla, G. (1967), 'The spread of Western Science', in *Science,*156 (3775): 611-622.

Gaillard, J. (2000), 'Monitoring and Evaluation System for Impact Assessment (MESIA): Conceptual Framework and Guidelines', *Report no. 4, Stockholm: IFS*, 38 pages. Available at: http://www.ifs.se/Publications/Mesia/mesia.asp

Gaillard, J., Zink, E. and Furo Tullberg, A. (2002), 'Strengthening Science Capacity in Tanzania - An Impact Analysis of IFS Support', *Report no. 4*, *Stockholm: IFS.* Available at: http://www.ifs.se/Publications/Mesia/mesia.asp

Gaillard, J. and Zink, E. (2003), 'Scientific Research Capacity in Cameroon - An Assessment of IFS Support', *Report no. 5*, *Stockholm: IFS.* Available at: http://www.ifs.se/Publications/Mesia/mesia.asp

Gaillard, J. and Gaillard, A-M. (2010), 'Développement et renforcement des capacités de recherche scientifique à Madagascar: une évaluation de l'impact des activités de la Fondation Internationale pour la Science (IFS) à Madagascar (1974-2008)', Paris: IRD, 2009. Available at:http://horizon.documentation.ird.fr/exldoc/pleins_textes/divers11-02/010051151.pdf

Harding, S. (1996), 'La Science moderne est-elle une ethnoscience?' in Waast, R. (ed.), *Les sciences au Sud: Etat des lieux*, Paris: ORSTOM.

MRSTD (1988), 'Réflexions sur la politique de la recherche à Madagascar', Antananarivo, 155 pages.

Randimbimahenina Andriamaromasina (2010), 'Organisation de la recherche malgache', in Feller, Ch. and F. Sandron, F. (eds.), *Parcours de recherche à Madagascar*, Marseille: IRD.

Rasoamampianina Vololoniauna (2010), 'Le Fonds Grandidier: l'histoire scientifique et technique de Madagascar avant l'annexion coloniale (1896)', in Feller, Ch. and Sandron, F. (eds.), *Parcours de recherche à Madagascar*, Marseille: IRD.

Waast, R. (2001), 'Afrique : vers un libre marché du travail scientifique ?' Économies et Sociétés, Série F. n°39, *Développement*» - III, (9-10): 1361-1413.

8

Relationship between Knowledge-capital and Firm's Performance in the Resource-based Industry

Oluseye Oladayo Jegede[1], *Angathevar Baskaran*[2] & *Mammo Muchie*[3]

1. Introduction

Several studies have been carried out on the determinants of firms' performance. Although this body of literature is thorough, most of the studies have used data from developed countries. Data on the drivers of performance from developing countries is very scant in literature, thus making it an arduous process to make useful comparisons between the drivers of firms' performance from developed and developing countries. Also, studies on firms' performance in developing countries haven't focused on knowledge capital as the determinant of performance. Furthermore, of the studies carried out in the manufacturing sector in Nigeria, very little attention

1 Department of Information and Knowledge Management, College of Business and Economics, University of Johannesburg, South Africa. Email: oluseyej@uj.ac.za, oluseyejegede@gmail.com

2 Associate Professor, Department of Development Studies, Faculty of Economics and Administration, University of Malaya, Malaysia; Senior Research Associate of SARChI (Innovation & Development), Tshwane University of Technology, Pretoria, South Africa. Email: baskaran@um.edu.my & anga_bas@yahoo.co.uk

3 DST/NRF SARChI Professor (Innovation & Development), Tshwane University of Technology, South Africa; Technology and Management Centre for Development (TMCD), Oxford University, UK; Associate Faculty Professor, Sussex University, UK; Adama Science and Technology University (ASTU), Ethiopia. Email: MuchieM@tut.ac.za

has been given to the mining industry. Yet, the industry remained a potential channel of rapid economic growth. The study, therefore, seeks to understand the relationship between knowledge-capital and financial performance in an understudied industry, that is, the mining industry in Nigeria. The study aims to obtain some useful insights that can inform policy strategies to increase the productivity of the industry in Nigeria thereby increasing the industry's input to the nation's gross domestic product.

Perspectives in the literature on the determinants of firms' performance have moved away from the classical approach of labour and capital (Solow, 1956;1988;1994) to the neoclassical approach in which technology plays a vital role (Romer, 1989;1994) and to the most recent evolutionary approach, which considers innovation (Schumpeter, 1939; 1929; 1942), national innovation system (Nelson, 1992; Patel & Pavitt, 1994; Freeman, 1995; Lundvall et al 2002; Lundvall, 2007), triple-helix (Leydesdorff & Etzkowitz, 1998; Etzkowitz & Leydesdorff, 2000; Etzkowitz, 2008; Leydesdorff, 2009) and economic geography (Krugman, 1991; Krugman, 1997; Porter, 2000) as the main drivers of firms' performance. One commonality to the evolutionary approach is the central role knowledge plays. This study thus explores the knowledge-capital approach advanced by Laperche (2007) and Laperche *et al.* (2011). Although a route less travelled in literature, the knowledge-capital approach appears to combine all the other older approaches. The knowledge capital approach is based on three pillars: knowledge, capital and the firm. "Knowledge-capital refers to the accumulated knowledge of one or several linked firms (embedded in the individuals - know-how - machines, technologies and routines of the enterprise), which is continuously enriched by information flows and used in the production process or more globally in the value creation process" (Laperche et al, 2011). According to Laperche (2007), knowledge-capital is explored from two angles: stock and flow. Knowledge stock represents knowledge rooted in employees, equipment, machinery, processes (techniques, know-how) and organizational routines which are deployed in the production activities. Knowledge flows represent scientific and technical information replenishing the knowledge stock in firms. Knowledge flow may be facilitated through research and development (R&D), training and acquisition of external knowledge or of new machinery and information from external sources. Different channels of knowledge stock and flow have been explored extensively and separately in different literatures but this study puts them together to test their significance on the firms' performance.

From history, as far as medium and large firms are concerned, research and development (R&D) have been seen as a significant driver towards innovation and performance (Schumpeter, 1942). R&D enables firms to come up with new products that could change the market dynamics or new production processes that will significantly reduce production costs per unit of labour or input. Generally, successful R&D in firms either helps firms to maximize profit or significantly reduce production/operational cost. OECD (2005) identified two types of R&D viz: intramural and extramural R&D. Intramural R&D includes all expenditures for R&D performed within a statistical unit during a specific period and Extramural R&D includes all the R&D expenditures spent outside of the statistical unit. While literatures (Kotabe, Srinivasan & Aulakh, 2002; Belderbos, Carree, & Lokshin, 2004; Sher, & Yang, 2005; Sampson, 2007; Artz, Norman, Hatfield & Cardinal, 2010) have identified that both intramural and extramural R&Ds are important determinants of firms' performance, other scholars have identified that intramural R&D may likely have a greater effect on firms' performance. For instance, Beneito (2006) carried out a study on Spanish manufacturing firms using R&D–patents relationship. He examined the different roles of intramural and extramural R&D in the innovative performance of firms, using patents and utility models counts as measures of innovation output. His findings indicated that important innovations were mainly intramural while extramural R&D was leaning towards incremental innovations. On the other hand, Laursen and Salter (2006), using a large sample of industrial firms, established that outward knowledge searches (including outsourced R&D) were important for innovation and performance of industrial firms. Another work by Kumar and Aggarwal (2005) explored the determinants of R&D behaviour of Indian enterprises over the 1990s and their impact on the R&D behaviour of multinational firms and domestic firms.The study demonstrated the variances in the landscape of R&D activities of multinational affiliates and domestic firms. Aggarwal posited that local firms direct their R&D activity principally towards the absorption of imported technology and to provide a backup to their external development via exports and FDI. Meanwhile, multinational affiliates focus on exploiting the advantages of India as an R&D platform for their parent's firm. Based on these insights, the study thus propounds that R&D, either carried out in-house or outsourced, may be significant drivers of firms' performance in the mining industry in Nigeria.

H_1: Intramural R&D is a significant driver of a firm's performance in the mining industry in Nigeria

H_2: Extramural R&D is a significant driver of a firm's performance in the mining industry in Nigeria

Drawing on the literature on knowledge-based view of the firm, several authors (Abdel-Maksoud, Dugdale & Luther, 2005; Becker, Huselid&

Beatty 2009; Michaelis, Wagner, & Schweizer, 2015) have explored the importance of the workforce for productivity and the performance improvement among firms and non-firms organisations.These studies draw on the notion that knowledge is domiciled in the minds of the workforce. Thus, the greater the size of the skilled workforce, the higher the chances of improved performance in the firms owing to the potential knowledge exchange and knowledge combinations that can take place among the employees. Indeed, employees are able to leverage each other's skills and strengths through effective knowledge management systems at the workplace. Success stories on innovativeness and improved performance in the literature (Cohen & Bailey, 1997; Tylecote & Conesa, 1999; Axtell, Holman, Unsworth, Wall, Waterson, & Harrington 2000; Laursen & Foss, 2003) have focused on experience in the shop floor especially in the manufacturing environment when factory workers were allowed to work together in a cooperative matter, compared to when they were separated or segmented (West & Altink, 1996). The study thus believes that the size of the workforce is a significant determinant of firms' performance.

H_3: The greater the size of the workforce, the higher the performance of the mining firms in Nigeria

Gray and Herr (1998) provided a comprehensive approach to workforce education and performance. They hypothesized that the level of education of an individual workforce would directly or indirectly improve on-the-job performance. Other researchers (Stone, Kaminski & Gloeckner 2008; Feller, 2011; Marginson, Tytler, Freeman & Roberts, 2013) have stressed the importance of having science, technology, engineering and mathematics (STEM)-oriented workforce for greater productivity, especially for manufacturing firms. These scholars advocate for firms to increase the quantity and quality of the STEM workforce in order to achieve increased productivity in the manufacturing environments. The study, therefore, hypothesized that the share of employees with a university degree and those with STEM education are significant drivers of performance.

H_4: The higher the percentage of employees with a university degree, the higher the performance of the mining firms in Nigeria.

H_5: The higher the percentage of employees with STEM education, the higher the performance of the mining firms in Nigeria.

Tsai (2004), Cassiman and Veugelers (2007), Bin (2008) and Shih and Chang (2009) have all highlighted the importance of external sources of technology for performance of firms. They stressed that it is particularly important to complement internal technologies by acquiring technologies from abroad. The foreign technology could be acquired through physical assets, equipment, hardware or software, patents, industrial design, trademarks and amongst others known as embodied technology (Bloom & Van Reenen, 2002). Another viable channel could be through the disembodied technologies which represent technology embedded in an employee (Zakaria, 2000). The presence of expatriates is a very important medium for the diffusion of foreign knowledge within the boundaries of another country (Harzing, & Sorge, 2003). Therefore, technology diffusion can be viewed either through the embodied or the disembodied technology lenses. International technology diffusion refers to all the channels through which countries acquire technological knowledge from abroad such as hiring an expatriate from abroad (Lichtenthaler & Frishammar, 2011). The study, hence, considers that the hiring of expatriates and the acquisition of machinery, hardware, equipment, software as well as the acquisition of external technologies/knowledge such as patents, trademarks, industrial design, etc. have significant impacts on the firms' performance.

H_6: Investment in the acquisition of machinery, equipment, hardware or software has significant impacts on the performance of the mining firms in Nigeria.

H_7: Investment in the acquisition of external knowledge/technology has significant impacts on the performance in the mining firms in Nigeria.

H_8: The larger the share of expatriates in the population,the higher the performance of the mining firms in Nigeria.

Other authors (Zucker, Darby & Armstrong, 2002; Tamer Cavusgil, Calantone & Zhao, 2003; Dhanaraj, Lyles, Steensma & Tihanyi, 2004; Harlow, 2008) have explored the relationship between tacit knowledge, innovation capability and firms' performance and found strong positive relationships between tacit knowledge and innovation capability as well as between tacit knowledge and firms' performance. Thus, the study states that the length of the experience of the chief executive officer of the business has a significant impact on the performance.

H_9: The longer the length of experience of the CEO of the business, the higher the performance of the mining firms.

2. Methodology

Study Sample and Sampling Technique

The study used primary and secondary data sources for its analysis. Secondary data were sourced mainly from different published sources. 150 firms with mineral titles not younger than December 2010 were purposively selected for the study but only 106 that were completed with accuracy were used in the analysis. A set of structured questionnaires was designed to gather information from the mining firms. Standard questions were obtained from the Community Innovation Survey (CIS) IV in drafting the questionnaire. The questionnaire was designed to obtain information such as knowledge capital and turnover of the firms. Measures were put in place to ensure the content validity of the research instrument. The questions were framed to be easily understood by the respondents and to exactly convey their sense and purpose to the respondents. The adaptation of the CIS IV questionnaire has been proven to be appropriate in previous similar studies in both developed and developing countries. Descriptive and inferential analyses were used for data analysis with data presented tables. The inferential statistics involved econometrics models of ordinary least squares method of multiple regressions. The regression models were adopted in order to find out whether changes in independent variables had a significant impact on the dependent variable and also to examine the direction of the relationship between the dependent and independent variables.

Study Variables and their Measurements:

Knowledge capital was captured with knowledge stock and knowledge flow. Knowledge stock was captured using five indicators viz:

- The strength of the workforce was measured by the employee size in the year 2013
- The knowledge of the workforce was measured by eliciting the percentage of the workforce who had a minimum university degree in the year 2013
- The science and technology orientation of the workforce was measured by obtaining the percentage of the employees whose specialization lies in the STEM field in the year 2013
- Tacit knowledge was measured by the percentage of expatriates in the workforce in the year 2013
- Tacit knowledge was also measured by capturing the length of working experience of the chief executive as of the year 2013

Knowledge flow was captured by using four indicators which were based on the amount the firms expended on the following activities:

- intramural R&D in the year 2013
- extramural R&D in the year 2013
- acquisition of machinery, equipment, hardware in the year 2013
- acquisition of external knowledge in the year 2013

The impact of knowledge stock on firm's financial performance was determined using firms' turnover as the dependent variable, andthe following independent variables: employee size, percentage of the workforce that have at least a university degree, percentage of the workforce with specialization in STEM education, percentage of expatriates in the workforce, length of work experience of the CEO, the amount expended on intramural and extramural R&D respectively, the amount expended on acquisition of machinery and equipment, and the amount expended on external knowledge (e.g. patents, industrial design, etc). Both the dependent and independent variables were logged for the regression to reduce stochastic error to the barest minimum.

Model Specification:

$$Y = a + b_1X_1 + b_2X_2 + b_3X_3 + b_4X_4 + b_5X_5 + b_6X_6 + b_7X_7 + b_8X_8 + b_9X_9 + e(1)$$

Where;

Y = Performance (proxy variable used was turnover)

a = Intercept (constant variable),

b = Co-efficient of the independent variables

e = Stochastic error in the equation,

X_1= employee size

X_2= percentage of workforce that have at least a university degree

X_3= percentage of workforce whose specialization is STEM education

X_4=percentage of expatriates in the workforce

X_5= length of work experience of the CEO

X6=amount expended on intramural R&D

X7= amount expended on extramural R&D

X8= amount expended on acquisition of machinery, equipment, etc

X9 = amount expended on external knowledge e.g. patents, industrial design, etc

3. Results and Discussion

Background of the Mining Industry in Nigeria

Table 1 shows that the most prevalent activity in the mining industry in Southwestern Nigeria is primarily quarrying (27.4%), closely followed by construction (20.8%), then exploration (19.8%) and small-scale mining (16.0%). Activities such as rock/mineral processing and dredging ranked lowest in the industry with a prevalence of 8.5% and 7.5% respectively. The mining industry in Southwestern Nigeria is unique in its way. This is because some of the sub-sectors in the industry are unorganized while others are quite organized. For example, the quarrying industry, as well as the construction industry are well-organized. However, the small-scale mining industry is largely unorganized and it is mainly dominated by artisanal miners, most of whom operate beyond the government regulations until recently when the government released funds to the artisanal miners. Most of them now operate as 'mining cooperatives' making them organized. Quarrying and construction companies are quite similar. The quarrying companies are into the business of blasting rocks and supplying it to end-users who may be individuals or contractors for the purpose of building houses, offices, bridges, amongst others. The construction companies are companies that blast rocks and use them as raw materials in their business activities. Hence, in the case of the latter, quarrying is just a unit of business activity. The exploration companies exist mostly as small business units or a consulting arm of small and medium enterprises or as a consulting unit of an academic institution. Consequently, it may not necessarily be a registered mining companycompared to other companies in the industry.

Table 1:Main Business Activities of the Mining Companies

Business Activities	Percentage (%)
Exploration	19.8
Small Scale Mining	16.0
Quarrying	27.4
Dredging	7.5
Processing	8.5
Construction	20.8
Total	100.0

Source: Field Survey (2015)

The processing companies are those that blast rocks and process it for aesthetic purposes (tiles for floors and walls) and those that mine gems and cut them into gemstones for jewellery making.The activities of dredging companies include sucking and pumping sand from streams and rivers. Sands mined from these rivers are usually friable and that is why they are basic raw materials in the glass industry. Only about 33% of the companies belong to a larger group (Table 2). By implication, the majority (67%) of the mining companies in Southwestern Nigeria are stand-alone firms; because they have their head offices located within Nigeria. Table 2 shows that 33% of companies are part of larger groups. Of these, 40.4% have their head offices in Africa (32% of them are in Nigeria), 30.6% in Asia, 18.8% in Europe, 5.6% in the United States & Canada, 2.8% in Australia and New Zealand and 1.8% in Latin America. The significance of a company having its head office abroad is that there will be greater ease of knowledge transfer from the parent company (situated abroad) to the local company (in Nigeria) and *vice versa.* Knowledge transfer has become important because technology has been evolving very fast in the last few decades. Companies with parent companies abroad are more likely to learn and deploy advanced technology faster than the ones whose parent companies are based in Nigeria or those who do not belong to a group.

Table 2:Firms that are part of a Group and Location of the parent firm

Enterprise that are part of a large group	%
Yes	33
No	67
Location of the parent companies	%
Africa (including Nigeria)	40.4
Asia	30.6
Europe	18.8
Australia & New Zealand	2.8
United States & Canada	5.6
Latin America	1.8

Source: Field Survey (2015)

Table 3 shows the descriptive statistics for the knowledge stock and flow variables using the mean for the year 2013 which was the reference period for the study. The employee size (average sample size) was 410. This value includes the total number of employees including permanent staffs, temporary/contract staffs, casual workers, management staffs, and expatriates. According to the Small and Medium Enterprises Development Agency of Nigeria, it was deduced that the average size of the mining firms in Nigeria falls within the large category. According to Pavitt (1991), large firms are potential sources of modern technologies and radical innovations which can quickly diffuse through the sector and spread to other sectors. Pavitt explained that large firms are able to quickly develop technological capabilities as a result of capital accumulation as well as having a large number of employees with different capabilities. A large number of employees will indeed help the firms to develop their employees' capability along some lines of speciality. Also, Pavitt heightened that large firms often engage in continuous improvement of the skills and competence of their employees to make the firms competitive. Owing to this, the mining industry in Nigeria could be seen as an industry that has a relatively strong technological capability to perform operations optimally. Even though the industry is largely heterogeneous, having a range of small to large firms that are into different business activities (according to Table 1), the firms can leverage on each other's strengths as the industry naturally facilitates the firms working together. Also, Table 3 reveals that from the average 410 employees, 6.11% (25) were expatriates. Lichtenthaler and Frishammar (2011) have stressed that one viable channel of tacit knowledge and technology diffusion is through hiring highly-skilled expatriates in the workforce. Colakoglu and Caligiuri (2008) investigated the link between the use of expatriates and subsidiary performance as a function of cultural distance. The study demonstrated that the ethic, social and educational distance controls the connection between expatriates in the workforce and the performance of the subsidiary firm. Thus, a higher ratio of expatriates from abroad is related to lower subsidiary firm performance, particularly in cases when ethic, social and educational distances are high. Therefore, the study posits that an educated workforce is important to complement the presence of expatriates in the workforce for improved performance. Hence, it may not be about the proportion of the expatriates in the workforce but how educated the workforce is to identify, appreciate and absorb knowledge from the expatriates. Table 3 further shows that more than half of the workforce have university degrees and that about 45% of this workforce have had training in the fields of Science, Technology, Engineering and Mathematics. Cohen and Levinthal (2000) have stressed the importance of domestic capability as a prerequisite to absorbing external capability. The rate at which a firm can absorb external knowledge is dependent on the amount of internal knowledge it already possesses. Having more than half of its workforce with a university degree, it shows that the industry is able to absorb technology/ knowledge from its expatriates, other firms and industries. Furthermore, with about 45% of the workforce having specialization in STEM which is a related field to mining and exploration, the industry is expected to thrive based on the strength of its workforce (Stone, Kaminski & Gloeckner 2008; Feller, 2011; Marginson, Tytler, Freeman & Roberts, 2013). Moreover, the experience of the manager/owner is positively correlated to performance in the literature (Zucker, Darby & Armstrong, 2002; Tamer Cavusgil, Calantone & Zhao, 2003; Dhanaraj, Lyles, Steensma & Tihanyi, 2004; Harlow, 2008). Hence, the study assumes that the average length of work experience of the chief executives of those mining firms which is 11.57 years connotes that the industry has chief executives with adequate tacit knowledge to bring requisite knowledge and creativity to solving the issues in the industry.

From Table 3, it is evident that extramural R&D was much higher than intramural R&D. Literatures (Veugelers, 1997; Cassiman & Veugelers, 2006;

Berchicci, 2013) have shown that outsourcing R&D is not only important for innovativeness and performance, it also helps firms to build technological capability through learning, imitating and cooperation. For instance, Veugelers' (1997) study on Flemish firms showed that R&D cooperation and extramural R&D were found to have substantial positive impacts on intramural R&D when the firms have employees in a separate independent R&D department/unit. Berchicci (2013) also found that firms that progressively depend on extramural R&D activities tend to perform better in terms of innovations. Similarly, Cassiman and Veugelers (2006), using a productivity approach, showed that firms that are only involved in either intramural or extramural R&D implemented fewer products innovations compared to firms that combined both types of R&D. The authors consequently hypothesize that the higher mean amount of extramural R&D was important for the mining firms to build internal capability by leveraging on the R&D from the parent firms, usually located in other countries (see Table 2). Over time, they are likely to perform all their R&D internally when they have developed their internal capability to the required threshold. Other potential ways of acquiring capability may be through the acquisition of embodied technology (Tsai, 2004; Cassiman & Veugelers, 2007; Bin, 2008; Shih & Chang, 2009) and external knowledge such as patents, industrial design and trademarks amongst others (Bloom & Van Reenen, 2002). The average investment of the mining industry in the acquisition of external knowledge was found to be very low when compared to the industry's mean turnover. On the other hand, the industry's investment in modern technologies was quite high, much higher than what it spends on R&D, patents, trademarks and industrial design put together. The outcome is in line with a similar study that was carried out in the manufacturing industry in Nigeria (Adeyeye, Jegede, Oluwadare & Aremu, 2016) which showed that the acquisition of machinery and training are the most prevalent innovation activities in the manufacturing sector in Nigeria. Overall, the mining industry spent about a quarter of its turnover on knowledge flow activities.

Table 3: Descriptive Statistics showing knowledge capital (stock and flow) in the mining industry in Nigeria

Knowledge Stock Variables	Industry mean for year 2013
Employee size (average sample size)	410.25
Percentage of workforce with a university degree	57.08%
Percentage of workforce whose specialization is STEM	45.48%
Percentage of expatriates in the workforce	6.11%
Length of work experience of the CEO	11.57yrs
Knowledge Flow Variables	**Intensity (Industry mean as percentage of turnover in 2013)**
Amount expended on intramural R&D	0.48
Amount expended on extramural R&D	2.27
Amount expended on acquisition of machinery, equipment	21.63
Amount expended on external knowledge	0.41
Total knowledge flow expenditure	23.60

Table 4 shows the Pearson correlation coefficient of the knowledge capital indicators with turnover. At 0.05 level of significance, seven out of the nine variables were strongly and positively correlated with the turnover. All the nine variables had a positive correlation with turnover. This shows that all the knowledge-capital (stock and flow variables) are positive determinants of performance in the mining industry in Nigeria. As shown by Table 4, four variables (total number of employees in the workforce, expenditure on intramural R&D, expenditure on extramural R&D, and expenditure on acquisition of new machinery, equipment, hardware or software) correlate with turnover at more than 0.8 indicating a very high degree of association between the independent variables and the dependent variable. This means that the total number of employees in the workforce with an r of 0.948 results in a coefficient of determination of 0.90, indicating that 90% of the change in turnover is associated with the change in employee size. Also, expenditure on intramural (in-house) R&D with an r of 0.854 has a coefficient of determination of 0.73, signifying that 90% of the change in turnover is associated with the change in expenditure on intramural R&D. Similarly, 97% of the change in turnover is associated with the change in expenditure on extramural R&D and 93% of the change in turnover is associated with the change in expenditure on acquisition of new machinery, equipment, hardware or software. On the other hand, the percentage of the workforce in the mines that were expatriates, length (in years) of experience of the chief executive and expenditure on acquisition of external knowledge were all weakly positively correlated with turnover. They indicate that 25%, 7% and 10.3% of the change in turnover is associated with the changes in following independent variables respectively: percentage of expatriates in the workforce, length (in years) of experience of the CEO and expenditure on acquisition of external knowledge.

Effect of knowledge capital on the mining firms' financial performance

Table 4:Correlation between Knowledge Capital and Turnover

	Firms' turnover in 2013
Employee size	0.948**
Percentage of workforce that have at least a university degree	0.151
Percentage of workforce whose specialization is STEM education	0.184
Percentage of expatriates in the workforce	0.497**
Length of work experience of the CEO	0.269**
Amount expended on intramural R&D	0.854**
Amount expended on extramural R&D	0.985**
Amount expended on acquisition of machinery, equipment, etc.	0.964**
Amount expended on external knowledge	0.321**

**. Correlation is significant at the 0.01 level (2-tailed).

*. Correlation is significant at the 0.05 level (2-tailed).

From Table 5, an interior value of $R^2 = 0.913$ may be inferred as 91.3% of the variance in the turnover that can be explained by the knowledge-capital (stock and flow) variables. The remaining 8.3% can be ascribed to unknown, prowling variables or integral variability. The study used the ordinary least square method because increases in the number of regressors increase the value of R^2. Nevertheless, R^2 alone cannot be used as a significant judgement of models with a number of very different independent variables.Hence, the F-test was used to compare the fits of different linear models of the intercept only with the equation using predictor variables. The F-statistics of 41.98342 (p=0.0001) obtained indicated that the fit of the intercept-only model was significantly reduced compared to the authors' model. Hence, the F-test showed that the relationship between turnover and the knowledge-capital (stock and flow) variables were statistically significant. Also, since the P-value for the F-statistics was less than the model's 0.05 level of significance, we can conclude that the R-squared value was significantly different from zero.

From Table 5, it can be seen that the coefficient of the log of following: employee size, percentage of expatriates in workforce, amount expended on extra mural R&D, the amount expended on acquisition of machinery and the amount expended on intra mural R&D, had positive and significant impacts on the log of turnover at 0.05 significance level. This indicates that for every additional employee employed, the turnover is expected to increase by an average of 0.89 Naira. Likewise, for every one percent increase in the proportion of expatriates in the workforce, the turnover is expected to increase by an average of 0.53 Naira. For every additional Naira spent on extramural R&D, the turnover increases by an average of 0.57 Naira. Every additional Naira spent on intramural R&D increases the turnover by an average of 1.05 Naira. For every additional Naira expended on acquisition of machinery, equipment, hardware or software, the turnover increases by an average of 0.37 Naira.

On the other hand, Table 5 shows that the log of the following: percentage of workforce with a university degree, the percentage of the workforce with specialisation in STEM, the length of experience of manager/owner and the amount expended on acquisition of external knowledge, had a positive but not significant impact on the log of turnover at 0.05 significance level. It was indeed surprising that the percentage of the workforce with a degree and whose specialization is STEM was not significantly associated with turnover (using both Pearson's correlation and linear regression). Looking at the industry being a capital-intensive industry in which technology is used extensively in the operations, conventional wisdom would have predicted that there will be a high level of association between the percentage of the workforce with a university degree and whose specialization is STEM with turnover. It was however found out that for the mining industry in Nigeria, the ratio of casual workers/contract staff to professional workers/core staff is very high. The firms often employ a large number of labourers, artisans (masons, iron benders, etc.) and deploy them on sites (in the mines). Hence, creativity, innovativeness and productivity are largely dependent on the instructions from the top management, the expatriates monitoring the work and on the shop-floor by these relatively low-level, seemingly unskilled workforce. In like manner, the length of experience of the owner/most senior manager/chief executive didn't have a significant impact on productivity (turnover) because the real work is done by the low-level artisans and unskilled labourers with close supervision by the expatriates and not by the chief executive. The chief executive controls things remotely from his/her office, not from the mining site. Besides, the responsibility of the chief executive could be more administrative rather than technical. Also, it was observed that the firms in the mining industry in Nigeria make use of established mining procedures as laid down by the relevant regulatory authorities. Hence, this reduces the dependency of the mining firms on the use of external knowledge such as foreign patents which are not particularly useful in the local settings in Nigeria. Thus, the amount expended on acquisition of external knowledge did not significantly affect turnover as well.

Table 5: Impact of Knowledge Capital on Firms' Turnover

Variable	Coefficient	Prob.
Employee Size	0.886814	0.0000
Percentage of workforce with Degree	0.080491	0.9412
Percentage of workforce with specialization inSTEM	0.467829	0.6456
Percentage of expatriates in workforce	0.533874	0.0015
Length of experience of CEO (in years)	0.289910	0.5251
Amount expended on extra mural R&D	0.573310	0.0067
Amount expended on acquisition of machinery	0.365612	0.0460
Amount expended on acquisition of external knowledge	0.157888	0.3867
Amount expended on Intra mural R&D	1.046298	0.0000
C	1.282000	0.5841
R-squared	0.913012	
F-statistic	41.98342	
Prob(F-statistic)	0.0001	

Dependent Variable: Turnover

Method: Least Squares

Sample (adjusted): 1 105

Included observations: 16 after adjustments

4. Conclusions, Limitations & Suggestions

The study was carried out to establish relationships between variables of knowledge-capital and performance in line with the extant literature. From the study, five out of nine variables (the employee size, the percentage of expatriates in the workforce, amount expended on extra mural R&D, intra mural R&D and acquisition of machinery) have shown significant impacts on performance. Hence, the study accepts the hypotheses H_1, H_2, H_3, H_6 and H_8. However, the following variables: the workforce with a university degree, percentage of the workforce with specialization in STEM education, the length of experience of chief executive officer and the amount spent on the acquisition of external knowledge such as patents, trademarks, and industrial design, did not have significant impacts on turnover. This appears to be because of the peculiarity of the context of the mining industry and the regulatory framework in Nigeria. The study thus rejects hypotheses H_4, H_5, H_7 and H_9.

This study has employed the knowledge-capital approach to examine the firm-level performance. Although the findings are useful, they can only serve as indications of possibly broader directions because of the limitations of the sample size. Studies that use more robust samples (for instance, covering more than one country within the African region) would, therefore, be very beneficial. Also, the effects of learning by doing, using, interacting, imitating and searching (DUIIS) as a driver of firm-level performance wasn't explored in this study. It would be interesting for further studies to examine the impact of individual and organizational learning on performances. Finally, detailed similar industry studies would facilitate comparison of results.

References

Abdel-Maksoud, A., Dugdale, D., & Luther, R. (2005), 'Non-financial performance measurement in manufacturing companies', *The British Accounting Review*, 37(3): 261-297.

Adeyeye, A. D., Jegede, O. O., Oluwadare, A. J., & Aremu, F. S. (2016), 'Micro-level determinants of innovation: analysis of the Nigerian manufacturing sector', *Innovation and Development*, 6(1): 1-14.

Artz, K. W., Norman, P. M., Hatfield, D. E., & Cardinal, L. B. (2010), 'A longitudinal study of the impact of R&D, patents, and product innovation on firm performance', *Journal of Product Innovation Management*, 27(5): 725-740.

Axtell, C. M., Holman, D. J., Unsworth, K. L., Wall, T. D., Waterson, P. E., & Harrington, E. (2000), 'Shopfloor innovation: Facilitating the suggestion and implementation of ideas', *Journal of Occupational and Organizational Psychology*, 73(3): 265-285.

Becker, B. E., Huselid, M. A., & Beatty, R. W. (2009), *The differentiated workforce: Translating talent into strategic impact*, Boston: Harvard Business Press.

Belderbos, R., Carree, M., & Lokshin, B. (2004), 'Cooperative R&D and firm performance', *Research policy*, 33(10): 1477-1492.

Beneito, P. (2006), 'The innovative performance of in-house and contracted R&D in terms of patents and utility models', *Research Policy,* 35(4): 502-517.

Berchicci, L. (2013), 'Towards an open R&D system: Internal R&D investment, external knowledge acquisition and innovative performance', *Research Policy*, 42(1): 117-127.

Bin, G. (2008), 'Technology acquisition channels and industry performance: An industry-level analysis of Chinese large-and medium-size manufacturing enterprises', *Research Policy*, 37(2): 194-209.

Bloom, N., & Van Reenen, J. (2002), Patents, real options and firm performance,' *The Economic Journal*, 112(478): C97-C116.

Cassiman, B., & Veugelers, R. (2006), 'In search of complementarity in innovation strategy: Internal R&D and external knowledge acquisition', *Management Science*, 52(1): 68-82.

Cassiman, B., & Veugelers, R. (2007), 'Are External Technology Sourcing Strategies Substitutes or Complements?: The Case of Embodied versus Disembodied Technology Acquisition', *SSRN Electronic Journal,* DOI: 10.2139/ssrn.982324

Cohen, S. G., & Bailey, D. E. (1997), 'What makes teams work: Group effectiveness research from the shop floor to the executive suite', *Journal of Management*, 23(3): 239-290.

Cohen, W. M., & Levinthal, D. A. (2000), 'Absorptive capacity: A new perspective on learning and innovation', In: *Strategic Learning in a Knowledge Economy* (pp. 39-67), DOI: 10.1016/B978-0-7506-7223-8.50005-8

Colakoglu, S., & Caligiuri, P. (2008), 'Cultural distance, expatriate staffing and subsidiary performance: The case of US subsidiaries of multinational corporations', *The International Journal of Human Resource Management*, 19(2): 223-239.

Dhanaraj, C., Lyles, M. A., Steensma, H. K., & Tihanyi, L. (2004), 'Managing tacit and explicit knowledge transfer in IJVs: the role of relational embeddedness and the impact on performance', *Journal of International Business Studies*, 35(5): 428-442.

Etzkowitz, H. (2008), *The triple helix: university-industry-government innovation in action*, London: Routledge.

Etzkowitz, H., & Leydesdorff, L. (2000), 'The dynamics of innovation: from National Systems and "Mode 2" to a Triple Helix of university–industry–government relations', *Research Policy*, 29(2): 109-123.

Feller, R. (2011), 'Advancing the STEM workforce through STEM-centric career development', *Technology and Engineering Teacher*, 71(1): 6.

Freeman, C. (1995), 'The 'National System of Innovation' in historical perspective', *Cambridge Journal of Economics*, 19(1): 5-24.

Gray, K. C., & Herr, E. L. (1998), *Workforce education: The basics* (pp. 150-152). Boston: Allyn and Bacon.

Harlow, H. (2008), 'The effect of tacit knowledge on firm performance,' *Journal of Knowledge Management*, 12(1): 148-163.

Harzing, A. W., & Sorge, A. (2003), 'The relative impact of country of origin and universal contingencies on internationalization strategies and corporate control in multinational enterprises: Worldwide and European perspectives', *Organization Studies*, 24(2): 187-214.

Kotabe, M., Srinivasan, S. S., & Aulakh, P. S. (2002), 'Multinationality and firm performance: The moderating role of R&D and marketing capabilities', *Journal of International Business Studies*, 33(1): 79-97.

Krugman, P. (1991), 'Increasing returns and economic geography', *Journal of Political Economy*, 99(3): 483-499.

Krugman, P. R. (1997*), Development, geography, and economic theory* (Vol. 6), Boston: MIT press.

Kumar, N., & Aggarwal, A. (2005), 'Liberalization, outward orientation and in-house R&D activity of multinational and local firms: A quantitative exploration for Indian manufacturing', *Research Policy*, 34(4): 441-460.

Laursen, K., & Foss, N. J. (2003), 'New human resource management practices, complementarities and the impact on innovation performance', *Cambridge Journal of Economics*, 27(2): 243-263.

Laursen, K., & Salter, A. (2006), 'Open for innovation: the role of openness in explaining innovation performance among UK manufacturing firms', *Strategic Management Journal*, 27(2): 131-150.

Leydesdorff, L. (2009), 'The Triple Helix Model and the study of Knowledge Based Innovation Systems'. Available at:https://www.leydesdorff.net/arist09/arist09.pdf.

Leydesdorff, L., & Etzkowitz, H. (1998), 'The triple helix as a model for innovation studies', *Science and Public Policy*, 25(3): 195-203.

Lichtenthaler, U., & Frishammar, J. (2011), 'The impact of aligning product development and technology licensing: A contingency perspective', *The Journal of Product Innovation Management*, 28(Suppl. 1): 89-103.

Lundvall, B. Å. (2007). National innovation systems—analytical concept and development tool. *Industry and Innovation*, 14(1), 95-119.

Lundvall, B. Å., Johnson, B., Andersen, E. S., & Dalum, B. (2002), 'National systems of production, innovation and competence building', *Research Policy*, 31(2): 213-231.

Marginson, S., Tytler, R., Freeman, B., & Roberts, K. (2013), *STEM: Country Comparisons: International Comparisons of Science, Technology, Engineering and Mathematics (STEM) Education*. Final report.

Michaelis, B., Wagner, J. D., & Schweizer, L. (2015), 'Knowledge as a key in the relationship between high-performance work systems and workforce productivity', *Journal of Business Research*, 68(5): 1035-1044.

Nelson, R. R. (1992), 'National innovation systems: a retrospective on a study', *Industrial and Corporate Change*, 1(2): 347-374.

Patel, P., & Pavitt, K. (1994), 'National innovation systems: why they are important, and how they might be measured and compared', *Economics of Innovation and New Technology*, 3(1): 77-95.

Pavitt, K. (1991), 'Key characteristics of the large innovating firm', *British Journal of Management*, 2(1): 41-50.

Porter, M. E. (2000), 'Location, competition, and economic development: Local clusters in a global economy', *Economic Development Quarterly*, 14(1): 15-34.

Romer, P. M. (1989), *Human capital and growth: theory and evidence* (No. w3173). National Bureau of Economic Research.

Romer, P. M. (1994), 'The origins of endogenous growth', *Journal of Economic Perspectives*, 8(1): 3-22.

Sampson, R. C. (2007), 'R&D alliances and firm performance: The impact of technological diversity and alliance organization on innovation', *Academy of Management Journal*, 50(2): 364-386.

Schumpeter, J. (1942), *Capitalism, socialism and democracy*. Available at: https://eet.pixel-online.org/files/etranslation/original/Schumpeter,%20Capitalism,%20Socialism%20and%20Democracy.pdf

Schumpeter, J. A. (1934), *The Theory of Economic Development* (translation of second German edition by Redvers Opie), Cambridge, MA: Harvard University.

Schumpeter, J. A. (1939), *Business Cycles* (Vol. 1, pp. 161-74). New York: McGraw-Hill.

Sher, P. J., & Yang, P. Y. (2005), 'The effects of innovative capabilities and R&D clustering on firm performance: the evidence of Taiwan's semiconductor industry', *Technovation*, 25(1): 33-43.

Shih, H. Y., & Chang, T. L. S. (2009), 'International diffusion of embodied and disembodied technology: A network analysis approach', *Technological Forecasting and Social Change*, 76(6): 821-834.

Solow, R. M. (1956), 'A contribution to the theory of economic growth', *The Quarterly Journal of Economics*, 70(1): 65-94.

Solow, R. M. (1988), 'Growth theory and after', *The American Economic Review*, 78(3): 307-317.

Solow, R. M. (1994), 'Perspectives on growth theory', *Journal of Economic Perspectives*, 8(1): 45-54.

Stone, K. B., Kaminski, K., & Gloeckner, G. (2008), 'Closing the gap: Education requirements of the 21st century production workforce', *Journal of STEM Teacher Education*, 45(3): 4.

Tamer Cavusgil, S., Calantone, R. J., & Zhao, Y. (2003), 'Tacit knowledge transfer and firm innovation capability', *Journal of Business & Industrial Marketing*, 18(1): 6-21.

Tsai, K. H. (2004), 'The impact of technological capability on firm performance in Taiwan's electronics industry', *The Journal of High Technology Management Research*, 15(2): 183-195.

Tylecote, A., & Conesa, E. (1999), 'Corporate governance, innovation systems and industrial performance', *Industry and Innovation*, 6(1): 25-50.

Veugelers, R. (1997), 'Internal R&D expenditures and external technology sourcing', *Research Policy*, 26(3): 303-316.

West, M. A., & Altink, W. M. (1996), 'Innovation at work: Individual, group, organizational, and socio-historical perspectives', *European Journal of Work and Organizational Psychology*, 5(1): 3-11.

Zakaria, N. (2000), 'The effects of cross-cultural training on the acculturation process of the global workforce', *International Journal of Manpower*, 21(6): 492-510.

Zucker, L. G., Darby, M. R., & Armstrong, J. S. (2002), 'Commercializing knowledge: University science, knowledge capture, and firm performance in biotechnology', *Management Science*, 48(1): 138-153.

Appendix (Questionnaire)

PART 1: General information about the enterprise, business, company or firm

1.0.	Name of Enterprise: Address: Main Activity:
1.1	Short Description of your Main Business Activity:

PART 2: Knowledge capital indicators of the enterprise, business, company or firm

2.1.1	What was your enterprise's total number of employees in 2013? Annual average number of employees, both full-time and part-time. If not available, give the number of employees at the end of the year.	
	2013	
2.1.2	Approximately what percentage of your total employees had a Diploma (HND) in 2013?	%
2.1.3	Approximately what percentage of your total employees with specialisation in Science, Engineering, Technology or Mathematics in 2013?	%
2.1.4	Approximately what percentage of your total employees are expatriates in 2013?	%
2.1.5	Approximately what the length of experience of the Manager or CEO	yrs

2.2	Please estimate the amount of expenditure in 2013 only for the first four innovation activities listed below Include personnel and related costs. *Please provide expenditure in Naira e.g. Five million naira which should be entered as 5,000,000*	STRICTLY CONFIDENTIAL ₦
2.2.1.	Intramural (in-house) R&D. *Include labour costs, capital expenditures on plant and equipment specifically for R&D.*	
2.2.2	Acquisition of R&D. *Extramural or outsourced R&D.*	
2.2.3	Acquisition of machinery, equipment and software. *Exclude expenditures on equipment for R&D.*	
2.2.4	Acquisition of other external knowledge.	
	Total of these four innovation expenditure categories (A+B+C+D)	

PART 3: Performance indicators of the enterprise, business, company or firm

3.1	What was your enterprise's approximate total turnover for 2013? Turnover is defined as the market sales of goods and services (Include all taxes except VAT). (STRICTLY CONFIDENTIAL) *Please give turnover in Naira [e.g. One million Nairashould be entered as* ₦1,000,000]	
	2013	₦

9

Foreign Direct Investment, Firm-level Capability and Human Capital Development:

Evidence based on Kenyan Manufacturing Industry

Geoffrey G. Gachino[1]

1. Introduction

The importance of human capital development has remained a subject of discussion in the economic discourse (Arrow, 1962; Becker, 1962, 1964). In endogenous growth literature, human capital is viewed as a major driver of technical progress and as an engine of economic growth (Lucas, 1988; Aghion and Howitt, 1992, 1998; Romer, 1990; Spagat, 2006). This is supported by the existing empirical work which recognizes human capital either accumulated through long term investments in formal education or other forms of skill development, as one of the key determinants of economic growth (Schultz, 1963; Barro, 1991; Barro and Sala-i-Martin,

1 Assistant Professor and Assistant Dean, College of Business Administration, University of Dubai, United Arab Emirates. Email: geoffrey.gachino@gmail.com or ggachino@ud.ac.ae

1995; Fleisher *et al.*, 2010). In its broad terms, human capital comprises knowledge, skills, experiences and values vested in people in an economy.

Following this recognition, most countries especially the newly industrialized countries, made tremendous effort while devoting enormous resources towards human capital development which was marked with great success (Amsden, 1989; Kim, 1997, 1999; Yussof and Ismail, 2002). This has enabled these countries to increase value addition in their manufacturing hence becoming key participants in the global export market. It must however, be emphasised that in these countries human capital was developed vis-à-vis other forms of technological capabilities such as production, linkage, investment and other complimentary capabilities (Fransman, 1985; Amsden, 1991, 1994; Rasiah, 1995, 2005). The rapid human capital development in the NICs and the perceived benefits has presented amenable lessons for other countries to emulate as well as rich benchmarking platform by the researchers. All in all, developing countries seem to have realized the important role played by human capital in the growth process. As such, there is increased effort towards its development in earnest through purposely and strategically designed policies incorporated in the national development and planning agenda.

Two forms of human capital development exist namely formal and informal. The former is the most common approach and often includes basic/primary school, secondary and tertiary level education. The tertiary level usually overlaps different institutions such as those meant to provide technical, industrial or vocational training. The latter approach occurs through different kinds of trainings, learning mechanisms and other forms of human resource enrichment programmes. It is very common in workplaces.

Since the formal approach of human capital development has been commonly studied, this paper will focus on the informal and attempt to understand how it is usually developed in a developing country context, in this case, Kenya located within the Sub Saharan Africa.Further, the focus of the study will be manufacturing industry taking firm as the unit of analysis. Within this domain, we will try to answer the following questions; what is the level of human capital in the Kenyan manufacturing? How does it vary across different industrial/sectors? How is it developed; in other words what are the determining conditions of human capital development? Several factors such as learning by doing, active collaborations and interactions (formal or informal) are perceived to be among vital determinants of human capital development.

This chapter is organised as follows: Section 2 presents the analytical framework and outlines hypotheses formulated for examination. Section 3 presents the methodological setting of the paper. Section 4 presents the scope and sample characteristics of the survey data used for this analysis. Section 5 presents the empirical findings and discussion while section 6 presents conclusions and policy implications. Suggestions for future further research are also provided in this section.

2. Analytical Framework and Hypotheses

In this paper we argue that an appropriate examination of human capital development in manufacturing industry must be done within the theoretical framework of technological change, skill development and innovation. The reason for this is that technological change, innovation and skill development all play a complementary role to each other. The process of undertaking technological change and innovation in firms presents learning and capability building opportunities which resonates well with human capital development. Technological changes in the production process or changes in products result in acquisition of new knowledge and ideas. Similarly, changes in management, organisation and marketing are always associated with accumulation of new values, ideas, skills and knowledge. In all these cases experiential and tacit knowledge are accumulated which are all forms of human capital development.

According to the endogenous growth literature, human capital provides the manpower and skills that are required for effecting technological change, maintaining a steady technical progress necessary for eventual economic growth. Phrased differently, endogenous literature recognises an ever increasing endogenous role of human capital accumulation in economic growth. While contributing to the endogenous literature Romer (1986, 1990), Lucas (1988) and Aghion and Howitt (1998) have made fundamental contributions to this subject, recognising the endogenous role played by technical change, research and development (R&D) and distinguishing between labour and human capital in contrast to the neo-classical economists who had overlooked skills attributes of labour. Their work was based on earlier seminal works by Arrow (1962), Uzawa (1965), Kaldor (1957) and Schumpeter (1934, 1952).

At the heart of endogenous growth theory is the increasing returns argument to economic growth, which as they argue, is possible due to endogenous technical change and presence of human capital. They argue that although growth may be mainly driven by accumulated stock of human capital, the effects of human capital is perhaps more important in undertaking technological change than perhaps is in the actual output production under a given technology. Supporting the role of technology and human capital development, the early work by Nelson and Phelps (1966)[1] purported that stock of human capital and ability to generate and maintain technical progress were the sole reasons behind the observed differences in economic growth across countries. So, revisiting complementary argument, we note that, while human capital can quicken acquisition and adaptation of technological change which in turn induces economic growth, on the opposite, dynamism in technological change and economic growth stimulates in turn human capital.

Following seminal work by Nelson and Winter (1982) technological change have been conceptualised in terms of evolutionary perspectives; one that involves dynamic heterogeneous actors interacting among themselves for socio-economic gains within an economy. This is what has come later to be referred to as national system of innovation (NSI). Hence, national system of innovation can be conceptualized as an evolutionary system which puts particular emphasis on the way in which technology, different social-economic agents, organisations, institutions and policies interact with each other for the purpose of fostering knowledge, learning, capability building and innovation. It is thus characterised by agents engaged in formal government and education institutions, network of physical, scientific, economic and technology infrastructure. The flow of technological information, knowledge and skills within the NSI is regarded as the most important thing for the purpose of technological learning and capability building in the local, national and global context.

We therefore argue that the process of human capital development at the firm level can be better understood assuming evolutionary and institutionalist view, which views firms not as isolated, static and pure economic organisations, but rather as members of changing economic and social-institutional networks. Adopting this framework enables an expanded framework that enables examination of human capital taking into consideration the role of firm-level capabilities, systemic embeddedness, supportive infrastructure and institutions, role of government policy and international influence which takes place through foreign direct investment (FDI) presence in the country. We examine each of these at a time including proposed hypotheses.

Foreign presence as a Stimulant for Human Capital Development

The role played by foreign presence in a host country particularly developing economies has been a subject of intense discussion (Lall and Streeten, 1977; Sinani and Meyer, 2004; Rasiah, 2005; Kuo and Yang, 2008; Blalock and Gertler, 2009; Gachino, 2010a, 2010b). Nonetheless, this discussion has largely remained inconclusive with some arguing that foreign presence in a host country results in externalities or spillover benefits, which are required for economic growth and development. The spillovers would be generated as multinational corporations (MNCs) transfer technology or undertake R&D in a host country. The MNCs also participate in exports, creates employment opportunities with advanced human resource opportunities. On the other hand, opponents of foreign presence argue that FDI is likely to crowd out local investment and stifle a host country's industrialization effort. This, they argue, would increase dependency of such countries and, hence, vulnerability of recipient countries on the FDI – exporting developed countries on account of the footloose nature of FDI.

However, despite this divergence in opinion, lack of clear-cut consensus, for many technically backward countries that are still wallowing in abject poverty, FDI is still viewed as the appropriate means through which economic growth can be achieved (Gachino, 2006). This is justified by the fact that these countries do not have the necessary resources required to initialise and maintain a steady economic growth process. Countries in the sub-Sahara region are characterised by low national savings and thus low investment levels hence low economic growth. The economies in this region are very fragile, with extremely small markets dominated by weak firms that are capital poor and still 'locked into' low levels of traditional skills and non-competitive techniques. The institutions and infrastructure are weaker than in many other developing countries.

Although FDI levels in the region are not high, Kenya's manufacturing industry is claimed to enjoy a sizeable amount of foreign presence (Kaplinksy, 1978; Rasiah and Gachino, 2005; Gachino, 2006, 2010b). Taking this country as a case study, it becomes interesting to find out what role FDI has played in technological learning, capability building and in the current analysis human capital development. This happens when MNCs provide access to new technology, managerial and marketing know-how. This can take place in the MNCs when they offer training to the locals to enable them operate machinery and technology. Training can take place through vertically linked firms and can include a wide array of issues; efficiency, achievement and conformity to international standards (such as ISO), marketing, organisation and management, labour market conditions. Training can take place indirectly as a result of MNC presence. When MNCs introduce competition, it forces local firms as well to introduce technological changes thus triggering local firms to learn and innovate if they are to improve their competitiveness. Skill development can also arise as a result of demonstration effects. This takes place simply when firms just observe how MNCs undertake their operations such as production and then imitate them.

However, as noted in the spillover literature, most of the spillover benefits have been observed in the context of developed or advanced developing countries. Little about such benefits is actually known about FDI in the context of underdeveloped countries where MNC subsidiaries exist. Actually, there are MNC subsidiaries already existing in such countries either because of existing niche markets (windows of opportunities), raw materials, cheap labour or sometimes to tap on an existing pool of knowledge and skills. In Kenya, for instance, there are many MNC subsidiaries which came into the country in the early years of independence. Kenya served as an excellent regional manufacturing base to serve an existing regional market in the whole of Eastern Africa, part of Central and Great Lakes region in Africa. Availability of raw materials, mainly agricultural and readily available cheap labour served as additional factors towards attracting subsidiaries to Kenya (Swainson, 1980; Gachino, 2009).

Since MNCs often exploit state-of-the-art technologies requiring skill levels that are higher than those used by locally owned firms, they are more generally likely to offer training to their staff than indigenous firms. This amounts to human capital development whose results could further translate to human capital spillovers in future (Noorbakhsh *et al.*, 2005). Comparing MNCs and local firms, MNCs have been shown to attach much priority to human capital development (Patibandla and Patersen 2002; Miyamoto, 2003; Li and Liu, 2005; Gachino, 2006; Kottaridi and Thanasis, 2010). At the same time local employees in a MNC may acquire skills, tacit knowledge, attitudes and ideas just by doing routine work in a firm that conforms to international production standards – this however does not always follow.

Human capital spillovers occur due to the mobility of workers or labour turnover from MNC affiliates to domestic firms hence diffusing knowledge and skills. This channel of technology transfer is quite unique from the others in that it involves technology embodied in the workers as they move between firms; in this case from foreign firms to the locally owned firms or when employees of MNCs leave their jobs to form their own firms. This kind of spillover is influenced to a great extent by the level of absorptive capacity in the firms. A study by Gerschenberg (1987) and Gachino (2006) on labour turnover examined MNC subsidiaries and the training and spread of managerial skills in Kenya. They observed that MNC subsidiaries offered more training of various sorts to their managers than private locally owned firms do.

Hypothesis 1: Presence of foreign firms is likely to stimulate human capital development in the Kenyan manufacturing industry

Firm Technological Capability and Human capital Development

Technological capability is conceptualized as the ability to generate and maintain technical change and innovation (Bell and Pavitt, 1992). It requires time, effort and enormous resources such as knowledge, skills and experience acquired over time through learning by doing, interacting, performing and so forth. It also includes institutional structures and linkages in firms, between firms and outside firms. The literature on learning and technological capability mainly classifies capabilities into: investment capability, production capability, innovative capability and linkage capabilities (Lall, 1992; Ernst *et al.*, 1998; Westphal *et al.*, 1985; Kim, 1997, 1999; Wangwe, 1995; Rasiah, 2005).

A firm that endeavours to improve its technological capability through learning, training and other means of knowledge accumulation such as R&D enhances its human capital development. The literature on technological capability accumulation has offered substantial insight on various learning aspects as well as stylised facts on a national systemic learning economy where changes, internal transformations and restructuring are important for the success of firms and industries. Whenever technological changes such as process, product, marketing, organisation and management take place there is always new acquisition of knowledge, ideas and information all of which add to accumulation of experiential tacit knowledge. Technological changes and capability building effort through learning, R&D and so forth increases human capital as well as absorptive capacity (Lucas, 1988; Cohen and Levinthal, 1990).

Hypothesis 2: *Firms that have accumulated technological capabilities (for example production; process and marketing) are more likely to result in human capital development than firms with weak technological capabilities.*

Export Performance

Participation in exports is widely regarded as one of the means through which human capital development could occur (Wignaraja, 2007). This takes place directly or indirectly through demonstration effects from other exporting firms in the industry. The first case occurs when a firm participating in international export market is stimulated to observe a dynamic learning process at the firm level which stimulates human capital development. As an example, a firm which re-orients its market operations to participate in export market begins by searching for and studying the appropriate export markets. This involves establishing international distribution linkages and networks as well as establishing overseas transport infrastructure. It also involves mastering of the global regulatory framework, tastes and preferences, and efficiency levels required. Due to these requirements, participation in export market forces firms to increase their learning effort in order to master techniques required in achieving and maintaining international competitiveness at the global export market. With continuous learning, firms therefore accumulate technological capability including human capital development.

In the indirect approach, firms learn from others operating in the same industry. This represents a case where a firm improves its human capital as a result of external or exogenous factors. Consider for instance, a case of a locally owned firm benefiting from export information through linkage activities established with a MNC firm operating in a country. Usually, the exporting firm – in this case the MNC – will have obtained international ISO standard accreditation, say in production of which one of the requirements is human resource development primarily through continuous training in the firms. This is expected to have trickledown effect to all the local firms supplying to such a MNC, since the suppliers are supposed to comply by supplying goods and services that are acceptable and in line with the ISO standard specifications. The locally owned firm supplying to the MNC are therefore forced to provide human resource training.

Demonstration effect is another way through which firms can be forced to provide human resource training. Take for instance, a firm intending to participate in a certain niche export market internationally. An obvious thing such a firm would be expected to do first is to observe and learn how other firms exporting to that particular market conduct their business. This is learning through demonstration effect where the firm intending to start exporting can imitate marketing techniques, existing networks, managerial or organisational forms from exporting firms. The role of exports in human capital development is supported by the proponents of the assimilation literature with reference to the successful cases of East Asian countries. Participation in exports provided tremendous contribution to technology capability building and human capital development as a result of international spillovers occurring from interactions with MNCs as well as sophisticated foreign clients abroad (Dahlman and Westphal, 1982; Westphal *et al.*, 1985; Westphal, 1990; Aitken *et al.*, 1997; Rasiah, 2005; Wignaraja, 2007).

Hypothesis 3: A firm which participates in exports is more likely to result in human capital development than a firm that does not.

Systemic Embeddedness: Importance of Interactions in Human Capital Formation

Human capital developed at the firm level and in an industry arises as a result of various learning and skill acquisition processes. Learning is regarded as an extremely interactive and dynamic process largely embedded and influenced by socio-economic factors, which includes prevailing policies. All these factors operate in a systemic manner, which then requires a strong systemic and network cohesion conducive for knowledge generation, exploitation and diffusion. This has been supported by the literature on network dynamics and NSI which emphasizes the importance of dynamic interactions through established formal and informal networks or otherwise among economic agents (Freeman, 1991, 1995; Lundvall, 1992; Nelson and Rosenberg, 1993; Mytelka, 2000; Kugler, 2006). Through these interactions, interactive learning can take place while technology, skills, ideas and information can be jointly exploited or exchanged for the purpose of value-added activities in production. In light of this discussion, we hypothesise that a firm embedded in a systemic atmosphere characterized by interactions among firms, institutions, and government and business associations is likely to benefit exploitation of interactive learning, demonstration effects and thus enhance its human capital development.

Hypothesis 4: *Systemic embeddedness of firms in the manufacturing industry is likely to promote human capital development in a positive direction.*

Firm Size–Scale Factor

The role of size on human capital development can be traced to the existing debate in industrial organisation on importance of scale on firms' competitiveness. On one side it is claimed that minimum efficiency scale (MES) is all that matters if a firm has to be competitive. Minimum efficiency scale represents the lowest level of output where the minimum average cost (MAC) is required to exhaust scale economies in manufacturing (Scherer, 1973; Pratten, 1971). Nonetheless, MES varies with the type of industries. For large and heavy industries such as automobiles and shipbuilding, high scale economies is expected since such cases require high MES unit production if low unit costs have to be maintained. On the other side, not all industries require high MSE unit production. In industries such as small-batch machine tools, it is scope that matters but not the scale (Piore and Sabel, 1984). This would be more now than ever before since information and communication technology (ICT) has played a significant contributory role in making small size very efficient. This happens when ICT enables increased decomposition and dispersal of production activities almost in real time. This alternative argument has been supported by voluminous empirical work against significance of scale in efficiency and innovative activities (Audretsch and Zoltan, 1991; Audretsh, 2002).

Although this debate may be valid, small and large firms in the Kenyan context have always shown a wide diversity with regard to performance. Small firms are usually characterised by low performance levels, which would make it impossible for them to recover costs that would possibly be incurred in human capital development. On the contrary, large firms, due to their scale of operation, are often endowed with resources which could be used to spread over human resource development. Quite often, large firms are in a better position to mobilise external resources and services than small firms.

In the Kenyan context, market dynamics favour large firms in that only firms above a certain size are able to have access to certain skills, information and credit facilities needed to be competitive. When it comes to financing for capability development, capital market imperfections confer an advantage on large firms in securing finance for technological activities. Availability of capital means more resources to engage in systemic research, labour training and a greater need for structured information gathering. This enables such firms to maintain inter-firm buyer supplier networks and with institutions that provide training, technical information and technical services, which are important inputs in the human capital development. Although firms in the Kenyan context were observed to be different from the above discussion, we opt to propose a neutral influence of firm scale in human capital development.

Hypothesis 5: *Human capital development may or may not be influenced by firm size; human capital development may be high in small firms as well.*

Systemic Infrastructural and Institutional Support Structure

The role played by systemic infrastructure and institutional support structure in human capital development need not be emphasised. We argued above that human capital development is a complex process that can be influenced by a host of factors, both internal and exogenous to the firms. It was emphasized that firm's systemic embeddedness was important in the process of knowledge generation, exploitation in production, utilisation for learning and innovation, and diffusion to other firms. Systemic interactions via networks and linkages created through sub-contracting relations or buyer-supplier linkages stimulate learning and innovation[2].

If firms have to effectively develop their capabilities, basic infrastructural and institutional support structures must be present. For instance, sound human capital development institutions must be put in place. Technology promotion centres such industrial research and development organisation and productivity centres must also be present. Investment promotion councils with strong capacity to promote investment and advice on technology transfer must exist. Similarly, institutions such as those providing financing play a very active role towards facilitation of learning, innovation and human capital development. Such institutions and the intermediary organisations role of coordinating demand-supply relations between firms, government, and institutions have been well articulated in the literature (Rasiah, 2001; Doner, 2001; Aoki, 2001; Kugler, 2006). They play an important role in strengthening network cohesion.

From a systemic point of view, infrastructural and institutional capacity to function effectively depends on systemic relationships established over time. To a large extent, if infrastructural and institutional structures play an effective role, then the risk of government failure is minimal. We will therefore argue by analogy that where support structure is present, it would be more likely that firms would be able to develop their required human capital. Testing a proposition based on existence of support structure is extremely difficult since no appropriate data exists for that. A proxy can however be developed based on collected firm level data. From these data, infrastructural and institutional structures will be taken as present if a firm claims to have received support of some kind (such as technical, financial and so forth) from the existing technical and financial institutions in the Kenyan manufacturing industry.

Hypothesis 6: *The presence of strong basic infrastructure and supportive institutions in an industry including financing for technology development and innovation is anticipated to promote human capital development.*

The Role of Government Policy

The government is often supposed to play a facilitating role in human capital development. The government ought to operate a broad-based policy since formal education and training need to be complemented by learning within firms. In countries that are still in their early years of development; with private sector and labour market only partially developed, learning and training at firm level and national level can only be achieved through a proactive role by the government to facilitate and whenever possible provide human resource development programmes. If left to the weak system, there is likelihood of market failure in provision of learning and hence, the government needs to intervene without having to rely on market mechanisms.

The government must actively determine the quality and scope of human capital development programmes. It must create an incentive system conducive to formal and informal learning. The facilitation role could be through incentives meant at encouraging firms to learn and innovate. It should help in development of an appropriate curriculum with relevant academic programmes required in the industry. It should also come up with institutions, which directly support promotion of human capital needed. Examples exist in the NICs where enormous human capital and indeed technological capability has been built as a result of conscious and continuous facilitation role by the state (Fransman, 1985; Nelson and Pack, 1999; Yussof and Ismail, 2002; Chang, 2003).

Hypothesis 7: The government role through relevant policies is expected to enhance human capital development in the country.

Age of the Firm

With regard to firm age, we hypothesise that firms with longer experience are considered to enjoy greater experiential and tacit knowledge and thus the older a firm is, the more it will have developed its human capital. Linking the size and age of a firm, Jovanovic (1982) argued that firms increase in size as a result of a selection process, in which efficient firms grow and survive, while inefficient firms stagnate or exit the industry. He noted that since the process takes time, larger firms are therefore expected to be older. This would then mean that there exists a positive age, human capital relationship. This would be expected based on a firm's accumulated stock of knowledge and experience over time, emanating from various kinds of learning processes undertaken in the firms as they imitate their competitors and MNCs – as they undertake R&D, search information or simply as they undertake incremental innovations. The accumulated stock of knowledge and experience over time amounts to absorptive capacity which is necessary if a firm is expected to recognise external knowledge, absorb it and assimilate it for productive purposes. To most firms in the Kenyan industry, the process of knowledge accumulation is slow; hence time becomes a crucial factor leading us to formulate the proposition that human capital development increases with the age of a firm.

Hypothesis 8: *Human capital development increases with firm age; human capital development tends to be more in old firms, or in other words, human capital development is a function of years of experience.*

Labour Market Conditions

Labour market conditions often influence knowledge acquisition and thus learning, capability, innovation and human capital development. Examples of labour market conditions that influence firms' incentives on learning and training provision include regulations on basic or minimum wages, restrictions on dismissals, and existing social security/insurance programs. Related studies examining the role of labour market conditions indicate that good labour conditions can positively contribute to industrialisation by stimulating competitiveness (Sengenberger and Pyke, 1991; Wilkinson and You, 1995). The same studies have shown the converse to be also true involving reduced industrialisation when poor labour market conditions are the norm. In the current context, we argue that when a firm observes good labour market conditions, it is bound to pay high salaries and wages, offer fridge benefits, and provide staff with human resources training opportunities including enrichment programmes and the like.

Hypothesis 9: *Good labour market conditions promote human capital development in Kenya's manufacturing.*

Industrial Specificity

Industrial specificity has a strong bearing on human capital development. We argue that existing differences in industries is likely to influence human capital development differently. Differences in industries often arise due to the nature and sophistication of technology in use thus requiring specialised skill training. It also arises due to the level of value added which is in turn determined by the nature of technology in use. Sometimes presence of MNCs may have a contribution due to their ownership characteristics, which includes state of their state-of-the-art machinery and technology. There is a wide array of literature in support of this fact. Take for instance the garments and automobile industries.

According to Gerrefi (2002) framework of producer-buyer driven value chains, garments are categorised in terms of buyer-driven chains, while automobiles are characterised by producer-driven chains. However, in both industries there is increased use of technology and tacit knowledge. While garments have become high technology users, the auto-part has equally become more knowledge intensive. The auto parts industry is closely related to machinery and engineering industries and electronics assembly. From this discussion, this paper proposes a hypothesis intended to test the role of industry specificity in human capital development.

***Hypothesis 10**: The industrial specificities in Kenya have a strong correlation on human capital development in Kenya.*

3. Methodological Setting

This section presents variable definitions and their operationalisation based on the above hypotheses. This is done by generating measurement proxies for each of these variables. Use of proxies and indexes has now been widely adopted in capability studies (Lall, 1992; Rasiah, 2005). Based on variables defined, an econometric model – Tobit model – is specified for our analysis.

Definition of Variables and Operationalisation

Human Capital Development – Dependent Variable

Human capital development (HMCD) was computed as a composite index based on three related proxies; training expenditure (TEXP), training mode (TRMOD) and human development resource practices (HDPRC). HMCD was thus estimated as follows:

HMCD Index = Normalised composite average (TEXP, TRMOD, HDPRC)

TEXP was proxied by the training expenses as a share of total payroll in the firm. TRMOD was measured as a categorical variable taking a value of 0 when no formal training was undertaken, 1 when only external staff are used to train employees, 2 when staff with training responsibilities were on payroll, 3 when a separate training department was used, 4 when a separate training centre was used. In order to understand how the firms considered specific human development resource practices (HDPRC), all the firms were asked if they had policies in place to encourage team-working, small group activities to improve company performance, multi-skilling, interactions with marketing, customer service and R&D department, lifelong learning and upward mobility. For each of these practices, a human resource practice was measured by a score value of one, which was then summed and divided by the total number of practices to obtain the average. All the figures were brought to comparable levels using a normalising formula as follows:

$$Index = \left[\frac{ObservedValue;X_{ij} - MinimumObservedValue;X_{j}}{MaximumObservedValue;X_{j} - MinimumObservedValue;X_{j}} \right]$$

The normalisation procedure simply involves establishment of a fixed minimum and maximum for each of the variables in order to normalise them to a comparable range between 0 and 1. X_{ij} is the actual value for category i in sector j, $X_{j,min}$ is the minimum value in sector j and $X_{j,max}$ is the maximum value in sector j. This procedure could as well be used to make the composite indices range from 0 to 10 or 0 to 100 depending on the desired level to draw comparisons between the categories of firms, industries or countries considered for cross country comparisons.

Explanatory Variables

The explanatory variables were defined as follows:

FDI – Foreign Presence

Foreign presence (FDI) was measured as foreign equity participation averaged over all plants in the sector, weighted by each plant's share in sectoral employment[3]. This proxy was adopted in this study since the survey captured only a few foreign firms.

Export Performance

Export performance EXPT was estimated by an export dummy defined as follows:

EXPT = 1 if a firm exports; EXPT = 0 if a firm does not export.

Process Technology Capability

Process technology capability (PRTC) was also computed as a composite index based on three related proxies; quality control instruments (QCI), investment in machinery and equipment including ICT components (IME) and quality of production machinery (QPM). PRTC was thus estimated as follows:

PRTC Index = Normalised composite average (QCI, IME, QPM)

QCI was measured as a binary variable; QCI = 1 if relatively advanced quality control methods were used, QCI = 0 otherwise. IME was measured by a score of one for each of the following investments (brought new capital equipment; set up new production line; put in new production system and put in new ICT components). An average was obtained by dividing with the total number of investments. QPM was measured as a categorical variable with a score of 5 when a firm rated its average quality of its production machinery as world class, 4 when rated as highly advanced, 3 when rated as just advanced, 2 when rated as not very advanced, 1 when rated as dated and 0 otherwise. Normalisation was done using the formula presented above.

Product Technology Capability

Product technology capability (PDTC) was again computed as a composite index based also on three related proxies; new product development (NPDEV), scope of the new product developed (NPDEVSC) and resources firms advance to undertake R&D (R&D). Thus, PDTC was estimated as follows:

PDTC = Normalised composite average (NPDEV, NPDEVSC, R&D)

NPDEV was a categorical variable equal to 3 if a firm has been involved in the development of over 10 new products, 2 if involved in the development of between 4 and 10 products, 1 if involved in the development of between 1 and 3 products, and 0 otherwise. Similarly, NPDEVSC was defined as a categorical variable equal to 4 if the new products were new to the global market, 3 if they were new to the regional market, 2 if they were new to the local market, 1 if they were only new to the firm and finally 0 otherwise. R&D was based on the resources firms' advance for the purpose of conducting R&D activities and was determined on the basis of three R&D proxies as follows:

R&D = Normalised composite average (RDU, RDE, RDN)

The first proxy related to whether firms undertake in-house process R&D and was measured as a simple binary variable as follows:

RDU = 1 if a firm undertakes in-house R&D, RDU = 0 if otherwise.

The second proxy dealt with R&D expenditure incurred by firms to undertake R&D. However, it was not possible from the sample data to disentangle investment advanced between process and product R&D, and hence this proxy was measured to relate to both product and process R&D as follows: RDE = R&D expenditure as a percentage of total sales.

The third proxy was based on the nature of R&D activity and was defined as follows: RDN was measured by a score of 1 for each of the following R&D activities; quality control, reverse engineering, original design, original brand, adaptive engineering, others and divided by the total number of the R&D activities. The formula explained above was used to normalize the proxies before computing the average.

Marketing Performance

Marketing performance (MKTP) was equally computed on the basis of three proxies following the above approach. The proxies considered were marketing expenditure as a percentage of total firm sales (MKTEXP), marketing mode (MKTMOD) and marketing support (MKTSUP).

MKTP = Normalised composite average (MKTEXP, MKTMOD, MKTSUP)

MKTEXP was measured as a percentage of total sales in each firm. MKTMOD was measured as a categorical variable taking a value of 1 when a firm uses external marketing support, 2 when a firm has staff with marketing duties, 3 when a firm has a separate marketing department, 4 when a firm has a separate marketing centre and 0 when no marketing is undertaken. MKTSUP from institutions was measured by a score of 1 for each of the institutions (such as industry associations, government support programmes, purchase reputation, external private marketing agents and so forth) and divided by the total number of investments. Normalisation was done using the equation above.

Firm Size – Scale of Operation

In this paper, firm size (SIZE) was proxied by employment level of the firms. Although other proxies exist for determining firm size such as firm's output performance or investment level, there is no specified rule of thumb *per-se* as to which is more appropriate than the other. For this analysis, firm size was defined as a binary variable using employment size as follows:

SIZE = 0 if a firm employment was =< 100; SIZE = 1 if employment was => 100

Firm Age

Firm age was simply taken as the number of years in absolute numbers since firm's establishment.

Basic Institutions and Infrastructure

The basic institutions and infrastructure proxy was estimated as a composite index (BSCII) using information systematically captured from the firms during the survey. The composite index included thirteen institutional and infrastructural variables and was computed as follows:

BSCII = Normalised composite average (TS, PS, WS, TCI, HF, GI, FS, BE, TE, UE, RDSE, RDA, RDI)

Where TS, PS, WS, TCI, HF, GI, FS, BE, TE, UE, RDSE, RDA, RDI refer to transport services, power supply, water supply, telecommunication infrastructure, health facilities, coordination from basic government institutions, financial services, basic education, technical training education, university education, R&D scientists and engineers, incentives for R&D activities and R&D institutions respectively. All the firms were asked to make an objective assessment of the existing institution and infrastructure with regard to their role in enabling manufacturing operations. The value for each of the variables was measured using a Likert scale ranging from 1-5 (weakest to strongest). This score served as the institutional rating for each firm. The value for each variable was normalised using the formula presented earlier.

Role of Government

The role of government (GOV) was computed on the basis of three related proxies following the above procedure as follows:

GOV = Normalised composite average (G_{INST}, G_{EDTC}, G_{RLN})

G_{INST} was related to usefulness of government institutions. All firms were asked to rate how government institutions benefited their ability to compete. The government institutions included science and technology support institutions; testing and quality evaluation facilities; marketing research and intelligence; overseas market promotion; export credit programs; financial incentives; SMI support and inter-firm collaboration schemes. G_{EDTC} was related to services of government regulatory bodies. Firms were asked to rate the services of government regulatory bodies in supporting their effort to develop technology and compete. The services included custom procedures, licensing arrangements, local duties and levies, access to land, municipal regulations, official corruption, regulation on hiring foreign workers and so forth. G_{RLN} was related to the value of relationships. Firms were therefore asked to rate value of their relationship with intermediary none and semi-government agencies. Such agencies included R&D organisations; financial service institutions; distributors; suppliers of material & components; customers; technical service providers; business service providers; relationship between firms and industry associations; strength of strategic alliances and so forth. For the three variables, (G_{INST}, G_{EDTC}, G_{RLN}), Likert scale scores ranging from 1-5 were used and averaged with the number of proxies used. Normalisation was done using the formula presented above.

Systemic Embeddedness

Systemic embeddedness (SYEMB) was computed as a composite index based on four proxies as follows:

SYEMB = Normalised composite average [BSCII, G_{EDTC}, G_{RLN}, SN]

All firms were asked to rate the strength of their connections and coordination with basic infrastructure institutions, related government organizations and between each other. Likert scale scores ranging from 1-5 were used and averaged with the number of proxies used. Where BSCII, G_{EDTC} and G_{RLN} were as explained above. SN referred to inter-firm buyer supplier firms. Normalisation was done using the above formula.

Labour Market Conditions

The proxy for labour market conditions was determined using a dummy variable based on a simple question which required firms to state if their workers were unionised or not. Firm wages can also be considered as an alternative proxy variable for labour market conditions. This can be derived from a firm's annual gross salary figures normalised by firm's employment size. Unfortunately, supply of salary figures by the firms was patchy as most of them did not want to divulge salary and wages figures. Hence, for this analysis a dummy proxy was opted for and expressed as follows:

Union = 1 if workers were unionised; Union=0 if workers were not unionised.

Industrial Specificity
Industrial specificities were estimated using industry dummies.

Determinants of Human Capital Development: An Empirical Tobit Model

Based on variables formulated above, our hypotheses pertaining to human capital development can be empirically tested using Tobit model analysis. Tobit model is suggested since HMCD was estimated as an index limited within a specified range, in this case between 0 and 1. This meant that HMCD was censored above 1 and below 0 [$0 \leq HMCD \geq 1$]. The empirical model was therefore set as follows:

$$HMCD = b_0 + b_1FDI + b_2PRTC + b_3PDTC + b_4EXPT\ b_5MKTP + b_6BSCII + b_7SIZE + b_8GOV + b_9SYEMB + b_{10}Union + b_{11}INDMMY + \alpha$$

4. Scope and Sample Characteristics

The data used in this paper comes from a survey covering only three manufacturing industries in Kenya; metal engineering, textile, and food processing and beverages.Since the objective of this paper was to examine the role of FDI and firm-level capabilities in human capital development, the scope of this analysis is therefore limited to only a few industries characterised by high levels of FDI and performance capabilities – in terms of value added. The three industries are believed to have higher levels of FDI than other industries. Food processing and textile industries are classified under agro based industries and as in most developing countries, the agro based industry is the most dynamic in Kenya today with high FDI presence, linkage intensive, largest employer and a major contributor to the GDP. In addition to the survey, specific case studies of at least five firms for each industry was undertaken to help extract industry-type characteristics which would have positive and direct consequences on human capital development. So, the survey and the selected case studies formed the basis for the results and analysis done in this paper.

The initial idea was to sample by weight each firm carries based on the sectoral output. However, this could not materialise since most of them were missing in the frame – in the country's statistical office. Nevertheless, without using any systematic sampling technique, a purposive selection procedure was followed in selecting the firms in such a way that the main activities by ISIC would at least be represented in all the three industries. This spreading of the selection coverage was important to make sure that all firms selected did not come primarily from the same manufacturing activities. The list of firms was extracted from the most recent National Directory of Industries (NDI) prepared by the Ministry of Trade and Industry. The list of firms was also drawn from firms that are included in the monthly survey of industrial production (MSIP); this is a survey conducted on monthly basis by Kenya National Bureau of Statistics (KNBS). This was also compared to the firms in the 'master file' still in KNBS – the master file is the frame which contains the list of all firms and institutions operating in Kenya. Another useful source of firm listing was the directory of firms and industries held by Kenya Association of Manufacturers (KAM, 2002)[4].

From an initial selection of 150 firms, 127 firms in the manufacturing industry were successfully surveyed. After eliminating 22 firms due to incomplete information, 105 firms remained for empirical analysis, which is about 83 % of the total firms surveyed. The breakdown is shown below in Table 1.

In the sample, there were only 37 foreign firms while all the rest were local firms. A firm was defined as foreign owned when foreign ownership of nominal capital was at least 10 % – this is the benchmark used by the Kenyan national authorities as well as OECD and UNCTAD[5].There were more local firms in all the industries with the exception of textile industry where foreign firms out-numbered the local firms. Table 1 further classifies all the firms by size following the definition of size provided earlier. About 65 % of the firms in our survey were classified as small firms. This was as expected in the Kenyan context since most of the firms in poor developing countries are normally characterised by small and medium enterprises (Lundvall and Battese, 2000; Mazumdar and Mazaheri, 2003). However, comparing local and foreign firms in terms of size, foreign firms in the sample seemed to be mostly large firms. While 75.7 % of foreign firms were classified as large firms, only 58.8 % of local firms were classified as large firms, Table 1. This is not surprising given that foreign firms have the necessary capacity in terms of resources to set up huge production processes employing heavy capital machinery for large-scale production in addition to a huge labour force.

Table 1: Ownership Structure of the Sample Firms

	Firm Orientation	Metal Engineering	Textile Industry	Food Processing Industry
Small	Local	12	6	10
	Foreign	4	1	4
Large	Local	12	5	23
	Foreign	7	11	10
Total		35	23	47

Source: Computed from author's survey.

Turning to export performance, it was noted during the survey that since the introduction of SAPs in Kenya most of the firms had attempted to re-orient themselves towards exporting. It was also noted that even firms that were largely inward-oriented had tended to operate primarily as suppliers to exporting firms. A few of the companies interviewed confirmed to have had short term and, in some cases, long-term contractual arrangement to supply their final products to domestic exporting firms. The survey data showed that 12%[6] of the firms had sales to domestic export companies. While some of the domestic exporting firms used these products as raw materials in their production, interviews conducted also confirmed that other domestic exporting firms served as marketing and exporting agencies for other companies[7].

Exporting firms formed about 51% of the total sample (Table 2). By ownership the proportion of local firms with export experience was 44% while that of foreign firms with export experience was 65%. There were more local firms without any export experience in food processing than in any other industry. In all the three industries, foreign firms with export experience outnumbered firms without any export experience. The break down is provided in Table 2. This shows that foreign firms are likely to be more export oriented than the local firms in Kenyan manufacturing. In addition, foreign firms seemed to dominate in export performance in the Kenyan manufacturing – from the three industries examined foreign firms share of total exports was about 77%. Except for food processing, foreign firms had higher export intensity than the local firms in all the other industries.

Table 2: Firms with Export Experience

Firms	Exporting Status	Food Processing	Textile	Metal Engineering	Total
Local firms	Exporting	11	6	13	30
	Non-exporting	22	5	11	38
Foreign firms	Exporting	8	9	7	24
	Non-exporting	6	3	4	13
Total		46	23	35	105

Source: Computed from author's survey in Kenya.

Foreign firms generally enjoyed higher firm-level capabilities than locally owned firms in all the three industries studied. Given industrial differences in technologies, firm-level capabilities were examined for each industry separately and then for all industries combined. We discuss each of the firm-level capabilities at a time starting with human capital development. Foreign firms enjoyed tremendous advantage in HMCD over locally owned firms in all the three industries, Figure 1. There was a wide variation between foreign and local firms on the basis of HMCD index computed for all the three industries combined. The results of T-Test analysis presented in Appendix 1 showed the difference to be statistically significant at least for metal engineering and food processing and beverages. This was expected since foreign firms usually undertake more human resource development activities than locally owned firms[8] generally meant to drive production in a foreign country and to compete in international export markets. Human capital is critical to operate and maintain the machinery and equipment and undertake organisational changes.

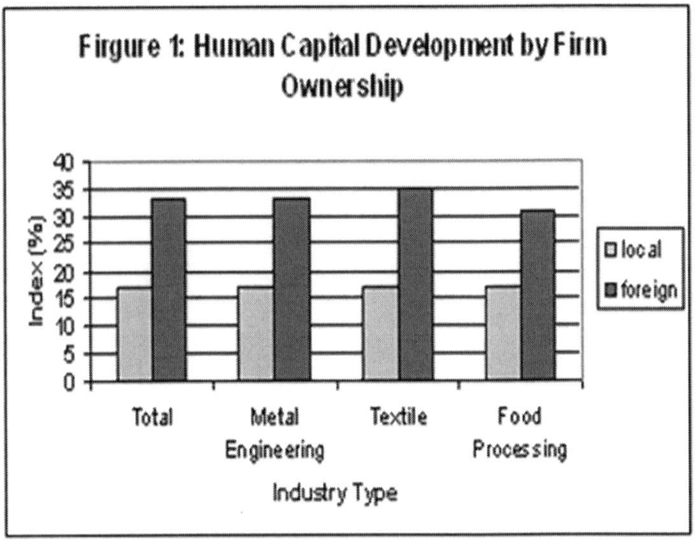

Source: Computed from author's survey.

The results of PRTC were slightly different from those of HMCD discussed above. Foreign firms enjoyed higher PRTC than locally owned firms in food processing and in metal engineering industry, Figure 2. However, the difference was significant at 10% only in machine engineering, Appendix 1. The T-test result also showed that when all the industries were considered jointly, foreign firms generated more PRTC than locally owned firms and the difference was statistically significant. These results were as expected since foreign firms would normally be more endowed with more advanced, sophisticated production processes in comparison to locally owned firms.

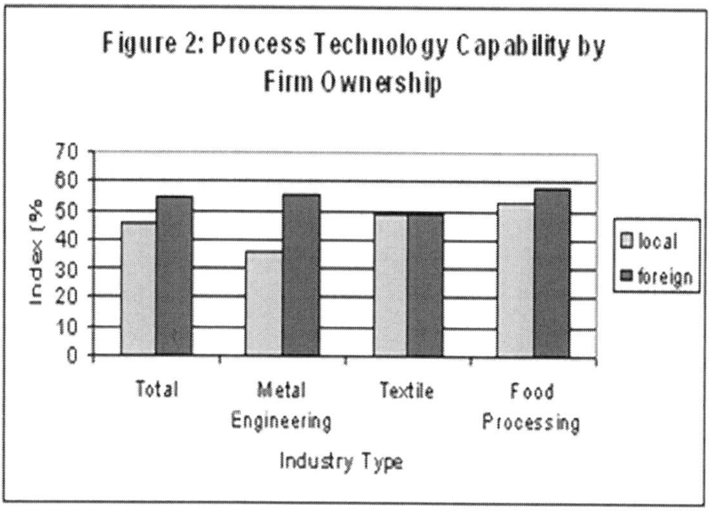

Source: Computed from author's survey.

As indicated elsewhere, foreign firms' share of the overall R&D index (RD) was higher than that of the local firms for all the three industries. It is interesting to note that while foreign firms enjoyed significantly different levels of product technology capability in the three industries, local firms seemed to have a comparable average of product technology capability in all the three industries with the highest in metal engineering and lowest in food processing and beverages. This is clearly demonstrated in Figure 3. Results of T-Test analysis presented in Appendix showed the difference to be statistically significant in metal engineering and food processing at 5 and 10% respectively. Hence, overall, despite their preference for carrying out much of their R&D activities overseas, foreign firms still generally enjoyed higher capabilities than local firms. However, in addition to R&D being little developed only a few firms performed it – only 25% of the firms surveyed reported to be doing some kind of R&D with MNCs dominating.

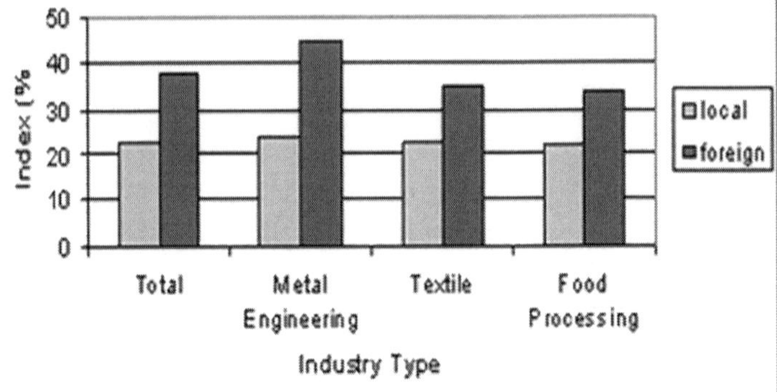

Figure 3: Product Technology Capability by Firm Ownership

Source: Computed from author's survey.

The preliminary analysis done showed also that foreign firms enjoyed more MKTP than locally owned firms, Figure 4. Results of T-Test analysis presented in Appendix 1 showed the difference between foreign and local firms to be significant in machine engineering and food processing at 10 and 5% respectively. The difference for all the industries combined was also significant at 5%. These results are not surprising given the fact MNCs usually have high level marketing prowess. In addition, these firms dedicate enormous resources to constant stimulation of marketing performance.

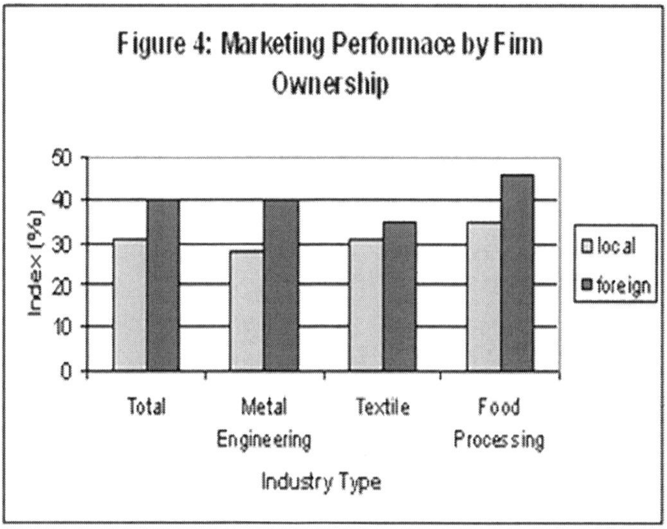

Source: Computed from author's survey.

While capabilities differ with industrial specificity and the type of technology, important conclusions can be summed up from this section. First, although over 50% of the firms in the sample enjoyed export experience and thus were exposed to international trade and competition, foreign firms dominated in exports. Second, specific firm-level technological capabilities between foreign and local firms varied significantly in the industries examined. Foreign firms enjoyed relatively higher levels of HMCD than the local firms. On other technological capabilities, foreign firms enjoyed higher PRTC, PDTC and MKTP than the local firms in all the three industries combined. It can therefore be argued that foreign firms dominated in all the firm-level technological capabilities than the local firms. The implication for this is that, although it is hard to determine the spillovers, there is a possibility that some of the capabilities generated by the MNCs could be absorbed in the Kenyan manufacturing. These would further contribute to the development of human capital.

5. Empirical Findings and Discussion

This paper attempted to examine the role of FDI presence and firm-level capabilities in human capital development controlling for a number of firm-level variables. The paper hypothesized that FDI and firm-level capabilities among other determinants played significant role in human capital development in the Kenyan manufacturing industry. These hypotheses were investigating empirically employing Tobit estimation technique[9] -- since the independent variable was "left censored" and "right censored".Most of the results estimated based on Tobit estimation technique were statistically significant as shown in Table 3. Two sets of estimates are estimated – with and without the inclusion of systemic embeddedness variable – each case estimated with and without industry dummies. The Tobit estimation technique produced statistically significant results between human capital development and FDI, EXPT, PRTC, PDTC and MKTP (Table 3). SIZE, BSCII, GOVN, SYEMB and UNION were not significant. We will only present results of determinants that were significant. Estimated results of variable correlation showed that none of the variables had any serious correlation (Appendix 2). The variables were also free from heteroscedasticity[10].

The results obtained with FDI, though as expected, did not generate coefficients of high magnitude. Results obtained without systemic embeddedness produced FDI coefficients that were positive and significant at 10 and 5% with and without industrial dummies included respectively. Results estimated with systemic embeddedness included seemed to improve in significance as the coefficients became significant at 5 and 1% with and without dummies included. According to the results obtained a high positive correlation between FDI and human capital development exits – HMCD. Foreign firms are characterised by ownership advantages such as high technology, knowledge, managerial skills and marketing know-how. In a host country when foreign firms employ local workers, they train them to acquire certain skills required in order to operate effectively in foreign firms – foreign firms employ more experienced workers and possess better training schemes. Having learnt, acquired experiential and tacit knowledge from the foreign firms, such workers might leave foreign firms and join local firms or start their own enterprises (Gershernberg, 1987). Linkages established between local supplying firms to foreign firms have acted as an avenue through which organised programmes are arranged to train workers from local supplying firms[11]. Through these links local firms get exposed to international export markets which in turn act as new source of learning and knowledge acquisition to the local firms and hence development of human resources capability (Lall, 1982, 1992; Rasiah, 1995; Bell and Pavitt, 1992).

EXPT had a positive correlation with human capital development with and without systemic embeddedness included. The coefficient obtained for EXPT was positive and significant at 5% but at 10% when systemic embeddedness and industry dummies were included. This implies that the process of exporting in the Kenyan manufacturing exposes firms to a pool of international knowledge, information and cutting-edge techniques from global markets. Accumulation of knowledge and techniques from established networks overseas culminates in a process of constant learning in the firms resulting in HMCD. In the long run this results enhanced ability to innovate and compete in the international market.

The results obtained with PRTC were as expected. The coefficients obtained were positive and statistically significant at 5% in all cases – with and without systemic embeddedness and industry dummies. These results indicated high correlation between PRTC and HMCD. Process capabilities range from basic skills such as quality control, operation and maintenance, to more advanced ones such as adaptation, improvement or equipment 'stretching and to the most demanding ones such as process research, design, and innovation. Stated differently, PRTC includes planning, scheduling and work procedures, execution of orders: ability to oversee, control and improve the operation of the facilities and processes. Equipment stretching, processing adaptation and cost saving, licensing new technology, in-house process innovation (Westphal *et al.*, 1985; Lall, 1992; Ernst *et al.*, 1998). Learning and performance are also viewed as a function of processing experience. Undertaking these activities, amounts to acquiring experience both experiential and tacit learning knowledge all of which result in accumulation of human capital development (Romijn, 1997).

Similarly, Tobit estimates for PDTC had the expected results – relatively robust coefficients which were positive and statistically significant at 5% with and without systemic embeddedness or industrial dummies. The results supported existence of a high positive correlation between human capital development and PDTC. This is not unexpected since PDTC ranges from raw material control, assimilation of product design, minor adaptation to market needs, product quality improvement, licensing and assimilating new imported product technology to in-house basic research and product innovation (Westphal *et al.*, 1985; Lall, 1992; Ernst *et al.*, 1998). As in the case of PRTC, undertaking these activities in firms amounts to acquiring experience both experiential and tacit learning knowledge all of which result in accumulation of human resources capability.

Table 3: Determinants of Human Capital Development: Tobit Estimates

Deteminant	Without Systemic Embeddedness		With Systemic Embeddedness	
FDI	0.063**	0.059*	0.069***	0.064**
	(0.028)	(0.030)	(0.026)	(0.027)
EXPT	0.160**	0.146**	0.136**	0.120*
	(0.069)	(0.073)	(0.066)	(0.069)
PRTC	0.442**	0.462**	0.435**	0.463**
	(0.184)	(0.188)	(0.182)	(0.186)
PDTC	0.352**	0.329**	0.305**	0.276**
	(0.143)	(0.149)	(0.140)	(0.144)
MKTP	0.411*	0.440**	0.504***	0.532***
	(0.207)	(0.213)	(0.193)	(0.198)
SIZE	-0.009	0.004	-0.018	-0.001
	(0.073)	(0.076)	(0.072)	(0.075)
AGE	0.004*	0.003*	0.004*	0.004*
	(0.002)	(0.002)	(0.002)	(0.002)
BSCII	0.015	0.017		
	(0.048)	(0.049)		
GOV	-0.027	-0.041		
	(0.320)	(0.322)		
SYEMB			0.140	0.119
			(0.216)	(0.219)
UNION	-0.049	-0.054	-0.053	-0.060
	(0.071)	(0.071)	(0.065)	(0.066)
Constant	-0.535***	-0.533***	-0.553***	-0.536***
	(0.180)	(0.184)	(-0.136)	(0.138)
Industry Dummies	*No*	*Yes*	*No*	*Yes*
LR-test	74.68***	75.02***	77.64***	78.22***
Log Likelihood	-28.012	-27.839	-29.059	-28.766
Pseudo R Squared	0.5714	0.5740	0.5719	0.5762
No. of observations	101	101	104	104

Note: The figures in parenthesis represent standard errors.
*, **, *** represent 10 %, 5 % and 1 % levels of significance respectively.
Source: Computed from data compiled from author's survey in Kenya.

MKTP had the expected results. The estimated coefficients with systemic embeddedness were robust and highly significant at 1% with and without industry dummies. With systemic embeddedness the coefficients obtained were significant at 10% without industry dummies and at 5% with industry dummies. These results provided statistical evidence of positive correlation between human capital development and MKTP. This would be expected since strong marketing capability requires a firm to possess knowledge and skills required for collecting marketing intelligence, development of new markets, and establishment of distribution channels and provision of customer services (Ernst *et al.*, 1998; Kugler 2006; Rasiah, 2005). All these are supposed to be fed into the firm to be translated into successful goods and services. This feedback aspect to the firm serves to provide new source of learning and innovation, which further translates into accumulation of human capital development.

Although the results obtained for AGE were as expected, they were however not robust. The Tobit coefficients obtained were weak but significant at 10% in all the cases. Nonetheless, these results supported a positive correlation between human capital development and firm's AGE. The interpretation of this would be that an old firm has accumulated tacit experience over time through learning by doing and by operation performance.

6. Conclusions and Policy Implications

The purpose of this paper was to examine the role of foreign presence, FDI, and firm-level capabilities in human capital development. Survey data collected from three manufacturing industries in Kenya, enabled testing of several hypothesis based on FDI and technological capabilities literature. Results of descriptive statistics indicated that foreign firms were large in size and generated higher human capital development than locally owned firms. Human capital development was different for each manufacturing industry. Overall, firms with export experience clearly outnumbered those that just sold in the domestic markets. Foreign firms enjoyed greater export-orientation than locally owned firms. The comparisons done employing T-Test analysis showed, on firm-level capabilities, foreign firms generally enjoyed higher process and product technology capability, and marketing performance than locally owned firms in all the industries combined. Although R&D activities were extremely low in all the three industries, foreign firms were once again more endowed with R&D capabilities than the locally owned firms. It can be concluded that foreign firms in countries which are typically at the same level of development with Kenya tend to be more involved in technology development than locally owned firms.

The empirical analysis produced statistically significant correlations between human capital development, FDI and firm-level capabilities (PRTC, PDTC, MKTP) including export performance. Several lessons can be drawn from this analysis. First, the analysis provided strong empirical evidence that foreign presence and firm-level capabilities stimulated human capital development in Kenya. Second, that firm export performance also mattered in determining human capital development. Third, that HMCD increased with firm Age. Fourth, that all the countries which are technically backward like Kenya are likely to have FDI play a positive and significant role in human capital development. Fifth, industry specificity appeared to have influence on human capital development which tended to differ with variables included. On the policy side we argue that policies that allow increased activities of FDI should therefore be encouraged alongside firm-level development of technological capabilities.

Partly due to government failure involving provision of basic infrastructure, creation of stable macro-economic climate, creation of special industrial zones and functional support institutions the costs of production have remained high contributing to loss of competitiveness in Kenya's exports. Indeed, Kenya has found it hard to compete even with imports from advanced developing countries brought into the country via other countries within the COMESA trading block. Systemic embeddedness had positive relationship with PRTC and MKTP. This helps firms spread their production and marketing activities with reduced transaction costs.

Given that foreign firms had high levels of export intensity and generated more HMCD, PRTC, PDTC and MKTP capabilities than the local firms, it can be discerned that FDI has at least resulted in some technological spillovers absorbed by domestic firms in Kenyan manufacturing. Participation by foreign firms and their high levels of HMCD, PRTC, PDTC and MKTP capabilities generated is likely to transform the local environment, develop industrial technological capabilities and facilitate export manufacturing. The government must therefore continue to play participatory role as a facilitator – mainly of public goods. The government must also increase its coordination role among institutions. It must focus especially on improving the institutions and systemic coordination to encourage collective learning, capability building and innovation process in firms. In addition, the country must formulate and embrace broad-based technology policies necessary to stimulate learning and innovation culture if industrialization can be anticipated by 2020 as envisioned in the current industrial policies. Only then, the country will be able to accelerate human capital development and thus enhance competitiveness in production with high levels of value added.

Acknowledgements

The author would like to acknowledge with thanks the release time provided by the University of Dubai to work on this paper. However, the usual disclaimer applies.

Endnotes

1 Well educated mangers, engineers and workers have a comparative advantage in seeing new opportunities and effective learning of new things.

2 These attributes of involving all actors dynamically and interactively for the sole purpose of social benefit to a wide economic standpoint, led to the formation of NSI built upon works of Freeman (1995), Lundvall (1992) and Nelson and Rosenberg (1993).

3 This is similar to the method used by Aitken and Harrison (1999).

4 We are grateful to Kenya National Bureau of Statistics (KNBS), Department of company registration and Kenya Association of Manufacturers (KAM) for allowing us to have access to their firm directories.

5 Examples of other benchmarks taken in other studies include Haddad and Harrison (1993) who regarded foreign firms as those with at least (5 %) equity owned by foreigners and Sjoholm (1997) who considered a benchmark (15 %) of equity owned by foreigners.

6 Computed from author's survey in Kenya.

7 Interviews conducted by the author in Kenya.

8 This was observed to be the case in most of the MNCs companies interviewed by the author (2002). MNCs seemed to be more keen on human resource development; most of them had training centres, better training schemes and engineering departments; something that most of their local counterparts did not have.

9 For details see Green (2000)

10 Results of Heteroscedasticity were not presented in this paper but can be availed on request.

11 During the survey, a few local firms reported having benefited from such training arrangements, a few foreign firms also reported having offered specific trainings mainly in production techniques and in quality control. It was also reported that foreign firms and local firms occasionally undertook joint trainings organised by industry association in Kenya.

References

Aitken, B., Hanson, H. and Harrison, A. (1997), 'Spillovers, Foreign Investment and Export Behaviour', in *Journal of International Economics,* 43: 103-132.

Aitken B. and Harrison A. (1999), 'Do Domestic Firms Benefit from Direct Foreign Investment? Evidence from Venezuela,' *The American Economic Review*, 89(3): 605-618.

Aghion, P. and Howitt P. (1992), 'Endogenous Growth Through Creative Destruction,' in *Econometrica*, 60(2): 323-351

Aghion, P. and Howitt P. (1998), *Endogenous Growth Theory,* Cambridge MA: MIT Press.

Amsden, A. (1989), *South Korea and Late Industrialisation,* New York, Oxford University Press.

Amsden, A. (1991), 'The Diffusion of Development: The Late-Industrialising model and Greater East Asia,' *American Economic Review,* 81(2).

Amsden, A. (1994), 'Why Isn't the whole World Experimenting with the East Asia Model to Develop? Review of the East Asian Miracle,' in *World Development,* 22(4):627-634.

Aoki, M. (2001), *Towards a Comparative Institutional Analysis,* Cambridge, MIT Press.

Arrow, K. (1962), 'The Economic Implications of Learning by Doing,' in *Review of Economic Studies*, 29(3): 155-173.

Audretsch, D. (2002), 'The Dynamic Role of Small Firms: Evidence from US,' in *Small Business Economics* 1(3): 13-40.

Audretsch, D. and Zoltan, A. (1991), *Innovation and Technological Change: An International Comparison.* Ann Arbor: University of Michigan Press.

Barro, R. (1991), 'Economic Growth in a Cross Section of Countries', in *Quarterly Journal of Economics* 106(2): 407-443.

Barro, R. and Salai-i-Martin (1995), *Economic Growth.* New York: McGraw Hill.

Becker, G. (1962), 'Investment in Human Capital: A Theoretical Analysis,' in *Journal of Political Economy* 70(1): 1-49.

Becker, G. (1964), *Human Capital,* Chicago, The University of Chicago Press.

Bell, M. and Pavitt, K. (1992), 'Accumulating Technological Capability in Developing Countries', in Summers, L. and Shah, S. (eds.), *Proceedings of the World Bank Annual Conference on Development Economics*, Washington D.C.: World Bank.

Blalock, G. and Gertler J. (2009), 'How firm capabilities affect who benefits from foreign technology,' in *Journal of Development Economics*, 90(2): 192-199.

Chang, H.J. (2003) *Globalisation, Economic Development and the Role of the State.* London, Zed Books: Third World Network.

Cohen, W. and Levinthal, D. (1990), 'Absorptive Capacity: A new Perspective on Learning and Innovation,' in *Administrative Science Quarterly,* 35: 128-152.

Dahlman, C. and Westphal, L. (1982), 'Technological Effort in Industrial Development: An Interpretative Survey of Recent Research', in: Stewart, F. and James, J. (eds.), *The Economics of New Technology in Developing Countries,* London: Frances Pinter Publishers.

Doner R. (2001), 'Institutions and the Tasks of Economic Upgrading', *Paper Prepared for Delivery at the 2001 Annual Meeting of the American Political Science Association,* San Francisco.

Ernst, D., Ganiatsos, T. and Mytelka, L. (eds.) (1998), *Technological Capabilities in the Context of Export-Led Growth: A conceptual Framework. Technological Capabilities and Export Success in Asia*, London: Routledge Publishers.

Fleisher, B., Li, H. and Qiang, M. (2010), 'Human capital, economic growth and regional inequality in China,' in *Journal of Development Economics*, 92(2): 215-231.

Fransman, M. (1985), International Competitiveness, Technical Change and the State: The Machine Tool Industries in Taiwan and Japan, in *World Development,* 14(12): 1375-1396.

Freeman, C. (1991), 'Networks of Innovators: A Synthesis of Research Issues,' in *Research Policy*, 20: 499-514.

Freeman, C. (1995), 'The National System of Innovation in Historical Perspective,' *Cambridge Journal of Economics,* 19(1): 5-24.

Gachino, G. (2006), 'Foreign Direct Investment, Spillovers and Innovation: The Case of Kenyan Manufacturing Industry', *Unpublished PhD Thesis*, Maastricht University.

Gachino, G. (2009), 'Industrial policy, Institutions and Foreign direct investment: The Kenyan context,' in *African Journal of Marketing Management,* 1(6): 140-160.

Gachino, G. (2010a), 'Technological spillovers from multinational presence: towards a conceptual framework,' in *Progress in Development Studies,* 10 (3):193-210.

Gachino, G. (2010b), 'Foreign Direct Investment and Firm level Productivity in Kenyan Manufacturing: A Panel Data Analysis,' in *International Journal of Institutions and Economics,* 2 (1): 17-57.

Gereffi, G. (2002), 'International Competitiveness in the Global Apparel Commodity Chain', in *International Journal of Business and Society,* 3(1): 1-23.

Gerschenberg, I. (1987), 'The Training and Spread of Managerial Know-How, A Comparative Analysis of Multinational and Other Firms in Kenya,' *in World Development,* 15(7): 931-939.

Green, W. (2000), *Econometric Analysis,* London, Prentice-Hall International.

Haddad, M. and Harrison, A. (1993), 'Are There Spillovers from Direct Foreign Investment? Evidence from Panel Data for Morroco,' in *Journal of Development Economics,* 42(1): 51-74.

Jovanovic, B. (1982), 'Selection and the Evolution of Industries,' in *Econometrica,* 50(3): 649-70.

Kaldor, N. (1957), 'A model of Economic Growth,' in *Economic Journal,* 67: 591-624.

KAM (2002), *The Manufacturers Directory.* Nairobi: Kenya Association of Manufacturers.

Kaplinsky, R. (ed.) (1978), *Readings on the Multinational Corporations in Kenya,* Nairobi: Heineman.

Kim, L. (1997), *Imitation to Innovation: The Dynamics of Korea's Technological Learning,* Boston Massachusetts: Harvard Business School Press.

Kim, L. (1999), *Learning and Innovation in Economic Development,* Cheltenham: Edward Elgar Publishing.

Kottaridi, C., and Thanasis, T. (2010), 'Foreign Direct Investment, Human Capital and Non-linearities in economic growth,' in *Journal of Macroeconomics,* 32(3): 858-871.

Kugler, M. (2006), 'Spillovers from foreign direct investment: Within or between industries?' in *Journal of Development Economies*, 80(2): 444-447.

Kuo, C. and Yang, C. (2008), 'Knowledge capital and spillover on regional economic growth: Evidence from China,' in *China Economic Review*, 19(4), 594-604.

Lall,S. (1982), *Developing Countries as Exporters of Technology: A First Look at the Indian Experience,* London: Macmillan Press.

Lall, S. (1992), 'Technological Capabilities and Industrialisation,' in *World Development,* 20(2): 165-186.

Lall,S. and Streeten, P. (1977), *Foreign Investment, Transnational and Developing Countries,* Basingstoke: Macmilan.

Li, X. and Liu, X. (2005), 'Foreign Direct Investment and Economic Growth: An Increasingly Endogenous Relationship,' in *World Development*, 33(3): 393-407.

Lucas, R. (1988), 'On the Mechanics of Economic Development', in *Journal of Monetary Economics,* 22(1): 3-42.

Lundvall, B. (1992), *National Systems of Innovation: Towards a Theory of Innovation and Interactive Learning,* London: Francis Pinter.

Lundvall, K. and Battese, B. (2000), 'Firm Size, Age and Efficiency: Evidence from Kenyan Manufacturing Firms,' in *The Journal of Development Studies,* 36(3): 146-163.

Mazumdar, D. and Mazaheri, A. (2003), *The African Manufacturing Firm: An Analysis Based on Firm Survey's in Seven Countries in Sub-Saharan Africa,* London, New York: Routledge.

Miyamoto, K. (2003), 'Human Capital Formation and Foreign Direct Investment in Developing Countries,' OECD Paper No. 211.

Mytelka, L. (2000), 'Local Systems of Innovation in a Globalised World Economy,' in*Industry and Innovation*, 7(1): 15-32.

Nelson, R. and Phelps, E. (1966), 'Investment in Humans, Technological Diffusion, and Economic Growth,' in *American Economic Review,* 56: 67-75.

Nelson, R. and Pack, H. (1999), 'The Asian Miracle and Modern Growth Theory,' in *The Economic Journal*, 109 (457): 416-436

Nelson, R. and Rosenberg, N. (1993), 'Technical Innovation and National Systems', in: Nelson, R. R. (ed.), *National Innovation Systems: A Comparative Analysis,* Oxford, UK: Oxford University Press.

Nelson, R. and Winter, S. (1982), *An Evolutionary Theory of Economic Change*, Cambridge: Harvard University Press.

Noorbakhsh, F., Paloni, A. and Youssef, A. (2005), 'Human Capital Development and FDI Inflows to Developing Countries: New Empirical Evidence,' in *World Development*, 29(9): 1593-1610.

Patibandla, M. and Petersen, B. (2002), 'Role of Transnational Corporations in the Evolution of a High-Tech Industry: The Case of India's Software Industry,' in *World Development,* 30(9):1561-1577.

Piore, M. and Sabel, C. (1984), *The Second Industrial Divide: Possibilities for Prosperity,* New York: Basic Books.

Pratten, C. (1971), *Economies of Scale in Manufacturing Industry,* Cambridge: Cambridge University Press.

Rasiah, R. (1995), *Foreign Capital and Industrialisation in Malaysia,* Basingstoke: Macmillan.

Rasiah, R. (2001), 'Market, Government and Malaysia's New Economic Policy,' *Cambridge Journal of Economics,* 25(1): 57-78.

Rasiah, R. (2005), *Foreign Firms, Technological Capabilities and Economic Performance: Evidence from Africa, Asia and Latin America,* Cheltenham, UK and Northampton, MA, USA: Edward Elgar.

Rasiah, R. and Gachino, G. (2005), 'Are Foreign Firms more Productive, and Export and Technology Intensive than Local Firms in Kenyan Manufacturing?', in *Oxford Development Studies,* 33(2):211-228.

Romer, P. (1986), 'Increasing Returns and Long Run Growth,' in *Journal of Political Economy,* 94: 1002-1037.

Romer, P. (1990), 'Endogenous Technological Change,' in *Journal of Political Economy,* 98: S71- 102.

Romijn, H. (1997), 'Acquisition of Technological Capability in Development: A Quantitative Case Study of Pakistan's Capital Goods Sector,' in *World Development,* 25(3): 359-377.

Scherer, F. (1973), 'The Determinants of Industry Plant Sizes in Six nations,' in *Review of Economics and Statistics,* 55(2): 135-175.

Schultz, T. (1963), *The Economic value of Education,* Columbi: Columbia University Press.

Schumpeter, J. (1934), *The Theory of Economic Development,* Oxford: Oxford University Press.

Schumpter, J. (1952), *Capitalism, Socialism, and Democracy,* London: Unwin.

Sengenberger, W. and Pyke, F. (1991), 'Small Firms, Industrial Districts and Local Economic Regeneration,' in *Labour and Society,* 16(1): 1-24.

Sinani, E., and Meyer, E.(2004), 'Spillovers of technology transfer from FDI: the case of Estonia,' in *Journal of Comparative Economics,* (32)3: 445-466.

Sjoholm, F. (1997), 'Technology Gap, Competition and Spillovers from Direct Foreign Investment: Evidence from Established Data,' in *Journal of Development Studies*, 36 (1): 53-73.

Spagat, M. (2006), 'Human capital and the future of transition economies,' *Journal of Comparative Economics*, 34(1): 44-56.

Swainson, N. (1980), *The Development of Corporate Capitalism in Kenya, 1918-1977.* Nairobi: Heinemann.

Uzawa, H. (1965), 'Optimum Technical Change in an Aggregative Model of Economic Growth', in *International Economic Review*. 6(1): 18-31.

Wangwe, S., (ed.) (1995*), Exporting Africa: Technology, Trade and Industrialisation in Sub-Saharan Africa,* London and New York: Routledge.

Westphal, L. (1990), 'Industrial Policy in an Export-Propelled Economy: Lessons from South Korea's Experience,' in *Journal of Economic Perspective,* 4(3): 41-59.

Westphal, L., Kim, L. and Dahlman, C. (1985), 'Reflections on Korea's Acquisition of Technological Capability', in Rosenberg, N. and Frischtak, C. (eds.), *International Technology Transfer: Concepts, Measures and Comparisons,* New York: Pergamon Press.

Wignaraja, G. (2007), 'Foreign Ownership, technological capabilities and clothing exports in Sri Lanka,' in *Journal of Asian Economics*, 19(1): 29-39.

Wilkinson, F. and You, J. (1995), 'Competition and Cooperation: Towards an Understanding of the Industrial District,' *Review of Political Economy*, 6: 259-78.

Yussof, I. and Ismail, R. (2002), 'Human Resource Competitiveness and Inflow of Foreign Direct Investment to the ASEAN Region,' in *Asia-Pacific Development Journal*, 9(1): 89-107.

Appendix 1: Two-Tailed T Test Results Comparing Foreign and Local Kenyan Firms

	Local	Std. Dev.	Foreign	Std. Dev.	Mean Difference	T-Values	Sig. (2-tailed)
Human Capital Development							
Metal engineering	0.168	0.230	0.334	0.242	-0.165	-1.945	0.060*
Textile and garment	0.167	0.176	0.353	0.335	-0.186	-1.644	0.115
Food and beverage	0.166	0.209	0.313	0.327	-0.147	-1.847	0.071*
All Firms	0.167	0.209	0.332	0.299	-0.165	-3.309	0.001***
Process Technology Capability							
Metal engineering	0.355	0.230	0.562	0.163	-0.207	-2.680	0.011**
Textile and garment	0.493	0.260	0493	0.277	-0.001	-0.005	0.996
Food and beverage	0.525	0.176	0.577	0.287	-0.052	-0.757	0.453
All Firms	0.46	0.222	0.545	0.249	0.085	-1.805	0.074*
Product Technology Capability							
Metal engineering	0.242	0.240	0.455	0.251	-0.212	-2.396	0.022**
Textile and garment	0.23	0.228	0.349	0.267	-0.119	-1.145	0.265
Food and beverage	0.219	0.196	0.336	0.215	-0.117	-1.826	0.075*
All Firms	0.229	0.215	0.376	0.242	-0.147	-3.197	0.002***
Market Performance							
Metal engineering	0.278	0.160	0.397	0.224	-0.120	-1.808	0.080*
Textile and garment	0.307	0.161	0.345	0.219	-0.038	-0.467	0.645
Food and beverage	0.352	0.148	0.456	0.183	-0.104	-2.055	0.046**
All Firms	0.318	0.156	0.402	0.207	-0.084	-2.346	0.021**

Note: *, **and *** - Significant at 1%, 5% and 10% levels respectively. Source: Computed from author's Survey.

Appendix 2: Correlation Matrix of All the Variables used in the Analysis

	HMCD	EXPTDMY	PRTC	PDTC	MKTP	BSCII	FDI	UNION	GOVN	SIZE	AGE	SYEMB
HMCD	1.000											
EXPTDMY	0.493	1.000										
PRTC	0.554	0.361	1.000									
PDTC	0.513	0.327	0.558	1.000								
MKTP	0.540	0.443	0.539	0.426	1.000							
BSCII	0.123	0.000	0.154	0.095	0.239	1.000						
FDI	0.416	0.330	0.279	0.180	0.165	-0.001	1.000					
UNION	-0.184	-0.049	-0.350	-0.131	-0.174	-0.289	-0.109	1.000				
GOVN	0.325	0.340	0.387	0.323	0.410	0.236	0.186	0.092	1.000			
SIZE	0.376	0.372	0.387	0.267	0.326	-0.067	0.501	-0.007	0.221	1.000		
AGE	0.062	0.019	-0.208	-0.044	-0.039	-0.023	-0.180	0.354	-0.069	-0.055	1.000	
SYEMB	0.277	0.190	0.348	0.326	0.297	0.494	0.115	-0.077	0.379	0.133	-0.067	1.000

Source: Computed from author's Survey.

10

Connecting the Dots between Knowledge, Openness, Networking, Partnerships and Innovation within Clusters:

The Case of Otigba Computer Village in Nigeria

Billy Adegbola Oluwale[1], *Oluseye Oladayo Jegede*[2], *Blessing Funke Ajao*[3] *&*
Emmanuel Makanjuola Ogunjeilua[4]

1 African Institute for Science Policy and Innovation, Obafemi Awolowo University, Ile-Ife, Nigeria. Email: adegbolaoluwale@gmail.com

2 Department of Information and Knowledge Management, College of Business and Economics, University of Johannesburg, South Africa. Email: oluseyej@uj.ac.za, oluseyejegede@gmail.com

3 Cyber Security Analyst, Willis College, 1200 St Laurent Blvd, Ottawa, ONK1K 3B8, Canada. Email: blessingfunkeajao@gmail.com

4 Department of Entrepreneurship, Joseph Ayo Babalola University, Ikeji Arakeji, Nigeria. Email: makanjuola19@gmail.com

1. Introduction

Innovation, Clustering and the Informal Economy

The term innovation has been variously defined and described in extant literature. Perhaps one of the oldest definitions was provided by Schumpeter (1934) who described innovation as the introduction of a new product, a new method of production, the opening of a new market, or the use of a new source of raw materials or new ways of organising industries. It includes the creation of novel or advanced products, processes, or services perceived as new and desirable by the market (Van de Ven, 1986; Woodside & Biemans, 2005). It requires the conversion of knowledge into new products, processes, and services as well as the successful diffusion of these inventions into the market (Kline & Rosenberg, 1986). Edquist (1997) states that innovations are new creations of economic significance while Li *et al.* (2008) views innovation from the indigenous perspective. They describe indigenous firm innovation as developing and introducing new products and processes indigenously. According to the Oslo Manual (OECD, 2005), the minimum requirement for an innovation is that the product, process, marketing method or organisational method must be *new (or significantly improved)* to the firm. Innovations constitute an indispensable component of the corporate strategies for several reasons such as to apply more productive manufacturing processes, to perform better in the market, to seek a positive reputation in customers' perception and, as a result, to gain sustainable competitive advantage (Gunday *et al.*, 2011).

Weaver *et al.* (2000) identified two basic types of innovation – Schumpeterian and Usherian. The Schumpeterian innovation is radical and trend – breaking. It refers to the achievement of a technological breakthrough and its first commercial introduction as an entirely new technological solution. Usherian innovation, on the other hand, is gradual and incremental. This latter thread of argument is supported by Adeoti (2002), which noted that innovation in a less developed country would refer not only to the narrow definition of the commercial application of an invention, but also includes the adaptation and improvement of existing innovations.

The Oslo Manual (OECD, 2005) identified four types of innovation (Innovation Typology) at the firm level. These are product innovation, process innovation, marketing innovation and organisational innovation. First, product innovation is the introduction of a good or service that is new or significantly improved with respect to its characteristics or intended uses. This includes significant improvements in technical specifications, components and materials, incorporated software, user-friendliness or other functional characteristics. Second, process innovation is the implementation of a new or significantly improved production or delivery method. This includes significant changes in techniques, equipment and/or software. It also includes new or significantly improved methods for the creation and provision of services. Third, marketing innovation is the implementation of a new marketing method involving significant changes in product design or packaging, product placement, product promotion or pricing. It is aimed at better addressing customer needs, opening new markets, or newly positioning a firm's product on the market, with the objective of increasing the firm's sales. Fourth, organisational innovation is the implementation of a new organisational method in the firm's business practices, workplace organisation or external relations. The distinguishing feature of an organisational innovation compared to other organisational changes in a firm is the implementation of an organisational method as the result of strategic decisions taken by management (with respect to business practices, workplace organisation or external relations) that has not been used before by the firm.

Traditional indicators of innovative activities such as R&D expenditures and patents often fail to capture the innovative performance of small firms adequately if at all they do. When small and medium-sized enterprises (SMEs) carry out their innovative activities, they often do so without specific financial and managerial resources and without formalised procedures (Santarelli & Sterlacchini, 1990). Thus, SMEs tend to undertake a significant amount of innovative activities in their design, production and sales departments though they may not have R&D departments. However, when an output indicator such as the number or the nature of the innovations introduced by firms of different sizes is used, it was found that small firms have introduced mainly incremental rather than major innovations (Santarelli & Sterlacchini, 1990). Innovation in the informal economy would include incremental innovations that are new to the firm or the country (De Beer, Fu & Wunsch-Vincent, 2013). In addition, Daniels (2010) revealed the adaptive innovative nature of the informal sector within the sub-Saharan African region. De Beer, Fu and Wunsch-Vincent (2013) suggest that there is more adaptation and imitation than the original invention in the informal economy.

Measurement of innovation has been of much concern to academics and researchers worldwide since the 1980s (Bloch, 2007). Much progress has been made in the Western world, especially with the development of the Oslo Manual. The first edition of the Oslo Manual, published in 1992, was a synthesis of the experiences from a broad group of innovation surveys in the late 1980s. It provided a standardized framework for collecting firm-level data on technological product and process (TPP) innovation in manufacturing industries (OECD, 1992). The second edition of 1997 filled the gap in the first to include innovation in service sectors. The third edition of 2005 broadened our understanding of innovation to include marketing and organizational innovations; a much expanded coverage of knowledge flows and the role of linkages in the innovation process (Bloch, 2007). Similarly, following the same trend of argument, the Bogota Manual was developed for the Latin American economies. However, innovations in the sub-Saharan African context, especially within the informal economy cannot be measured with conventional metrics such as R&D investment, patents and intellectual properties. It therefore behoves us to establish an applicable method or system of measurement for the African continent.

It has been established firmly in literature that innovation drives economies. There is an increasing awareness of this also among developing economies. Compared to developed nations, there is a lower level of science and technology (S&T) in these countries due to infrastructural deficiencies, lack of human/knowledge capital, instability, corruption and lack of political will among others. S&T activities are mainly funded by national governments and international donors while foreign companies prefer to import R&D from their parent companies. There is, thus, a lack of applied research, a deficit of trained engineers and scientists, and weak technological capabilities in these economies (De Beer, Fu and Wunsch-Vincent, 2013).

Brusco (1992) cited by Oyelaran-Oyeyinka (1997) defines a cluster as "an industrial district which is a set of companies, located in a relatively small geographical area, that the said companies work, either directly or indirectly, for the same end market, that their shared range of values and body of knowledge is so important that they define a cultural environment, and that they are linked to one another by very specific relations in a complex mix of competition and co-operation". Madsen *et al.* (2003), on the other hand, define industrial clusters as groups of firms on the same location composing a production system with spillovers that can be either vertical or horizontal. This has been corroborated by Rosenfeld's (2001) assertion that industrial or business clusters are based on the physical proximity of firms in one area or region. It has been observed that many communities that have developed certain strong informal networks share and diffuse knowledge and innovations with each other (De Beer, Fu and Wunsch-Vincent, 2013). Firms in the informal economies (IE) tend to operate in clusters or "agglomerations" (Livingstone, 1991). Clustering activities of firms lead to several advantages such as diffusion of information, rapid transfer of skills and knowledge, and sharing of facilities among others (ILO, 1992).

According to Oyelaran-Oyeyinka (1997), there is hardly any evidence that two clusters are sharing the same attributes, but Pyke, Becattini and Sengenberger (1990) observed some general organizing principles in clusters such as (i) the existence of strong networks of small firms sharing division of labour through subcontracting and specialization; (ii) clusters have geographic bounds but networking may exist far beyond territorial space; (iii) willingness to co-operate, which does not affect rivalry and healthy competition; (iv) widespread entrepreneurial dynamism (which can come as a response to relatively easy access to capital); (v) flexibility (which is associated with the highly skilled, specialized and trained workforce in contrast to the largely unskilled or semi-skilled workers of the mass market production lines); and (vi) trust and cultural affinity (which refers to trust and communality). There is cooperation between employees and employers rather than rigidity and antagonistic tendencies.

Technological learning is a common feature exhibited by industrial clusters. In his study of Nnewi clusters, Oyelaran-Oyeyinka (1997) observed that all the firms studied had acquired product capability to copy foreign designs. Apart from this, the firms had also acquired vital elements of process technology such as quality control, maintenance and industrial engineering. The general mechanism for technological learning was the external training of new staff in Taiwan or on-the-job. Akinbinu (2001) similarly observed that in the auto-mechanic clusters studied in Ibadan, the entrepreneurs made efforts to improve their skills through technological learning. It has been noted (Oyelaran-Oyeyinka, 2006) that learning-by-doing is an important component of non-formal learning in the African small firms which are rooted in crafts apprenticeship. Other scholars have similarly observed that learning and innovation in the informal economy are often based on apprenticeships where senior or master artisans train younger ones (Zeng, 2008; Kawooya, 2012). This is usually done out of generosity to help a dependent relative or friend who would otherwise depend on them. It is a symbiotic relationship whereby the apprentices who are eager to learn tend to provide cheap labour for the master craftsman. Once they master the art or particular skills, the senior or master artisan will subsequently assign them to specific tasks. The senior artisan's role is then limited to supervising them or dealing with complicated tasks that require new ways or ideas for dealing with certain problems (De Beer, Fu and Wunsch-Vincent, 2013).

There are some characteristics of innovation in the informal economy as observed by scholars. De Beer, Fu and Wunsch-Vincent (2013) revealed that large amounts of constraint-based innovations take place under conditions of survival, scarcity and constraints in the informal economy. Innovations are primarily demand-driven to satisfy the needs of less-affluent customers by focusing on and exploiting local resources and markets. Daniels (2010) identifies following characteristics of the Jua kali in Kenya: (i) small business size (less than 5 workers); (ii) low start-up capital and ease of entry; (iii) labour-intensive nature of work; (iv) absence of any protection by social contract or law; (v) skills transfer by informal apprenticeship; (vi) affordability by local consumers; (vii) unreliable power supply and insecure premises; (viii) limited funding; (ix) adaptability to market conditions; and (x) efficiency through coordination among businesses.Aubert (2005) also posits that innovation climates in developing countries are hampered by the weaknesses of key elements of knowledge-based economies such as levels of educational attainment, the business environment and the information infrastructure. In addition to all those general problems mentioned above, SMEs in less developed countries face further barriers, such as the lack of technological and policy infrastructure, the low degree of innovativeness, bad location and inappropriate firm size for the market (Demirbas, 2011).

Openness, Networking and Partnership

Open innovation can be described as an innovation paradigm shift from a closed to an open model (Chesbrough, 2003). Two types of open innovation have been described; inbound open innovation and outbound open innovation. The former is the practice of attracting discoveries outside the company instead of relying entirely on in-house R&D while the latter is the practice of looking for an external organization that can commercialize a discovery through bringing it to the market (Chesbrough & Crowther, 2006). In this model, firms are thus expected to purposively use inflows and outflows of knowledge to accelerate internal innovation, and to expand markets for external use of innovation, respectively (Chesbrough, 2006). It is generally agreed that sourcing of external knowledge for innovation is a critical process of a firm's inbound open innovation activities, where external knowledge flows into the organization (Chesbrough, Vanhaverbeke, & West, 2006; Dahlander & Gann, 2010; Brunswicker & Vanhaverbeke, 2015). Open innovation is no longer restricted to high tech industries alone; there are now several organizations outside the high-tech industries that have adopted the concept.The primary driver responsible for the adoption of this concept is the search for growth in revenues and new products (Chesbrough & Crowther, 2006).

Networking and innovativeness are two major characteristics of industrial clusters (Eraydin & Armatli-Koroglu, 2005). Networks fall into two principal categories: inter-organizational networks and inter-personal networks (O'Donnell, Gilmore, Cummins, & Carson, 2001). Eggers, Kraus and Covin (2014), in their study of manufacturing SMEs, found a positive link between networking and innovativeness. However, in a study by Giuliani and Bell (2005), it was reported that firms within the same cluster, all equally characterized by geographical proximity, displayed very different interaction patterns when it came to knowledge sharing. Some firms were observed to share ties within the same cluster while others had little or no ties with other firms (Balland, Boschma & Frenken, 2014). Thus, knowledge networks within clusters have been observed to be 'uneven and selective, not pervasive and collective' (Giuliani, 2007). This suggests that geographical co-location is neither enough nor necessary for knowledge to be transmitted between enterprises within a cluster (Balland, Boschma & Frenken, 2014). These different perspectives call for a further look into the subject matter.

Partnership can be defined as a cooperative relationship in which resources are shared and exchanged in the pursuit of mutual objectives (Das & Teng, 2000). It enables firms to access new and unique information that gives rise to new product development and innovation (Smith-Doerr & Powell, 2005). It also leads to the transfer of existing knowledge from one firm to another (Dyer & Nobeoka, 2000; Meyskens & Carsrud, 2013). It has been observed (Yamada & Yamashita, 2006) that partnership provides competitive advantages for entrepreneurial activities and engenders the amalgamation of other elements necessary for innovation. They posit that innovation emerges along with the formation of partnership and depends on the characteristics of the partnership. Partnership has become popular as many universities in the USA, Europe, and Japan have sought to proactively increase their industrial partnering activities. The eagerness to partner is due to the understanding that collaborations with industry can be symbiotic, with both partners benefitting (Kleyn, Kitney & Atun, 2007).

2. Methodology

The research was carried out by developing and administering survey instruments designed to measure different types of innovation in the Otigba Computer Village, Nigeria. Questionnaire were administered on two hundred (200) informal ICT microenterprises in the cluster, the main target being owners/employees of the microenterprises. The purposively-selected enterprises were those having an employee size of less than ten and offering ICT-related technical services. The results of the survey were used to carry out quantitative analyses germane to the objective of the study. The information gathered was supplemented with additional information from published sources such as reports and journals. Data collected were analyzed using descriptive statistics such as percentages, frequencies, means, bar charts and pie charts. The Standard Package for Social Scientists (SPSS 20.0) was used for the statistical analysis.

3. Results and Discussion

Nature of Openness in Otigba Cluster

Table 1 shows the nature of openness at the Otigba market cluster. Open innovation is a paradigm that assumes that firms can and should use external ideas as well as internal ideas, and internal and external pathways to market. As the firms look to advance their technology, majority of the enterprises in the cluster strongly agreed that while there was "competition within the computer village" (Mean = 4.64), "cooperation within the cluster" was fully embraced. This was in tandem with an earlier work by Pyke and Sengenberger (1992) which specified that cooperation, healthy competition and trust are some of the organising principles of a cluster.

Table 1: Nature of Open Innovation in the Cluster

	N	Min	Max	Mean
There is competition within the computer village	200	1	5	4.64
There is cooperation within the computer village	200	1	5	4.10
There is mutual trust within the computer village	200	1	5	3.43
Valid N (listwise)	200			

Scale
Strongly Agree = 5
Agree = 4
Undecided = 3
Disagree = 2
Strongly Disagree = 1

Organisational Learning

Most of the businesses asserted that they had knowledge development in their enterprises (see Figure 1). According to Burgers et al. (2008), technology development means firms having relevant knowledge regarding the products, technologies, and/or processes that pertains to their business. Figure 2 shows that majority of the firms upgraded their knowledge weekly. The essence of upgrading weekly was to keep abreast of the demand. They accumulate capabilities in the repairs of phones, laptops, etc., and these are products that come with a lot of technical changes as new products are introduced periodically by the manufacturers. Another way through which the firms develop their knowledge and capabilities is through trainings organized within the enterprise, as shown in Figure 3. This contrasted with Oyelaran-Oyeyinka (1997) that reports that external training was the general mechanism for technological learning.

Figure 1:Existence of In-house Training

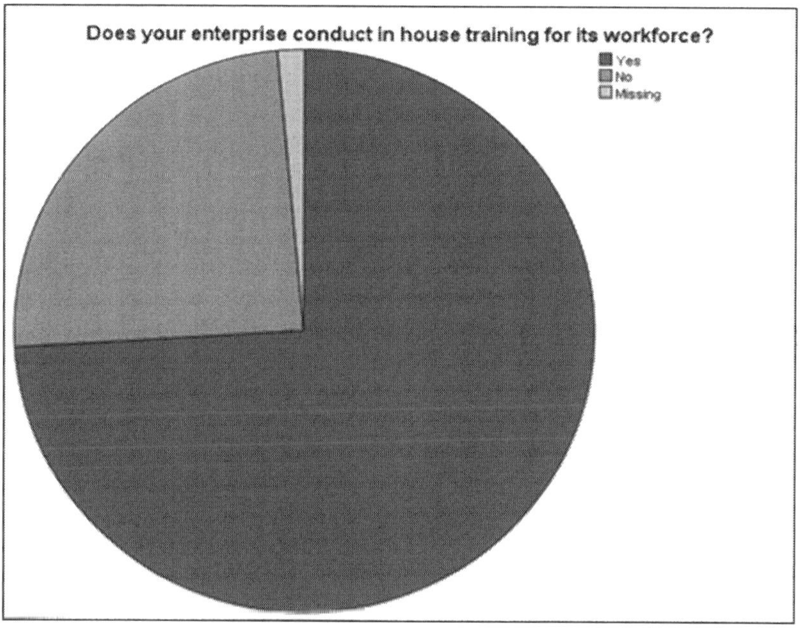

Figure 2: Rate of Knowledge Development in the Cluster

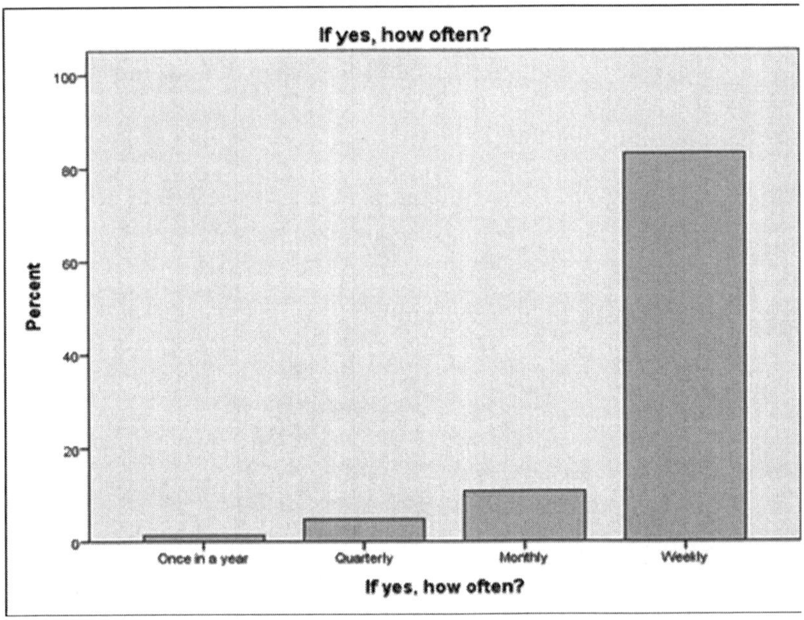

Figure 3: How the Firms in the Cluster Conduct Training

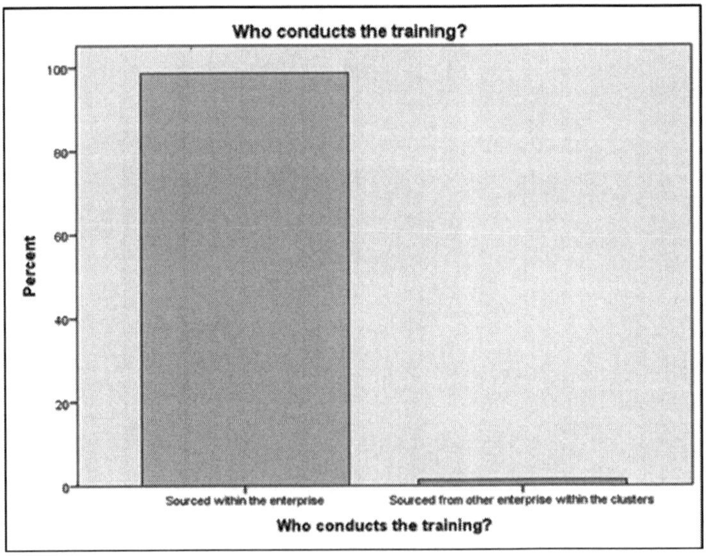

Table 2: Payment for Training

		Frequency	Percent	Valid Percent	Cumulative Percent
Valid	Trainings are paid for by the employer	146	73.0	97.3	97.3
	Others	4	2.0	2.7	100.0
	Total	150	75.0	100.0	
Missing	System	50	25.0		
Total		200	100.0		

Figure 4: Other Modes of Transferring Knowledge Aside Training

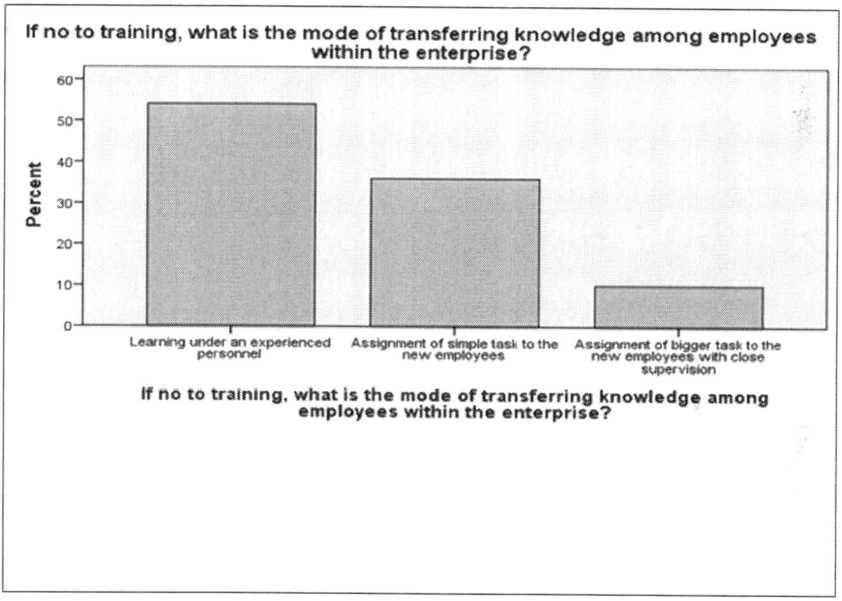

Knowledge Adoption

Close to about 80% of the enterprises claimed that they retained knowledge by sharing the knowledge with selected few employees in the enterprise and through refusal to share knowledge with competitors (Figure 5). Refusal to collaborate on specific knowledge-related issues, retaining key employees and sharing the knowledge with family members were other ways of retaining knowledge within the cluster (Figure 5). The likely implication of this is that when a firm retains its knowledge, it tends to be more competitive within the period during which the knowledge is still known to only the firm but as time goes on knowledge diffusion tend to reduce the competitive strength of such a firm. It is best if knowledge retention about a particular skill or technology is directly or indirectly converted to knowledge diffusion for monetary advantage for the firm in possession of the knowledge. Furthermore, Figure 6 shows the amount of technical knowledge that the firms were willing to volunteer to competitors.It appears that in the Otigba cluster, competitors are not seen as a market threat as it normally looks like in other places since there is a degree of knowledge sharing amongst the firms.

Figure 5: Means of Retaining Knowledge in the Enterprises

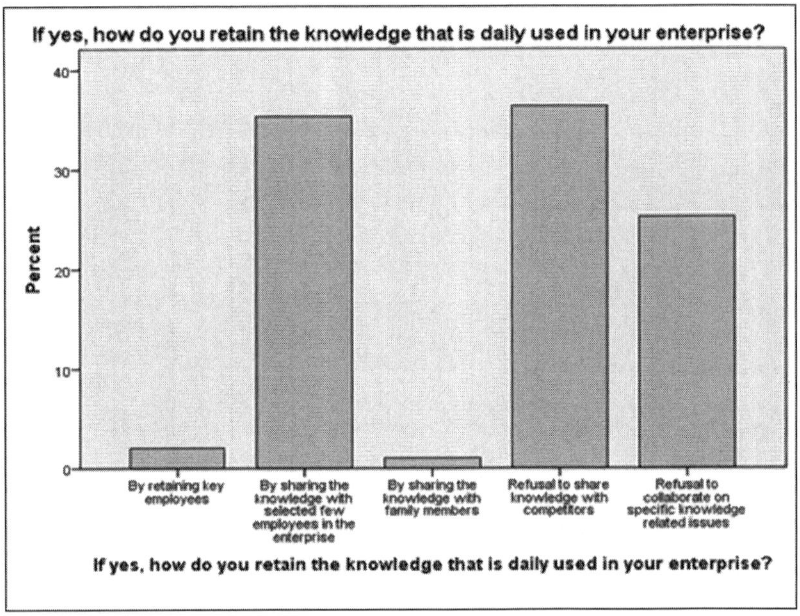

The implication of this is that it helps to open up the cluster for innovative ideas. There is, thus, a general willingness to volunteer only as much technical knowledge as to make them feel comfortable to compete with their rivals. From earlier studies, it is a known fact that though clusters co-operate and share information, this does not affect the rivalry and healthy competition among them (Oyelaran-Oyeyinka, 1997; Oluwale, Ilori & Oyebisi, 2013).

Figure 6: Knowledge Sharing with Competitors

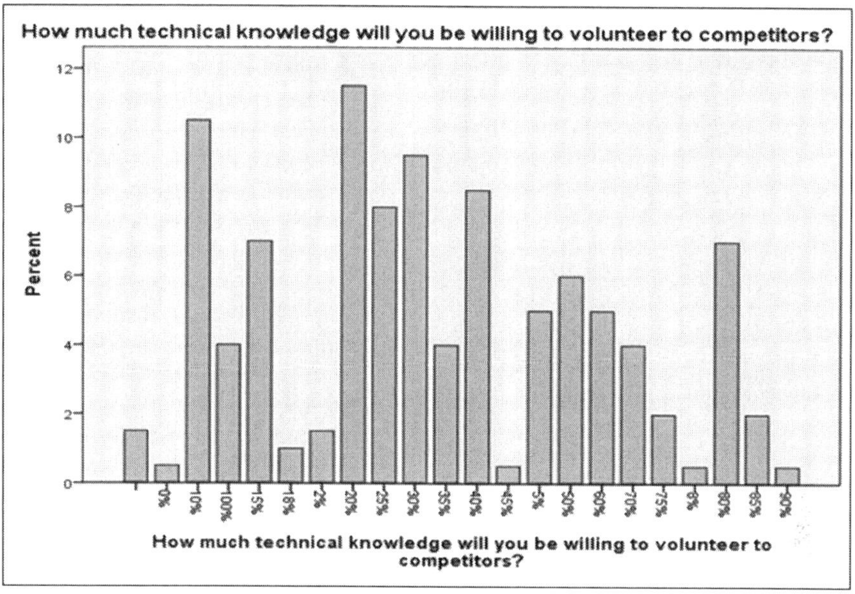

Prevalence and Nature of Innovations

Firms were mainly (about 70%) involved in process innovation followed by marketing innovation (about 30%) but their product innovation was low (Figure 7). According to the Oslo Manual (2005), process innovation includes new or significantly improved methods for the creation and provision of services. They can involve significant changes in the equipment and software used in services-oriented firms or in the procedures or techniques that are employed to deliver services. Thus, the firms might have improved on the techniques used to deliver their services over the years, but they might be low on product innovation because they are not the producers of the products *per se*.

Figure 7: Kinds of Innovations Firms were Involved In

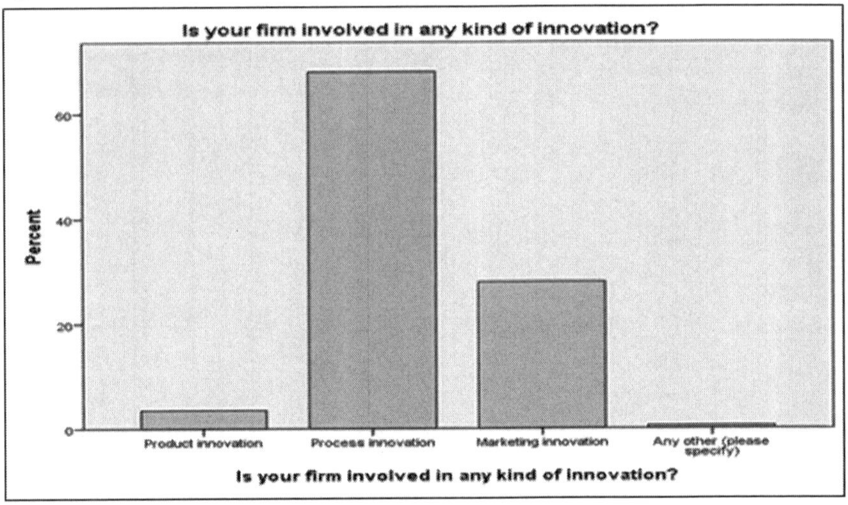

Four kinds of innovation were identified in the cluster. These were product, process, marketing and organisational innovations in line with the Oslo Manual (2005) categorisation. Organisational innovation was the most prevalent among the firms with 46.2% being adaptive and 53.8% being adoptive (Table 3). This is rather curious since the firms studied were essentially indigenous. Marketing innovation was more adaptive than adoptive, and this may not be unconnected with the fact that the firms are operating within their own national environment. However, product and process innovations were found to be mainly adoptive. The above may be due to the fact that the trade items were imported into the country and the firms had little or nothing to add to them.

Table 3: Kind of Innovation Carried Out by Firms

Innovation type	Nature of innovation	
	Adaptive (%)	Adoptive (%)
Product innovation	0.5	60.0
Process innovation	4.5	69.0
Marketing innovation	24.5	6.5
Organisational innovation	46.2	53.8

Source: Field survey (2016)

Role of Openness, Networking and Partnerships on Production Processes and Innovation within the Cluster

Openness plays a very significant role on the access to information, customers, new domestic market, tools/technology, suppliers of raw materials and inputs but plays only a slightly significant role on the finished products acquired beyond the shores of Nigeria with a mean of 2.40 (Table 4). The role of impact of networking on access to information, tools/technology, customers, suppliers of raw materials and inputs, and new domestic market was reported as very significant (Table 5) whereas its role on access to international market (finished products) was only slightly significant. This agrees with earlier studies in the literature on networking advantages.

Also, partnership plays a very significant role on access to customers, information, new domestic market, tools/technology, suppliers of raw materials and inputs, but has slight significance on finished products sourced from abroad with a mean of 2.35 (Table 6). Networking plays a very crucial role in clusters worldwide. In Otigba computer village, networking and openness impacted production processes to a large extent (mean 3.00) at the enterprise level while the impact of partnership on acquisition of technical knowledge within the enterprise was small (Table 7). Similarly, openness and partnership impacted on innovations carried out within the enterprise to a large extent but the extent of networking on innovations carried out was small with a mean of 2.25 (Table 8). However, on a general basis in extant literature, strong network is a common attribute among clusters (Pyke, Becattini & Sengenberger, 1990; Oyelaran-Oyeyinka, 1997; Oluwale, Ilori & Oyebisi, 2013).

Table 4: Role of Openness within the Cluster

	N	Min	Max	Mean	Std. Dev
Role of openness on access to information	200	3	3	3.00	.000
Role of openness on access to customers	200	1	3	2.99	.141
Role of openness on access to new domestic market	199	1	3	2.99	.142
Role of openness on access to tools/ technology	200	1	3	2.93	.285
Role of openness on access to suppliers of raw materials and inputs	200	1	3	2.92	.366
Role of openness on access to international market (finished products)	200	1	3	2.40	.756
Valid N (listwise)	1				

Scale
Very Significant = 3
Slightly = 2
Not Significant = 1

Table 5: Role of Networking within the Cluster

	N	Min.	Max.	Mean	Std. Dev
Role of networking on access to information	197	2	3	2.99	.101
Role of networking on access to tools/technology	198	1	3	2.93	.286
Role of networking on access to customers	198	1	3	2.96	.234
Role of networking on access to suppliers of raw materials and inputs	198	1	3	2.92	.354
Role of networking on access to international market (finished products)	198	1	3	2.39	.771
Role of networking on access to new domestic market	196	1	3	2.92	.384
Role of networking on access to others (please specify)	1	2	2	2.00	.
Valid N (listwise)	1				

Scale
Very Significant = 3
Slightly = 2
Not Significant = 1

Table 6: Role of Partnership within the Cluster

	N	Min	Max	Mean	Std. Dev.
Role of partnership on access to customers	186	1	3	2.98	.164
Role of partnership on access to information	186	2	3	2.98	.126
Role of partnership on access to new domestic market	183	2	3	2.97	.163
Role of partnership on access tools/ technology	186	1	3	2.90	.368
Role of partnership on access to suppliers of raw materials and input	185	1	3	2.90	.397
Role of partnership on access to international market (finished products)	185	1	3	2.35	.774
Role of partnership on access to others (please specify)	0				
Valid N (listwise)	0				

Scale
Very Significant = 3
Slightly = 2
Not Significant = 1

Table 7: Impact of Networking, Openness and Partnership on Production Processes and Acquisition of Technical Knowledge

	N	Min	Max	Mean	Std. Dev.
To what extent has networking impacted on your production processes within your enterprise?	2	3	3	3.00	.000
To what extent has openness impacted on your production processes within your enterprise?	2	3	3	3.00	.000
To what extent has partnership impacted on your acquisition of technical knowledge within your enterprise?	200	1	3	2.31	.733
Valid N (listwise)	2				

Scale
Large Extent = 3
Small Extent = 2
Not at all = 1

Table 8: Impact of openness, partnership and networking on innovations within the enterprise

	N	Min	Max	Mean	Std. Dev.
To what extent has openness impacted on innovations you carry out within your enterprise?	195	2	3	2.86	.346
To what extent has partnership impacted on your production processes within your enterprise?	3	2	3	2.67	.577
To what extent has networking impacted on innovations you carry out within your enterprise?	194	1	3	2.25	.713
Valid N (listwise)	3				

Scale
Large Extent = 3
Small Extent = 2
Not at all = 1

4. Conclusion and policy recommendations

Most of the enterprises surveyed at the Otigba ICT cluster started-off as micro enterprises, but some have crossed the margin to become small-scaled and medium-scaled enterprises. Knowledge sharing played a major role in the phenomenal transformation of enterprises within the cluster. The enterprises within the cluster were relatively innovative – with process innovation ranking the strongest. Openness, networking and partnership played a very significant role on access to information, customers, new domestic market, tools/technology, suppliers of raw materials and inputs among the enterprises. In extant literature, it is a known fact that clustering, with its various attributes, supports innovation and innovativeness. Majority of the respondent enterprises which exhibited these attributes were involved in one form of innovation or the other. Conclusively, knowledge sharing has become a source of collective advancement to enterprises within the cluster without limiting the growth of individual enterprises.

The success story of the Otigba computer village coupled with its phenomenal growth has shed more light on the practice of open collaboration and what could be achieved by enterprises through it. To replicate this, it is recommended that clustering be encouraged in other sectors of the informal economy especially at the enterprise level. As knowledge is shared willingly within the cluster and constitutes as one of its major strengths, enterprises can be encouraged to share information with greater fervour by rewarding originators of useful information. This can be done by cluster unions/associations creating awards for deserving members either annually or on a seasonal basis.

References

Adeoti, J. O. (2002), 'Building Technological Capability in the Less Developed Countries: the role of a national system of innovation', *Science and Public Policy*, 29(2): 95-104.

Akinbinu, A.F. (2001), *Informal Small Enterprises Clusters: A Case Study of Auto-Mechanic Villages in Ibadan*, Nigerian Institute of Social and Economic Research (NISER) Monograph Series No. 5.

Aubert, J.E., (2005), 'Promoting Innovation in Developing Countries: A Conceptual Framework', *World Bank Policy Research Working Paper 3554*, World Bank.

Balland, P.-A., Boschma, R., and Frenken, K. (2014), 'Proximity and Innovation: From Statics to Dynamics', *Regional Studies,* 49 (6): 907-920.

Becattini, G. (1990), 'The Marshallian industrial district as a socioeconomic notion', In: F. Pyke, G. Becattini and W. Sengenberger (Eds.), *Industrial Districts and Inter-Firm Co-operation in Italy*, Geneva: International Institute for Labour Studies.

Brunswicker, S. and Vanhaverbeke, W. (2015), 'Open Innovation in Small and Medium-Sized Enterprises (SMEs): External Knowledge Sourcing Strategies and Internal Organizational Facilitators', *Journal of Small Business Management*, 53: 1241–1263.

Chesbrough, H.W. (2003), *Open Innovation: The New Imperative for Creating and Profiting from Technology*, Boston: Harvard Business School Publishing Corporation.

Chesbrough, H.W. (2006), *Open Business Models: How to Thrive in the New Innovation Landscape*, Boston, MA: Harvard Business School Press.

Chesbrough, H. W. and Crowther, A., K. (2006), 'Beyond high tech: early adopters of open innovation in other industries', *R&D Management* 36 (3), 229-236.

Chesbrough, H. W., Vanhaverbeke, W. and West, J. (Eds.) (2006), *Open Innovation: Researching a New Paradigm*, Oxford: Oxford University Press.

Dahlander, L., and D. Gann (2010), "How Open Is Innovation?" *Research Policy* 39(6): 699–709.

Das, T. K., and Teng, B. (2000), 'A resource-based theory of strategic alliances', *Journal of Management,* 26(1): 31–61.

De Beer, J., Kun F. & Wunsch-Vincent, S. (2013), "The informal economy, innovation and intellectual property - Concepts, metrics and policy considerations," *WIPO Economic Research Working Papers 10,* World Intellectual Property Organization - Economics and Statistics Division.

Demirbas, D. (2011), 'Formal, Informal, Environment and Skill Barriers for Entrepreneurs: Microeconometric Evidence from 197 Turkish SMEs', *Journal of Business and Policy Research, 6* (No. 2. Special Issue): 13-35.

Dyer, J. H., & Nobeoka, K. (2000), 'Creating and managing a high-performance knowledge-sharing network: The Toyota case', *Strategic Management Journal*, 21(3): 345–367.

Edquist, Charles (Ed.) (1997), *Systems of Innovation-Technologies, Institutions and Organizations*, London: Pinter.

Eggers, F., Kraus, S., and Covin, J.G. (2014), 'Traveling into unexplored territory: Radical innovativeness and the role of networking, customers, and technologically turbulent environments', *Industrial Marketing Management, 43*(8): 1385-1393.

Eraydin, A. and Armatli-Koroglu, B. (2005), 'Innovation, networking and the new industrial clusters: the characteristics of networks and local innovation capabilities in the Turkish industrial clusters', *Entrepreneurship & Regional Development*, 17: 237–266.

Giuliani, E. (2007), 'The selective nature of knowledge networks in clusters: evidence from the wine industry', *Journal of Economic Geography* 7: 139–168.

Giuliani, E. and Bell, M. (2005), 'The micro-determinants of meso-level learning and innovation: evidence from a Chilean wine cluster', *Research Policy* 34: 47–68.

Gunday, G., Ulusoy, G., Kilic, K., Alpkan, L. (2011), 'Effects of Innovation Types on Firm Performance', *International Journal of Production Economics, 133:* 662-676.

ILO (1992), *Technological Capability in the Informal Sector - Metal manufacturing in developing countries*, Geneva: ILO.

Kawooya, D. (2012), 'Diffusion and Transfer of IP-Related Innovation and Technology Between Formal and Informal Sectors in Uganda', Open African Innovation Research and Training.

Kleyn, D., Kitney, R.and Atun, R.A. (2007), 'Partnership and Innovation in the Life Sciences', *International Journal of Innovation Management,* 11(2): 323–347.

Li, Y., Liu, Y., Duan, Y., and Li, M. (2008), 'Entrepreneurial orientation, strategic flexibilities and indigenous firm innovation in transitional China', *International Journal of Technology Management,* 41(1/2): 223 – 246.

Livingstone, I. (1991), 'A reassessment of Kenya's rural and urban informal sector', *World Development,* 19(6): 651-670.

Meyskens, M. and Carsrud, A.L. (2013), 'Nascent green-technology ventures: a study assessing the role of partnership diversity in firm success', *Small Business Economics,* 40: 739–759.

O'Donnell, A., Gilmore, A., Cummins, D., & Carson, D. (2001), 'The network construct in entrepreneurship research: A review and critique', *Management Decision*, 39(9): 749–760.

OECD (1992), *Proposed Guidelines for Collecting and Interpreting Technological Innovation Data — The Oslo Manual*, 1st edn., Paris: OECD.

OECD/Eurostat (2005), *Guidelines for Collecting and Interpreting Innovation Data — TheOslo Manual*, 3rd edn., Paris: OECD.

Oluwale, B.A., Ilori, M.O., and Oyebisi, T.O. (2013), 'Clustering and Innovation in the Auto-mechanic Industry in Nigeria', *African Journal of Science, Technology, Innovation and Development*, http://dx.doi.org/10.1080/20421338.2013.837284.

Oyelaran-Oyeyinka, B. (1997), *Nnewi: An Emergent Industrial Cluster in Nigeria,* Ibadan: Technopol.

Oyelaran-Oyeyinka, B. (2006), *Learning Hi-Tech and Knowledge in Local Systems: The Otigba Computer Hardware Cluster in Nigeria*, UNU Working Paper Series. #2006-007.

Oyelaran-Oyeyinka, B. & Lal, K. (2006), 'Learning new technologies by small and medium enterprises in developing countries', *Technovation*, 26(2): 220-231.

Pyke, F., Becattini, G., & Sengenberger, W. (1990), *Industrial districts and inter-firm co-operation in Italy,* Geneva: International Institute for Labour Studies.

Santarelli, E. and Sterlacchini, A. (1990), 'Innovation, formal vs. informal R&D, and firm size: Some evidence from Italian manufacturing firms', *Small Business Economics*, 2(3): 223-228.

Schumpeter, J. (1934), *The Theory of Economic Development,* New York: Oxford University Press.

Smith-Doerr, L., & Powell, W. W. (2005), "Networks in economic life", In: N. Smelser & R. Swedberg (Eds.), *The Handbook Of Economic Sociology,* New York: Russell Sage Foundation.

Van de Ven, A. H. (1986), 'Central problems in the management of innovation', *Management Science*, 32(5): 590–607.

Weaver, P., Jansen, L., van Grootveld, G., van Spiegel, E., and Vergragt, Ph. (2000), 'Sustainable Technology Development', Sheffield: Greenleaf, Publishers, chapter 3 – Technology and technological change. Available at:

https://ocw.tudelft.nl/wp-content/uploads/TDSI-R2-Sustainable_Technology_Development.pdf

Woodside, A. G., & Biemans, W. (2005), 'Managing relationships, networks, and complexity in innovation, diffusion, and adoption processes', *Journal of Business & Industrial Marketing*, 20(7): 335–338.

Yamada, J.and Yamashita, M. (2006), 'Entrepreneurs' Intentions and Partnership Towards Innovation: Evidence from the Japanese Film Industry', *Creativity and Innovation Management,* 15(3): 258-267.

Zeng D. Z. (2008), *Knowledge, Technology, and Cluster-based Growth in Africa.* A report submitted to WBI Development Studies, The World Bank, Washington D.C.

11

Perceived Important Attributes in Dissemination Rates of Maize Inventory Credit Innovations in Ghana

Mawuena Aggey[1], *Nana K.T. Ghartey*[2] *& Charles Kweku Brown*[3]

1. Introduction

Conceptual and analytical issues relating to dissemination phenomena remain contemporary. Woolgar (1995) argues for re-thinking the concept of "dissemination" and cognate terms including "transfer" and "uptake" while Dearing (2008) observes classical diffusion and innovation theory is evolving into a science of dissemination. West and Bogers (2010) call for greater theoretical precision and increased focus on the micro-foundations of relationships that enable innovation creation and commercialization.The need for higher precision in definition, application, and analysis of terms in innovation studies frequently arises.

1 Research Scientist, CSIR-Institute of Industrial Research, P. O. Box LG576, Legon, Ghana. Email: aggeym@yahoo.com

2 Senior Research Fellow in Social Economics, Centre for Development Studies, University of Cape Coast, Ghana. Email: kwamtech@yahoo.com

3 Professor in Development Studies, Centre for Development Studies, University of Cape Coast, Ghana.

Eveland (1979) reviewed the use of "adoption", the second oldest concept in innovation studies, observing that the term has come to be used with less precision than norms of social or policy analysis allow. Tornatzky and Klein (1982) reviewed innovation characteristics literature and performed a meta-analysis of research results describing the direct relationship (or first order correlation) of innovation attributes to adoption. They found only three from ten most referenced innovation attributes in literature showed consistency in their relationship to adoption. Compatibility and relative advantage were positively related to adoption ($p<0.05$) and complexity was negatively related to adoption at a near-acceptable level of statistical significance ($p=0.062$). Possible factors contributing to inconsistent relationships between innovation characteristics and empirical adoption rates include lack of specificity in the conceptualization of many innovation characteristics and poor research methodology. More research to verify and elaborate relationship of innovation attributes to adoption of innovations is recommended (Tornatzky and Klein, 1982).

Crossan and Apaydin (2010) observe that innovation is a broad term with multiple meanings drawing on theories from various disciplines, and studied using a wide range of research methodologies with its synthesis further complicated by multiple levels of analysis, dimensions, and inconsistent operationalization of primary constructs; which in turn lead to mixed empirical results. Their review demonstrates innovation research is fragmented, poorly grounded theoretically, and not fully tested in all areas, with even the latest innovation models failing to consistently capture across and within sector factors.Furthermore, our observations suggest that much empirical diffusion research appears to overlook the possible impact of the extent and interplay of diffusion and dissemination in specific spread phenomena investigated, probably generating further inconsistencies.As in many change initiating projects, innovation dissemination may jump start and enhance innovation diffusion; both phenomena occurring concurrently. Fully accounting for these possibilities in the research framework should lessen observed inconsistencies.

Grounded in the third premise of classical centralized diffusion theory and the dissemination communication model, our work concerns actively promoted diffusion as against passive diffusion which is spontaneous depending mainly on the potential adopter and market forces. Dissemination phenomena, being planned, targeted, directed and supported by change agents over time to serve the needs of resource-poor beneficiaries (Rogers, 2003) result in smoother diffusion patterns (Morrill et al., 1988). This work seeks to contribute to the effort of re-thinking the concept of "dissemination" by highlighting subtle differences between dissemination and diffusion phenomena in how innovation dissemination rates relate with innovation attributes perceived by adopters as important in their adoption and implementation activity. Noting that innovation adoption may result from both vertical and horizontal communication interactions between change agents and adopters, as well as among adopters, it is suggested that a determination of relative proportions (or relative intensity) of these vertical and horizontal communication interaction in dissemination phenomena will account for joint promotion agent and adopter perceptions influence on adoption rates, thereby improving theoretical precision and consistency in measured correlations.

The context of innovation dissemination discussed relates to a Maize Inventory Credit Programme (MICP) package of innovative practices in post-harvest maize processing, handling and marketing. It is actively promoted and disseminated by Technoserve Incorporated (TNS), a Non-Governmental Organization (NGO), to smallholder maize farmers in Ghana. Technoserve Incorporated Ghana programme started in 1971, operates in more than 145 rural communities, and assists farmers in rural financial intermediation and value addition to their produce. Professional staff provide business training to farmers, agro-processors and institutions supporting them, forging vital links between farmer-owned businesses, private sector buyers, financial institutions, and input credit firms. Aiming at poverty alleviation through rural enterprise and job creation, TNS promotes and disseminates the MICP as a tool to mitigate farmers' problems of harvest season maize glut and low prices, and their inability to take advantage of lean season high prices (Reed et al., 1994; Morris et al., 1999).

This paper presents the components of TNS's MICP, identifies innovation attributes important to adopters, and explores the correlation between adopter perceptions of various attributes and dissemination rates of respective innovative practices, specifically exploring the hypothesis that when innovations are spread through proactive aggressive technical assistance packages by change agents, dissemination rates may not necessarily correlate with adopter perceptions of innovation attributes as found in spontaneous innovation diffusion phenomena. Both vertical and horizontal communication mechanisms were involved in this spread phenomenon, but the dissemination mechanism was overriding as every potential adopter had had one-on-one interaction with a TNS project officer before adoption of promoted practices. The findings suggest that in pure innovation dissemination phenomena, adopter perceptions of innovation attributes may not clearly influence adoption rates, even when these attributes are perceived as important in the adoption decision. The study draws much on the methodology and findings of Fliegel and Kilvin (1966), a classic diffusion study (Tornatsky and Klein, 1982; Rogers, 2003; Dearing, 2008) involving individual farmer adopters, which explored similar concepts in a spontaneous diffusion context.While Fliegel and Kilvin (1966) sampled well-to-do dairy farmers in the United States of America, our study involved resource-poor maize farmers in Ghana, in a dissemination context.

2. Concepts Definition

An innovation is perceived to be new or significantly better than existing or standard knowledge and practice of an adopting entity (OECD/Eurostat, 2005; Rogers, 2003). It connotes a product idea comprising a physical entity, service, concept or idea, or any combination of these offering a bundle of attributes in features, functions, benefits and applications to satisfy the needs and desires of adopters (Aggey, 2002; Evans and Berman, 1990). Innovation attributes, particularly those perceived by adopters as important to their adoption decisions have been known to influence dissemination and diffusion phenomena (Fliegel and Kilvin, 1966; Tornatzky and Klein, 1982; Rogers, 1995); and adopter perceptions ofrelative advantage, compatibility, complexity, trialability and observability are generally accepted to predict adoption rates (Rogers, 2003; Dearing, 2007). However, depending on the spread phenomenon context and sample of respondents, empirical results may show inconsistencies.Adeboye (1995) assertion that high initial costs deter innovation diffusion among resource-poor respondents is consistent with Rousan (2007) observation that costly innovations will not receive goodwill of farmers, and Simtowe et al. (2010) conclusion that adoption is largely influenced by economic constraints. However, for a sample of well-to-do dairy farmers in Susquehanna county (Pennsylvania, United States of America), respondents were willing to adopt relatively expensive innovations to expand their farm and substitute capital for labour (Fliegel and Kivlin, 1966), and Rousan (2007) finds a positive correlation between cost and innovation adoption. Compatibility refers to the degree of similarity or congruity between an innovation and previous practice. Fliegel and Kivlin (1966) found that compatibility is not important in explaining the rate of adoption but Rousan (2007) concludes compatibility and use without external assistance correlates positively with diffusion rates while Wilkening and Johnson (1961) explain that radical departure from tradition will be less readily accepted than an idea, which is only a variation on familiar practice.

Innovation dissemination rate is relative speed at which use of an innovation is adopted among members of a social system in direct response to dissemination effort. It is the mean annual gradient or slope of the curve of cumulative proportion of adopters directly assisted to adopt and use an innovation over a period of expended dissemination effort, and adoption is the act and practice of applying or causing to apply a specific component of innovative practice in respondent's business operations (Aggey, 2002). The classic definition of "adoption" is "making full use of a new idea as the best course of action available" (Rogers, 2003, Eveland, 1979, and Rogers and Shoemaker, 1971), referring to the original, correct, starting point (Eveland, 1979).

Forster (1986) explains that the S-shaped innovation adoption curve shows a relationship between effort expended and results achieved, describing the beginnings of the S-curve as a period of learning, mistakes, much effort, and little progress. Progress accelerates with less and less effort in the steep section, with diminishing returns occurring towards the end. Arguing that mere passage of time does not lead to progress, but it is the application of effort which does, Forster (1986) cautions that plotting results against pure time would be erroneous. Forster's (1986) insight seems to relate mainly to the innovation dissemination model. However, product advocacy, promotion and advertisement in modern marketing techniques strongly suggest that even spontaneous diffusion of innovation may no longer proceed without the pushing effort of an agent. Adoption is a rational process (Phonkaew, 2001), and Eveland (1979) notes that analysts and change agents must define a set of predominant values, such as "ultimate interests of the client", to take precedence over more local values but not forgetting that others may not share the same whole hearted commitment, tending to act and make decisions based on their own values. However, opinion leaders and change agents may influence innovation decisions towards desirable directions (Rogers, 1983; Rogers, 1995), but the extent to which change agent activity will cloud adopter perceptions in specific innovation dissemination phenomena is a question to explore.

3. Data and Methodological Approach

When individual "adoption" is measured with the basis for concept definition as a definable and retrievable decision-act, either "hard data" or recall data may be used to produce reliable information about the concept (Eveland, 1979).Re-call information from adopter interviews, measured on Likert type scales, and change agent field reports (hard data) as well as observation of farmers barns were used to validate and enhance data robustness. Data was also collected on respondents' initial source of information about the change agent and the innovation package. A split sample interview procedure was developed to manage the respondents' burden of responding to a 390-item questionnaire schedule used in the survey. The core study methodology is adapted from of Fliegel and Kilvin (1966) with additional questionnaire items to measure proportion of adopters obtaining information from only promotion agents prior to adoption.

Study Area

Five adjacent districts in the northwestern corner of Ghana's agro-ecological transition zone formed the study area including Techiman, Nkoranza, Wenchi, and Kintampo in Brong Ahafo, and Ejura-Sekyedumase district in the Ashanti region.They lie at the heart of Ghana's mainmaize producing area in the forest-savannah transition zone comprising Ashanti, Brong Ahafo and Eastern regions collectively called the "maize triangle" (Onumah and Coulter, 2000). This area produces 59% of Ghana's maize output of 1,013,000 tonne pa (FAO, 2002). The groups studied lie in the same agro-ecological zone, served the same markets, and are exposed to the same national and promotion agency policies and regulations.

Identification of Innovations and Attributes

Preliminary in-depth interviews with 19 Technoserve Business Advisors (TBAs) identified innovations disseminated to 146 maize-groups country-wide. Up to 31practices disseminated by TNS to their clients were identified (Table 1) and 26 of these were studied while 15 attributes studied by Fliegel and Kivlin (1966) were adopted to compare findings (Table 2).

The central concept of TNS's MICP is 'using secured maize as collateral for commercial loans' (Londner et al., 1999; Aggey, 2002; Aggey et al., 2011). Participating farmers stored produce from harvest time when prices are low, to the lean season when prices peaked. Well processed and stored maize is used as collateral for bank loans which the farmer could access once the maize was accepted into storage. Farmers may sell produce or redeem it for consumption before the stipulated selling time, if necessary.At the point of sale, loan repayments and expenses for storage and processing were deducted from proceeds before farmer is paid.Aggey et al. (2011) notes that employing farm produce as collateral for bank loan was novel.

Business Advisors mobilized, trained, monitored and linked-up farmer-based community groups with requisite services and resources, and their effort over each calendar year is captured as "effort year". TBA field reports were reviewed and selected group executives interviewed to triangulate information on respondents' innovation adoption status and adoption year. The sample of 26 innovative practices was surveyed among a random sample of target beneficiaries who also identified innovation attributes they considered important in their adoption decisions.

Respondent Sampling, Instrumentation and Data Analysis

Only 46 TNS maize farmer groups were active in the study area during the survey. A purposive sample of 25 groups was selected and cross-clustered geographically (by districts) and chronologically (by first year of MICP adoption) ensuring all districts and adoption years were represented.Active group members were identified, stratified by sex and randomly sampled from a sampling population of 606 (234 females and 372 males) with a sample size of 234 respondents (90 females and 144 males) using tables from Krejcie and Morgan (1970).Questionnaires and interview schedules similar to those used in Fliegel and Kivlin's (1966) study were used.

Each respondent provided information on own adoption status before and after TNS intervention, adoption year and source of information for the innovations, and their perceptions of each innovative practice on 15 dimensions of attributes as defined in Table 2. Data on adoption status is distilled through a stage-wise process to arrive at frequency counts and cumulative percentages of adopter populations. These annual calculations of direct dissemination figures were cumulated against effort years expended by Technoserve Business Advisors (TBAs) in the study area. Average dissemination rates were calculated for each component innovative practice from the resulting figures (Aggey *et al.*, 2011). Correlation analysis was performed between dissemination rates and adopters' perceptions of these attributes using SPSS.

Table 1:Specific Components of TNS's Maize Inventory Credit Programme

Category of component		Specific Items
I.	Chemicals	Actellic 25E (Super actellic); Cymbush; Suombi cumbi.
II.	Equipment	Mechanical sheller and prime mover; Weighing scale; Spraying machine; Grinding mill and prime mover; Sieve for sifting chaff from maize.
III.	Skills	Hands-on skill/experience in chemical application; Group management and dynamics; Formal business management skills; Equipment operation and routine maintenance skills.
IV.	Financing	Inventory collateral.
V.	Organization	Idea of joining a group; Using group facility.
VI.	Process	Chemical treatment before storage; Chemical fumigation on re-infestation in warehouse; Adequate drying to 12-13% moisture content; Adequate cleaning.
VII.	Storage systems	Store maize as shelled grains; Store maize in jute sacks; Packing sacks of maize on wooden pallets; Spacing packed maize away from warehouse walls; Using a central warehouse; Adequate warehouse ventilation; Adequate stack access; Protection from rodents; Hemetic cocoon.
VIII.	Product	Selling maize as clean, dry, loose grains.
IX.	Packaging	Selling maize in standard weight (130-135 kg capacity jute sacks)
X	Sales	Seasonal sales of maize stock.

Source: Field survey, 2000.

Table 2:Operational Definitions of Innovation Attributes and Description of Perceived Advantage Rating when Innovation is better than Previous Practice

Innovation attribute	Operational definition	Attribute rating for advantageous innovation
Initial Cost (IC)	How much it costs to buy or start using the innovation	Low
Continuing Cost (CC)	How much it costs to run or keep using the innovation	Low
Rate of Cost Recovery (RCR)	How much it takes to get time, labour or money costs back on using the innovation	Low
Pay Off (PO)	How well does the innovation pay off in money terms	High
Social Approval (SA)	How much are people likely to look up to one because one uses the innovation	High
Saving Time (ST)	How much time does the innovation save in getting the job done	High
Saving Discomfort (SD)	How much does the innovation save hard, dirty, or sweaty work in getting the job done	High
Regularity of Reward (ROR)	How often does the innovation produce the desired results over repeated trials	High
Divisibility for Trial (DFT)	How easy is it to try out the innovation on small scale	High
Simplicity (S)	How easy is it to understand and use the innovation	High
Clarity of Results (COR)	How clearly do results of the innovation show up	High
Incompartibility (I)	How much different is the innovation from older ways of doing the job	Low
Association with Maize Business (AWB)	How much does the innovation has to do with doing maize business	High
Mechanical Attraction (MA)	How much interest would the innovation have for a person who likes to work with machines	High
Pervasiveness (P)	How much does using the innovation lead to the use of other innovations in maize business operations	Low

Source: Fliegel and Kivlin (1966) and Field survey, 2000.

3. Findings

Important Attributes in the Maize Business Innovation Adoption Decision

Respondents rated how important each of fifteen attributes studied was in their respective adoption decision of 26 innovative practices, scoring on a scale of 1 to 4 with 1 equivalent to "very low" and 4 being "very high" in importance. For each of 25 farmer groups surveyed only between zero and eight percent of respondents had heard of the package from other farmers and traders before change agents got to their community; suggesting very low spontaneous diffusion and very high dissemination effort.

Attributes that were relatively more important in their decision to adopt the MICP innovations are identified in Table 3, givingfigures for all respondents as well as respondents in a joint modal group category obtained when all the largest respondent sub-categories in age group, gender, education, and occupation are jointly selected statistically. This sample returned close to 25% (61) of all respondents.Conclusions drawn for this joint modal group relate only to this specific group of respondents, comprising males aged between 25 and 59 years, with some first cycle school education. They were mixed crop farmers with maize as major crop; they did not have any off-farm income generating activity and have participated in the MICP any time from 1992 to 1998. The figures in columns two and three of Table 3 are the number of practices out of 26 for which adopters rated the importance of the attributes (given in column one) in their adoption decision at more than the median mark (2.5) of the rating scale.The subsequent two columns identify the attributes for which exactly half the number of innovations is rated above this median mark.In these borderline cases, the number of practices for which the attributes are rated as important in the adoption decision equals number of practices for which they were not perceived important. The figures in the last column are for those attributes for which, clearly, more than half the innovations are rated more important than the median mark.These are the attributes clearly rated directly by adopters as important to their adoption decisions.

Table 3: Important Attributes in the Adoption of 26 Practices in TNS's MICP

Innovation attribute	Importance ratings above median mark (2.5)		Ratings above 2.5 with totals equal 13		Ratings above 2.5 with totals more than 13	
	All R	Joint modal R	All R	Joint modal R	All R	Joint modal R
Initial Cost (IC)	14	17	-	-	14	17
Continuing Cost (CC)	0	5	-	-	-	-
Rate of Cost Recovery (RCR)	13	17	13	-	-	17
Pay Off (PO)	15	16	-	-	15	16
Social Approval (SA)	5	11	-	-	-	-
Saving Time (ST)	14	13	-	13	14	-
Saving Discomfort (SD)	15	12	-	-	15	-
Regularity of Reward (ROR)	25	25	-	-	25	25
Divisibility for Trial (DFT)	0	1	-	-	-	-
Simplicity (S)	10	10	-	-	-	-
Clarity of Results (COR)	23	20	-	-	23	20
Incompatibility (I)	3	3	-		-	-
Association with Maize Business (AWB)	13	15	13	-	-	15
Mechanical Attraction (MA)	13	12	13	-	-	-
Pervasiveness (P)	8	11	-	-	-	-

Source: Field survey, 2000.'R' refers to respondents.

Table 3 shows that six (6) of the fifteen (15) attributes were relatively more important to each category of respondents. Initial cost, pay off, regularity of reward, and clarity of results were important to both groups.Saving time and discomfort were also important to all respondents, but rate of cost recovery and association with maize business were important for the joint modal group.The joint modal respondents also rated saving time as important to the adoption of exactly half the practices studied. In the case of all respondents, rate of cost recovery, association with maize business, and mechanical attraction were borderline cases.The attributes that were less important to this group of adopters are continuing cost, social approval, and divisibility for trial, complexity, incompatibility, mechanical attraction and pervasiveness.

This procedure only separates the attributes into three groups of less important, more important and borderline cases. It does not rank individual attributes within the groups as attributes are not compared directly to each other.Respondents only rated importance of each attribute to the adoption of a given MICP component, and cited initial cost, pay off, regularity of reward, clarity of results, saving time, saving discomfort, rate of cost recovery and association with maize business as important. Are these among perceived advantages of the MICP innovations?Do they strongly associate with dissemination rates of the maize business innovations? These issues are explored in the following sections.

Dissemination Rates in the Maize Business Innovation Package

Average dissemination rates of innovative practices identified are presented for eight groups of respondents including; all respondents, modal age group, females, males, modal education group, illiterates, modal occupation and a joint modal category (Table 4).

The fastest disseminating quartile of practices was in financing, sales and storage systems innovation categories."Using maize inventory as collateral" disseminated fastest at 14.2% adopters per effort year in the "all respondents" category. "Seasonal maize sales" followed at 14.1% but remained the fastest moving innovation among the female, illiterate, and joint modal groups of respondents. In third place was "storing maize in central warehouse". The remaining innovations in this quartile were: providing adequate access to packed maize in storage (13.9%), spacing packed maize from warehouse walls (13.8%), packing maize on pallets (13.7%) and storing shelled maize (12.2%). Among ten categories (Table 1) of innovative practices investigated, results suggest dissemination was swifter for financing, sales and storage systems categories of innovations. Although two key practices in the MICP spread fastest, the supporting practice of "inventory collateral" moved faster than the central idea of "seasonal sales", probably because the former was the real novelty among all the practices investigated (Table 4).

Frequency Distribution of MICP Innovations by Attribute Cost-Reward Perceptions

Respondents rated how they perceived 15 attributes studied in terms of costs and rewards after adopting each of the 26 maize business practices.Their scores are on the scale of 1 to 4, with1 = very low and 4 = very high. Table 5 presents the crude frequency distribution of responses for the adoption of "actellic for maize preservation".

Table 4: Dissemination Rates of Practices in the MICP

Practices in MICP	Dissemination rates of MICP practices in various respondent categories							
	All cases	Age	Gender		Education		Work	Joint mod-al
		25-59 yrs	Female	Male	None	First cycle	Farm-trade	
Actellic	7.87	7.86	7.99	7.77	7.93	7.85	7.96	7.62
Motorized sheller	3.14	1.44	3.42	2.68	2.88	3.13	2.84	3.35
Weighing scale	0.2	0.43	-0.08	0.37	-0.32	0.92	0.35	0.77
Spraying machine	6.88	7.00	7.17	6.62	6.78	6.97	6.97	6.81
Collateral	14.21	14.13	14.78	13.64	14.31	13.85	13.66	12.34
Group membership	5.89	5.97	6.02	5.82	5.63	6.04	5.99	6.05
Group facility	7.67	7.68	7.86	7.64	7.79	7.53	7.56	7.55
Shelled grain sales	0.39	0.39	0.39	0.39	0.39	0.39	0.39	0.39
Standard measure	1.41	1.7	1.52	1.34	0.52	1.79	1.48	1.62
Chemical preservation	4.25	4.22	4.37	4.21	4.35	4.15	4.24	4.04
Fumigation	10.62	13.07	11.96	9.85	10.07	11.17	9.84	9.38
Adequate drying	11.26	11.26	11.7	10.69	11.62	9.35	10.83	10.62
Adequate cleaning	11.86	11.82	12.6	11.66	12.46	11.41	11.33	10.19
Seasonal sales	14.1	14.04	14.99	11.39	14.69	13.82	13.59	12.53
Group management skills	3.35	3.31	1.99	4.16	2.9	3.53	3.0	4.95
Actellic application skills	4.65	4.56	4.61	4.86	4.04	4.99	5.14	5.52
Business management skills	2.74	2.55	1.14	3.65	1.63	2.94	2.1	4.05

Equipment operation and maintenance skills	4.05	4.09	3.24	4.72	3.65	4.3	4.63	3.62
Shelled grain storage	12.2	8.76	13.06	11.62	12.64	11.15	11.66	8.1
Grain storage in jute sacks	11.53	11.49	12.42	10.98	12.12	11.04	10.92	6.74
Wooden pallets	13.65	13.59	14.54	13.26	14.03	13.31	13.00	9.73
Space from walls	13.84	13.74	14.67	13.41	14.07	13.61	13.19	10.27
Central ware-house	14.08	14.03	14.87	13.47	14.59	13.73	13.53	10.40
Warehouse ventilation	0.71	0.70	0.81	0.64	0.77	0.93	0.70	0.00
Stored grain access	13.9	13.98	14.75	13.40	14.23	13.62	13.25	10.22
Protection from rodents	7.34	7.52	7.92	6.95	7.34	7.15	7.13	6.46

Source: Field survey, 2000

Table 5:Frequency Distribution of Cost-Reward Ratings of 15 Attributes to Adoption of "Actellic for Maize Preservation" (all respondents)

Innovation attribute	Cost-reward rating				Median score	Valid responses
	1	2	3	4		
Initial Cost (IC)	1	6	26	14	3.0	47
Continuing Cost (CC)	1	9	26	11	3.0	47
Rate of Cost Recovery (RCR)	1	9	24	14	3.0	47
Pay Off (PO)	0	6	19	22	3.0	48
Social Approval (SA)	1	10	25	11	3.0	48
Saving Time (ST)	2	10	22	14	3.0	48
Saving Discomfort (SD)	2	7	25	9	3.0	44
Regularity of Reward (ROR)	3	1	20	23	4.0	44
Divisibility for Trial (DFT)	0	9	17	18	3.0	44
Complexity (C)	0	6	27	13	3.0	46
Clarity of Results (COR)	0	5	15	26	4.0	46
Incompartibility (I)	1	8	22	15	3.0	46
Association with Maize Business (AWB)	1	3	15	28	4.0	46
Mechanical Attraction (MA)	1	10	30	6	3.0	47
Pervasiveness (P)	8	16	15	8	2.0	47

Source: Field survey, 2000.

The scores represent shared perception of respondents regarding how low or high these attributes appear to them, in terms of costs and rewards, after they (respondents) had adopted "actellic for maize preservation" as standard practice in their maize business. The median scores represent the average measure of cost or reward to an adopter of "actellic for maize preservation" as measured along the specified attribute dimensions. Regarding perceptions of cost or reward accruing from adoption, a given score (say, 2 or 4) can be interpreted diametrically depending on whether the attribute registers a cost or reward in the adopter's perception.For example, a high score of 3 for initial cost of adoption is viewed as a cost and hence de-motivates adoption of actellic for maize preservation. But a similar score of 3 for rate of cost recovery is a reward and motivates adoption. In the next section below, the attributes are sorted into perceived advantages (when a high score can motivate adoption) and disadvantages (when a high score can de-motivate adoption).

Up to 52 tables were generated for the two categories of respondents; modal and all respondents groups, for all 26 practices studied. A summary of the frequency distribution obtained for the "all respondents" category is in Table 6.It presents the frequency distribution of the 26 MICP components by the median score of their cost-reward perception for all respondents categories. For example, 14 out of the 26 innovations investigated has median score ranks of 3.0 on the cost-reward perception scale for the initial cost attribute.

Perceived Advantages of the Maize Business Innovations

Tables 2 and 7 are useful for identifying advantages perceived by adopters of the MICP innovations and exploration of whether these advantages are along dimensions of those attributes cited as important in respondents' adoption decisions.Table 2 states the operational definitions of the attributes, implicitly comparing previous practice with the innovation, and thus describing the measure of the respective attribute of new practice from the former when the attribute is a perceived advantage.

Table 6: Frequency Distribution of 26 MICP Components by Median Score of Attribute Cost-Reward Perception (all respondents)

Innovation attribute	Median score of cost-reward rating						
	1.0	1.5	2.0	2.5	3.0	3.5	4.0
Initial Cost (IC)	2	0	8	0	14	1	1
Continuing Cost (CC)	4	1	9	0	12	0	0
Rate of Cost Recovery (RCR)	1	0	7	0	15	1	2
Pay Off (PO)	1	0	8	0	12	0	5
Social Approval (SA)	1	0	3	0	21	0	1
Saving Time (ST)	2	0	12	0	8	0	4
Saving Discomfort (SD)	2	0	11	1	11	0	1
Regularity of Reward (ROR)	1	0	2	0	16	0	7
Divisibility for Trial (DFT)	3	0	12	0	11	0	0
Complexity (C)	1	0	0	1	14	2	8
Clarity of Results (COR)	1	0	1	0	20	1	3
Incompartibility (I)	1	0	6	1	17	0	1
Association with Maize Business (AWB)	1	0	3	0	12	0	10
Mechanical Attraction (MA)	9	0	6	1	8	0	2
Pervasiveness (P)	1	0	16	0	4	2	3

Source: Field survey, 2000.

For example, initial cost is a perceived advantage when it is lower for the innovation than for previous practice. It is not a perceived advantage when it is higher. Respondents' perceptions of the advantage (or benefit) gained or disadvantage (or cost) incurred from adopting the MICP innovations are summarized in Table 7.These perceptions are also in terms of the 15 attributes and are provided for the total sample as well as the joint modal group.As in Table 3, the figures are for the total number of innovations ranked above the median 2.5 (by respondents) for each attribute; then for attributes with total innovations ranked above the median 2.5 equal to 13; and finally for those for which this total is more than 13.

Between the two respondent categories, nine (9) of the attributes were jointly ranked above the median 2.5 for 16 to 24 innovations in the package studied (last two columns of Table 7). These attributes are initial cost, rate of cost recovery, payoff, social approval, regularity of reward, complexity, clarity of results, incompatibility, and association with maize business. The joint modal respondents, in addition to the above, ranked pervasiveness above 2.5 and saving time as a borderline case. Applying the definitions in Table 6 therefore, and exempting saving time, these 10 attributes were ranked high in the perception of respondents. By this procedure the attributes ranking low in the perception of respondents are continuing cost, saving discomfort, divisibility for trial and mechanical attraction (Table 7). Among the attributes ranked high, those that were perceived as advantages for the maize business innovations, for both respondent categories are; pay off, social approval, regularity of reward, simplicity, clarity of results, and association with maize business.The only low ranked attribute perceived as advantage is continuing cost. Similarly, the high ranked attributes that are perceived disadvantages (or cost) are initial cost, rate of cost recovery, incompatibility, and pervasiveness (this last one being only for the joint modal respondents).

The low ranked attributes that were perceived disadvantages are saving discomfort, divisibility for trial and mechanical attraction.Saving time ranks low and is a perceived disadvantage for the total sample but remains a borderline case for the joint modal group. From Section 3.3, four of the 8 attributes that were more important in respondents' adoption decision are perceived advantages.These are: payoff, regularity of reward, clarity of results and association with maize business.The remaining attributes, initial cost, saving discomfort, and rate of cost recovery were perceived disadvantages. Saving time is either perceived a disadvantage or a borderline case depending on which group of respondents is concerned. Among those attributes that were less important in the adoption decisions of respondents, lowered continuing cost, higher social approval, and increased simplicity of the adopted innovations are advantages perceived.Divisibility for trial, incompatibility (or compatibility), mechanical attraction and pervasiveness are perceived disadvantages.

Table 7: Cost-Reward Rating of Attributes of 26 MICP Innovations

Innovation attribute	Perception ratings above median mark (2.5)		Ratings above 2.5 with totals equal 13		Ratings above 2.5 with totals more than 13	
	All R	Joint modal R	All R	Joint modal R	All R	Joint modal R
Initial Cost (IC)*	16	18	-	-	16	18
Continuing Cost (CC)*	12	12	-	-	-	-
Rate of Cost Recovery (RCR)	18	18	-	-	18	18
Pay Off (PO)	17	18	-	-	17	18
Social Approval (SA)	22	20	-	-	22	20
Saving Time (ST)	12	13	-	13	-	-
Saving Discomfort (SD)*	12	12	-	-	-	-
Regularity of Reward (ROR)	23	23	-	-	23	23
Divisibility for Trial (DFT)*	11	12	-	-	-	-
Simplicity (S)	24	24	-	-	24	24
Clarity of Results (COR)	24	23	-	-	24	23
Incompatibility (I)	18	19	-	-	18	19
Association with Maize Business (AWB)	22	21	-	-	22	21
Mechanical Attraction (MA)*	10	12	-	-	-	-
Pervasiveness (P)	9	14	-	-	-	14

Source: Field survey, 2000. 'R' refers to respondents; *Attributes ranked low in perception by this procedure.

Dissemination Rates and Adopter Perceptions of Innovation Attributes

We examine the hypothesis that when innovations are spread through proactive and aggressive technical assistance packages by change agents then dissemination rates may not necessarily correlate with adopter perceptions.

Symbolically, the null hypothesis isHo: $r_{xy} = 0$
And the alternate hypothesis isHi: $r_{xy} \neq 0$
Where$r_{xy}$is the symbol of relationship between x and y; (r is also used to denote the Pearson's correlation coefficient)
Xis the independent variable;
Yis the dependent variable;
=is the equality symbol; and
$\neq$ is the inequality symbol.

The reasoning informing this hypothesis is that, while proactively disseminating these practices, TNS, where it is found necessary, also creates and maintains requisite resource and service links for sustaining the adoption of the package. In such a dissemination situation, the spread of the package and its continued use among the beneficiaries appear to depend more on the activities and capability of (TNS) and/or the provision of linkages, than how adopters perceive the attributes of the innovations.

Table 8: Dissemination Rates and Median Cost-Reward Perceptions of Innovation Attributes (all respondents)

Inno-vation	Median cost-reward scores of MICP innovation attribute rating by adopters													
	IC	CC	RCR	PO	SA	ST	SD	ROR	DFT	S	COR	I	AMB	MA	P
A	3	3	3	3	3	3	3	4	3	3	4	3	4	3	2
B	3	3	3	3	3	4	4	3	3	3	4	3	4	4	2
C	1	1	1	1	1	1	1	1	1	1	1	1	1	1	1
D	4	2	3	3	3	4	3	4	2	3	3.5	3	2	3	2
E	3	3	3.5	4	3	2	2	3	3	3	3	3	4	2	4
F	3	3	3	3	3	2	2	3	2	3	3	3	4	2	3.5
G	3.5	3	3	3	3	3	3	3	2	3	3	3	4	2.5	4
H	3	3	3	4	2	2	2	4	3	4	3	2	4	3	2
I	2	1.5	2	2	3	2	2	2	2	2.5	2	2.5	2	2	3
J	3	3	3	4	3	3	3	4	3	3	4	3	3	3	3
K	3	3	3	3	2	3	3	4	2	3	3	4	3	3	2
L	2	2	3	3	3	2	1	3	3	4	3	2	3	1	2
M	3	3	3	3	3	2	2.5	3	3	4	3	2	3	4	2
N	3	3	4	4	3	2	2	3	3	3.5	3	3	4	2	3.5
O	2	2	2	2	4	1	2	2	1	3	3	2	3	1	2
P	2	2	3	3	3	4	3	4	3	3	3	3	3	3	2
Q	2	2	2	2	3	2	2	3	2	3	3	3	2	1	2
R	2	2	3	2	3	4	3	4	2	4	3	3	3	3	2
S	3	3	4	4	3	2	2	3	3	4	3	2	4	3	3
T	3	2	3	3	3	3	2	3	3	4	3	3	3	2	3
U	3	2	2	2	3	3	3	3	2	3	3	3	4	2	2
V	1	1	2	2	3	3	3	3	2	4	3	3	3	1	2
W	3	2	3	3	3	2	2	3	2	4	3	3	4	1	4
X	2	1	2	2	3	2	3	3	1	3	3	2	3	1	2
Y	2	1	2	2	3	3	3	3	2	3.5	3	3	3	1	2
Z	3	3	3	3	2	2	2	3	2	3	3	3	3	1	2

Source: Field survey, 2000.

Note: Column abbreviations are as defined in earlier tables, i.e. IC= Initial Cost, CC=Continuing Cost etc.'**A**-Actellic maize preservation, **B**-Motorized sheller, **C**-Scale, **D**-Spray machine, **E**-Collateral, **F**-Group membership, **G**-Group facility, **H**-Shelled grain sales, **I**-Standard measure, **J**-Chemical preservation, **K**-Fumigation, **L**-Adequate drying, **M**-Adequate cleaning, N-Seasonal sales, **O**-Group management skills, **P**-Actellic applicationskills, **Q**-Business management skills, **R**-Equipment operation skills, **S**-Shelled grain storage, **T**-Jute sacks, **U**-Wooden pallet, V- Spacing from wall, **W**-Communal warehouse, **X**-Ventilation, **Y**-Access, **Z**-Protection against rodent'.

Table 8 presents a sample of the data used in testing this hypothesis. The practices investigated are listed in column 1. The attributes are in row 1. Excluding the last column, the array of numbers presented are respective median cost-reward ratings of attribute dimensions of adopted practices as given by innovation adopters. These numbers are derived from Column 6 of Table 5 and similar tables corresponding to all 26 adopted practices. The last column of Table 8 has dissemination rates of the 26 practices as stated in Table 4.

In analysing the findings, emphasis is on partial correlations because innovation attributes are probably perceived as part of a complex (Fliegel and Kivlin, 1966). Thus, when so many inter-correlations occur among the attributes as shown in Table 10, then the simple correlation coefficients become less reliable (Levin, 1990). Partial correlation coefficients, by definition account for the effect of other independent variables.The discussions are also limited to the all respondents categories, as this provides the larger picture of the study population. Finally, though the hypothesis is in a 2-tail format, interesting directional relationships suggested by the data are also discussed.

Table 9 summarizes the specific tests of research hypotheses for "all respondents" and "joint modal group respondents".In each case, the expected directions of the relationships are stated, as well as the simple and 14th order partial correlation coefficients that constitute the tests of hypotheses are reported. Inter-correlations among the various attributes for the "all respondents" group are in Table 10.

The Pearson coefficients in the tables are interpreted as follows.With a sample size N of 26, and 24 degrees of freedom for the zero-order figures, a coefficient of 0.381 is required for significance at the 0.05 level for the two-tail test to be established.When the degree of freedom is 10 for the 14th order figures, a coefficient of 0.576 is required for significance at the 0.05 level.The corresponding coefficients are 0.323 and 0.497 respectively for the one–tail test.The relationship is weak when the coefficient is less than 0.4; moderate for between 0.4 to 0.7; high for between 0.71 to 0.91; and very high when it is more than 0.91 (Sarantakos, 1992).

Table 9: Expected and Actual Relationships between Attribute Perceptions and Dissemination Rates of MICP Innovations

Attribute	Relationship with dissemination rates (Coefficients)				
	Expected direction	All respondents		Joint modal respondents	
		Simple correlation	Partial correlation	Simple correlation	Partial correlation
Initial Cost (IC)	_	+0.248	+0.390*	+0.240	-0.440
Continuing Cost (CC)	_	+0.129	-0.293	+0.299	+0.087
Rate of Cost Recovery (RCR)	_	+0.402*	-0.289	+0.383	+0.018
Pay Off (PO)	+	+0.302	-0.091	+0.428	+0.193
Social Approval (SA)	+	+0.233	-0.026	+0.246	+0.379
Saving Time (ST)	+	+0.081	-0.251	+0.029	-0.185
Saving Discomfort (SD)	+	-0.005	+0.125	+0.002	-0.163
Regularity of Reward (ROR)	+	+0.117	-0.271	+0.256	-0.224
Divisibility for Trial (DFT)	+	+0.347	+0.338*	+0.172	-0.020
Simplicity (S)	+	+0.506*	+0.260	+0.407	-0.090
Clarity of Results (COR)	+	+0.184	-0.137	+0.430	+0.210
Incompatibility (I)	_	+0.376*	+0.420*	+0.483*	+0.419*
Association with Maize Business (AWB)	+	+0.434*	+0.229	+0.479*	+0.311
Mechanical Attraction (MA)	+	-0.080	-0.102	-0.117	-0.072
Pervasiveness (P)	_	+0.385*	-0.246	+0.197	+0.079

Source: Field survey, 2000. *Coefficients considered appreciable in this study.

Table 10: Inter-correlations among 15 attributes of the MICP innovations (all respondents)

Attribute	IC	CC	RCR	PO	SA	ST	SD	ROR	DFT	S	COR	I	AMB	MA	P
Initial Cost (IC)	1.00	0.74	0.68	0.69	0.14	0.27	0.25	0.48	0.43	0.22	0.55	0.41	0.52	0.54	0.48
Continuing Cost (CC)		1.00	0.77	0.79	0.02	0.06	0.09	0.42	0.60	0.19	0.50	0.30	0.60	0.62	0.40
Rate of Cost Recovery (RCR)			1.00	0.90	0.22	0.24	0.07	0.56	0.73	0.54	0.52	0.35	0.64	0.52	0.55
Pay Off (PO)				1.00	0.11	0.10	0.02	0.53	0.77	0.43	0.53	0.25	0.62	0.49	0.55
Social Approval (SA)					1.00	0.18	0.29	0.15	0.13	0.44	0.52	0.23	0.35	0.04	0.35
Saving Time (ST)						1.00	0.79	0.68	0.32	0.21	0.55	0.62	0.13	0.54	-0.09
Saving Discomfort (SD)							1.00	0.54	0.08	0.10	0.21	0.55	0.27	0.52	-0.09
Regularity of Reward (ROR)								1.00	0.50	0.48	0.73	0.59	0.38	0.54	0.04
Divisibility for Trial (DFT)									1.00	0.49	0.50	0.23	0.48	0.59	0.28
Simplicity (S)										1.00	0.46	0.21	0.51	0.16	0.24
Clarity of Results (COR)											1.00	0.54	0.56	0.45	0.15
Incomparti-bility (I)												1.00	0.33	0.20	0.33
Association with Maize Business (AWB)													1.00	0.29	0.54
Mechanical Attraction (MA)														1.00	0.09
Pervasive-ness (P)															1.00

Source: Field survey, 2000

4. Discussion

The attributes are discussed in broad categories of costs, returns, efficiency, risk and uncertainty, communicability and effects, and congruence, to facilitate direct comparison with Fliegel and Kivlin's (1966) classical diffusion study conducted on spontaneous diffusion of farm related innovations adopted by small scale farmers in the United State of America.

Cost Attributes

High costs (initial, continuing or operating) are expected to deter fast innovation dissemination (Fliegel and Kivlin, 1966; Adeboye, 1995; Morris *et al.*, 1999; Rogers, 2003).For this sample of respondents, initial costs do not correlate significantly with dissemination rates.The simple correlation is low but positive, and the partial correlation is also positive, considerably higher but its absolute value (0.39) is lower than the 0.576 required for significance at the 0.05 level.Even, with a lower critical value (0.497) for the directional one tail test, the null hypothesis is still accepted implying even if the insignificant correlation is accepted there is no inverse relationship between initial costs and dissemination rates. These findings do not support the popular assertion that high initial costs deter innovation diffusion among resource-poor respondents (Adeboye, 1995).It is rather similar to the findings for a sample of well-to-do dairy farmers in Susquehanna county (Pennsylvania, United States of America), where respondents were willing to adopt relatively expensive innovations probably to expand their farm and substitute capital for labour (Fliegel and Kivlin, 1966). Rousan (2007) recently finds a positive correlation between cost and innovation adoption but concludes that costly innovations will not receive the goodwill of farmers in diffusion, and adoption is largely influenced by economic constraints (Simtowe *et al.*, 2010).

It appears respondents in the present study could adopt relatively expensive innovations because of interventions from TNS and other institutions. The more rapidly disseminating innovations include stockpiling maize for seasonal sales and collateral, a secured communal warehouse, constructing wooden pallets and drying maize adequately.These would require substantial cash outlay but TNS links up the Agricultural Development Bank and other financing institutions to provide inventory loan support. While some of the groups hired warehouses at high costs, many obtained idle cocoa sheds free-of-charge or at concessionary rentals. A Government of Ghana and donor supported Village Infrastructure Project (VIP) is also providing free community warehouses in the study area. It is therefore feasible for these resource poor adopters to adopt those expensive innovations relatively rapidly.

It should also be noted that for these respondents, correlations between initial cost and continuing cost (0.74), rate of cost recovery (0.68) as well as pay off (0.69) are direct and moderately strong (Table 10) suggesting respondents link high costs and longer periods of investment to high payoff. Initial costs were important in the adoption decision, probably because they were perceived as high compared to previous practice.It is thus a perceived disadvantage to respondents. However perceived importance and/or disadvantage of initial cost do not translate into any correlation (directional or otherwise) with dissemination rates.

The null hypothesis is upheld for continuing costs though the hypothesis that high continuing costs deter rapid dissemination receives partial support. Both the simple and partial coefficients are low, but the latter is in the expected negative direction, similar to Fliegel and Kivlin (1966).A reason for the different effects of the two costs could be that many operating costs, for example fees for shelling, drying, cleaning, replacing worn out sacks and membership dues are financed by respondents using current income. These may be relatively low, but their effect on cash holdings of respondents are direct as opposed to capital costs, and rent charges, which are financed by credit from financing institutions.

Continuing costs are not important in the adoption decision, but it is a perceived advantage. As with initial costs, these do not translate into a significant relationship with dissemination rates. The findings therefore show no relationship between dissemination rates and costs, whether or not the latter are perceived advantages or important in the adoption decision.

Rate of cost recovery is not important in the adoption decision, but it is a perceived disadvantage.This is probably because with the innovations farmers get cash payment of only 75 percent of the going price of grain at harvest. The remaining 25 percent of the price is received some three to six months later, after seasonal sales.These are delayed returns, compared to previous practice where farmers are paid full price at harvest time, though at lower cash returns. We conclude that when costs are perceived as affordable by adopters, both diffusion and dissemination phenomena may not be deterred by costs but beyond perceived affordability, diffusion rates developnegative correlation with costs while dissemination rates may remain unaffected whether cost attributes were important to the adoption decision or not..

The magnitude of financial reward (payoff) is important in the adoption decision and a perceived advantage.However, that dissemination rates associate with payoff is not supported by the findings. The partial coefficient is almost zero.Though the simple correlation is appreciable, and in the hypothesized positive direction, it is not significant for 'all respondents' group, and the same results are obtained for social approval.The results for payoff are contrary to those of Fliegel and Kivlin (1966) who find a positive correlation, but those for social approval are similar. Other diffusion works (Zhou et al., 2010; Adesina and Baidu-Forson, 1995, Adesina and Zinnah, 1993;

Rousan, 2007) support Fliegel and Kivlin on payoff but were silent on social approval.Fliegel and Kivlin (1966) suggest that social approval or disapproval could only become important in explaining diffusion when modern technology is a rarity in the social system under study. The present study lends some credence to this proposition. All the maize business innovations, except inventory collateral, and to some extent communal warehousing were already known in the study area. They were therefore not rare modern innovations.

Efficiency Attributes

The broad meaning of the term ''efficiency'' is adopted from Fliegel and Kivlin (1966) to include saving time and saving discomfort.The two attributes are conceptually similar and Tables 9 and 10 show they are strongly related in the two categories of respondents reviewed. Respondents' perceptions that innovations would save working time were hypothesized to be positively associated with dissemination rate.For both respondent categories the coefficients are low (Between 0.08 and 0.25), suggesting that potential timesaving is overshadowed by other attributes.Although the simple correlation coefficients are positive the partial correlations are reversed to the expected direction.This is consistent with the findings on the rate of return.The faster disseminating innovations in the MICP are not strong on timesaving.Essentially, it seems that they postpone cash returns from farmers' produce to a future date, though better returns are expected.

The conclusions are the same for saving of discomfort.Relief from odious or difficult tasks does not seem to be important in the context of other attributes perceived by respondents. Some other observations from the study further support this conclusion. For example, only three of the 26 innovations are equipment innovations likely to save time and labour directly. This also shows up in very low and reversed directed coefficients for perceptions of mechanical attraction. Finally, saving time and discomfort are not listed in the more important attributes in the adoption decision of all respondents though they become important in the joint modal class. That they are both perceived as disadvantages is also consistent with the observation about delayed returns and limited mechanization of operations that occur with this set of innovations. Fliegel and Kivlin (1966); Adesina and Baidu-Forson (1995); and Adesina and Zinnah (1993) find positive correlation between diffusion rates and these attributes.

Risk and Uncertainty

Regularity of reward and divisibility for trial are discussed under this heading.Concern that innovation will produce desired results over repeated trials relates to the concept of reliability in process equipment maintenance and in measurement.On the other hand, the possibility of trying out an innovation on small scale prior to full adoption minimizes unanticipated consequences (Fliegel and Kivlin, 1966).Regularity of reward was important in respondents' adoption decision and was also a perceived advantage.But it has no relationship with dissemination rates.Both the simple and partial coefficients were low (-0.27 to 0.27).On the other hand, divisibility for trial, which was important to adopters, was also a perceived disadvantage. In absolute terms this attribute too does not associate with dissemination rates.Both the simple and partial coefficients (0.347 and 0.338) are quite substantial, but statistically insignificant compared to the critical values of 0.381 and 0.576 respectively.Fliegel and Kivlin (1966) and Rousan (2007) find significant and moderate correlation between both of these risk attributes and diffusion rates.

Communicability of the Innovation and its Effects

These include simplicity, clarity of results, regularity of reward, and payoff. Simplicity refers to the problem of conveying an idea to a potential adopter, and the latter attributes all refer to results of adopting an innovation and demonstrating its effectiveness (Fliegel and Kivlin, 1966).Regularity of reward and payoff were discussed above. Simplicity correlates moderately with five other attributes in the scheme. These include rate of cost recovery (0.54), divisibility for trial (0.49), regularity of reward (0.48), social approval (0.44) and pay off (0.43) (Table 10).In a bivariate analysis where these other attributes are not accounted for, dissemination rates show moderately significant correlation with simplicity; that is 0.506 compared to the critical value of 0.381.However, when the other attributes are accounted for, the null hypothesis is supported. Although simplicity is a perceived advantage, it is not important in the adoption decision.These results are partially similar to those of Fliegel and Kivlin (1966) who found that complexity was not important in the adoption decision of their respondents. Clarity of results was important to adopters as well as being a perceived advantage, but it shows no association with dissemination rates. The coefficient of correlation is –0.137 to 0.184. The results of Fliegel and Kivlin (1966) are similar to these. The hypothesized positive relationship between clarity of results and rate of adoption was found in the simple correlation analysis but the relationship is weak, and the partial coefficient is both negative and low.As might be expected, the perceptions of this attribute positively relate to regularity of reward (0.73) and payoff (0.53).Explaining similar observations Fliegel and Kivlin (1966) suggest that demonstrated economic feasibility and certainty of results might have taken account of the relevant aspects of this type of attribute. Rousan (2007) finds strong positive correlation between diffusion rates and simplicity and communicability.

Congruence

Fliegel and Kivlin (1966) operationalize this idea in four attribute scales: compatibility, association with the major enterprise, mechanical attraction, and pervasiveness. An innovation is perceived in the context of other things and ideas - old and new -, and the perceived connections between the innovation and its context can affect adoption decisions. Compatibility refers to the degree of similarity or congruity between an innovation and previous practice.In this study the null hypothesis posit incompatibility and dissemination rate will not be significantly associated.This hypothesis is rejected at the level of simple correlation because the coefficient is significant statistically, indicating a moderate positive association. The relationship is still positive and appreciable, that is 0.42 compared with the critical value of 0.576 for a 2-tail test. This conclusion is contrary to that of Fliegel and Kivlin (1966) who found that compatibility is not an important factor in explaining the rate of adoption. Rousan (2007) concludes compatibility and use without external assistance correlates positively with diffusion rates. It is expected that radical departure from tradition will be less readily accepted than an idea, which is only a variation on familiar practice (Wilkening and Johnson, 1961). However, the positive correlation between incompatibility and dissemination rates suggests the opposite. One explanation is offered by an examination of the faster disseminating innovations. The top six are inventory collateral, seasonal sales, communal warehouse, adequate access, spacing and wooden pallet.With an average of 3.7%, the percentage of respondents already using these practices before TNS intervention ranged from 1.3 to 5.6%.The remaining 20 innovations averaged 40.1% of respondents previously practicing, ranging from 4.3 to 97.8%, showing that majority of adopters were previously practicing something perceived as different from the faster moving innovations. It can also be argued that the new must differ from the old or there will be no perceived advantage in accepting the new (Fliegel and Kivlin, 1966). Barnett (1953), pointing to compatibility as a necessary condition for assessing an innovation in the context of existing ideas, also suggests that incompatibility is a possible sufficient reason for accepting the new, especially where the old has come to have less value.

The degree to which an innovation contributes to farmer's main enterprise also suggests a connection between the new idea and the context into which it is introduced, and it can be assumed to have a positive value (Fliegel and Kivlin, 1966).The data shows that association with maize business is partially important in explaining rapid dissemination of innovations to this sample because the coefficients are in the assumed positive direction. When other attributes are taken into account, the partial correlation coefficient of 0.229 implies a positive but weak correlation. The simple correlation is also positive, moderately strong and significant with a coefficient of 0.434.Seven other attributes correlate moderately with association with maize business showing that when this attribute is perceived as a complex of others it becomes significant in explaining the rapid dissemination of maize business innovations.The "association with maize business" attribute has a perceived advantage, although it is not cited by respondents as important to their adoption decision. These findings are partially similar to those of Fliegel and Kivlin (1966) who found the partial correlation coefficient large and positive. This is not true for mechanical attraction. Neither the simple nor partial correlation coefficients are positive. Both values are close to zero, similar to those of Fliegel and Kivlin (1966). Pervasiveness is hypothesized to relate negatively to dissemination rates. The zero-order coefficient is significant (0.385), but in the opposite direction.The attribute also shows inter-correlation with five other attributes. The inverse relationship may be because faster moving innovations for this sample were most pervasive in that most of the other innovations were conditionality for obtaining the inventory loan assistance.When the other attributes are accounted for in the tenth-order coefficient the relationship becomes negative but very low and insignificant.It is concluded that pervasiveness would not deter rapid dissemination of maize innovations to the sample studied.

5. Conclusion

Of 15 attributes studied, 6 were cited as important in respondents' adoption decision including initial costs, pay off, regularity of reward, clarity of results, saving discomfort, and saving time. Seven attributes were perceived by respondents as advantages peculiar to the innovations disseminated including pay off, social approval, regularity of reward, simplicity, clarity of results, association with maize business, and continuing cost. Pay off, regularity of reward, and clarity of results was important as well as perceived advantages. Fiveattributes; rate of cost recovery, divisibility for trial, compatibility, pervasiveness and mechanical attraction were neither important in adoption decision, nor perceived as advantages in the innovative practices disseminated.

Dissemination rates did not associate with cost attributes, payoff, social approval, saving time and labour, regularity of reward, divisibility for trial and pervasiveness. Simplicity, and clarity of results both show very weak positive correlations with dissemination rates but correlations with compatibility and association with main enterprise were moderate and positive. Only in the case of 6 attributes, that is initial cost, continuing cost, simplicity, clarity of results, compatibility and association with main enterprise do correlation with dissemination rates show some similarities with correlations found for diffusion rates. No such similarities were observed in the remaining 9 attributes.

This work contributes to an effort at re-thinking the concept of "dissemination" by highlighting subtle differences between innovation dissemination and diffusion phenomena regarding how their rates relate with innovation attributes perceived by adopters as important in their adoption and implementation activities. Differences observed suggest influence of adopter perceptions of innovation attributes on innovation adoption phenomena may not be entirely the same for dissemination and diffusion phenomena. When costs are perceived as affordable by adopters, both diffusion and dissemination phenomena may not be deterred by costs, but beyond perceived affordability, diffusion rates develop negative correlation with costs while dissemination rates may remain unaffected whether or not cost attributes were important to adoption decision.

How much promotion agent effort obfuscates adopter judgment of inno vation attributes in dissemination phenomena may be clarified by estimating a ratio between vertical and horizontal communication in a dissemination process thereby obtaining a thresh-hold to explain differences between the rates of diffusion and dissemination of the same innovation within the same social system with implications for over adoption, adoption discontinuance or rejection after promotion agent withdrawal.

References

Adeboye T. (1995), 'Diffusion of pre-commercial inventions from government funded research institutions in Nigeria', in Ogbu, O.M., Oyeyinka, B.O.and Mlawa, H.M. (eds.), *Technology Policy and Practice in Africa,* Ottawa: International Development Research Centre.

Adesina, A. A. and Baidu-Forson, J. (1995), 'Farmers' perceptions and adoption of new agricultural technology: evidence from analysis in Burkina Fasso and Guinea, West Africa', in *Agricultural Economics*, 13: 1-9.

Adesina, A. A. and Zinnah, M. M. (1993), 'Technology characteristics, farmers' perceptions and adoption decisions: a tobit model application in sierra leone', in *Agricultural Economics*, 9: 297-311.

Aggey, M. (2002), 'Innovation dissemination rates, linkages and perceptions: the case of technoserve projects under the Techiman Zonal Office', *Unpublished M. Phil Thesis*, Centre of Development Studies of the Faculty of Social Sciences, University of Cape Coast, Cape Coast, Ghana.

Aggey, M., Ghartey, N. K. T. and Brown, C. K. (2011), 'Component dissemination rates of small holder maizebusiness innovation package (MBIP) in Ghana', in *African Journal of Science, Technology, Innovation and Development*, 3(1): 84-101.

Barnett, H. G. (1953), *Innovation*, New York: McGraw-Hill.

Crossan, M. M. and Apaydin, M. (2010), 'A multi-dimensional framework of organizational innovation: a systematic review of the literature', in *Journal of Management Studies*, 47(6): 1154-1191.

Dearing, J.W. (2007), 'Measurement of innovation attributes,' in *Occasional Paper*, Center for Health Dissemination and Implementation Research.

Dearing, J.W.(2008), 'Evolution of diffusion and dissemination theory', in *Journal of Public Health Management Practice*, 14(2): 99-108.

Evans, J.R. and Berman, B. (1990), *Marketing*, 4th edition, New York: Macmillan.

Eveland, J.D.(1979), 'Issues in using the concept of "adoption of innovations"', in *Journal of Technology Transfer*, 4 (1): 1-13.

FAO (2002), 'Ghana Special Report', FAO/WFP crop and food supply assessment mission to Northern Ghana, FAO Corporate Document Repository.

Fliegel, F. C. and Kilvin, J. E. (1966), 'Attributes of Innovations as Factors in Diffusion', in *American Journal of Sociology*, 72(3): 235-248

Forster, R. N. (1986), *Innovation: the attacker's advantage*, New York: Summit Books.

Krejcie, R. V. and Morgan, D. W. (1970), 'Determining sample size for research activities', in *Education and Psychological Measurement*, 30: 607-610.

Londner, S.I, Hicks, F., Kwadzo, G. T-M., and Panlibuton, H. (1999), 'Financing rural growth: farm inventory credit in Ghana', *Findings Paper*, TechnoServe, Inc. 1999.

Levin, R. I., (1990), *Statistics for management*, 4th edition, Singapore: Prentice Hall.

Morrill, R., Gaile, G. L. and Thrall, G. I. (1988), *Spatial Diffusion*, Scientific GeographySeries, Vol. 10, SAGE, Beverly Hills, International Study, Cambridge University Press, London.

Morris, M.L., Tripp, R., and Dankyi, A. A. (1999), 'Adoption and impacts of improved maize production technology: a case study of the Ghana grains development project', in *Economics Programme Paper*, 99-01.

OECD/Eurostat (2005), 'Oslo manual: the measurement of scientific and technological activities. guidelines for interpreting innovation data', 3rd edition, Paris: OECD and Eurostat.

Onumah, G. and Coulter, J. (2000), 'A Review of the Maize Commodity System in Ghana', *Discussion Paper*, Natural Resources Institute, Kent.

Phonkaew, S. (2001), 'Propensity for innovation adoption: integration of structural contingency and resource dependence perspectives', in *ABAC Journal,* 21(1): 1-29.

Reed, L., Owusu-Ansah, M., Chinbua, A., Boateng, M. and Panlibuton, H. (1994), *The role of NGOs in rural financial intermediation in Ghana*, Accra: TNS.

Rogers, E.M., (1983), *Diffusion of innovation*, New York: The Free Press.

Rogers, E.M. (1995), *Diffusion of innovation*, 4th edition, New York: The Free Press.

Rogers, E.M. (2003), *Diffusion of innovation*, 5th edition, New York: The Free Press.

Rogers, E. M. and Shoemaker, F.F. (1971), *Communication of innovations: a cross-cultural approach*, New York: The Free Press.

Rousan, L. M. (2007), 'Factors influencing adoption of improved farm practices among women farmers in Northern Jordan', in *American-Eurasian Journal of Agricultural and Environmental Science*, 2(3): 220-226.

Sarantakos, P., (1993), *Social research methods*, New York: Prentice Hall.

Schon, D. (1971), *Beyond the stable state*, London: Temple Smith.

Simtowe, F., Asfaw, S., Diagne, A. and Shiferaw, B. (2010), 'Determinants of agriculturaltechnology adoption: the case of improved groundnut varieties in Malawi', *PaperPresented at the Joint 3rd African Association of Agricultural Economists (AAAE) and 48th Agricultural Economists Association of South Africa (AEASA) Conference*, Cape Town, South Africa.

Tornatzky, L. G. and Klein K. J. (1982), 'Innovation Characteristics and Innovation Adoption-Implementation: A Meta-Analysis of Findings', in *IEEE Transactions on Engineering Management*, EM-29, No. 1.

West, J. and Bogers, M. (2010), 'Contrasting innovation creation and commercialization within open, user and cumulative innovation', *Paper Presented at the Academy of Management,* Montreal, Canada.

Wilkening, E. A. and Johnson, D. E. (1961), 'Goals in Farm decision making as related to practice adoption', in *Wisconsin Agricultural Experiment Station Research Bulletin,* 225.

Woolgar, S., (1995), 'Rethinking the Dissemination of Science and Technology', *Unpublished Paper*, Centre for Research into Innovation Culture and Technology (CRICT), Brunel University, Uxbridge, UK.

Zhou, Y., Yang, H. and Mosler, H-J (2010), 'Factors affecting farmers' decision on fertilizer use: a case study for the Chaobai Watershed in Northern China', in *Consilience: The Journal of Sustainable Development,* 4(1): 80-102.

Acknowledgements

The authors are grateful to Technoserve Inc. Ghana for the support and permission to publish the findings of this study.

12

Design Science and Living Lab Research for Innovation and Development in South Africa

Adele Botha[1], *Marlien Herselman*[2], *Ronel Smith*[3] *& Hendri Coetzee*[4]

1. Introduction

The combination of using design science research within a Living Lab context is often applied in European countries (Wolfert *et al.*, 2010; Holst *et al.*, 2010). However, this is not the case from a South African perspective as the focus on Living Labs in South Africa is usually only to show the involvement of users in the innovation life cycle without applying design science processes to support product development. The purpose of this paper is to address the following research question:

1 Meraka Institute, CSIR, PO Box 395, Pretoria, South Africa & North West Living Lab, Potchefstroom, South Africa, Email: abotha@csir.co.za.

2 Meraka Institute, CSIR, PO Box 395, Pretoria, South Africa & North West Living Lab, Potchefstroom, South Africa, Email: mherselman@csir.co.za.

3 Meraka Institute, CSIR, PO Box 395, Pretoria, South Africa & North West Living Lab, Potchefstroom, South Africa, Email: rsmith2@csir.co.za.

4 Meraka Institute, CSIR, PO Box 395, Pretoria, South Africa & North West Living Lab, Potchefstroom, South Africa, Email: hendri@researchlogisitcs.co.za

How can Design Science Research Support the Deployment of a Solar Panel Digital Doorway in the North West Living Lab in South Africa?

This is answered by juxtaposing design science research with Living Lab research in order to understand the different aspects of how these methodologies can support each other in the development and deployment of an artifact like a digital doorway where open innovation is a key feature. The application of design science will then be provided as an example of how it was applied in the physical design and functionality of the solar panel digital doorway in the North West Living Lab in South Africa. The methodology applied will be design science research to illustrate how the solar panel digital doorway was designed and implemented in this Living Lab context. Data collection and analysis took place using multiple sources: participation in workshops (brainstorming and work meetings); in-depth interviews; participant observation; and document analysis. Participants involved the technical team, designer team, users from the community, community leaders and suppliers. Detailed meeting notes were taken, and interviews and key meetings were recorded. Data and models were validated with subject matter experts (designers and users).

2. Background to design science research

Design science research has been practised in Computer Science, Software Engineering and Information Systems (IS) for over 25 years now (Iivari, 2007). A series of papers, including Nunamaker *et al.*(1991); Walls *et al.*(1992); March and Smith (1995) and Hevner *et al.* (2004), and recently published design science papers such as Lee*et et al.* (2008); Kolfschoten and de Vreede (2009); Choi*et al.* (2010) and Geerts (2011), have all discussed the importance of design science research in IS. The design science research (DSR) paradigm has been actively discussed in recent years and is highly relevant to IS because it directly addresses two of the key issues of the discipline: the role of the IT artifact in IS research (Weber, 1987; Orlikowski and Iacono, 2001; Banbasat and Zmud, 2003) and the priority of relevance in the application domain (Hirscheim and Klein, 2003).Wang and Wang (2010) has also indicated the close connection of design science research in IT innovation. Design science research focuses on creation and the purpose of design is "to change existing situations into preferred ones" (Simon, 1996). Design science addresses 'wicked problems' in IS (Rittel and Webber, 1984) and is fundamentally a problem-solving paradigm. Wicked problems as explained by Hevner and Chatterjee, (2010), relate to the ill-defined environmental contexts, creativity and teamwork to produce effective solutions.

Design science research creates artifacts which is something created by humans usually for a practical purpose and March and Smith (1995) differentiate among four different types of artifacts: concepts, models, methods and instantiations. Two important characteristics of design science artifacts are relevance and novelty (Geerts, 2011). First, an artifact must solve an important problem: i.e., being relevant. Second, to differentiate design science research from routine design, Hevner *et al.* (2004) suggest that design science research should address either an unsolved problem in a unique and innovative way or a solved problem in a more effective or efficient way.

Design science research contribution requires the following processes: 1) Preliminary study/analysis of practical problems and needs, 2) development of solutions/prototype phase, 3) evaluation and testing and 4) assessment or reflection (Reeves, 2006; March and Storey, 2008; Wang and Wang, 2010).

Hevner *et al.*, (2004) were the first to provide an Information systems framework to show where design science research fits. This framework was later improved by Pirenen, (2009) as well as Wang and Wang (2010). Figure 1 is adapted from Hevner *et al.*, (2004) and Pirenen, (2009) and indicates the relevance and rigour of design science research in Information systems and is also used as the theoretical framework for this paper.

Figure 1: Information System Framework

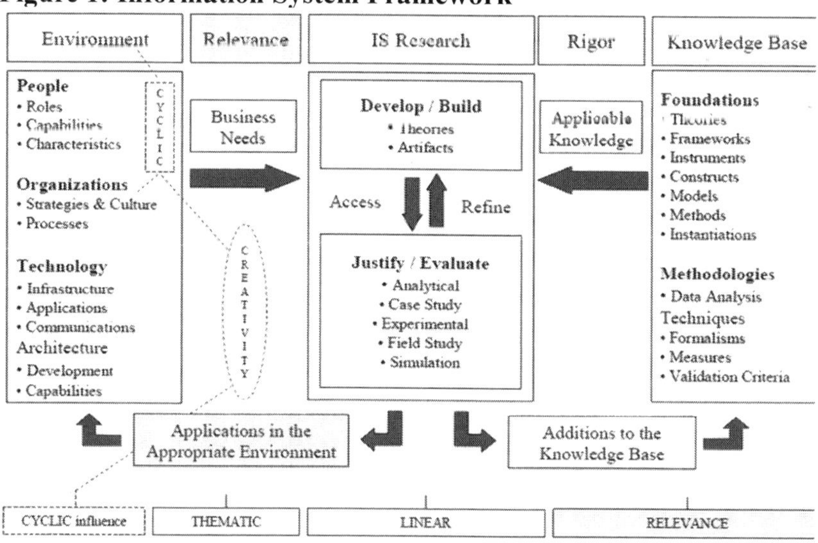

Source: Adapted from Hevner et al. (2004) & Pirenen (2009)

Figure 1 adapts the IS research framework found in Hevner *et al*., (2004) by overlaying focus on three inherent research cycles: relevance, rigour and design with creativity and how each of these contributes to the knowledge base of foundations and methodologies. In this framework people, organization and technology are three components of the environment of design research. Business needs are the drive force for design research so that design research can be relevant. Design research must add knowledge to the knowledge base so that it can be rigorous. Hevner *et al*. (2004) also proposed seven guidelines for design research: design as an artifact, problem relevance, design evaluation, research contributions, research rigour, design as a search process and communication of research (Wang and Wang, 2010).

3. Background to Living Labs (LL)

Living Labs on the other hand is a newer approach, only developed in 1990 (Lepik *et al*., 2010) and is referred to by Holst *et al*. (2010) supported by Eriksson *et al*. (2005) as a system, an arena, environment and/or a systemic innovation approach. Based on their experience they argue that a Living Lab is both a milieu (environment, arena) and an approach (methodology, innovation approach). It is a concept which refers to a research and development methodology where innovations such as services, products and application enhancements are created and validated in collaborative, multi-contextual empirical real-world settings (Geerts, 2011). Also, it is seen as a new character in the open innovation chain (Lepik *et al*., 2010).

Living Labs focus on open innovation which is a vital element of the knowledge-based economy. This term is coined by Chesbrough (2003) to characterize the fundamental shift from open towards external innovation. An "open" approach to innovation leverages internal and external sources of ideas. Open innovation calls for collaborative organizing principles for managing research and innovation. The Living Lab is a way of implementing the open innovation approach (Fahy *et al*., 2007; Garcia-Guzman *et al*., 2007; Mulder *et al*., 2007). LL represents a user-centric innovation approach for sensing, prototyping, validating and refining complex solutions in multiple and evolving real life contexts. It can be characterized by an iterative, design-oriented approach in which incremental solutions are re-used, sometimes leading to unexpected results or changes in intended innovation directions. LL promotes an alternative innovation paradigm: the end-user's role shifts from research object to a pro-active position where user communities are co-creators of product and service innovations. Open-Innovation process (Ståhlbröst and Bergvall-Kåreborn, 2008) which include 1) idea &

concept which involves research and planning and preparation of proposal; 2) prototype; 3) pre-commercial product or service, uptake refine; 4) evaluate, growth; and 5) co-creation with market/client exploitation (Eriksson, *et al.*, 2005; ENoLL 2010; Pallot, 2009; Følstad, 2008).

According to Bergvall-Kåreborn *et al.* (2009a), the five key components of Living Labs exist which are:

- The *ICT & Infrastructure* component which outlines the role that new and existing ICT technology can play to facilitate new ways of cooperating and co-creating new innovations among stakeholders.
- *Management* represent the ownership, organization, and policy aspects of a Living Lab (a Living Lab can be managed by consultants, companies or researchers).
- The Living Lab *Partners & Users* bring their own specific wealth of knowledge and expertise to the collective, helping to achieve boundary spanning knowledge transfer.
- *Research* symbolizes the collective learning and reflection that take place in the Living Lab and should result in contributions to both theory and practice. Technological research partners can also provide direct access to research which can benefit the outcome of a technological innovation.
- Finally, *Approach* stand for methods and techniques that emerge as best practice within the Living Labs environment.

Figure 2: Example of Living Lab Research with All its Facets

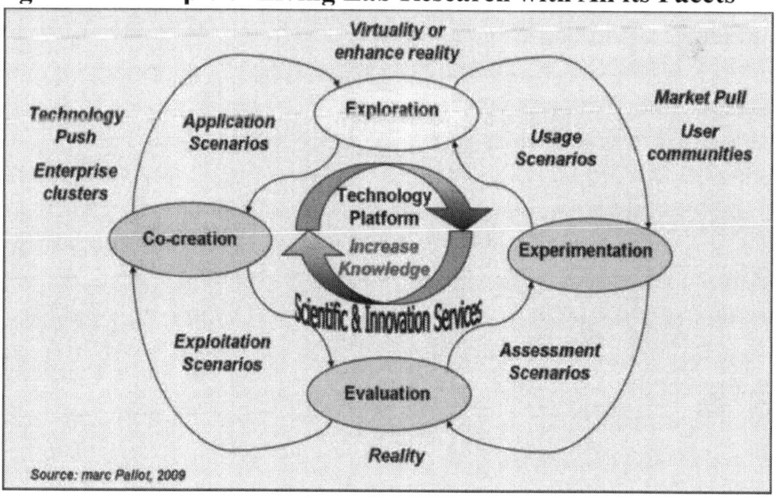

Source: Pallot (2009)

Figure 2 also illustrates how all the above cycles within a Living Lab can operate:

4. Bringing the key elements of design research and Living Lab research together

During the literature overview of design science and Living Lab research a number of similar issues/concepts were highlighted like outcomes, cycles/phases, characteristics, environments, processes, and value/impact or relevance. The main difference is really the Living Lab focus on an open innovation process and the aspect of commercialization of a product where the user is the co-designer in all the phases and cycles. Design science research does not explicitly refer to commercialisation of product or artifact but rather has reflection as the last phase in its cycle or process, but design science research also involves people who can be users/experts. The focus in Living Labs is more on innovation within real-life context but both mention a multidisciplinary context.

Table 1 was constructed to illustrate specific concepts which were found in the discussion of both design science and Living Lab research. From Table 1 one can deduce that similarities are mostly found in the outcomes, methodologies, value/impact, processes and contexts except for Living Lab research which focus on an open innovation/real-life context. Differences are mostly found in the guidelines and principles. The idea was not to compare or differentiate between the two approaches but rather to provide an overview of both in order to understand that one can within a Living Lab environment apply design science research (DSR) as a methodology. LL involve more diverse stakeholders and must take place within real-life contexts. A problem is thus investigated from various angles to involve users/experts to assist with improvement and new products, processes and services and more than one research approach can be used in LL environments apart from design science research. Many cities are also now seen as LL spaces or ecosystems where citizens can collaborate to improve their environment (Smart city concept).

5. Developing and deploying the Solar-powered DD in North West Living Lab

In order to address the research question and purpose of this paper it is important to illustrate the application of design research within a LL context. The following example involves the Solar panel Digital Doorway which were developed and deployed in a LL environment to improve its design as a product within a rural context.

The Digital Doorway (DD) project is an initiative of the South African Department of Science and Technology and the CSIR Meraka Institute in South Africa. The aim of the initiative is to expose rural communities to ICT and to promote functional computer literacy through unassisted learning. Locally designed robust and vandal proof "kiosks" with a wide variety of content are deployed at easily accessible locations in rural communities. Community members are encouraged to explore and experiment with the content and functionality offered by the DD with the minimum of assistance (Gush, 2008).

The DD has gone through various design iterations based on feedback from monitoring and evaluation studies and the communities in which it is deployed. Data were collected from the design team, the implementers and users from the DD. Most DDs deployed were 220V until the experience and feedback from the technical team resulted in a redesign for a self-contained solar panel DD was identified (see Figure 4).

Table 1: Key concepts in both Design Science and Living Lab research

Key concepts	Design research	Living Labs
1.Environment/ context	People, organizational systems, technical systems, problems and opportunities (Hevner *et al.*, 2004)	Real-life settings, multidisciplinary, user-driven/centred innovation milieu (ENoLL, 2010)
2. Guidelines/ principles	Hevner *et al.*, (2004) also proposed seven guidelines for design research: design as an artifact, problem relevance, design evaluation, research contributions, research rigour, design as a search process and communication of research (Wang and Wang, 2010).	ICT infrastructure, management, research, approach, Living Lab partners and users as well as principles of Openness, Influence, Realism, Value and Sustainability (Bergvall-Kåreborn *et al.*, 2009b)

Key concepts	Design research	Living Labs
3. Process	Preliminary study/analysis of practical problems and needs, development of solutions/ prototype phase and evaluation or assessment (Reeves, 2006; March and Storey, 2008; Wang and Wang, 2010)	Open-Innovation process (Ståhlbröst and Bergvall-Kåreborn, 2008) which include 1) idea & concept which involves research and planning and preparation of proposal, 2) prototype, 3) pre-commercial product or service, uptake, refine and 4) evaluate, growth and 5) co-creation with market/client exploitation (Eriksson, *et al.*, 2005; ENoLL 2010; Pallot, 2009; Følstad, 2008)
4. Methodologies	Case studies, experiments, Field studies, simulation (Iivari, 2007; Wang and Wang, 2010)	Experimentation, ethnographic studies, case studies, simulations, Focus group and participatory (Følstad, 2008)
5. Value/impact to Information Systems	Builds meta-artifacts that support the development of concrete IT applications with design product and design process knowledge (Iivari, 2007) and evaluate artifacts, design theories for business problem-solving (Wang and Wang, 2010)	Provide structure and governance to the user participation, effective: in customization exercises and in exploration, especially in interdisciplinary projects that involve organizational change, where they work as "innovation arenas" customization, localization or validation of existing products or services. (Almirall, 2008)
6. Outcomes	IT artifact which can include the constructs, models, and methods applied in the development and use of Information systems (Hevner *et al.*, 2004; Hevner and Chatterjee, 2010)	New services, products and societal infrastructures, innovation (Følstad, 2008; Geerts, 2011)

DSR was adopted to develop and test the first iteration of the solar container DD. The modified container DD was then deployed in an active Living Lab environment (North-West Living Lab) with the intent of developing it further through community participation and co-creation, once again using a DSR within a LL context where all five key components of Living Labs (i.e. ICT infrastructure, management, all LL partners and users from the community, research for relevance and rigour and approach which was the application of DSR).

To develop the solar panel DD the following different design science cycles and phases, which were indicated earlier under section 3 (Reeves, 2006; March and Storey, 2008; Wang and Wang, 2010), were applied. These are: 1) Preliminary study/analysis of practical problems and needs; 2) development of solutions/prototype phase; 3) evaluation and testing; and 4) assessment or reflection. This is evident from Figure 3.

Initially, during the first phase the focus of the research was to understand the phenomena in its natural setting and to conceptualise solutions that would be grounded in sate of the art scientific knowledge. Once the requirements of the domain framed by the insights from literature were comprehended, these were translated to technology attributes and affordances of the digital doorway. The output in this phase is thus preliminary designs and approaches that are framed by theoretical underpinnings derived from literature. The feedback from the technical team as well as users was valuable to relate these two needs and practical problems which were experienced by the previous old type DD. This informed the development of the solar-powered DD.

The second phase is predominantly a technical endeavour, designing, developing and evaluating the concept, through paper mock-ups and other means and designing, developing and evaluating an early proof of concept technology product. The outputs of this phase were tentative products, design principles and product approaches. The product is subjected to evaluation and feedback from the network of partners (design team, technical team, suppliers) that were purposefully chosen to give critical and valuable feedback. The output of this phase would be a revised product (solar DD), revised design principals and a revised product approach. As the product matures through iterations it is progressively exposed to the rigours exposures of the real life setting it is designed for.

Figure 3: Design research model for solar powered DD - Physical design and functionality/content & service delivery design in a LL context

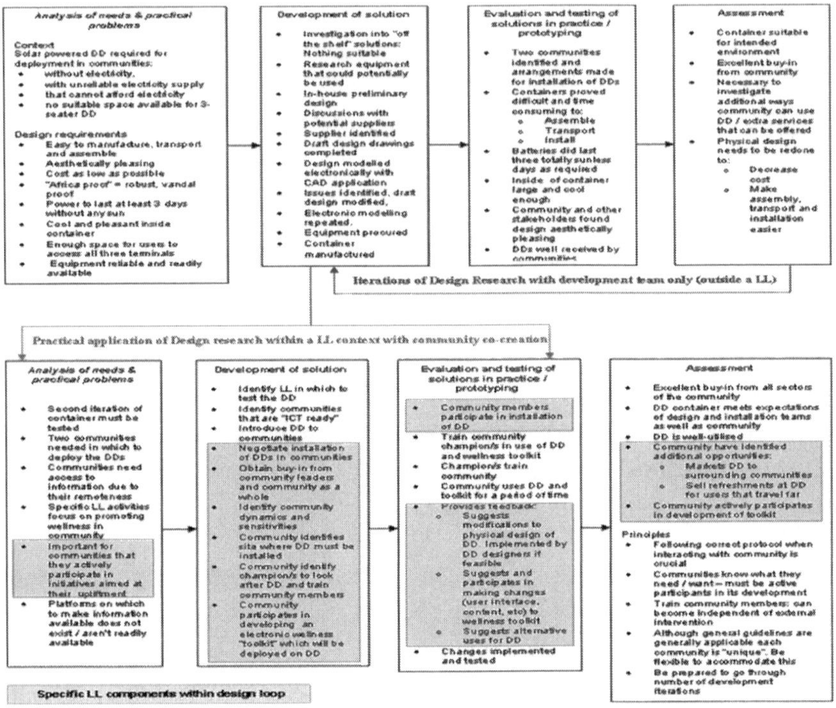

Source: Adapted from: Reeves, 2006; March and Storey, 2008; Wang and Wang, 2010.

The third and fourth phase focussed on more social aspects of appropriation and best practice implied in the original design, delivering a product, design principles and a documented product approach. The maturity of the product would enable the stable integration within a bounded real-life scenario. This phase enables the productising of related products. Within budget and time constraints the final phase delivers semi summative feedback and evaluation on the process, product, usability and usefulness of the resulting digital doorway in the NWLL. Participants who were involved here included community leaders, users from the community, suppliers, technical team members and design team members. The phases and cycles are provided with detailed discussions in Figure 3.

The North-West Living Lab (NWLL) was established in September 2010 and forms part of Living Labs of Southern Africa (LLiSA). The aim of the NWLL is to promote and facilitate the sustainable social development of communities in the North West Province of South Africa by means of existing scientific and/or technological innovations and interventions. The NWLL has a dual purpose. Firstly, it acts as a voice or platform for communities in the North West Province to articulate the actual needs (priorities) and expectations within their particular communities (a so-called open, user-driven innovation or 'bottom-up' approach). Secondly, it acts as a liaison (or channel of communication) between communities, institutions, industries, and government in an attempt to further develop, test and perfect innovations or interventions aimed at improving the everyday lives of communities in the Province (Coetzee and du Toit, 2011).

Figure 4 illustrates how the iterations of design science research was applied in the physical design of the solar Digital Doorway before it was deployed in the NWLL (above 4 phases) but also how the same phases were applied to improve the product with the same design science phases but with the NWLL community as co-creators of the new improved product (4 phases).

Figure 4: Context of NWLL and Role of Digital doorway and users

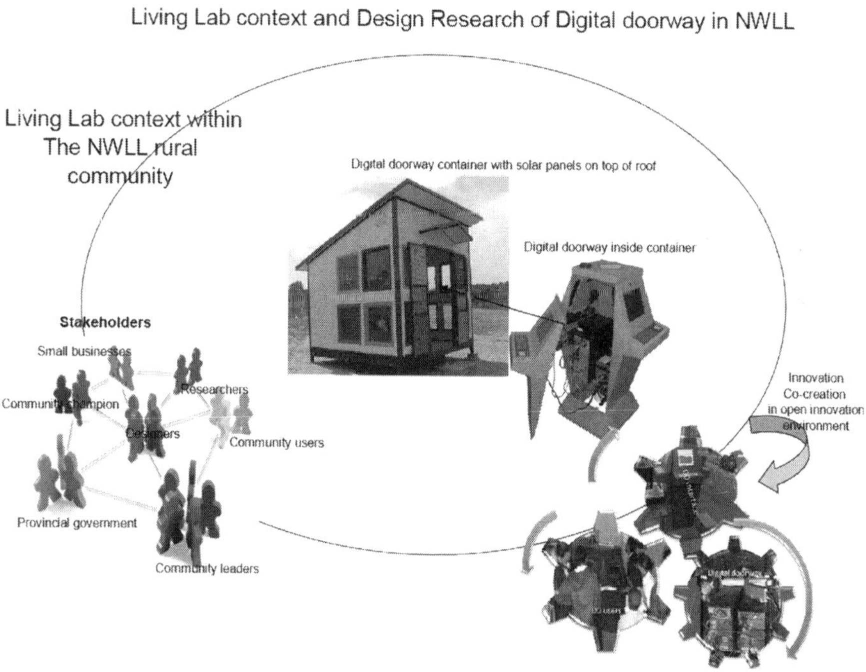

6. The use of Living Lab as a setting for evaluation of design artefacts

We identify three aspects of LLs that make them suitable for obtaining feedback on design artifacts. First, Living Labs result in pilot implementations and thus are not limited to theoretical experiments where design science research processes and cycles work well. LLs offer a real-life setting which provides the richness of complex problems but also a limited scope which enables researchers to study the domain in depth and develop close collaboration with all relevant domain experts. Second, LL enables immediate feedback from domain experts concerning a complex real-life setting and facilitates iterations of the build-and-evaluate loop of design artifacts. A third point concerns the solar panel DD specifically as a design artefact. Although the result of this Living Lab is a pilot rather than a full-scale implementation, the Living Lab is sufficient to provide proof of concept of innovative ideas. In applying the solar panel DD we are mainly interested in ensuring proper usage of users in the community and get their feedback as co-creators to ensure constant redesign.

LLs in South Africa are in many ways similar to European LLs but also have characteristics and language unique to the context in which they operate. According to case descriptions (Coetzee and Du Toit, 2011), one of the main differences between South African LLs and European LLs is the emphasis on co-creation with communities, specifically rural communities, in contrast to European LLs' collaboration with 'users' who are mostly located in urban areas. The South African LLs also compare well with the literature regarding the timeline for LL establishment and activities (Følstad, 2008). LLs in South Africa are also each unique, they simultaneously operate in unique ways with distinct focus areas. South African LLs also support emerging economies, but additionally, encompass the impact of LLs on community wellbeing (NWLL), education (SLL) and social media (RLab).

7. Conclusion

This paper provided information on how the design science research supported the deployment of solar panel DD in a Living Lab context in the North West Province of South Africa, which is mainly rural. Each research domain (DSR and LL) was found to have its own specific uniqueness and components. We do not favour one above the other but do realise after careful analysis that Living Labs can actually involve design science research and that a Living Lab is actually bigger and more than just a methodology. We have outlined the fact that Living labs can be an environment, an approach or a milieu where open innovation is the key focus. The phases of how the solar panel DD was developed within the DSR methodology and within the LL of the NW indicated the importance of all user involvement and feedback to ensure co-creation with community members. Living Labs are thus more than just design research or similar to it because it is systems for building future economies in which real-life user-driven innovation will be a normal co-creation technique for new products, services and societal infrastructure.

References

Almirall, S., (2008), 'Living labs and open innovation: roles and applicability', in *Electronic Journal for Virtual Organizations and Networks*, 10: 21-46.

Benbasat, I. and Zmud, R.W. (2003), 'The identity crisis within the discipline: Defining and communicating the discipline's core properties', in *MIS Quarterly,* 27(2): 183-194

Bergvall-Kåreborn, B., Holst, M., and Ståhlbröst, A. (2009), 'Concept Design with a living lab approach', *Paper presented at HICSS-42*, 5-8 January 2009, at Big Island, Hawaii.

Bergvall-Kåreborn, B., Ihlström Eriksson, C., Ståhlbröst, A., and Svensson, J. (2009), 'A milieu for innovation - defining living labs', *Paper presented at The 2nd ISPIM Innovation Symposium - Stimulating Recovery - The Role of Innovation Management*, 6-9 December 2009, at New York City, USA.

Chesbrough, H. (2003), *Open Innovation: The New Imperative for Creating and Profiting from Technology*, Harvard: Harvard Business School Press.

Choi, J., Nazareth, D.L. and Jain, H.K. (2010), 'Implementing service-oriented architecture in organizations', in *Journal of Management Information Systems*, 26(4): 253–86.

Coetzee, H, Du Toit, I-M. (2011), *Case study report: Living Labs in Southern Africa.* Available from: http://www.llisa.net

European Network of Living Labs (ENoLL). (2011), Available at: http://www.openlivinglabs.eu

Eriksson, M., Niitamo, V.P., and Kulkki, S. (2005), State-*of-the-Art in Utilizing Living Labs Approach to User-centric ICT innovation - a European approach*, Centre of Distance Spanning Technology at Luleå University of Technology, Sweden, Nokia.

Fahy, C., Ponce De Leon, M., Ståhlbröst, A., Schaffers, H. and Hongisto, P. (2007), 'Services of living labs and their networks', In: Cunningham, P. and Cunningham, M. (eds.), *Expanding the Knowledge Economy: Issues, Applications, Case Studies,* Amsterdam: IOS Press, pp. 713–721.

Følstad, A. (2008), 'Living labs for innovation and development of information and communication technology: a literature review', in *The Electronic Journal for Virtual Organisations and Networks,* 10:100-131.

Garcia Guzman, J., Navarro de la Cruz, M., Schaffers, H. andKulkki, S. (2007), 'Methodological framework for human and user centric rural living labs', In: Cunningham, P. and Cunningham, M. (eds.), *Expanding the Knowledge Economy: Issues, Applications, Case Studies,* Amsterdam: IOS Press, pp. 730–737.

Geerts, G. (2011), 'A design science research methodology and its application to accounting information systems research', in *International Journal of Accounting InformationSystems*.Availableat:http://linkinghub.elsevier.com/retrieve/pii/S1467089511000200.

Gush, K. (2008), 'Towards a more personalised user experience and better demographic data on the Digital Doorway public computer terminals', *5th Prato Community Informatics & Development Informatics Conference 2008: ICTs for Social Inclusion: What is the Reality?* Prato, Italy, Centre for Community Networking Research, Monash University.

Hevner, A. and Chatterjee, S., (2010), *Design Science Research in Information Systems: Theory and Practice.* New York: Springer.

Hevner, A., March, S., Park, J., and Ram, S. (2004), 'Design science in information systems research', in *Manage Information Systems Quarterly (*MIS), 28(1): 75–105.

Hirschheim, R. and Klein, H.K. (2003), 'Crisis in the IS field? a critical reflection on the state of the discipline', in *Journal of the AIS*, 4(5), 2003: 237-293.

Holst, M. Ståhlbröst, A. and Bergvall-Kåreborn, B. (2010), 'Openness in living labs: facilitating innovation', in *Proceedings of the 33rd IRIS Seminar (Information Systems Research Seminar in Scandinavia),* Rebild Bakker, 21-24, August 2010, Rebild, Denmark.

Iivari, J., (2007), 'A Paradigmatic analysis of information systems as a design science', in *Scandinavian Journal of Information Systems*, 19(2): 39–64.

Kolfschoten, G.L. and de Vreede G-J. (2009), 'A design approach for collaboration processes: a multi-method design science study in collaboration engineering', in *Journal of Management of Information Systems*, 26(1): 225–56.

Lepik, K-L., Krigul, M. and Terk, E. (2010), 'Introducing living lab's method as knowledge transfer from one socio-institutional context to another: evidence from Helsinki-Tallinn cross-border region', in *Journal of Universal Computer Science*, 16(8): 1089-1101.

Lee, J., Wyner, G.M. and Pentland, B.T. (2008), 'Process grammar as a tool for business process design', in *MIS Q*uarterly, 32(4): 757–78.

March, S.T. and Smith, G. (1995), 'Design and natural science research on information technology', in *Decision Support Systems,* 15(4): 251–66.

March, S.T. and Storey, V.C. (2008), 'Design science in the information systems discipline: an introduction to the special issue on design science research', in *MIS Quarterly*, 32(4): 725-730.

Mulder, I., Fahy, C., Hribernik, K., Velthausz, D., Feurstein, K., Garcia, M., Schaffers, H., Mirijamdotter, A. and Ståhlbröst, A. (2007), 'Towards harmonized methods and tools for living labs', In: Cunningham, P. and Cunningham, M. (eds.), *Expanding the Knowledge Economy: Issues, Applications, Case Studies*, Amsterdam: IOS Press, pp. 722–729.

Nunamaker, J., Chen, M. and Purdin, T. (1991), 'Systems development in information systems research', in *Journal of Information Management Systems,* 7(3): 89–106.

Orlikowski, W. and Iacono, C. (2001), 'Research commentary: desperately seeking the "IT" in IT research—a call to theorizing the IT artifact', in *Information Systems Research,* 12(2): 121–134.

Pallot, M. (2009), 'Ecospace survey on barriers affecting collaboration effectiveness and efficiency, in *ECOPSACE Newsletter*, 11 & 12.

Pirenen, R. (2009), 'Research framework of integrative action', in *Proceedings of the Fifteenth Americas Conference on Information Systems,* San Francisco, California, 6th -9th August.

Reeves, T.C. (2006), 'Design research from a technology perspective', In: Van Den Akker, J., Gravemeijer, K., Mc Kenney, S. & Nieveen, N. (eds.), *Educational Design Research,* London: Routledge.

Rittel, H.J. and Webber, M.M. (1984), 'Planning problems are wicked problems', In: Cross, N. (ed), *Developments of Design Methodology,* New York: John Wiley & Sons.

Simon, H. (1996), *The Sciences of the Artificial,* Cambridge, MA: MIT Press.

Ståhlbröst, A. and Bergvall-Kåreborn, B. (2008), 'Constructing representations of users needs – a living lab approach' in *Proceedings of IRIS31*, 10–13 August, Åre, Sweden.

Walls, J., Widmeyer, G.E.L. and Sawy, O. (1992), 'Building an information system design theory for vigilant EIS.', *Information System Research* 3(1): 36–59.

Wang, S. and Wang, H. (2010), 'Towards innovative design research information systems', in *Journal of Computer Information Systems,* 5(1): 11-18.

Weber, R. (1987), 'Toward a theory of artifacts: a paradigmatic base for information systems research', in *Journal of Information Systems*, 1(2): 3-19.

Wolfert, J. Verdouw, C.N., Verloop, C.M. and Beukens, A.J.M. (2010), 'Organizing information integration in agri-food - a method based on a service orientated architecture and living lab approach', in *Electronics in Agriculture*, 70:(2): 389-405.

13

Nigeria Assessing the National Economic Empowerment Development Strategy as a Development Plan

Enwere Dike[1] *& Kanayo Ogujiuba*[2]

1. Introduction

In 2003 the Nigerian federal government launched the National Economic Empowerment Development Strategy (NEEDS), describing it as a 'development plan'. The broad objective of the present paper is to find out whether and to what extent the NEEDS actually satisfies the theoretical prerequisites of a development plan. Does the NEEDS possess an explicitly specified set of objectives, and are the latter reducible to targets that can serve as a measure of the extent the objectives are achievable? Does the NEEDS possess policy instruments with which to achieve its objectives? Finally, is there alignment between the policy objectives and policy instruments of the NEEDS-the plan consistency criterion? The issue of whether the NEEDS objectives have been achieved is not pursued in the present paper. Other

1 Department of Economics, Kogi State University, Anyigba, Kogi State, Nigeria, Email: meidike@yahoo.com

2 Department of Economics, Kogi State University, Anyigba, Kogi State, Nigeria.

studies have addressed that aspect (e.g. IMF, 2005; United Nations, 2006; Ikeanyibe, 2009; Onakuse and Lenihan, 2007).

Development planning is a process in which a government chooses specific socio-economic objectives, then sets targets, and, finally, organizes a framework for implementing, coordinating, and monitoring progress towards achievement of stated objectives and targets. Through the formulation of policies or policy framework[1], articulation of appropriate projects and programmes, and the mobilization of available material and financial resources, the government attempts to achieve the goals and targets of the plan. The point of departure in a development plan is thus the articulation and analysis of objectives of national economic development and the selection of optimal instruments or strategies to attempt to realize those objectives. Further, a key responsibility of development planning is to find the interdependencies between the objectives of development plan on the one part and on the other the instruments for attaining them.

There are some six prerequisites of a development plan: (i) an over-arching development vision or philosophy; (ii) clearly specified objectives or goals; (iii) policy instruments for achieving objectives; (iv) a time horizon; (v) alignment between objectives and strategies; and (vi) a time preference function for judging whether the potential future benefits of the plan justify the resources invested to achieve them.

The present paper establishes that whereas the NEEDS fulfils prerequisites (i) to (iv), it is, at best, weak in (v) and (vi). But the NEEDS is not supported by macroeconomic models of the economy to permit analysis of the interdependencies in the economy.

The rest of the paper is structured into six sections. Section 2 deals with the conceptual and theoretical issues; section 3 deals with the problems of setting objectives and instruments and the plan consistency problem. Section 4 identifies the philosophy and objective of the NEEDS; and section 5 assesses the policy instruments and their consistency with the policy objectives and targets. Section 6 concludes the study.

2. Some Conceptual and Theoretical Issues in Planning

Generally, planning entails making decisions which are intended to influence the future course of events in accordance with defined or pre-set goals or objectives, policies and strategies. In the context of a national economy, planning refers to the conscious coordination by the government of economic policies and administrative interventions to attempt to achieve specified goals of economic development as embodied in a development plan blueprint. The latter, which may be comprehensive (covering the entire macro economy), perspective, medium-term, long-term, rolling or annual, defines the means by which national economic development is to be advanced.

National economic planning presupposes existence of a 'visible hand' or an interventionist state, which directly determines or influences prices, output and production. Although national planning can take a variety of forms, its most important features usually include: (i) setting growth/production targets for different sectors of the economy, that determine or influence the supply of different goods and services; (ii) regulation of production of certain goals and services, to determine demand for them; (iii) price-and wage-fixing by the government; and (iv) (sometimes) intervention in factor markets, to influence the behaviour of producers.

A development plan is thus a government document which includes policies, strategies and tactics, and incorporating an investment programme of projects (as its material counterpart) and a budget (as its financial counterpart). A development plan represents a deliberate attempt by a government to coordinate economic decision-making on a long-term basis and to direct (and in some cases even control) the level and growth of the principal economic variables of the economy in order to achieve predetermined set of objectives. Essentially, a development plan represents an attempt to move the economy from what is perceived to be an undesired or 'bad' equilibrium towards a desired or 'good' equilibrium.

Contrasting interpretations of planning

There are two interpretations of development planning to be found in the economic development literature: the neoclassical and the development economics or structuralist. These two interpretations are summarized in Figure 1. Typically, the neoclassical interpretation conceives economic planning as a rational and objective resources allocation process, a solution of the 'economic problem' – i.e. allocation of scarce resources to maximize economy-wide social welfare function.

Figure 1: Contrasting Interpretations of Development Planning: the Neoclassical and Development Economics Perspectives

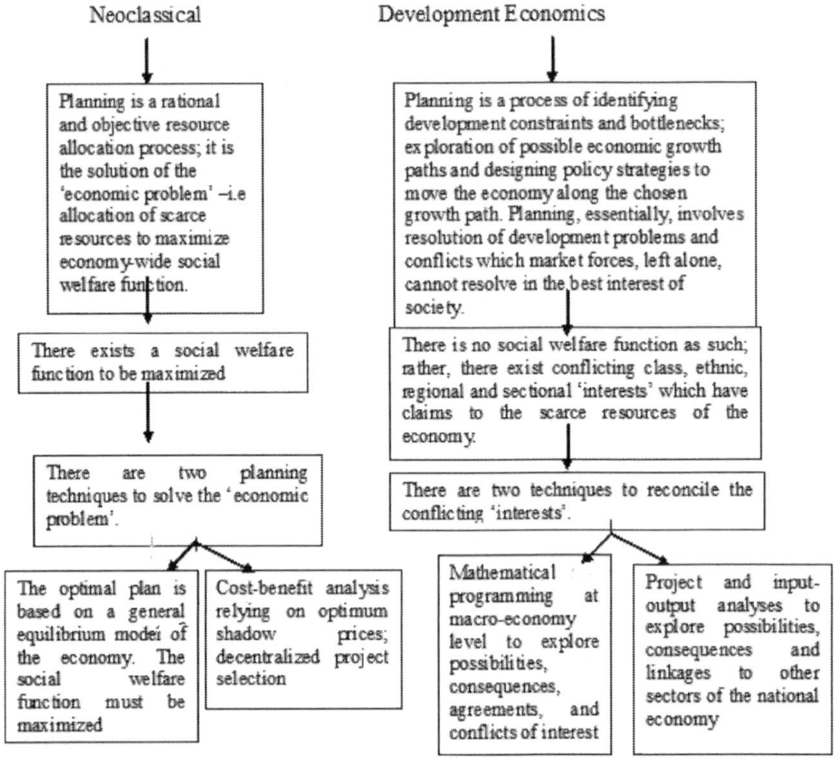

So, the neoclassical interpretation presupposes existence of a social welfare function to be maximized; it assumes, besides, a perfectly competitive market structure for realizing or maximizing the social welfare function.

It might, perhaps, be relevant to remind the reader that the proposition that perfect competition will result in maximization of utility (welfare) was due to Pareto (1909). Pareto attempted to formulate a utility maximization function under competitive equilibrium, which became conceptualized in the notion of a Pareto optimum or Pareto superiority. This notion was to become a standard tool of neoclassical welfare economics providing a criterion of when one economic configuration is considered better in a social welfare sense than another. Dobb (1969) informs us, however, that the concept of a social welfare function owes its origin to Bergson (1938), but was later to acquire considerable importance in neoclassical literature, serving as a formal device of positing something like a community indifference curve, or a set of social preference functions which will enable a social optimum to be formulated.

Extrapolating from individual's preference function to form a social (community) preference function assumes, however, that all individuals in society seek to achieve the same objectives at any point in time or that there are no individual differences in objectives. But, the neoclassical social welfare function tallies with the neoclassical position portraying economic society as a homogenous entity with no class divisions, nor regional, ethnic and cleavages[2]. Neoclassical theory builds a unique set of assumptions on how micro-level agents (individuals) behave and, through a process of methodological individualism, aggregates those individual behaviours to explain macro-level or economy-wide conditions and developments. In the neoclassical perspective, therefore, statements about economy-wide conditions could be derived as a simple, linear aggregation of micro-level relationships. Neoclassical economics employs this linear view of the economy to build its social welfare function.

In the neoclassical interpretation, planning should follow the dictates of the market transmitted through the price system and must not attempt to counter the latter. But neoclassical theory does not admit the problem of 'market failures' whose main sources are monopoly, externalities and income distribution.

For much of the 1980s through the 1990s the neoclassical propositions seem to have influenced policy thinking at national and international levels. These were decades when free-market policies appeared to have triumphed; when the right growth policy was interpreted to mean lower fiscal deficits; lower import tariffs; fewer restrictions on international trade and capital flows; and greater role for markets in resource allocation –'regardless of history, political economy, or local institutions' (Zagha *et al.*, 2006; see also Aron, 2000). Much of this neoclassical policy vision came to be reflected in the Washington consensus, which synthesized the types of policy reform agenda most economists in the World Bank, International Monetary Fund (IMF), the United States Treasury, etc. thought were necessary to rescue Latin American countries –indeed, developing countries, generally-from cycles of high inflation and low growth. The driving force behind the several components of the Washington consensus was the conviction that government is more likely to make things worse than better; there is also the usual neoclassical 'trickle-down' approach to economic growth policy, namely that poverty would be taken care of by growth and is not a major obstacle itself to growth and development (see Williams, 1990, 2000; Srinivasan, 2000).

For the structuralist/ development economics perspective, development planning is essentially, a process of identification of development bottlenecks, exploration of possible macroeconomic expansion paths and designing policy strategies to move the economy along the chosen expansion path. It is a process of resolution of development bottlenecks arising from market failures, which demands that market forces be moderated or regulated by the planning mechanism. In this perspective there is no social or economy-wide welfare function as such to be maximized; rather, there are conflicting interests underpinned by class, ethnic and regional cleavages, which have claims on scarce national resources.

The structuralist/development economics perspective inspired and gave support to import substitution industrialization (ISI) in developing countries. But it takes as its starting point the existence of disequilibria that work through macroeconomic mechanisms, but whose causes are thought to be embedded in the underlying economic, social and political characteristics of underdeveloped capitalism. Structuralist development economics evolved from the non-orthodox analysis carried out over the years at the Economic Commission for Latin America and Caribbean (ECLA). It bears direct lineage to classical Marxian political economy because of its focus on political and social conflicts over distribution and the attempts to identify the fundamental roots of macroeconomic disequilibria rather than their more immediate and apparent causes. The original structuralist group at ECLA held optimistic views on ISI to kick-start development. But as ISI failed to deliver by the end of the 1970s, dependency theory began to evolve to explain why.

The development economics interpretation found a receptive audience among policy makers in developing countries, generally, in the post-war II decades up until the onset of adjustment reforms by the end of the 1970s. It is the perspective, generally, that seems to have influenced the expanded role of government in developing countries, manifested in an array of macroeconomic and trade regulations which are largely aimed at maximizing capital accumulation and long-run growth performance (see, for instance, United Nation ,1965; Helfgoth and Schiavo-Campo, 1970; Arndt, 1988; World Bank, 1997).

Evolution of development planning

Development planning has evolved through some six phases starting in the post-war II decades, the 1950s and 1960s (Table 1), shaped by the interactions between three forces: accumulated experiences of developing countries themselves; a broadening of the economic and social objectives of the latter underpinned by changes in national and international economic and political environments; and development of analytical techniques to evaluate alternative policy choices (Weiss, 1990; Chenery, 1983). The post-colonial development experiences of developing countries began to accumulate, in concrete terms, with import substitution industrialization (ISI) in the 1950s through the 1970s. By the end of the 1970s the ISI project had run into serious difficulties in developing countries, especially in Sub-Saharan Africa (Valk, 1996). As from the 1970s there emerged growing global interdependence, oil shocks, growing instability and foreign exchange constraints culminating in the external debt crisis of the 1980s and 1990s. By the end of the 1990s, developing countries began to face problems of globalization, environmental degradation, global warming and climate change. Besides, there was the problem of growing poverty, even as economic growth resumed in developing countries generally.

The analytical techniques of planning can be viewed at two levels[3]: macro and micro. Again, starting in the post-war II decades, we observe a transition from the 'closed economy' macro-planning models, whose work-horse was the Harrod-Domar growth model emphasizing savings as the sole strategy to drive growth[4], to the 'open economy' dual-gap models, linear programming and input-output models of the 1970s.

Table 1:Sketch of Evolution of Development Planning

Approximate date	Objectives/constraints	Analytical Approach	Techniques	Development Experience of Developing Countries
1950 – 1965	Internal constraints: Low investment and savings capacity; skilled labour	Closed Economy Harrod-Domar modle; input-output tables	Investment criterion	Import substitution industrialization (ISI). Post-war agricultural export boom; import limits to growth
1966-1970	External Constraints: Trade constraints; foreign capital	Open- Economy Dual-gap models; Linear programming; Semi-input- output models	Project Evaluation; Efficiency prices	Increased raw-material export dependence. Growing income inequality Accelerated growth in East Asian newly industrializing countries (NICs)

1971-1974	Multiple Constraints Growth and Equity	Computable General Equilibrium (CGE) market simulation	Welfare prices poverty-based investment	Difficulties in ISI; First oil shocks and growing instability and foreign exchange crisis. Continued accelerated growth in NICs
1975-1986	External Debt External capital limits; structural disequilibrium	Models of structural adjustment programmes (SAPs) Global modeling	Sources of productivity growth	External debt crisis; widening gap between developed and developing countries outside NICs. Rising unemployment, Take-off growth in East Asian NICs
1987-1990s	External Debt Shocks. Internal and external flexibility; renewedcapital flows	Response models to SAPs; open markets.	Sources of productivity growth	External debt crises; SAP reforms; Debit rescheduling
2000s	Coping withGlobalization Integrating with global markets; poverty alleviation	Open economy Endogenous growth models; poverty-growth elasticity models; sources of international competitiveness; climate change models	Sources of international competitiveness	Globalization; millennium development goals (MDGs), global warming and climate change

Source: Authors; with input from Meier (1989

Whereas the Harrod-Domar model was a restatement of the internal structural rigidities intrinsic to developing economies, the dual-gap extensions of the Harrod-Domar model were in reality just a restatement of the internal and external structural disequilibria inherent in underdevelopment. On the other hand, the CGE models were evolved to permit analysis of the impact of domestic resources allocation and individual policy instruments on growth; they were widely applied by the World Bank in the 1980s in an attempt to establish the effects of structural adjustment policies and found to be of limited relevance, given that they discounted the effect of structural rigidities in limiting the impact of the stabilization polices of structural adjustment (Tarp, 1993). Found to be much more relevant were the dual economy models, which take into account sectoral differences in response to adjustment price incentives (Jha, 1994), the nature of financial markets in developing countries, etc. Models of structural adjustment and efficiency pricing evolved in the 1980s and 1990s; the 2000s witness macro-planning models of international competitiveness, endogenous growth, technology transfer and catch-up, global warming and climate change, etc.

What is observed then is growing complexity in the models required to take account of the multiplicity of objectives and constraints inherent in economic development. The rapidly changing global economic landscape, characterized by globalization and the need to develop efficient mechanisms to be able to adapt to these changes, has led to the reassessment of development policies and planning techniques. Developing countries have had considerable difficulty adapting to these changes.

3. Objectives, Instruments and the Plan Consistency Problem

The point of departure in planning, as already posited, is thus the specification and analysis of objectives and the selection of optimal strategies to attempt to realize these objectives. Objectives can always range from the general to the specific; from the abstract to the particular; from the non-quantifiable or non-measurable to the quantifiable or measurable. Usually in national development plans we find at the most abstract level, the ultimate aim or goal or objective of the society or nation- reflecting its philosophy of development- the ideological aspiration that tends to provide inspiration to the people. We may term this the 'vision' of the plan-the ultimate goal of economic development, often couched in the form of a slogan to elicit popular appeal (Griffin and Enos, 1970).

Targets as intermediate objectives

During the plan period itself, one will find some intermediate goals which may still sound abstract, but which may still be achievable during the medium term. During still the same plan period or stages in the latter, one can find some less abstract, intermediate objectives-otherwise termed targets. The latter represent specific quantitative results that the plan is designed to produce. The terms 'aspirations' 'goals' and 'targets' used above may be interpreted to represent the different hierarchical levels the objectives of the plan can be articulated. Indeed, in the final analysis, it is against the 'targets' that the performance of a plan can be measured. Moreover, the targets must align with the objectives, and both (objectives and targets) with the aspirations (ibid.).

Social objectives

A development plan must take into account social goals. But a development plan has its ultimate objective in the welfare of the society. Articulating social goals, however, has not been easy for developing countries, if only because, as pointed out above, of the myriad social, political and regional cleavages which characterize societies in developing countries captured in the concept of dualism. However, one such social objective would be, for instance, to improve the percentage of total income accruing to the lowest income group. An economic plan with a clear, well-articulated social objective could have as one of its targets that the redistribution of income will move in favour of the lower 80-90% of income classes by, for instance, taking 20-30% of the income of 10% of the upper income classes and diverting it to the lower 80-90%. Such an objective, social in nature as it obviously is, cannot be achieved using economic growth alone. Institutional changes are required to complement economic growth.

Development experience has always and everywhere shown that the poverty and income distribution problem requires more than economic growth for its solution: it requires institutional reforms focusing directly on reducing the concentrated control of assets, the unequal distribution of economic power, and the unequal access to educational and income-earning opportunities that are the hallmark of developing countries, generally. A classic case of such redistribution strategies as they relate to the rural economy, where the bulk of the poverty group is concentrated, is land reform. The latter will take different forms in different countries depending on the institutional contexts: in some contexts it will require land asset redistribution to transform tenant cultivators into smallholders who will then have an incentive to raise production and improve their incomes; in others, it will require building institutions that permit small farmers to secure access to much needed critical agricultural inputs-credit, fertilizers, irrigation water, seeds, marketing facilities, and agricultural education. Not only the rural economy but also the urban economy requires such institutional reform agenda: here the focus will be provision of commercial credit at affordable rates to small entrepreneurs – so-called micro-finance-so that they can expand their enterprises and create more employments.

On the other hand, however, it should be admitted that social objectives are rather difficult to formulate and implement. This is particularly true in contexts of developing countries where implementing social objectives (such as land redistribution) which involves changing the social class structure and tearing down barriers to income and social mobility; providing such public goods as good governance, opportunities for higher education and improved healthcare delivery; gender equality; etc.

Temporal goals

Yet another category of goals is time: so-called temporal goals, which are often neglected in the development plans of developing countries. A key question tackled here may be framed as follows. How does society distribute its current output between consumption and savings? Society has a choice of consuming all its output or saving some part of it and postponing consumption to a future time. Further, society has a choice between leaving its savings untouched and investing them in real assets to build up new productive capacities. Both decisions - to save and leave what is saved untouched, and invest in real capital assets (physical, human, social, technological) lead to improvement in future income earning capacities.

Further, the decision in what proportions to allocate present output to present consumption and future consumption (= current investment) links the economic and social goals of one instant in time to those of other instants in time (Griffin and Enos, op. cit). That is, the decisions made now on how to allocate current output between consumption and savings (and between savings left untouched and savings invested in capital assets) have implications for future economic and social well-being of society. Through the decision as to what profile of investment it chooses over time, the plan is going to influence significantly the structure of output and, particularly in contexts of a 'mixed economy', of public and private ownership systems, the distribution of consumption as well. It seems quite strategic, therefore, for a development plan to specify the temporal choice (time preference function) clearly and express the society's preference here in the form of a goal/objective.

Policy instruments: institutions and technology

Policy instruments refer to those tools that the policy makers intend to manipulate in some way to attempt to achieve policy objectives within the constraints laid down. Society must have evolved viable instruments with which to achieve its objectives; when choosing the latter, society must consider the instruments available to realize them, otherwise it would be engaging in mere wishful thinking. Where the policy instruments fail to match policy objectives, the latter have to be scaled down or reorganized to fit the instruments. This is similar to the budget constraint in consumption theory, for example, where the total purchases of the consumer must not exceed the consumption budget. For instance, in establishing objectives, it will be necessary to estimate the size of the labour force, its composition and skill level, and even sectorial disposition. If pursuing a specific objective- e.g. expanding manufactured exports- will require more of one type of labour skills than could be allocated to it without jeopardizing other, more strategically important goal (e.g. expanding food production to attain domestic food security or reduce food import dependency) then the goal of manufactured exports would have to be abandoned or scaled down.

The problem represents the interdependencies between objectives and instruments, which are usually, solved using mathematical growth models[5]. The objectives, measured precisely, are targets and appear as the dependent variables in the mathematical formulations; the instruments, when stated in equally precise form, appear as independent or explanatory variables. As a rule, the number of instruments must be at least as many as the number of targets (objectives). The instruments can be viewed as comprising the technology (stocks of knowledge) and institutions of society. For instance, the instruments can be thought of as the quality of the human capital in its various dimensions: personal skills of the work force; stocks of expertise society has at its disposal in the form of accumulated information (e.g. computer programmes, data banks, blue-prints of capital equipment, etc.); and entrepreneurship (resource reallocation capability). The instruments can also be viewed as the size of the capital stock and the rates guiding its sectorial allocation; also the processes and relationships which affect the reproduction of the system's capital stock such as, for instance, the savings ratio in GDP, the investment ratio in GDP, the division of gross investment between new investment and replacement (depreciation) investment, etc.

Technology can be produced and reproduced over time, given appropriate policy environment; so also, other investment inputs. On the other hand, institutions represent a more complex element or variable. Institutions not only help to produce outputs; they often try to influence the production and consumption of other products. An example may be cited in land rights. Whereas people attach a lot of emotions and 'moral attitude' to institutions, this is not so for technology; whereas technology tends to limit its effects to its products, institutions tend to have significant externalities, influencing what other people do and how they consume other goods (Griffin and Enos, op. cit.). Given the emotions that go with institutions, changing the latter has always been a long, difficult and painful process, and it is not always successful. It is only in the aftermath of wars, revolutions, depressions and crises that significant institutional changes can occur, a relevant example being the external debt crisis of the 1980s which ushered in fundamental changes in national and international institutional arrangements.

Interdependencies between policy objectives and policy instruments

Once the policy objectives of a development plan have been specified by the political leadership the responsibility of planners is, *inter alia*, to try to establish the interdependencies between those objectives and the instruments to realize them. For instance, if the policy objective is to expand manufactured exports capacities, one obvious primary instrument to be employed will include increasing the level of investment in those sub-sectors of manufacturing with potentials to generate exportable: textiles, food processing, petroleum products, *et cetera*. This primary policy instrument, in turn, becomes a secondary objective to be maximized, which, in turn, requires instruments to realize it, etc.

Figure 2: Interdependencies between Policy Objectives and Policy Instruments in a Development Plan

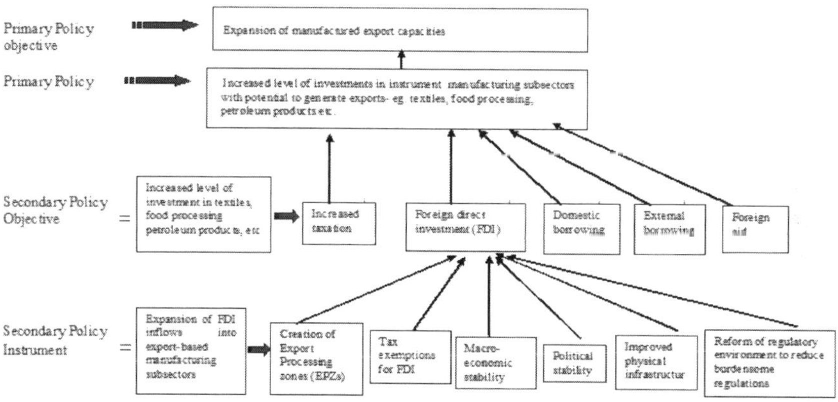

Figure 2 shows the complexities involved in establishing the interdependencies between policy objectives and policy instruments in a development plan illustrating with the hypothetical example of expanding export capacities in manufactures. As can be observed, increased level of investment in the subsectors of manufacturing with potentials to produce exports becomes the primary policy instrument; this in turn becomes a secondary objective, which in turn will require policy instruments to realize (e.g. increased taxes, foreign direct investment (FDI), domestic borrowing, external borrowing, foreign aid, etc.). Of course, the interdependencies are more complicated than has been described by Figure 2. The relationships here are similar to those between causes and effects. Planners must be able to analyse the causes of certain effects in order to be able to find out optimal policy instruments to tackle them. This is the so-called plan consistency problem.

Plan consistency problem

This requires, as hinted above, that the planning process establish alignment between aggregate, macroeconomic targets and targets established for the microeconomic units, including sectors, industries, etc. Usually, three to four processes are involved in establishing plan alignment or consistency (Griffin and Enos, op. cit.):

- We assure that the individual industries and sectors/trades and other micro agencies can reasonably be expected to meet their targets-e.g. that agriculture or sub-sector thereof will produce the required inputs or exports; or that manufacturing capacities will operate at expected levels.
- We scrutinize the other industries utilizing the same inputs with agriculture and manufacturing to ensure that producing the targets in agriculture and manufacturing will not deprive some other, more important industry/ activity of the resources it needs. But other sectors/ commodities apart from agriculture and manufacturing will have their targets too. We also check that the 'great aggregates', namely total output, total income, consumption and investments, exports, imports, etc. and their growth rates are consistent with one another and with their myriad components.
- We check that policy instruments are in alignment with policy objectives. The plan itself must be consistent-e.g., if the target growth rate of GDP is 6% per annum or 3% in per capita terms, then the weighted average growth rate of all items produced and consumed (agricultural crops, petroleum products, shelter, education, health, etc.) must not be less than 3%. If the objective is to redistribute income such that the shares of the top 10% of the income pyramid declines, we make sure that the policy instruments by which this redistribution is to be effected-e.g., comprehensive taxes on personal and corporate income- are established and enforced.

Consistency checks make use of such planning techniques as input-output tables, mathematical/linear programming, econometrics, forecasting and simulation. In subsequent sections we attempt to assess the NEEDS against the framework analysed above.

4. The NEEDS: Overarching Philosophy and Objectives

The NEEDS, described as Nigeria's 'plan for prosperity' and 'the response to the development challenges of Nigeria', is a 4-year medium-term plan covering the period 2003-2007. As a comprehensive plan, the NEEDS seeks to include not only all levels of government (Federal, State, and Local) towards moving in the same direction and, hence, seeking to achieve the same set of objectives, but also seeks to involve the private sector, the Non-Governmental Organization (NGOs) and the general public. Figure 3 provides a picture of the NEEDS at a glance.

The vision (philosophy)

The philosophy of a development plan specifies the objectives in the most abstract, general level; but it reflects, as pointed out earlier, the philosophy of development. According to the NEEDS, the vision is to:

> ...build a truly great African democratic country, politically united, integrated and stable, economically prosperous, socially organized, with equal opportunity for all, and responsibility from all, to become the catalyst of (African) Renaissance, and making adequate all-embracing contributions, sub regionally, regionally, and globally...(NPC, op. cit.: 2).

It seems that the above vision has permitted Nigeria's policy makers and political leadership to single out some key broad objectives (goals): wealth creation; employment generation; poverty reduction; and value reorientation. These four elements of the NEEDS's objective represent the first step by which the vision/philosophy would be translated into some achievable goals/targets.

Figure 3:The NEEDS at a Glance

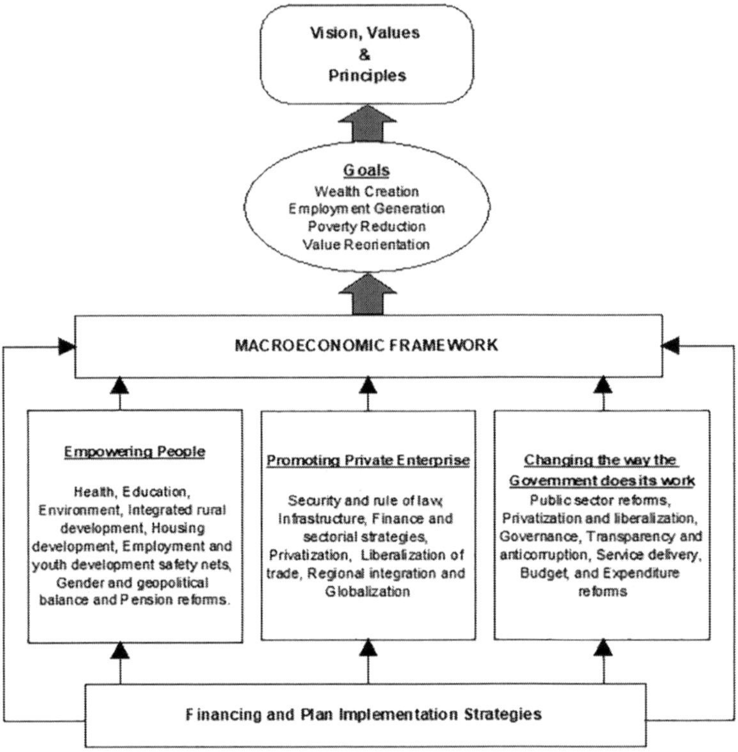

Source: NPC (2004).

The objective of the NEEDS is further elaborated into four as follows: (i) sustain a rapid, broad-based GDP growth rate outside of the oil sector that is consistent with poverty-reduction, employment generation, and sustainable environment; (ii) diversify the production structure away from oil and mineral resources; (iii) make the productive sector internationally competitive; and (iv) systematically reduce the role of government in direct production of goods, and strengthen its facilitating and regulatory functions.

These objectives of the NEEDS were chosen by the Obasonjo regime and are said to draw their inspiration from the Kuru Declaration of 2001 which proposed:

> ...adopt the New Orientation as an agenda for dealing with immediate and future issues of governance in Nigeria; removing impediments to efficiency and effective implementation and execution of programmes initiated by the

> federal government; expeditious actualization of government objectives and vision of national renewal and re-construction… *inter alia* (as cited in NPC, op. cit.: 5).

According to the Kuru Declaration, all public officials, elected and appointed, swear to abide by certain codes of values embodying Nigeria's development objectives and needs. The NEEDS was projected to represent a conscious effort to mobilize the Nigerian people around them.

Translating NEEDS's objectives into targets

Targets represent, as already stated, intermediate goals within the framework of a development plan; being far less abstract than the goals or objectives, plan targets represent specific quantitative results that the plan is designed to produce. As seems clear, the terms 'vision' 'goals' or 'objectives' and 'targets' as used in the present context represent the different hierarchical levels the goals of the NEEDS can be articulated. Indeed, they represent in a descending order of abstraction the goals of the plan, and, ultimately, it is against the 'targets' that the performances of the NEEDS can be measured. It is important that the targets align with the objectives and both (objectives and targets) with the vision or aspiration (see Table 2). Until this was done, it would not be possible to determine just how great an effort would be necessary to meet the NEEDS's objectives. In other words, the movement from the NEEDS's overarching philosophy to the targets (see Table 2) represents the hierarchy of goals/objectives found in development plans: commencing with the abstract (vision) and ending with the most precise (quantifiable) targets. Although the relationship between vision, objectives and targets is often difficult to articulate yet it is vitally important to do this.

Economic growth as the most common plan objective

A casual inspection of the NEEDS would show that economic growth rates (macroeconomic, sectorial) are the most common economic goal or target (see Table 2). But generally using economic growth rates as a goal has a charismatic quality in them: they are easily broadcast, comprehended, and remembered (by economists!). More importantly for the concrete case of the NEEDS, the economists and statisticians, who man Nigeria's National Planning Commission, Ministry of Finance, Central Bank, and other economic ministries, can 'develop and regurgitate' these growth rates. Further, such growth rates can be compared across time; as well, such growth rates can be extrapolated into the long run (quite often however, such extrapolations come off to be significantly off their targets!), as is done in Table 3.

But at the broad policy level, the target rate of growth of GDP or GNP or some other subject of planning has considerable economic significance. If, for instance, Nigeria would be able to achieve a GDP growth rate in real terms (in per capita terms) of 3.8% (as suggested by data on macroeconomic trends in Table 2) in a 10-year period running, for example, for the 2003-2012 period – this would translate into Nigeria's per capita income increasing by 3.8 x 10 = 38% higher relative to its level in 2003- a significant improvement in economic welfare, *ceteris paribus*.

Table 2: Selected Targets under the NEEDS, 2003-2007

(1) Macroeconomic	**2003**	**2004**	**2005**	**2006**	**2007**
Growth in real GDP (%)	10.2	5.0	6.0	6.0	7.0
Growth in Oil sector (%)	23.0	0.0	0.0	0.0	0.0
Growth in non-oil sector (%)	3.3	7.3	8.5	8.3	9.5
Reduction in poverty (%)	5.0	5.0	5.0	5.0	5.0
Minimum number of new jobs (nil.)	-	1.0	2.0	2.0	2.0
Growth in real private consumption (%)	-	4.8	4.8	4.8	4.8
Inflation rate (%)	15.0	10.0	9.5	9.5	9.0
(2) Sectorial					
Growth in agricultural sector (%)	7.0	6.0	6.0	6.0	6.0
Growth in manufacturing sector (%)	-	7.0	7.0	7.0	7.0
Manufacturing capacity utilization used (%)	53.0	-	-	-	-
Communication (teledensity)	1.40	-	-	-	1.25
Agricultural exports	-	-	-	-	$3bn.
Environment Reduce all forms of environmental degradation by 30% of 2004 level by 2007.					
(3) Fiscal					
Maximum public debt deficits (% GDP)	-	3.0	3.0	3.0	3.0
Total expenditure (% GDP)	25.1	23.5	23.4	22.9	22.3
Recurrent expenditure (% budget)	70.0	65.0	60.0	60.0	60.0
Capital expenditure (% budget)	30.0	35.0	40.0	40.0	40.0
(4) External Sector					
External Reserves ($ml)	7.187	7.687	8.687	9.687	10.687
Growth in imports (%)	-	15.0	18.0	25.0	30.1
Growth in exports (%)	-	10.0	20.0	25.0	30.0
Earning from non-oil exports (% total exports)	<5	-	-	-	>10
Food (% total imports)	14.5	-	-	-	7.5

(5) Financial					
Growth in credit to private sector (%)	30.0	30.0	30.0	30.0	30.0
(6) Education					
Adult literacy rate (%)	57.0	-	-	-	65.0
(7) Health					
HIV/AIDS prevalence (%)	6.1	-	-	-	5.0
Immunization coverage (%)	39.0	-	-	-	60.0
Access to safe water (%)	64.1	-	-	-	70.0
Access to adequate sanitation (%)	53.0	-	e-	-	65.0
(8) Infrastructure					
Power generation (megawatts)	-	4000	5000	7000	10,000
Roads (rehabilitation, maintenance, new roads,)	3000	3500	3500	4000	4000

Sources: NPC (op. cit. Table 2).

Table 3: Implications of Alternative Growth Scenarios for Key Objectives of the NEEDS

Scenario	Indicator	Assumed GDP growth rate	2000 (actual)	2015	2030
A	Per capita income	3.6	$300	$328	$352
	Incidence of poverty	3.6	70%	75%	80%
B	Per capita income	5.0	$300	$416	$576
	Incidence of poverty	5.0	70%	70%	70%
C	Per capita income	7.0	$300	$556	$1,031
	Incidence of poverty	7.0	70%	35%	17%

Source: NPC (op. cit. table 2.1, p. 11).

However, per capita GDP growth remains an amorphous development objective. Higher per capita growth rates of GDP may not translate into improvements in the status of Nigerians if economic growth was not accompanied by a structural transformation that would permit the distribution of the dividends of growth in favour of the low-income populations. For instance, if high GDP growth rates were driven by investments in the capital-intensive sectors-e.g. oil and gas, urban-based construction and energy, etc., known to have limited employment absorption potentials, or which require skill-intensive labour which poor rural households can hardly supply, this may not lead to improvements in total welfare, although it might result in uplifting the incomes of the workforce located in those capital-intensive activities.

So, one disadvantage in focusing solely on per capita GDP growth rates as a goal or target in the NEEDS is that it would encourage the allocation of investments to activities or sectors which increase output expansion while paying little attention to those which increase welfare or income redistribution – e.g. agriculture and rural and urban-based small and medium enterprises (SMEs). Besides, focusing on growth tends to encourage production of 'private goods' at the expense of 'public goods' whose contribution to output growth comes indirectly through creation of external economies. There is the need to incorporate explicitly social goals in the NEEDS and purse them with much the same enthusiasm as encouraging private initiatives. On the other hand, however, we should admit that social goals are rather difficult to formulate and yet more difficult to implement. This is, again, particularly true in the contexts of developing countries where implementing social goals – e.g. land asset redistribution, involves changing the existing social structure, tearing down barriers to income and social mobility, providing such 'public goods' as good governance, opportunities for higher education, improved healthcare delivery; gender equality; etc.

5. Choosing the Policy Instruments of the Needs

What are the policy instruments to achieve the objectives and targets specified in the NEEDS? The NEEDS specified the following six broad policy instruments: (i) Privatize, deregulate and liberalize key sectors of the economy; (ii) Coordinate national sectorial development strategies for agriculture, industry, especially small and medium enterprises (SMEs), and services (especially tourism); (iii) Develop infrastructure, especially electricity, transport and water; (iv) Address the problems of finance, and mobilize long-term savings and investment; (v) Create efficient regulatory regimes that include environmental standards, and (vi) Target programmes to promote private sector growth and development (NPC, op. cit.:16).

The NEEDS spells out other policy objectives and corresponding policy instruments: e.g. fiscal policy, balance of payments policy, monetary and exchange rate policies (ibid., pp. 17-25). More important, perhaps, is the 'social charter' dealing on strategies to reduce poverty described as 'the most difficult challenge facing Nigeria and its people and the greatest obstacle to pursuit of sustainable socioeconomic growth' (ibid.: 28). To reduce poverty, the NEEDS proposed to meet the following broad targets, among others: (i) increase average per capita consumption by at least 2% annually; (ii) create about 7million jobs by 2007; (iii) increase the percentage of the population with access to safe drinking water to at least 70% by 2007 (ibid.: 35).

Conflicting objectives and instruments

The NEEDS is replete with multiple, conflicting objectives and instruments. But a macroeconomic model, which would be required to evaluate the major alternatives from among which the economy will choose, is clearly lacking in the NEEDS. Such a model would estimate logically the opportunity cost of attaining the objective-that is, how much of one goal must be given up or sacrificed in order to attain another objective or set of objectives.

Among the NEEDS's objectives are both to reduce poverty and expand non-oil exports between 2003 and 2007 (Table 2). One alternative, which such a model would help to solve, would be how to reduce poverty at an annual rate of 5% combined with growth in exports of 10% annually. Another alternative to be solved under different policies might be an annual reduction in poverty at the rate of 10% combined with an export expansion of 15% annually.

The macroeconomic model would have to show that either alternative is economically feasible–that is realizable, given the resources facing the Nigerian economy during 2003-2007. Then for the policy makers to achieve those objectives within certain constraints, the objectives could be: a target growth rate of GDP or per capita income; some terminal level of consumption, subject to constraints on the composition of GDP; the distribution of income and the availability of factor supplies, etc.

Indeed, the first set of action in formulating a development plan-such as the NEEDS claims to be – must be to construct an aggregate model of the Nigerian economy to highlight and check the implications of the target rate of growth – the consistency problem. This is not available, to the best of our knowledge. Besides, a set of structural equations for the whole economy must be set up, which identifies the restrictions of the various policy instruments which the policy makers must take as datum – i.e. fixed for the NEEDS period. Such structural equations must represent such things as: technological relationships in manufacturing, agriculture, etc.; income consumption relationships; foreign trade relationships; and other behavioural and institutional relationships. The relevant question that comes to mind is: Are these instruments consistent with the objective of the NEEDS and its targets? For example, since the target GDP growth rate averaged 6.8% per annum, or 4% in per capita terms, then the weighted average growth rate of all produced and consumed items-e.g. agricultural crops, petroleum products, shelter, education, health, etc; should average 4% precisely. It is outside the objective of the present study to engage in this type of empirical study.

Temporal goals: the time preference function

As hinted in section 3, one element often found missing in the developing plans of developing countries is temporal goals or the time preference function. This is, also, explicitly missing in the NEEDS. Specifically, there is no framework to analyse how the Nigerian economy or society will distribute its output during the period 2003-2007 between consumption and savings. We are not told how much in terms of financial resources would be required to finance the investments required to achieve the target GDP growth rates, the sources of such financial resources in terms of whether they will come from taxation of domestic incomes, internal borrowings, external loans, FDI, grants and aid, etc. We are told that total expenditure as percentage of GDP will decline from 25.1 to 22.3 during the plan periods, that recurrent expenditure as percentage of the total budget will decline; that capital expenditure as percentage of the total budget will rise from 30 to 40, etc. (Table 2).

The obvious fact that the NEEDS lacks a time preference function means, also, that there is no social rate of discount-that is, the NEEDS lacks a framework with which to discount the potential future social benefits of the NEEDS to establish whether such benefits are worth their present social costs.

In the execution of the NEEDS the Nigerian government will acquire the funds or financial budget of the plan through different means: by taxation; by increasing the public debt by floating bonds, treasury certificates, treasury bills, etc; and by external borrowing. In all three cases the government would be essentially withdrawing money from private-sector savings that otherwise would have been used to finance investments or consumption. These withdrawals would probably reduce immediate private consumption as well as curtail investment for the Nigerian society as a whole for future productivity and economic growth. Thus, they represent a social cost in opportunities lost over time due to diverting private savings into public expenditures or public consumption.

Let us provide some hypothetical example of how such a discount rate might be established. Suppose the budget for financing the NEEDS were derived as follows: 70% from taxation of domestic incomes, 15% from domestic debt, and 15% from external loans; and suppose the time value (opportunity cost) of taxation was 18%, and 20% and 22%, respectively, for domestic debt and external loans. Then the weighted average of the three would be the acceptable social discount rate, calculated as follows:

$$i = 0.70 \times 0.18 + 0.15 \times 0.20 + 0.15 \times 0.22$$
$$i = 0.0306 + 0.03 + 0.033$$
$$i = 0.0936$$

$i = 9.36\%$ is the social discount rate.

Such a result, however, would pose an important problem, precisely because it was obtained by using market interest rates, which would otherwise be acceptable if there was perfect competition, or the opportunity cost was the same for both the private and public sectors. Even though the market interest rate may have been freely determined, those rates may deviate from their optimal level given the absence of perfect capital markets, presence of externalities, etc.

6. Conclusions

The NEEDS fulfils most of the criteria to qualify as a development plan: an over-arching philosophy; explicitly specified core objectives or policy goals; a set of policy instruments to achieve policy goals; and a time horizon. The NEEDS's key defect lies in a clear lack of alignment between its core objectives, namely wealth creation, employment, poverty reduction, and value reorientation on the one side, and on the other the policy instruments, namely, empowering the Nigerian population, promoting private enterprise and changing the way the government does its work. Nor does the NEEDS provide a coherent analysis of the interdependencies that do exist between each of the above objectives and the policy instruments. As seems clear, the policy instruments themselves become objectives to be achieved, which, in turn, demands specification of policy instruments to achieve them.

For instance, wealth creation will need empowerment of the people and promotion of private enterprise as its policy instruments. Poverty eradication will require improved education system to endow Nigerians with the human capital to improve their productivity and, hence, earning potentials, etc. Establishing such interdependencies, complex as they obviously are, requires construction of simultaneous equation models of the Nigerian economy, where the core objectives become dependent variables and the policy instruments independent or explanatory variables; otherwise, it would require an input-output analysis for projecting or assessing how developments in one sector would affect on other sectors.

One constraint on formulating such models and giving empirical content to them would lie in difficulty in building an appropriate data base. The data constraint problem in Nigerian planning was identified long ago in Stolper's (1966) analysis of Nigeria's' first 5-year development plan, 1962-1967. This problem suggests the need to build up a reliable macroeconomic data base as a prerequisite for effective development planning in Nigeria.

Finally, the problems identified in the NEEDS are not peculiar to Nigerian development planning. Indeed, the literature shows that developing countries, generally, have little difficulty articulating plan objectives and specifying targets, and were designing on paper policy instruments. Unfortunately, they have considerable difficulty in plan implementation. The reasons for the latter have to do with, inter alia, insufficient and unreliable data. Todaro and Smith (2009) observe thus:

> The economic value of a development plan depends to a great extent on the quality and reliability of the statistical data on which it is based. When these data are weak, unreliable, or non-existent, as in many poor countries, the accuracy and internal consistency of economy wide quantitative plans are greatly diminished. And when unreliable data are compounded by an inadequate supply of economists, statisticians… (as is also the situation in most poor nations) the attempt to formulate and carry out a comprehensive…plan is likely to be frustrated at all levels' [bracketed words in original].

Endnotes

1 This refers to a definite course or method of action selected from among alternative policy scenarios and in the light of given economic, political, social and physical (environmental) conditions to guide and, usually, determine or guide present and future decision choices.

2 On the other hand, the neoclassical proposition traces to earlier proposition in John Stuart Mill's *A System of Logic* (1874) portraying economic society as a 'social molecule' composed of 'social atoms' (all atoms are alike) whose actions do not affect the dynamics of economic society, nor do the actions of one individual affect those of others.

3 For a good review of some of these technologies, see Todaro and Smith (2009).

4 For an application of the Harrod-Domar model to policy, see Taylor (1975).

5 See, for example, Taylor, op. cit. on the Harrod-Domar growth model as summarized in Todaro and Smith, op. cit. pp. 56-8. See also Griffin and Enos (op. cit, Part Two).

6 The reference here is to NEEDS1 launched in 2003.

References

Aron, J. (2000), 'African in the 1990s: The Institutional foundations of growth', *Working Paper Series WPS/97-15,* Centre for the Study of African Economies, University of Oxford, UK.

Aron, J. (2000), 'Growth and Institutions: A Review of the Evidence' in *The World Bank Research Observer*, 15(1): 99-135.

Arndt, H. W. (1988), 'Market Failure and underdevelopment', in *World Development,* 16: 219-229.

Bergson, A. (1938), 'A reformulation of certain aspects of welfare economics,' in *Quarterly Journal of Economics,* 52(310): 310-334.

Chenery, H. B. (1983), 'The Evolution of Development Planning', *Development Discussion Paper* 158, Harvard Institute for International Development, December.

Dobb, M. (1969), *Welfare Economics and the Economics of Socialism: Towards a Common Sense Critique,* London: Cambridge University Press.

Griffin, K. and Enos, J.L. (1970), *Planning Development,* Boston, MA: Addison-Wesley.

Helfgoth, R. and Schiavo-Campo, S. (1970), 'An Introduction to development planning,' *UNIDO industrialization and Productivity Bulletin, 16.*

Ikeanyibe, O. M. (2009), 'Development Planning in Nigeria: Reflections on the National Economic Empowerment and Development Strategy (NEEDS) 2003-2007,' in *Journal of Social Science,* 20(3): 197-210.

IMF (2005), 'Nigeria: Poverty Reduction Strategy paper-National Economic Empowerment and Development Strategy', *IMF Country Report 05/433*, Washington D.C.: IMF.

Jha, R. (1994), *Macroeconomics for Developing Countries,* London: Routledge.

Meier, G. M. (1989), *Leading Issues in Development* (5th edition), New York: Oxford University Press.

NPC (2004), *Meeting Everyone's needs: National Economic Empowerment and Development Strategy,* Abuja: National Planning Commission.

North, D. C. (1990), *Institutions, Institutional Change and Economic performance,* New York: Oxford University Press.

Onakuse, S. and Lenihan, E. (2007), 'Policies, Programmes and Sustainable Development in Nigeria: in A Critique', in *Africana,* 1(1): 41-58.

Pareto, V. (1971), *Manual of Political Economy,* New York: August Kelley.

Polshikov, P. (1981), *Capital Accumulation and Economic Growth in Developing Africa*, Moscow: Progress Publishers.

Srinivasan, T. N. (2000), 'The Washington consensus a decade later: Ideology and the art science of policy advice', in *The World Bank Research Observer,* 15(2): 265-70.

Stolper, W. F. (1966), *Planning Without facts: Lessons from Resource Allocation from Nigeria's Development,* Cambridge, MA: Harvard University Press.

Tarp, F. (1993), *Stabilization and Structural Adjustment,* London and New York: Routledge.

Taylor, L. (1975), 'Theoretical Foundations and Technical Implications', In Blitzer, C. R, Clark, P. B. and Taylor, L. (eds.), *Economy-Wide Models and Development Planning,* London: Oxford University Press.

Todaro, M.P. and Smith, S.C. (2009), *Economic Development (*10th edition), Boston, MA: Addison-Wesley.

United Nations (1965), *Planning the External Sector: Techniques, Problems, and Policies*, New York: United Nations.

United Nations (2006), *United Nations System in Nigeria: Comments on NEEDS 1 and Suggestions for NEEDS2,* Abuja: UN.

Valk, Peter de (1996), *African Industry in Decline: The Case of Textiles in Tanzania in the 1980s*, The Hague: Macmillan Press Ltd/in association with the Institute of Social Studies (ISS).

Weiss, D. (1990), 'The Theoretical Foundations of Development Planning Under Changing Global Economic Conditions,' in *Economics* (Tubingen), 41: 21-32.

Williamson, J. (1990), 'What Washington means by policy reform', In Williamson, J. (ed.), *Latin American Adjustment: How Much has happened*? Washington, D. C.: Institute for International Economics.

Williamson, J. (2000), 'What should the World Bank think about the Washington Consensus?' in *The World Bank Research Observer,* 15(2): 251-64.

World Bank (1997), '*World Development Report',* (Box 1.4) New York: Oxford University Press.

Zagha, R., Mankani, G. and Gill, I. (2006), 'Rethinking Growth,' in *Finance and Development,* 43 (1): 7-11.

14

Agricultural and Economic Development in Nigeria:

Politics of Fertilizer Subsidy Implementation and Governance Structure

Ayinde, Opeyemi Eyitayo[1]; *Olaoye, Ibukun James*[2]; *Mammo Muchie*[3] & *Oloyede, Adeola Oreoluwa*[4]

1. Introduction

The situation of agriculture and economic development in Nigeria is described as a paradox. In Nigeria, there is a huge potential to diversify the country's oil-reliant mono-cultural economy through the development of its agricultural sector. The sector is one of the pillars of its economy, as it accounts for about 40% of the GDP and 90% of non-oil exports (FAO, 2008; AFDB, 2018). It is a key contributor to poverty

1 Department of Agricultural Economics and Farm Management, University of Ilorin, Ilorin, Nigeria. Department of Agricultural Environmental, Development and Economics, Ohio State University, Columbus, Ohio, USA. Email: opeayinde@yahoo.com & opeyemiayinde@gmail.com

2 Department of Agricultural Economics and Farm Management, University of Ilorin, Ilorin, Nigeria. Email: olaoyeibikunjames@gmail.com

3 DST/NRF SARChI Professor (Innovation & Development), Tshwane University of Technology, South Africa; Technology and Management Centre for Development (TMCD), Oxford University, UK; Associate Faculty Professor, Sussex University, UK; Adama Science and Technology University (ASTU), Ethiopia. Email: MuchieM@tut.ac.za

4 Department of Agricultural Economics and Farm Management, University of Ilorin, Ilorin, Nigeria. Email: oloyedeadeola@gmail.com

alleviation, as a large percentage of the population derive their income from agriculture-related activities, especially the rural farm families (Ayinde et al., 2009; Azhi, 2008; NEEDS, 2004). It is to be noted that more than 70% of the 182 million people are employed in agriculture, mostly in small farms (FAOSTAT, 2015; Fuentes et al., 2012; FAO, 2011; Kolawale & Ojo, 2007). Nevertheless, Nigeria is faced with a looming food security crisis with a growing population as the country is becoming increasingly dependent on imported foods (FMARD, 2016).

Considering that Nigerian population is expected to double by 2030, the agriculture sector will be under severe pressure to produce more to meet the demands from the growing and increasingly urbanized population as well as the export market (Grow Africa, 2016; Fuentes et al., 2012). Insecure land tenure, scarcity of funds and credit, labour shortage (despite overall high unemployment) and stagnant technology have hampered the agricultural modernization and development. Given the limit to land expansion, optimal use of science-based agricultural inputs is necessary to increase the agricultural production (Ismaila et al., 2010; Ayinde et al., 2009). Also, it has been estimated that Nigeria is experiencing deteriorating annual nutrient depletion in soil fertility (Stoorvogel & Smaling 1990; Sheldrick & Lingard 2004) and thus risking its ability to sustain the modest gains achieved from the recent agricultural growth (Liverpool-Taise et al., 2010). Soil degradation due to inappropriate agricultural practices, soil erosion, deforestation and climate change are on the increase in Nigeria (FMARD, 2016). Thus, the once dominant subsistence-oriented farm economy is at risk of gradual marginalization.

The inherent lack of fertility along with the widespread soil nutrient mining have led to the expansion of the agricultural frontier in Africa and the opening up of less favourable soils for cultivation (Morris et al., 2007). Also, the low level of fertilizer usage in Africa compared to West European and Asian countries is one of the factors that explains the lagging agricultural productivity growth (Liverpool-Tasie & Takeshima, 2013; Takeshima & Liverpool-Tasie, 2015; Agbahey et al., 2015). Some scholars argue that as the fertilizer usage in Africa is generally low, the African countries should increase significantly the usage of fertilizer if their agricultural growth targets, poverty reduction goals, and environmental sustainability objectives are to be met (Jayn et al., 2018; Morris et al., 2007). For example, Yamano and Kijima (2010) point out that fertilizer use in sub-Saharan Africa is too low and grossly inadequate to replenish the nutrients lost through the harvested crops.In Nigeria, the fertilizer usage is relatively low (13kg/ha).So, the Nigerian government has been introducing a wide range of policies, programmes and projects to encourage fertilizer use. However, they have had limited impact in ameliorating the problem.

According to Jenkins (1978), a policy simply refers to a set of interrelated decisions concerning the selection of goals and the means of achieving these goals or objectives within a specified situation or time. Policies constitute the foundations of the long-term goals and objectives and the allocation of resources necessary for carrying out these goals and objectives (Chandler 1962, Resnick et al., 2015). However, policies to stimulate increased agricultural productivity in the Sub-Saharan African countries require a wide range of measures which embrace innovations, improved crop production techniques and the optimal use of fertilizer and improved seeds (Vanlauwe et al., 2014; Howard et al., 2003). None of them is likely to be effective if implemented in isolation. The use of fertilizers is considered critical (Zerfu & Larson, 2010; Jayne & Rashid, 2013). Efficient use of fertilizer in crop production has a great potential to increase crop yields and improve productivity (Agbahey et al., 2015; Barbier, 2000). Hence, the striking contrast between the limited use of fertilizer in Africa and extensive use of fertilizer in other developing regions has stimulated considerable discussion about the role of fertilizer in the agricultural development process. It has also generated debate about the types of policies and programmes that are needed to realize the potential benefits of fertilizer in agricultural development in Africa (Morris et al., 2007).

Effective and efficient implementation of fertilizer policy instruments could provide a tool for achieving higher agricultural productivity, improved food security and, through lower food prices, pro-poor economic growth (Dorwards et al., 2014; Mason & Jayne, 2013; Jayne et al., 2013; Ricker-Gilbert et al., 2011). According to Morris et al. (2007), the most significant changes in fertilizer policy over the years include the privatization, dismantling of state fertilizer distribution agencies and the liberalization of the fertilizer sector (e.g., removal of price controls and elimination of subsidies). Governments seek to maximise the benefits of fertilizer policy instruments, especially subsidy, to different stakeholders in order to enhance agricultural development (Morris et al., 2007). The main interest in fertilizer policy has been the need to boost food security in the short-term while also implementing longer-term investments to raise productivity.

Majority of small farmers have been confronted by increasing nutrient-depleted soils, low agricultural productivity, coupled with a rapidly growing population that is increasing the pressure on natural resources and threatens the environment (IFDC, 2013). Fertilizer use can alleviate these challenges, but its consumption is still far below the FAO and 2006 Abuja

Declaration -- 200kg per hectarage recommendation. The increasing population and economic growth are key forces driving the demand for increased food production and fertilizer use (Foresight, 2011; FAO, 2011; Raut & Sitaula, 2012).

Boserup (1965) opined that as population pressure increases, we must find ways to increase the supply of food through the increased use of modern technology.Therefore, to meet the demand of the growing population, we need to use more new technologies and intensified agricultural farming systems (Raut & Sitaula, 2012). Globally, the importance of new technologies and innovations in addressing food security challenges cannot be disputed. Thus, over the years, the governments in many developing countries have acknowledged the need to boost agricultural production as a necessary condition for economic growth and development.

For example, in Nigeria, both past and present governments have used different policy tools to increase usage of fertilizer and productivity simultaneously. The structure of Nigeria's fertilizer policies and market have witnessed changes over the years. The government's efforts to promote fertilizer use in Nigeria have a long and interesting history. According to Morris et al. (2007), direct subsidies that reduce fertilizer prices paid by farmers and centralized control of fertilizer procurement and distribution activities are the major intervention methods used by different governments in the fertilizer market. The Nigerian government has been using various policy approaches including financial measures such as subsidy to increase fertilizer use among small scale farmers. However, despite all the governmental efforts, low fertilizer use remains a problem and low productivity as well as poor farm income are still unaddressed.

In this background, this chapter analyses the politics of fertilizer subsidy implementation and governance structure towards agricultural development in Nigeria. First, it discusses the issues related to fertilizer subsidy in Nigeria. Second, it highlights the political situation of fertilizer policy implementation. Third, in a snapshot, it reveals how the fertilizer policy reforms have improved agricultural production in Nigeria. Lastly, the chapter presents the development consequences in terms of agricultural contribution to GDP and the status of governance in Nigeria.

2. Materials and Methods

The study mainly employs qualitative research approach and uses secondary data gathered from published sources such as journal articles, conference proceedings, newspaper articles, annual reports of nationalgovernment agencies and international organisations, specifically annual reports from the Federal Ministry of Agriculture and Rural Development, and National Bureau of Statistics, in Nigeria.

3. Result and Discussion

This section presents the discussion on the fertilizer subsidy in Nigeria, the politics of its implementation, the governance structure and the situation of Nigeria's agriculture and economic development.

Fertilizer subsidy in Nigeria

In the past, agricultural input subsidies have been used by governments to boost the adoption of new technologies and, thus, increase the agricultural productivity of small farmers in developing countries (Ellis, 1992).In Nigeria, the fertilizer subsidy was phased out during the liberalization policy era in the late 1980s owing to huge government expenditure and some inherent problems with government policy structure. However, the failure of the private sector to meet the demand for fertilizer led to the change in government policy in 2001 and the fertilizer subsidy was reintroduced.

The experience with universal subsidies in SSA was largely negative. It resulted in inefficiencies, such as the adverse selection of programme beneficiaries (which benefited influential/well-off farmers), the displacement of commercial sales, and the subsidies resulted in disproportionate fiscal costs compared to their benefits (Morris et al., 2007). This failure, together with a shift in development paradigm towards structural adjustment, eventually led to the dismantling of fertilizer subsidies. It resulted in the liberalization of fertilizer market and a policy shift towards supporting the development of private-sector-led market (Minot, 2009). However, even during that period, there were strong arguments for maintaining limited subsidies (Reardon et al., 1996). Many observers note that the removal of subsidies coincided with a reduction in food production and fertilizer use (Banful, 2011).

Therefore, large-scale agricultural input subsidies have regained a resurgent interest of the government in Sub-Saharan Africa (Dorward, 2009; Hansen & Baltzer, 2011; Abubakari & Abubakari, 2014; Dorward & Chirwa, 2014). This was due to the rising evidence which showed that access to subsidised farm inputs significantly increases farmers' productivity by reducing transition cost in the adoption of new technologies (Chibwana et al., 2012; Aloyce et al., 2014).

Lowering of input prices through subsidies provide incentives for farmers to use more of the inputs, which in turn, translates into increased output

(Seck, 2016) and higher farm profits (Liverpool-Taise et al., 2017). According to Hansen and Baltzer (2011) and Nwaobiala and Ubor (2015), subsidized agricultural inputs may include improved seeds, fertilizers and crop protection chemicals, and machinery. In Nigeria, the central element of agricultural policy is the input subsidy (Amurtiya et al., 2018; Umar et al., 2015). Fertilizer subsidy alone accounted for about 68% of the government agricultural expenditure in Nigeria in the recent past (Takeshima & Liverpool-Tasie 2013). Over the years, in Nigeria, fertilizer subsidy policy has been changing whenever the government changed. Table 1 shows the cost of fertilizer under the market stabilization scheme and growth enhancement scheme. However, it is noteworthy to highlight that the country experienced three eras of changes (as per the change of the government). They adopted different policy structures and approaches.Under the present government in Nigeria, the aim is to build on the success of the growth enhancement scheme under the Agricultural Transformation Agenda (ATA) (FMARD, 2016). Yet the structure and approach of fertilizer subsidy implementation differ in many aspects. For example, the rate of fertilizer subsidy across each government varied in magnitude and approach of their deliveries. The growth enhancement scheme of the ATA led to the emergence of the use of input voucher using mobile phone technology. Most of these changes and modifications arise as a result of political power play in the government.

Table 1: Cost of Fertilizer Subsidy under Market Stabilization Scheme (2001 – 2010) and Growth Enhancement Support Scheme (2011 – 2015)

Year	Qty of Fertilizer Supplied To Fg (Mt)	Cost of Quantity Supplied (₦)	Subsidy Cost (₦)	Rate of Subsidy (₦ / Mt)	Rate of Subsidy (%)
2001	164,012	4,876,554,998	1,683,000,000	10,261	35
2002	163,700	3,605,662,509	1,485,000,000	9,071.	41
2003	511,841	4,620,418,025	1,188,000,000	2,321	26
2004	560,150	11,024,019,200	2,459,160,000	4,390	22
2005	600,000	8,341,772,360	1,750,432,213	2,917	21
2006	09,000	16,258,649,932	3,507,200,000	4,946	22
2007	990,000	19,422,363,970	4,855,590,994	4,904	25
2008	691,153	57,055,503,960	14,263,875,990	20,637	25
2009	371,062	38,050,847,750	11,000,000,000	10,261	34
2010	586,145	58,429,230,250	22,327,500,000	38,092	38
2011	Na	Na	Na	Na	Na
2012	120,097	13,210,670,000	6,605,335,000	55,000	50
2013	536,095	58,970,450,000	29,485,225,000	55,000	50
2014	1,381,818	152,000,000,000	76,000,000,000	55,000	50
2015	Na	Na	Na	Na	Na

Source: Amurtiya et al., 2018; Ayoola and Ayoola, 2016

Reports have shown that late delivery of inputs in Nigeria is a major challenge faced by farmers (FMADR, 2016; Nwaobiala and Ubor, 2015; Oyediran et al., 2015; Fertilizer Suppliers Association of Nigeria, 2012). Low education and ICT skills among most Nigerian farmers as well as poor network facilities in rural communities have affected the implementation of fertilizer policies (Motilewa et al., 2015; Oyediran et al., 2015; Nwalieji et al., 2013; Nwaobiala and Ubor, 2015; Oyediran et al., 2015; Alabi & Adams, 2015; Fertilizer Suppliers Association of Nigeria, 2012).

Further, the structure of implementation of fertilizer subsidy has created room for corruption (Grow Africa, 2016). The low-density coverage of agro-dealers in the country is another impediment causing farmers to travel relatively long distance to obtain subsidized inputs (Adebo, 2014). The inadequacy of manpower and non-commitment of some of the staff of the ADPs and ministry of agriculture have affected the efficiency of the implementation of fertilizer policy (Nwaobiala and Ubor, 2015; Oyediran et al., 2015; Fadairo et al., 2015).

The successful implementation of any public policy or scheme is largely dependent on the adequacy of information provided to its targeted beneficiaries who are mostly small-scale farmers (Oyediran et al., 2015; National Agricultural Extension and Research Liaison Services, 2012; Nwalieji et al., 2013; Adebo, 2014). Competition between suppliers of fertilizer is subdued because the Federal Government has granted regional monopolies to certain suppliers (Amurtiya et al., 2018).Elite and politically inclined large-scale farmers gained control or influence over subsidy implementation in some areas due to their party affiliation (Amurtiya et al., 2018; Fadairo et al., 2015; Alabi & Adams, 2015) and consequently, rightful beneficiaries were excluded from the fertilizer subsidy programmes (Federal Ministry of Agriculture and Rural Development, 2016). This has had a negative influence on the perception and trust of the farmers towards government programmes, which is likely to affect future government programmes of this nature (Amurtiya et al., 2018). Additionally, fraudulent behaviours of politically influential elites who control the programme implementation tend to result in "leakages" and diversion away from the intended beneficiaries (Dorward & Chirwa, 2011).

Furthermore, it is considered that the quantity of inputs being disbursed is grossly inadequate to meet the needs of small-scale farmers (Fertilizer Suppliers Association of Nigeria, 2012; National Agricultural Extension and Research Liaison Services, 2012) and the types of inputs supplied are inappropriate and of low quality (FMARD, 2016; Fertilizer Suppliers Association of Nigeria, 2012; Liverpool-Taise et al., 2010).

Oxford Business Group (2016) reported that fertilizer subsidy in Nigeria has brought a certain level of improvements in farm outputs but it has failed to transform productivity as expected. The government is still faced with heavy financial implication of inputs subsidy which conversely has serious implications on the effectiveness and sustenance of the fertilizer input subsidy policy. Takeshima and Liverpool-Tasie (2015) reported that the fertilizer subsidy had no significant effect on the local maize and rice prices in Nigeria despite the huge financial implication of the policy on government expenditures. Therefore, there is a need for the government to readdress and strengthen the governance structures of various institutions involved in the implementation of the fertilizer subsidy programmes, to ensure its smooth delivery and effectiveness.

To summarize, it is important to have a clear understanding of politics or political power play in the implementation of fertilizer subsidy programmes and the distribution of subsidized fertilizer to small farmers in Nigeria.

Politics of Fertilizer Policy Implementation

The political economy surrounding fertilizer and agricultural input demand and supply structure have been changing over the years according to the changes that occur in the seat of power. The constant effort of the government to improve small farmers' productivity through policies to aid the adoption of fertilizer is yet to translate into an increase in sustainable agricultural production and rural household income (Liverpool-Taise et al., 2010, 2015, 2017). Most of the small farmers fail to benefit from these government efforts and policies due to poor implementations and wrong targeting (Liverpool et al., 2017, 2015; Ogunfowora, 2000). Previous studies have reported that expenditure on fertilizer subsidy has been too costly for the government (Kherallah et al., 2002; Morris et al., 2007; World Bank, 2008). It was found that most of the subsidized fertilizer fell into the hands of the private sector actors who sold it at a higher price while some of it were even exported through backdoors to neighbouring countries where they were sold at higher price. As a result, only a small part of the subsidized fertilizer finally reached the small-scale farm holders (Obi-Egbedi and Bankole, 2017; Liverpool-Tasie, 2014a, 2014b; Liverpool Taise et al., 2010). These studies concluded that the implementation of the fertilizer policy in Nigeria is ineffective and inefficient.

The politics behind the implementation of the fertilizer policy in Nigeria still remains an issue that needs better reconsideration. The joint participation of the state and private sectors in the fertilizer market remains a topic of concern (Liverpool-Taise & Tekshima, 2013; Fuentes et al., 2012; IFDC, 2001). Figure 1 shows the flow of fertilizer in the market among stakeholders. According to the supply chain presented in Figure 1, the movements of subsidized fertilizer from the public to the private sector are issues that can sabotage the efforts of the government. Generally, fertilizer subsidy policy tends to have a greater impact on the total fertilizer use when administered in areas where the private sector has been inactive and when it targets small scale farming households that cannot pay market price (Xu et al., 2009a, 2009b; Ricker-Gilbert et al., 2011; Mason & Jayne, 2013; Jayne et al., 2013; Mather & Jayne, 2015).

In addition, Nagy and Edun (2002) reported that in the early 1980s fertilizer policy started with states solely involved in procurement and distribution of subsidized fertilizer. Under the Federal Market Stabilization Programme (FMSP), the Nigerian government directly procured and distributed subsidized fertilizer via the state government and the private sector played a minor role (Liverpool-Taise et al., 2010; Oko, 2011; Liverpool-Tasie & Takeshima, 2013). However, the implementation of the structural adjustment programme in the late 1980s and 1990s led to the private control of ownership, procurement and distribution of fertilizer in Nigeria. The failure of the private sector to step up the supply to meet the demand for fertilizer in Nigeria resulted in the reintroduction of the fertilizer subsidy and, thus, the re-entry of government participation in the country's fertilizer market. Since 2001, the government introduced between 35% and 41% subsidy for fertilizer through the growth enhancement scheme of 2011-2015 (Amurtiya et al., 2018; Ayoola & Ayoola, 2016).

Recently, the most important policies and programmes which encapsulate fertilizer subsidy are the Agricultural Transformation Agenda (ATA) and Agricultural Promotion Policy (APP). According to FRMRD (2016), ATA (2011-2015) used the growth enhancement scheme and mobile phone technology vouchers for implementing the fertilizer subsidy. The APP (2016-till date) is using the agribusiness and agripreneurship approach to boost the performance of the ATA scheme. It tries to build on the success of the ATA scheme. However, the politics driving the changes in this policy structure is important because this goes a long way in determining the success or failure of the programme. The roles of fertilizer policy stakeholders (federal and state governments, international donors and NGOs, Ministry of agriculture, relevant institutions, ADPs and fertilizer companies and importers) and the power play between them, as well as the synergy between them remain challenging political issues. They need to be addressed in order to achieve effective and efficient distribution of subsidized fertilizer and accurate scientific monitoring and evaluation of policies.

Figure 1 shows the fertilizer supply and distribution chain in Nigeria. It reveals the flow of fertilizer from importing and blending companies to the state ministry, private sector, ADPs and the sales agents till it reaches the large- and small-scale farmers.

The flow of fertilizer from the state ministry, private sector, and input supply companies to the ADPs is worrisome and questionable as the fertilizer from each outlet come with different prices and costs. In addition to this, both large-scale and small-scale farmers can access fertilizer from different sources with different prices. This could result in farmers, especially, small-scale farmers selling their subsidized fertilizer to agents at higher prices to make a short-term profit instead of waiting till the end of the production season (Liverpool-Taise et al., 2015). Since 1960s, fertilizer subsidy programmes have been implemented in Nigeria where both the Federal and State governments procured fertilizer directly from importing companies and distributed it at subsidized price to farmers (Liverpool-Tasie & Takeshima, 2013).However, commercial marketing of fertilizer has not been banned in Nigeria and the quantity of fertilizer intended for subsidy programme has been large. Hence, there has been a substantial leakage of subsidized fertilizer into the commercial "unsubsidized" market (Takeshima & Liverpool-Tasie, 2013). It was facilitated by a patronage system where the governors and other political office holders used their favoured elites and local governments for distributing subsidized fertilizer, which severely constrained the scheme from reaching the intended beneficiaries.

Figure 1: Fertilizer Supply Chain in Nigeria

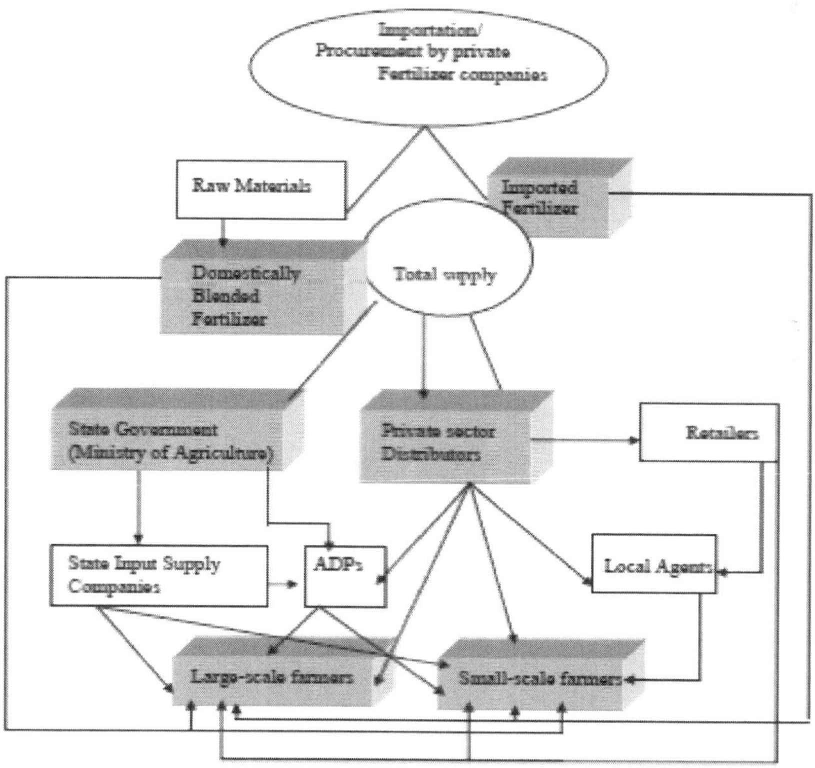

Source: IFDC et al. (2001); Liverpool-Tasie & Takeshima (2013)

Situation of Governance in Nigeria

In recent times, governance has been a topical issue among development policy experts and research scholars globally (Xuehui et al., 2014; Fosu, 2017). It is an instrument used to better evaluate development performance (Rodrik 2008, Acemoglu & Robinson 2012). There is a perception that poor governance is a major factor limiting economic growth and development, especially in developing countries like Africa (Fosu, 2004; Bates, 2008). Poor governance resulted in poor growth due to ineffective policy implementations while good governance enhances growth and development through effective and efficient policy implementations (Ndulu et al., 2008; Fosu, 2017). This implies that whether a government implements one policy or the other, its success depends more on the governance structure of the country than the policy itself. Therefore, we assess six-governance indicators in Nigeria: (i) voice and accountability; (ii) political stability and absence of violence/terrorism; (iii) government effectiveness; (iv) regulatory quality; (v) rule of law; and (vi) control of corruption. For this we use world governance indicators (WGI) data. We relate implications of the governance settings in Nigeria for monitoring and evaluation of the fertilizer policy, as well as overall agricultural development. Figure 2 shows the graph of the six-governance indicators for Nigeria between 1996 – 2016. It reveals that the governance situation in Nigeria is poor since all the indicators are negative. The indicators are measured on scale with scores ranging from -2.5 to +2.5 representing poor and good governance respectively. Most of the indicators are fluctuating except for government effectiveness that seems relatively stable but still negative. Particularly two indicators - political stability, violence and terrorism, and rule of law, are highly negative. The implication of poor governance settings cannot be separated from the poor implementation of fertilizer policy in Nigeria, which has negatively affected the policy impact on farmers' output and rural income.

To sum up, poor governance settings in Nigeria appear to have affected the effective implementation of agricultural development policies. So, it is imperative that Nigeria take measures to improve its governance structure because this is fundamental for effective implementation of development policies such as fertilizer subsidy policy.

Figure 2: Governance Indicator for Nigeria (1996 -2016)

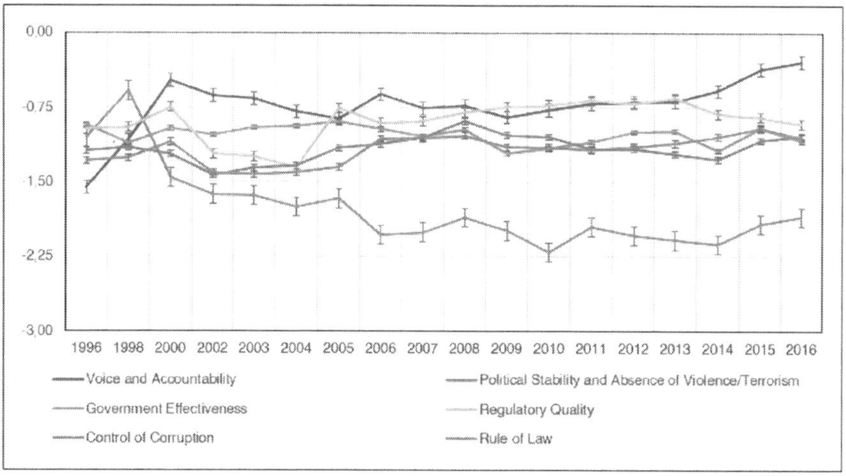

Source: Authors' Construct using the World Bank, Worldwide Governance Indicators online database (Accessed: 17 October 2018)

Snapshot of Agricultural production and Economic Development in Nigeria

Agricultural production alongside non-farm or off-farm activities constitute a major source of income for most rural households. Generally, they depend directly or indirectly on agriculture for food and livelihood. In Nigeria, agriculture plays a key role and has a potential to be a dominant force in achieving sustainable food security in the future. But, at present, most small farmers are facing several problems such as nutrient-depleted soil, low agricultural productivity, and declining land per capita (IFDC, 2013). Despite these problems, the contribution of agriculture to the national economy cannot be underestimated.For example, this can be seen from the cereal production in Nigeria. Cereal remains the most common group of crops that farmers cultivate by applying fertilizer during the planting periods. According to Ismaila et al. (2010), major cereals produced in Nigeria include rice, sorghum, maize, and pearl millet. Figure 3 shows the total production of maize, rice, sorghum and millet in tonnes as well as area of land under cereal production in '000 hectares between 1980 and 2014. It is observed that the area of land under cereal cultivation increased sharply in 1990 and it became relatively stable afterwards.It declined slightly around 2000 and 2010 and then it increased significantly.The cereal production, especially sorghum, maize and rice, has increased but relatively low compared with the size of land under cereal production. However, the increase in cereal production could be the result of increase in area of land under cultivation and it may not be due to the increase in inputs such as fertilizer. Factors identified militating cereal productivity in Nigeria include climatic factors, soil conditions, migration, government policies, use of local varieties, prevalence of weeds, pest and diseases (Ismaila et al., 2010), and failure to intensify the use of improved inputs such as fertilizer, seeds and pesticides (Ogunwole et al., 2004). Therefore, in order to ensure inputs such as fertilizer and improved seeds are accessible to targeted farmers and the subsidy programme achieves the desired aim, there is need to address weak governance structure and its functioning in the country. The government needs to transform this situation by strengthening the institutions and reforming policy implementation process.

Figure 4 provides a snapshot of agricultural value-added and economic development in Nigeria. The time series graphs show that all economic indicators of the country are poor and even worse in the recent years. The inflation of consumer prices has been increasing since 2014, real per capita income and the real GDP income have been declining during this period. The agricultural value added is stagnating at the minimum point since 2011. Therefore, it is imperative that the Nigerian government take strong measures to overcome the governance structural problems.It is evident that unless the government transforms the governance structure, it is unlikely to achieve sustainable agricultural and economic growth and development.

Figure 3: Cereal Production in Nigeria

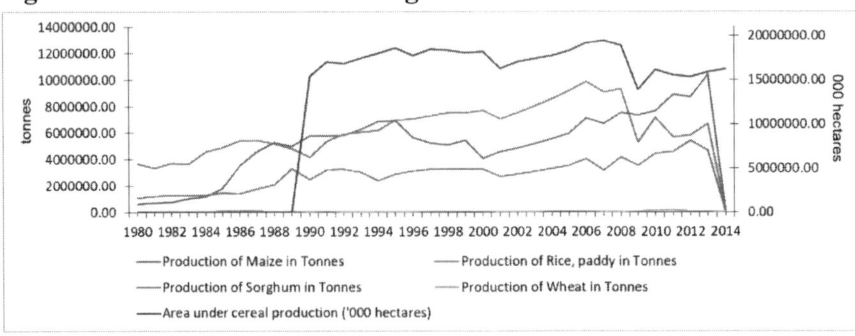

Source: http://dataportal.opendataforafrica.org/bbkawjf/afdb-socio-economic-database-1960-2019?country=1000590-nigeria

Figure 4: Indicators of Macroeconomic and Agricultural Performance in Nigeria

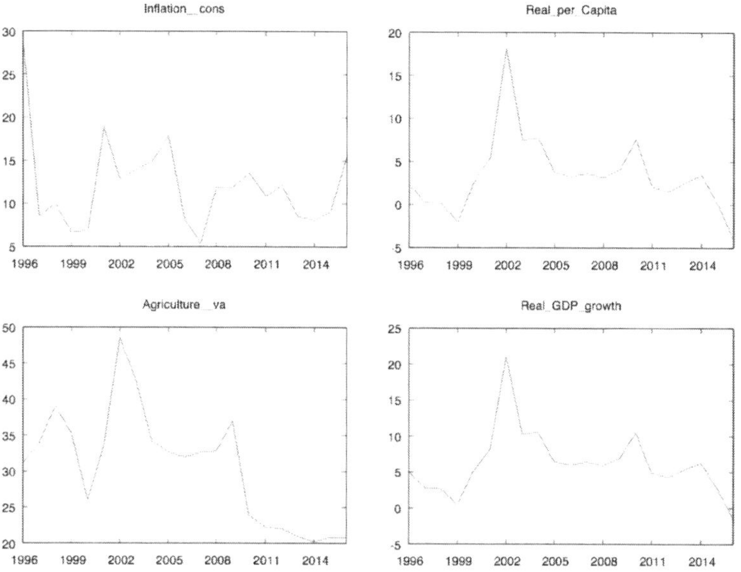

Source: http://dataportal.opendataforafrica.org/bbkawjf/afdb-socio-economic-database-1960-2019?country=1000590-nigeria (computed using Gretl)

Conclusion and Recommendation

This study analyses the politics of the fertilizer subsidy implementation and governance structure and their impact on agricultural development in Nigeria. It found that the fertilizer subsidy is still used as a major policy instrument by the government to boost agricultural productivity and small-scale farmers' income in order to achieve pro-poor growth and development. The study shows that robust agricultural subsidy implementation strategies (not influenced by unhealthy politics) and good governance structure will help drive sustainable agricultural development in Nigeria and in other African countries. Thus, we recommend that the Nigerian government should take steps to dissociate agricultural policy implementation from partisan politics and strengthen the governance structure to ensure proper monitoring and evaluation of its policies and programmes. Hence, a more holistic approach will be required to achieve sustainable agricultural productivity in Nigeria. Small-scale farming households should be encouraged to explore more and better innovative means to stimulate their productivity such as the use of complementary improved inputs and climate smart management practices.

Reference

Acemoglu, D. and Robinson, J. A.(2012), *Why Nations Fail: The Origins of Power, Prosperity, and Poverty*, New York: Crown Business.

Adebo, G. M. (2014), 'Effectiveness of E-Wallet Practice in Grassroots Agricultural Services Delivery in Nigeria – A Case Study of Kwara State Growth Enhancement Support Scheme', *Journal of Experimental Biology and Agricultural Sciences*, 2(2320): 410–418.

African Union (2006), *Abuja Declaration on Fertilizer for an African Green Revolution*, 13 June 2006, Abuja, Nigeria.

Agbahey J. U. I., Grethe, H. and Negatu, W.(2015), 'Fertilizer supply chain in Ethiopia: structure, performance and policy analysis', *Afrika Focus,* 28(1): 81-101

Aloyce, G. M., Gabagambi, D. M. and Hella, J. P. (2014), 'National Agricultural Input Voucher Scheme Impact on Productivity and Food Security of Smallholder Farmers in Tanzania,' *Journal of Economics and Sustainable Development*, 5(21): 32–43.

Ayinde, O.E., Adewumi M.O. and Omotosho F. I. (2009), 'Effect of Fertilizer Policy on Crop Production in Nigeria', *The Social Sciences,* 4(1): 53-58.

Ayoola, G. and Ayoola, J. S. (2016), 'The Transformation of Smallholder Agriculture in Africa: Lessons in Policy Experimentation and Governance from Nigeria, Invited poster presentation, *5th International Conference of the African Association of Agricultural Economists*, September 23-26, Addis Ababa, Ethiopia.

Ayoola, G.B., Chude V. O., and Abdulsalaam A. A. (2002), 'Toward a Fertilizer Regulatory Policy for Nigeria: An Inventorization of the Fertilizer Sector', A study commissioned by the Federal Fertilizer Department (FFD), Federal Ministry of Agriculture and Rural development, Abuja,May, 2002.

A study commissioned by the Federal Fertilizer

Department (FFD), Federal Ministry of Agriculture and Rural development, Abuja. May, 2002

Azih, I. (2008), 'A Background Nnalysis of the Nigerian Agricultural Sector (1998 to 2007)', OXFAM NOVIB Economic Justice Campaign in Agriculture.

Azih, I. (2008), 'A Background Nnalysis of the Nigerian Agricultural Sector (1998 to 2007)', OXFAM NOVIB Economic Justice Campaign in Agriculture.

Barbier, E.B. (2000), 'Links between Economic Liberalization and Rural Resource Degradation in the Developing Regions', *Agricultural Economics*, 23: 299-310.

Bates, R. (2008), 'Political Reform', in B. Ndulu, S. O'Connell, R. Bates, P. Collier and C. Soludo (eds.), *The Political Economy of Economic Growth in Africa 1960-2000*, Cambridge: Cambridge University Press, pp. 349-390.

Chandler, A. (1962), *Strategy and Structure*, Cambridge, MA: MIT Press.

Dorward A. (2009), 'Rethinking Agricultural Input Subsidy Programmes in a Changing World', Paper prepared for the Trade and Markets Division, Food and Agriculture Organization of the United Nations. Aavailable at:http://www.fao.org/es/esc/common/ecg/586/en/Dorward_FAO_Subsidy_Paper_FINAL.pdf.

Dorward A., Roberts, P. D.,Finegold, C.,Hemming, D. J. ,Chirwa, E.,Wright, H.J.,Hill, R. K., Osborn, J.,Lamontagne-Godwin, J.,Harman, L.,and Parr, M. J. (2014), 'Protocol: Agricultural Input Subsidies for improving Productivity, Farm Income, Consumer Welfare and Wider Growth in Low- and Middle-Income Countries: A Systematic Review', The Campbell Collaboration | www.campbellcollaboration.org

Dorward, A., Chirwa, E., Kelly, V.,Jayne, T. S.,Slater, R.and Boughton, D. (2008), *Evaluation of the 2006/07 Agricultural Input SubsidyProgramme, Malawi.* Final Report, Lilongwe, Malawi.

Druilhe, Z. and Barreiro-Hurlé, J. (2012), 'Fertilizer subsidies in sub-Saharan Africa', *ESA Working paper No. 12-04*, Agricultural Development Economics Division, Food and Agriculture Organization of the United Nations, Rome, Italy. www.fao.org/economic/esa

Ellis, F. (1992), *Agricultural Policies in Developing Countries,* Cambridge University Press, Cambridge, UK.

FAO (2008), 'An international technical workshop, Investing in sustainable crop intensification: The case for improving soil health', *Integrated Crop Management,* vol. 6, Rome.

FAO (2011), *Current World Fertilizer Trends and Outlook to 2015*. Food and Agriculture Organization, United Nations, Rome, Italy.

FAOSTAT (2015), 'Data Extract from World Development Indicator', Washington D.C.: World Bank.

FMARD (2016), 'The Agriculture Promotion Policy (2016 – 2020)', *Building on the Successes of the ATA, Closing Key Gaps,* Policy and Strategy Document for Nigeria.

Foresight (2011), 'The future of food and farming: Challenges and choices for global sustainability', Final project report, The Government Office for Science, London.

Fosu, A. K. (2004), 'Mapping Growth into Economic Development: Has Elite Political Instability Mattered in Sub-Saharan Africa?', *American Journal of Economics and Sociology*, 63(5): 137-156.

Fosu, A. K. (2013), 'African Economic Growth: Productivity, Policy Syndromes and the Importance of Institutions', *Journal of African Economies*, 22 (4): 523-551.

Fosu, A. K. (2017), 'Governance and development in Africa: A concise review', *GDI Working Paper 2017-002*, Manchester: The University of Manchester.

Fuentes, P.A., Bumb, B. and Johnson, M. (2012), 'Fertilizer Markets in West Africa: The Fertilizer Supply Chain in Nigeria', International Fertilizer Development Center (IFDC) and International Food Policy Research Institute (IFPRI) Paper Series IFDC – P-42.

Grow Africa. (2016), *Fertilizer Subsidy Reform Revives Nigeria's Agriculture*. Abuja, Nigeria: Grow Africa. http://dataportal.opendataforafrica.org/bbkawjf/afdb-socio-economic-database-1960-2019?country=1000590-nigeria

IFDC (2013), 'Developing Competitive Fertilizer Market in Sub-Sahran Africa: Policy and Non Policy Solutions. A background Paper on Fertilizer', Policy expert meeting on Technical Convening on Seed and Fertilizer Policy in Africa, Addis Ababa, Ethiopia, December 5-7.

Igudia, P. O. (2017), 'A Qualitative Analysis of the Agricultural Policy Dynamics and the Nigerian Economy: 1960-2015', *European Scientific Journal* 13 (34): 284-312. Doi: 10.19044/esj.2017.v13n34p284

International Fertilizer Development Center (IFDC), International Institute for Tropical Agriculture (IITA) & West African Rice Development Association (WARDA) (2001), 'Agricultural input markets in Nigeria: an assessment and a strategy for development', IITA.

International Fertilizer Development Centre (IFDC) (2003), 'Input Subsidies and Agricultural Development: Issues and Options for Developing and Transitional Economies', Paper Series, Muscle Shoals, USA.

Ismaila, U., Gana, A. S., Tswanya, N. M.and Dogara, D. (2010), 'Cereals production in Nigeria: Problems, constraints and opportunities for betterment', *African Journal of Agricultural Research* 5(12): 1341-1350, http://www.academicjournals.org/AJAR DOI: 10.5897/AJAR09.407

Jayne, T.S., and Rashid, S. (2013), 'Input subsidy programs in sub-Saharan Africa: a synthesis of recent evidence', *Agricultural Economics*, International Association of Agricultural Economists, November, 44 (6): 547–562.

Jayne, T. S., Mather, D.,Mason, N., and Ricker-Gilbert, J. (2013), 'How do fertilizer subsidy programs affect total fertilizer use in sub-Saharan Africa? Crowding out, diversion and benefit/cost assessments', *Agricultural Economics*, 44(6): 687–703.

Jayne, T.S., Mather, D., Mason, N.M, Ricker-Gilbert, J. and Crawford, E.W. (2015), 'Rejoinder to the comment by Andrew Dorward and Ephraim Chirwa on Jayne, T. S., D. Mather, N. Mason, and J. Ricker-Gilbert. 2013. How do fertilizer subsidy program affect total fertilizer use in sub-Saharan Africa? Crowding out, diversion, and benefit/cost assessments', *Agricultural Economics,* 46(6): 745-755.

Jayne, T.S., Sitko, N.J., Mason, N.M., and Skole, D. (2018), 'Input subsidy programs and climate smart agriculture: Current realities and future potential', In: Lipper, L., McCarthy, N., Zilberman, D., Asfaw, S., Branca, G. (Eds.), *Climate Smart Agriculture: Building Resilience to Climate Change*, Springer, Cham, Switzerland, pp. 251–273.

Jenkins, W. (1978), *Policy Analysis*, London: Martin Robertson.

Kherallah, M., Delgado, C., Gabre-Madhin, E.Z., Minot, N., and Johnson, M., (2002), *Reforming Agricultural Markets in Africa*, Baltimore: Johns Hopkins University Press.

Kolawale, O., and Ojo, S.O. (2007), 'Economic efficiency of small scale food crop production in Nigeria: A Stochastic Frontier Approach', *Journal of Social Sciences*, 14(2): 128-130.

Liverpool-Tasie, L. S. O., Omonona, B. T., Sanou, A., and Ogunleye, W. (2015), 'Is Increasing Inorganic Fertilizer Use in Sub-Saharan Africa a Profitable Proposition?Evidence from Nigeria', *Policy Research Working Paper 7201*, World Bank Group Africa Region Office of the Chief Economist.

Liverpool-Tasie, L.S.O., and Takeshima, H. (2013), 'Input promotion within a complex subsector: fertilizer in Nigeria',*Agricultural Economics,* 44: 581–594

Liverpool-Tasie, L.S.O. & Takeshima, H. (2013), *Moving Forward with Fertilizer in Nigeria: Fertilizer Promotion Strategies within a Complex Fertilizer Subsector.* Mimeo.

Liverpool-Tasie, L.S.O. (2014a), 'Fertilizer subsidies and private market participation: the case of Kano State, Nigeria', *Agricultural Economics*, 45 (6): 663–678.

Liverpool-Tasie, L.S.O., (2014b), 'Do vouchers improve government fertilizer distribution? Evidence from Nigeria', *Agricultural Economics,* 45 (4): 393–407.

Liverpool-Tasie, S. L.O., Auchan, A. A. and Banful, A. B. (2010), 'An Assessment of Fertilizer Quality Regulation in Nigeria', *Nigeria Strategy Support Program (NSSP) Report 09*. International Food Policy Research Institute.

Mather, D., and Jayne, T.S., (2015), 'Fertilizer subsidies and the role of targeting in crowding out: An assessment of smallholder fertilizer demand in Kenya', *The International Conference of Agricultural Economics*, 9-14 August. Milan, Italy.

Morris, M., Valerie, A. K., R. J., Kopicki, R. J., and Byerlee, D., (2007). 'Fertilizer use in African Agriculture: Lessons Learned and Good Practice Guidelines', Directions in Development; Agriculture and Rural Development. Washington, DC: World Bank. https://openknowledge.worldbank.org/handle/10986/6650 License: CC BY 3.0 IGO.

Nagy, J.G. and Edun, O. (2002), *Assessment of Nigerian Government Fertilizer Policy and Suggested Alternative Market-Friendly Policies*. Consultants to IFDC.

NEEDS (2004), 'National Economic Empowerment and Development Strategy (NEEDS), Nigeria', The NEEDS Secretariat, National Planning Commission, Federal Secretariat, Abuja.

Ndulu, B., O'Connell, S., Bates, R., Collier, P. and Soludo, C. (eds.) (2008), *The Political Economy of Economic Growth in Africa 1960-2000*, Vol. 1, Cambridge: Cambridge University Press.

Nedergaard, P. (2006), 'Market failures and government failures: A theoretical model of the common agricultural policy', *Public Choice* 127: 385-405.

Obi-Egbedi, O. and Bankole, O. A. (2017), 'Determinants of participation in fertilizer subsidy programme among rice farmers in Ogun State, Nigeria', *Journal of Development and Agricultural Economics*, 9(6): 162-167.

Ogunfowora, O. (2000), 'The Travails of Nigerian Agricultural Inputs Supply System: Which Way Forward?', ACS ABISE Consulting System (NIG) Ltd., 5th Tai Solarin Memorial Lecture, Mayflower School, Ikenne, Nigeria.

Ogunwole, J.O., Bello, A.L. and Owonubi, J.J. (2004), 'Environmental characterization of cereals producing areas of Nigeria', In: Idem, N.U.A. and Showemimo, F.A. (eds.), *Cereal crops of Nigeria: Principles of Production and Utilization*, pp. 16- 37.xxii, 337. Zaria: Ade Commercial Press.

Oko, W. E. (2011), 'Impact of Fertilizer Policy on Crop Production in Nigeria', *Master thesis*, Department of Agricultural Economics Faculty of Agriculture University of Nigeria, Nsukka.

Oxford Business Group (2016), 'State efforts to boost agricultural output in Nigeria'. Available at: http://www.oxfordbusinessgroup.com/overview/state-efforts-boost-agricultural-output-nigeria.

Oyediran, W. O., Dick, T. T., Owolade, E. O., and Oluade, E. A. (2015), 'Contributions of Growth Enhancement Support Scheme (GESS) programme to food security and poverty alleviation of Agricultural Cooperatives in Ogun State, Nigeria', *Journal of Educational Policy and Entrepreneurial Research (JEPER)*, 2(June): 13–22.

Raut, N., & Sitaula, B.(2012), 'Assessment of Fertilizer Policy, Farmers' Perceptions and Implications for Future Agricultural Development in Nepal', Sustainable Agriculture Research; 1 (2), http://dx.doi.org/10.5539/sar.v1n2p188

Resnick D., Babu, S., Haggblade, S., Hendriks, S. and Mather, D. (2015), 'Conceptualizing Drivers of Policy Change in Agriculture, Nutrition, and Food Security: The Kaleidoscope Model', *Food Security Policy (FSP) Discussion Paper*, January 2015.

Ricker-Gilbert, J., and Jayne, T.S. (2011), 'What are the enduring effects of fertilizer subsidy programs on recipient farm households: Evidence from Malawi?', *MSU Staff Paper No. 2011-09*, East Lansing, MI: Michigan State University.

Ricker-Gilbert, J., and Jayne, T.S., (2012), 'Do fertilizer subsidies boost staple crop production and reduce poverty across the distribution of smallholders in Africa? Quantile regression results from Malawi', *The Triennial Meeting of the International Association of Agricultural Economists*, 18-24 August, Foz Do Iguacu, Brazil.

Ricker-Gilbert, J., Jayne, T., and Chirwa, E. (2011), 'Subsidies and Crowding Out: A Double-Hurdle Model of Fertilizer Demand in Malawi', *American Journal of Agricultural Economics*, 93(1): 26-42.

Stoorvogel, J.J., and Smaling, E.M.A., (1990), 'Assessment of Soil Nutrient Depletion in Sub-Saharan Africa: 1983-2000', Vol. 1., Main Report, 2nd Edition. Winand Staring Centre, Wageningen, The Netherlands. https://library.wur.nl/isric/fulltext/isricu_i25329_001.pdf

Takeshima, H. and Liverpool-Tasie, L. S. O. (2013), 'Fertilizer subsidy, political influence and local food prices in sub-Saharan Africa: Evidence from Nigeria', *The Agricultural & Applied Economics Association's AAEA & CAES Joint Annual Meeting,* Washington, DC, August 4-6, 2013.

Vanlauwe, B., Kihara, J., Chivenge, P., Pypers, P., Coe R. and Six, J. (2011), 'Agronomic use efficiency of N fertilizer in maize-based systems in sub-Saharan Africa within the context of integrated soil fertility management', *Plant and Soil*, 339: 35–50.

World Bank (2008), *World Development Report 2008: Agriculture for Development.* Washington, D.C.: World Bank.

Xu, Z., Guan, Z., Jayne, T.S., and Black, R., (2009a), 'Profitability of applying fertilizer on maize for smallholder farmers in Zambia'. *Agricultural Economics*, 40 (4): 437–446.

Xu, Z., Burke, W.J., Jayne, T.S., and Govereh, J., (2009b), 'Do input subsidy programs 'crowd in' or 'crowd out' commercial market development? Modeling fertilizer use decisions in a two-channel marketing system' *Agricultural Economics,* 40 (1): 79–94.

Xuehui, H., Haider, K., and Juzhong, Z. (2014), 'Do Governance Indicators Explain Development Performance? A Cross-Country Analysis', *ADB Economics Working Paper Series. No 417.*

Zerfu, D. and Larson, D. (2010), 'Incomplete markets and fertilizer use: Evidence from Ethiopia', *Policy Research Working Paper 5235*, Washington, D.C.: World Bank.

15

The Transformation of the Global System and its Implications for Africa

Dani W. Nabudere[1]

1. Introductory Remarks

The global capitalist crisis that occurred in 2007-08 has changed the way we shall relate to the future. Mass democratic pressures such as those we are witnessing in the Arab World are already indicative of the way countries will try to cope with problems of equality in economics and freedoms in political life. The economic meltdown that occurred is deep and it is amazing that when the crisis struck the majority of mainstream economists did not see its magnitude and its long-term implications. Indeed, some economists at first viewed the meltdown as purely an American phenomenon. It was, they argued, a 'sub-prime mortgage crisis.' Others who saw deeper elements in the crisis called it a 'credit crunch,' but soon realised that it was not a 'credit crunch' related only to the 'sub-prime' mortgage crisis, but a 'financial crisis' as well. Even with this broadened understanding, the crisis was still regarded as mainly a US problem and not a global one.

By the beginning of 2009, some political leaders in the G 20 countries and economists, including 'monetarist economists,' realised that the crisis was a multifaceted one and that at bottom; it was a 'global economic crisis.'

1 (Late) Former Vice Chancellor, Marcus Garvey University, Upper Mooni, Mbale, Uganda.

Already from mid-September 2008, the effects begun to be felt globally as US leaders begun to talk of an eminent 'recession.' In early October 2008, I was one of the few observers who predicted the seriousness of the widening crisis. I wrote three short articles for a local Uganda Sunday newspaper called *The Sunday Monitor* in which I warned that what we were witnessing was not just a 'financial crisis' nor an 'economic crisis' but a 'global capitalist economic crisis' and that the crisis was a terminal one for capitalism. This is what I wrote:

> The present 'financial' crisis afflicting the global economy should not be seen from the narrow focus of the credit crunch and its relationship to the subprime mortgage crisis in the Western countries, especially the US. The crisis goes to the very foundations of the global capitalist system and it should be analysed from that angle. What is at the core of the crisis is the over-extension of credit on a narrow material production base. This is in a situation in which money has become increasingly detached from its material base of a money commodity that can measure its value such as gold. But this is not just a monetary phenomenon. It has its roots in the 'real economy' of which it is part" (*The Sunday Monitor*, 2008).

I was able to comment quickly and assess the magnitude of what was happening because I had in the 1980s done a serious study of money and credit which resulted in the publication of one major work: *The Rise and Fall of Money Capital* (1990) and its shorter version: *The Crash of International Finance* (1989) following the 'Bloody Monday' crisis of October 1987. In writing these volumes, I studied all the works of Karl Marx dealing with Capital and Money as well as the work of the then only serious bourgeois economist who appeared to understand money, Maynard Keynes, who had tried to grapple with the consequences of the 'industrial cycle' in the interwar period and how to manage it. In those works, we demonstrated how capital in the form of finance capital had lost its productive power and how it had increasingly resorted to 'financiering' and the 'making money out of money without production,' which later became the dominant factor behind the 2008 economic 'meltdown.'

It is clear now that despite the attempts to fight the recession and achieve some amount of economic recovery, the economies of major developed countries such as the US, Britain and most EU countries as well as Japan are still fragile and unstable. Germany has done much better because of its reliance on the Chinese recovery by supplying it with capital goods. What is characteristic of all countries of the world is the growing inequality, poverty and the galloping food prices for the majority of their populations. The crises that we are witnessing in the countries of the Middle East and North Africa have been sparked off by the food crisis, which is only one aspect of the deep inequality in the world. The crisis of capitalism at its core can be traced at the level of distribution in the food crisis in the mid-2008s, which turned out to be linked to the speculations in the global commodities markets.

This is why the financial crisis was also a reflection of the energy and food crisis occurring at that time, because oil and food products such as oil, wheat, rice and other commodities had been subjected to speculative trading, which acted as 'hedges' against risk in backing up highly leveraged paper financial instruments such as 'future contracts,' derivatives and Collateralised Debt Obligations or CDOs. The British Prime Minister, Gordon Brown, among the world leaders, was the only one who saw this connection when he brought up the issue in the World Bank meeting called to address the food crisis in 2008. The real problem underlying currency instability and commodity price volatilities was that the dollar, which acts as a global reserve currency, was not backed by any solid money commodities such as gold or silver and this is because these money-commodities could no longer fulfil those functions, which they were supposed to do under capitalism. This is what led to the food commodities coming into the picture as 'hedges' to back up 'future contracts' and derivatives expressed in US dollars and held by banks.

The number of speculative future contracts for wheat, which made commitments to buy or sell a given volume of wheat at a certain future date at a predetermined price, for instance, had quadrupled over the previous five years (2003-2008). What made matters worse was the fact that speculation had become especially active by exploiting the record low inventories in the existing agricultural commodities. In the past 25 years, most countries had gradually abandoned the policy of stocking grains and other agricultural commodities, which acted as food security stocks. With the food market being in turmoil, there were no food cushions to absorb the impact of any sudden disruption in their ability to import grains.

During the first three months of 2008, international nominal prices of all major food commodities reached their highest levels for fifty years. The United Nations Food and Agricultural Organisation-FAO reported that food price indices had risen, on the average, by 8% in 2006 compared with the previous year. In 2007, the food index rose by 24% compared with 2006 and in the first three months of 2008, it rose by 53% compared with 2007. This sudden surge was led by increases in vegetable oils, which on the average increased by 97%, followed by grains with an increase of 87%, dairy products with 58% and rice with 46%. This trend has continued since 2007-2008 and what we are witnessing in the streets of Tunisia, Cairo, Tripoli, Yemen, Syria, and Bahrain is partly a reflection of this capitalist crisis.

2. The Tunisian origin of the Arab Revolutions

The events in Arab world and especially, in Egypt, which has been dubbed the 'Youth Revolution', were very much ignited by these developments, which included the development of the 'Face Book' social networks. These networks are the products of technological changes that have occurred in the capitalist world and which are highly connected with the global economic situation discussed above. This is because of the role the electronic media, especially the mobile telephony, Face Book, Twitter and other social networks have played in these events. These revolts have challenged the rights of dictators who have ruled their countries for decades under 'emergency' conditions in order to prevent their citizens enjoying their freedoms, including the right to employment.

The conditions of desperation that global capitalism has created in Arab world as well as in many other parts of the global South were behind the uprising in Tunisia. It will be recalled that Mohamed Bouzizi was an unemployed young man who was trying to sell some vegetables on the street to earn a living given the high rates of unemployment in that country. Bouzizi was arrested and beaten up by the police for daring to earn a living on the streets and refusing to pay a bribe to be let free. This, in the eyes of the population, symbolised the 'heartlessness' of a State that had lost all human contact with its citizens. Instead of empathising with Bouzizi's plight, Bouzizi was instead harassed on several occasions by agents of the State, assaulted, humiliated and prevented from attempting to engage in some income generating activity on which he and his family could depend. It was out of the desperation of this harassment that Bouzizi in an act of defiance set himself on fire and killed himself.

This act of bravery triggered off demonstrations on the part of his family in Sidi Bouzid, which were joined by hundreds of supporters in solidarity in defiance of the 'heartless' State, which called on them to disperse. It is this act of defiance on the part of the people and in empathy with Bouzizi's action that spread like wild fire in the whole country and finally brought down the 23-year corrupt, authoritarian, pro-Western, and crony capitalist regime of Zine Al-Abadine Ben Ali and his family from power. But before his downfall, Ben Ali and his regime had been lauded and held out to be a successful. He was hailed as a wealthy head of a fast-growing and 'most-competitive' economy in Africa even when the population were suffering under the burdens of repression

But this very 'competitive' economy was a monopoly of French interests for it was also true that France alone accounted for 72.5% of the country's imports and 75% of its exports to the European Union. This was this kind of 'success' that the Western world praised and held out to the people of Tunisia as the basis of their existence. In fact, the economy was a dependent economy on the interests of the European and American monopolies and their local cronies, which required an iron-fisted regime to maintain. It constituted the bedrock of inequality between the very opulent and rich class and the impoverished, poor classes agonising against high levels of the unemployment and political repression. This included many jobless university graduates such as Bouzizi who were the victims of a lop-sided economy producing high-priced necessities of life, which the majority of the population could not afford. This was the capitalism that the Tunisian people knew and not the imagined capitalist world of 'successes' of a few cronies who run the Tunisian neo-colonial State. The revolt was an attempt by the people of Tunisia to reconstruct a state that had *feelings* for its people and not one that was merely instrumental in oppressing them.

3. The real capitalist success

Yet it can also be said that what was happening in Tunisia and what later took place in Egypt was the success of capitalism in creating the real conditions that were now being resisted and also in producing individuals and new institutions that were taking a lead in the resistance to a decayed capitalism. The Arab revolutions have been referred to as 'Face Book' revolutions because of their use of rapid communication systems that the Face Book as a social organising network enabled the people to interface and act as one body. The Face Book is a product of capitalism and an extension of the electronic media that Marshall McLuhan (1964), analysed in the 1960s.

We can now recall the work of McLuhan in which he predicted that the visual, individualistic print culture that characterised the early period of capitalism would be brought to an end by what he called "electronic interdependence" in which the electronic media would replace the visual media with an aural/oral culture. In this new age, McLuhan predicted, humankind will move from individualism and fragmentation to a collective identity, with a "tribal base." McLuhan called this emerging social organization the 'global village,' but this village was to be a product of capitalist 'economic globalisation,' which McLuhan and the world had as yet seen in the 1960s. Economic globalisation, as we now know it, dawned on us in the 1980s.

However, McLuhan's most widely known work was: *Understanding Media: The Extensions of Man* which he wrote in 1964. This work was a pioneering study in media theory in which he proposed that the media and not the content they carried should be the focus of study as 'the medium of the message.' McLuhan's argued that a medium affected the society in which it played a role not by the content delivered over it, but by the characteristics of the medium itself. He used the light bulb to demonstrate the new concept he was trying to develop. According to him, a light bulb does not have content in the way that a newspaper has articles or a television has programmes, yet it is a medium that has a social effect; that is, it enables people to create spaces during night time that would otherwise be enveloped by darkness. He described the light bulb as a medium without any content but that it created an environment by its mere presence. He further postulated that content had little effect on society in that it did not matter whether television broadcast children's shows or violent programmes. In either case, the effect of television on society would be identical. He noted that all media had characteristics that engaged the viewer in different ways; for instance, a passage in a book could be reread at will, but a movie had to be screened again in its entirety to study any individual part of it.

In the first part of *Understanding Media,* McLuhan also argued that different media invite different degrees of participation on the part of a person who chooses to consume a medium. Some media, like the movies, were "hot"—that is, they enhance one single sense in this case a vision in such a manner that a person does not need to exert much effort in filling in the details of a movie image. McLuhan contrasted this with "cool" TV, which he claimed required more effort on the part of the viewer to determine meaning, and comics, which due to their minimal presentation of visual detail required a high degree of effort to fill in details that the cartoonist may have intended to portray. A movie was thus said by McLuhan to be "hot", intensifying one single sense "high definition", demanding a viewer's attention, and a comic book was said to be "cool" and "low definition", requiring much more conscious participation by the reader to extract value from it. McLuhan described the term "cool media" as emerging from jazz and popular music and, in this context, it is used to mean "detached." For McLuhan, these two concepts 'hot' and 'cool' were not binary opposites but could co-exist on a continuum: they could be more correctly measured on a scale rather than seen as dichotomous.

Although McLuhan did not say so, his analysis was part of a wider understanding of what the capitalist industrial organisation had achieved in the process of its contradictory development. As we know human labour and technology were the basis of capitalist development. They are counterpoised as necessary opposites in Marx's schema of 'living' labour (of living human labour) and 'dead' labour (existing in the form of machinery) being prerequisites of capitalist industrial production. In the process of production, technology and machinery tend to extend the workers' physical senses and the functions of their bodies (e.g. the eye and the hand). Sequentially, this extension first leads to segmentation and alienation of the individual and hence to his/her feeling a traumatic experience of change in the use of these senses and bodily functions. In short, the traumatic experience creates what McLuhan called a "self-amputation" of the physical senses. This process enables the ruling classes to destabilise and manipulate the working classes as well as exploiting the gender qualities of women by creating new forms of dependence.

But as technology does so, it also impacts on the body to find a new bodily and sensual balance and equilibrium or new rations in order to cope in the new environment. This demand, which occurred with the over-production of commodities caused by technological development, led to the need on the part of individual workers to adjust to new economic and political conditions. Historically this occurred during the Great Depression in the 1930s and the period leading to the Second World War. A process of 'industrialisation of culture' took place in which, according to Brian Milani, there was a 'growing role of culture in the economy.' This resulted in 'new bureaucracies of mental labour' who handled vast amounts of information flows 'necessary to organise mass production and distribution and increasingly complex political systems.' In so doing, this 'industrialisation of culture' accomplished a 'depersonalisation' and 'objectification' of bourgeois class rule by creating new forms of organisation in which labour could be absorbed profitably (Milani, 2000).

Even then, this transformative process had the effect of extending the working individuals' minds and nervous systems (or consciousness), which had different implications than the extension of their muscles and bodies. This was because the period of the intense use of physical labour was no longer necessary with increased technological development for industrial deployment. Therefore the new technological processes tended to integrate rather than segment the workers' sensual balance and this is what enabled them to handle immense flows of information necessary for ever expended production and distribution of commodities-forcing the integration of economic and politics as a new 'culture' under 'integrated' monopoly conditions under which 'scientific management' became a precondition. Fordism and Taylorism were the expression of this development, which created new factors for the exploitation of labour under new conditions.

In terms of the evolution of electronic media in this period, McLuhan suggested that the very speed of electronic change tended to force the individual to forsake processing of reality in analytical, sequential ways. Instead it enabled a processing that acted 'mythically' using all the senses all at once, like hunter gatherers. This state of mind, he pointed out, emphasised 'field consciousness,' which in turn encouraged identity to be derived directly from the mind rather than from the *contents* of the mind. Such a healthy, balanced relationship to the information explosion, which such media brought about, tended to encourage individuals to go beyond processing innumerable bits of information towards *seeing and feeling* the patterns of the *flow of knowledge* and reality in their contexts.

This development made individuals to move away from the domination of visual senses towards an emphasis on *touching and hearing*, which were more inclusive and integrative forms of perception anchored in *sensing* than simply thinking. This brought about a situation of better balanced relationship between mind and body in which the mind became centred in the whole human organism not only in our heads *ala* Descartes. This development had epistemological implications in the way individuals created and used knowledge and information tending towards a transdisciplinary framework. This balanced perception had a fundamentally transformative impact on the individual who increasingly became a more holistic individual who was able to combine real individual autonomy with cooperation with others, say in forming trade unions in defence of their collective interests. Such individual was anchored both internally and externally rendering him/herself flexible and accommodative of others. Such individual, in the words of McLuhan, rendered oneself with a 'psychic mobility,' in that he/she became less self-preoccupied, more sensitive to social context and environment, and more amenable to service. This development implied a human spiritual transformation towards *Ubuntu*. This is what emerges from McLuhan's analysis and can be seen in the current electronic media developments.

This is why although his ideas had undergone a decline since the 1960s; his work is currently undergoing a revival. Wired magazine and various Internet-oriented publications have adopted McLuhan as the patron saint of the digital age. McLuhan's phrases such as the "global village" and the "medium is the message" have provided support for those commentators who view McLuhan as the oracle of the digital era. During the past decade, more than a dozen new books and countless articles have been published focusing on McLuhan's contribution.

In 2001, Posner published a book on: *Public Intellectuals: A Study in Decline*. He defined these individuals as modern intellectuals who are academics but who respond to "market forces" in their non-academic role as commentators on society. Posner further elaborated his definition of "public intellectual" by using a multitiered definition of regarding 'public intellectuals' as "academics writing outside their field" or "writing for a general audience." He contended that because the modern university places such a great emphasis on specialization, which heavily favours depth versus breadth of knowledge, very few academics are trained, or inclined, to play the role of 'public intellectuals.' For him, this narrow training and socialisation process, especially in the United States, explains "why so many of the most distinguished academic public intellectuals active in the second half of the twentieth century were foreigners".

Using Posner's terminology, McLuhan was a 'public intellectual' whose legacy was twofold: First, his emphasis that mass communication has altered our perception of 20th-century life, and secondly, his belief that the content of communication is dictated by its form and not content. According to another scholar, "McLuhan's efforts instilled an urgent awareness of the media environment as a basic force in shaping the modern sensibility." Thus although McLuhan was depicted by his critics as an academic rebel who did not follow an orthodox outlook or doctrine in his writings, his role as a 'public intellectual' operating outside the academic compartmentalisation has rendered his work invaluable to the understanding of current developments such as those in the Arab countries.

Thus while the mass media most prominent in McLuhan's time incorporated a one-to-many broadcasting model, he understood that ultimately it was still up to *each audience member* to control their intake of that media, and to contextualize it in a way that made sense in their own world view. This is what the social networks such as the Face Books, Blogs and the mobile phones have done to empower the individual into active politics. The Face Book and other forms of the social networks have simply extends this natural capability that media in general have acquired. This social media explicitly takes the *one-to-many* model and makes it a *many-to-many* model of communication. The content of social environments is the same as the content regardless of their location. What is important is what you choose to pay attention to and how you make sense of it in your life. This is the significance of McLuhan's work in explaining the current developments, that capitalism has made possible and hence its 'success' in creating conditions for its own demise.

4. The Egyptian Youth Revolution

The developments that arose out of Tunisia and were passed on to Cairo are of tremendous human significance because they point to the way towards a more humanistic future. They manifest the role of an emergent holistic individual seeking not just identity but a new being ness. It is true that we must not regard these developments as a consequence of the communication revolution *per se.* But at the same time, the communication revolution has been important in mobilising people outside the traditional structures such as religion, political parties and social organisations oriented towards a particular political agenda. What social networking had done is to mobilise everyone everywhere to act, think, relate and bring about change in a more direct way in a desired general direction. Social networking has raised the acquired social consciousness and turned it into a mass revolutionary action.

Of course the material conditions in which this has arisen is fundamental to the process, as we have noted in the case of Tunisia. But the current moment calls for a heightened consciousness which is necessary for the emergence of a new society. This is why the spiritual aspect is of uttermost importance to emphasise at this moment. The Face Book and other social media alone could not have raised and maintained the 'will to power' of the masses without the non-stop global cable TV networks such as Al-Jazeera, CNN, and BBC and their 'Breaking News' every few hours. These public media supplemented the social network, especially when the latter had been disconnected by the dictators. These 24-hour global news networks, the products of a decaying capitalism, were part and parcel of this exposure of the inequities and indignities of the global capitalist economic and political order that the people struggled to dismantle.

To be sure, when the now renamed April 6th Youth Movement took shape in Tahrir Square in Cairo it did so as a demand for freedom, dignity, and equality. According to Francis Kornegay (2011), writing in a new magazine in Johannesburg, although this outbreak of anger appeared a spontaneous 'Face Book' phenomenon, in fact the outburst had been at least five years in preparation on the basis of a new generation pan-Arab youth collaborating between Tunisia and Egypt. The Muslim Brotherhood seems to have played a role in this respect and the Friday Prayers were also an element in this mobilisation, but by no means the inspirers of the new movement. Indeed, Kornegay argues that this uprising may have signalled the death-knell of jihadism and its sectarian agenda, "which actually converges with the region's conservative authoritarian status-quo." In the case of Egypt, there had been a "bottom-up" revolution very much assisted by the new social networking, but which partly vested its faith in "military guardianship." Kornegay further argues that Tahrir was 'essentially bourgeois ruction.'

Nevertheless, he also argues that this kind of analysis may be 'mere squabbling' because the real impact of the revolt went far beyond such descriptions. Khadija Sharife writing in the same magazine argues that the mass youth-fuelled revolt cut across class, gender, religious and age divides, which had profound impact on Egyptian, Middle East and African sub-regions. This is why in order to prevent the 'contagion' from spreading, the elite army officers, capitalists and the remnants of the old political order-working together with their international backers and controllers-will seek to exercise hegemony over the pace, direction, form and content of the revolutionary process.

But it is necessary to analyse and try to understand in a transdisciplinary manner this 'revolutionary process' if we are not to lose sight of these very important developments. These developments are already being felt even in the African continent as a whole. They are also defining the policies of major powers such as the United States in dealing with these countries, especially in their relationship with Israel. If indeed the uprisings- although youth-fuelled- did in fact "cut across class, gender, religion and age, then we have to try to understand what it was that the revolts were about. Indeed, calling the Egyptian uprising 'bourgeois ruction' as Kornegay tries to do may indeed turn out to be so much 'squabbling' as he himself admits.

In order to understand the force behind these revolts, let us again recall the origins of the revolt in Tunisia and the reasons behind them. As we have seen, the revolts arose as an expression of solidarity in empathy with Bouzizi and his family in the way the agents of the State had treated Bouzizi. There are several elements from which we can draw a kind of résumé of his revolt: *unemployment, lack of food and other necessities of life, lack of opportunities of advancement, corruption on the part of the State officials, brutality of the police and other security agencies, demand for dignity, demand for equality, demand for citizenship, lack of empathy for the sufferings of the masses of the people by the State, capitalist cronyism, kleptocracy on the part of the ruling family, authoritarianism and dictatorial governance.*

If the elements in this résumé are put together, analysed and synthesised, it becomes clear that these concerns and demands of the people are *qualitative* in nature rather than *quantitative*. This can be illustrated by an incident, which occurred during the Tahrir square demonstrations when the then President Hosni Mubarak tried to calm down the tempers of the demonstrators by increasing the salaries of public workers by fifty percent. The gesture was rebuffed and laughed at by the crowd who responded by stating that what they were demonstrating against was his despotic rule and not salaries and that in any case the majority of them were unemployed to deserve such an increase! They retorted that what they were demanding was his immediate departure and towards this demand they declared one Friday in February to be his "Day of Departure." They were demanding, they retorted, 'freedom,' 'dignity,' and 'equality.' These were all qualitative demands.

As we have indicated above, and arising from Marshall McLuhan's analysis, there was a spiritual transformation in this emerging 'holistic individuals' who together with others were united in empathy and solidarity in these demands. McLuhan argued that the very speed of electronic change, which was occurring during his time but which had become speedier and speedier with the passage of time, tended to force the individual to forsake processing of reality in analytic and sequential way. This was essential, he added, in order to take the process 'mythically' all at once using all our senses. In this situation, the state of mind, tended to emphasise 'field consciousness,' which in turn encouraged identity to be derived from the mind rather than from the *contents* of the mind. Such a healthy, balanced relationship to the information explosion, which such media brought about, encouraged holistic individuals to go beyond the mere processing of innumerable bits of information towards *seeing and feeling.* Such a healthy balance of mind and body also tried to identify the patterns of the *flow of knowledge* and *reality* in their contexts.

This development had also epistemological implications in the way the holistic individuals created and used knowledge and information. The creation and using of such information was towards wholeness rather than segmentation. Such a development had fundamentally a transformative impact on the individual who now increasingly becomes more of a holistic individual who combines real individual autonomy with the need to cooperate with others. Such an individual is anchored both internally and externally rendering his/her self-flexible and accommodative of others. The new individual becomes less self-preoccupied, more sensitive to social context and environment, and more amenable to service to others. As we concluded above, this development implies a human spiritual transformation towards *Ubuntu-the African philosophy of recognising others as part of oneself.*

5. Ubuntu-an African contribution

But what do all these developments suggest for Africa if indeed the transformation of the capitalist individual leads to a spiritual transformation of such individual to *Ubuntu*, which the Umuntu believes in? It is clear that despite the fragmentation and marginalisation that modernity has imposed on the people of Africa, elements of *Ubuntu* still exist in the African societies through their languages, cultures and knowledge systems. *Ubuntu* seeks a *restoration* of balance in relations between individuals *inter se* and between individuals and nature. In the new situation in which the holistic individuals now find themselves united in solidarity-no longer alienated and isolated, they find *Abantu* in existence with elements of *Ubuntu* still with them. The formerly alienated but now holistic individuals find themselves already embedded in the culture of *Ubuntu* in a new form, which McLuhan's analysis seems to suggest. Such new environment requires that in order to fit in the new combined human environment of interconnectedness and wholeness, such new combined individuals have to make their rules of a restorative society on an on-going basis.

Already academic researchers are beginning to examine this new situation by exploring the parallels between online social networking and the practices of 'tribal' societies that McLuhan envisaged. In the collective profile-surfing essential for 'face booking,' 'My spacing' and 'New life' in which they try to engage in "friending," they begin to see the resurgence of ancient patterns of oral communication. Lance Strate, a communications professor at Fordham University and devoted 'MySpacer' has argued that "Orality, which is characteristic of African communication, is the basis of all human experience." He is convinced that the popularity of social networks stems from their appeal to deep-seated, prehistoric patterns of human communication and points out that humans evolved with speech and not with writing. This is in fact what we have called Afrikology (Nabudere, 2011).

Indeed. the growth of social networks — and the Internet as a whole — stem largely from an outpouring of expression that often feels more like "talking" rather than writing. Such activities as blog posting, comments writing, homemade videos and, lately, an outpouring of epigrammatic one-liners broadcast using services like Twitter and Face Book status updates point to such a new culture based on oral 'tribal' communication. Irwin Chen has observed: "If you examine the Web through the lens of Orality, you cannot help but see it everywhere." Irwin Chen is a design instructor at Parsons University who is developing a new course to explore the emergence of oral culture online. He argues that "Orality is participatory, interactive, and communal and focused on the present. The Web is all of these things."

This validates the work of an early student of electronic Orality, Walter J. Ong, who was a professor at St. Louis University and student of Marshall McLuhan. He is the one who coined the term "Secondary Orality" in 1982 to describe the tendency of electronic media to echo the cadences of earlier oral cultures. The work of Walter Ong, who died in 2003, seems especially prescient in light of the social-networking phenomenon that is taking place and which points towards Ubuntu as a culture of the future. "Oral communication," according to him, "unites people in groups." In other words, oral culture means more than just talking. It implies subtler, and perhaps more important — social dynamics at work of coalescing (Ong, 2002).

Another scholar has noted: "In tribal cultures, your identity is completely wrapped up in the question of how people know you." He adds: "When you look at Face Book, you can see the same pattern at work: people projecting their identities by demonstrating their relationships to each other." According to him, "You define yourself in terms of who your friends are." In 'tribal' societies, he adds, people routinely give each other jewellery, weapons, and ritual objects to cement their social ties." Similarly, on Face Book, people accomplish the same thing by trading symbolic sock monkeys, disco balls and hula girls. "It's reminiscent of how people exchange gifts in tribal cultures," says Dr. Strate, whose 'MySpace' page lists his 1,335 "friends" along with his academic credentials and his predilection for "Battlestar Galactica." These are comparisons which are 'virtual' and need to be 'actualized' through Ubuntu and holistic living in real communities. There are big differences between real oral cultures and the virtual kind. In tribal societies, forging social bonds is a matter of survival; on the Internet, far less so, although there is an element of the search for spiritual survival (Strate *et al.,* 2003).

Then there's the question of who really counts as a "friend." In tribal societies, people develop bonds through direct, ongoing face-to-face contact. The Web eliminates that need for physical proximity, enabling people to declare friendships on the basis of otherwise flimsy connections. There are deep differences between real 'tribal' networking and modern 'social networks' in that sense. With social networks, there's a fascination with intimacy because it simulates face-to-face communication. But there's also this fundamental distance of distance which makes it safe for people to connect through weak ties where they can have the appearance of a connection because it's safe. Therefore, while 'tribal' networking and cultures typically engage in highly formalized rituals; modern social networks seem to encourage a level of casualness and familiarity that would be unthinkable in traditional oral cultures.

Therefore, new holistic societies can only learn something from 'tribal' societies, but cannot live them. To construct a new society they need to proceed by writing or making rules as they go on but with the fundamental lesson that this must recognize human interconnectedness and beingness in Ubuntu. According to Dr. Strate the sheer popularity of social networking seems to suggest that for many people, these social networking environments strike a deep, perhaps even primal chord inside them to which they want to link. According to him such yearnings "fulfil our need to be recognized as human beings, and as members of a community." He adds, "We all want to be told: You exist." In fact, Dr Strate should have put it in a proper Ubuntu way: "I exist, because you exist." This is the way to go.

What then can we say the people in Tahrir Square were demanding when they talked of a new democracy that respects their human dignity and equality? Can it not be surmised that what they really demanded was a state that has a feeling and empathy for their needs and concerns. Can we say that perhaps they were demanding a *new State that has feelings like a human being,* which moreover can demonstrate its feelings for the people rather than through dictates? Can we say that such a State is possible because by its very nature a State monopolises all means of violence, which it has invariably used against its citizens without any feelings for those citizens. In short, a modern State (especially the post-colonial State) brutalises its citizens and at the same time claims to represent them, which is a contradiction in terms.

Perhaps if such a new State that has feelings for its citizens is impossible to imagine, then what the demonstrators really demanded was that they themselves should constitute a 'State' or 'Community' in which the functions of the State are assumed by the individuals themselves. This happened in the 'tribal' societies, but also in the polis in Athens. Is this perhaps what Marx meant when he predicted the 'withering away of the state?' But Marx regarded such a situation as leading to 'communism' in which there was equality for everyone. Is this perhaps the kind of 'communal' society that is imagined by the social networks? If so how can it be actualised beyond the 'virtual' "Communities" that the social networks have created? This is perhaps the task that is implied by the current revolutions.

Marshall McLuhan aptly observes in his book, *Laws of Media* that as the information that constitutes our environment is perpetually in flux, so there is need to be flexible and not anchored in fixed concepts. He advocated the adopting of ancient skills which can enable us to navigate through an ever uncharted and unchartable milieu. Therefore, our "uncharted and unchartable" world that is before us seems to sum up our new opportunities. But in order to arrive at our uncharted future we need to take the following considerations into account. We must be able to:

- *perceive* the complexity of the environments with which we have to deal;
- *focus* appropriately on the critical factors that influence complex relationships;
- *resolve* the tension between intention and emergence of reality.

These ideas are derived from Social Networking whose objective is to move towards a new world driven by Ubuntu philosophy. We can try them out as we go on so long as we do not stop asking questions.

6. Conclusion

Thus, we come to the conclusion that the capitalist crisis under way in the world is not another 'industrial cycle' which can be resolved with another Keynesian recipe. It is terminal for capitalism and new forces are emerging to challenge any attempt at its re-emergence. What seems to be emerging from the womb of the collapsing global capitalist system are new social forces who are demanding a new world in which personal greed behind the capitalist accumulation, which is behind the crisis, gives way to a more humanistic, sharing and caring system nurtured by economic and social relationships. They also demand a more caring state system, which at bottom, demands new responsibilities from the holistic individuals to manage such caring public relationships. Does this imply the 'disappearing' of the state in the form we have known it or does it lead to a new state systems based on *glocal* citizenships?

References

McLuhan, M. (1964), *Understanding Media: the Extensions of Man*, New York: McGraw-Hill.

Milani, B. (2000), *Designing the Green Economy: the Postindustrial Alternative to Corporate Globalization*, Maryland: Rowman and Littlefield.

Nabudere, D.W. (1989), *The Crash of International Finance-Capital and its Implications for the Third World*, Oxford: Fahamu Books and Pambazuka Press Publication.

Nabudere, D.W. (1990), *The Rise and Fall of Money-Capital*, London: Africa in Transition Trust.

Nabudere, D.W. (2011), *Afrikology, Philosophy and Wholeness: an Epistemology*, Pretoria: Africa Institute of South Africa Press.

Ong, W.J. (2002), *Orality and literacy: the Technology of the Word*, New York: Routledge, Francis & Taylor Group.

Posner, R.A. (2001), *Public Intellectuals: a Study of Decline*, Cambridge, MA: Harvard University Press.

Strate, L., Jacobson, R. L. and Gibson, S. B. (2003), *Communication and Cyberspace: Social Interaction in an Electronic Environment*, New York: Hampton Press.

The Sunday Monitor (2008), 'Bunyoro, Mengo Courting Trouble'. *The Monitor (Uganda)*, October 12, 2008. Available at http://www.accessmylibrary.com/article-1G1-187086425/bunyoro-mengo-courting-trouble.html.

16

The Technology Innovation Agency (TIA):

A Public Support Mechanism for Technological Innovation in a Developing Country

Dhesigen Naidoo[1]

The Rationale for TIA

The notion of a National System of Innovation (NSI) and the role of science and technology in a NSI first appeared in the South African government national policy dialogue during the development of the Science and Technology White Paper (Republic of South Africa, 1996).

This was subsequently reaffirmed in the National Research and Development Strategy (NRDS) (Republic of South Africa, 2002).The National R&D Strategy went on to further examine the concept of South Africa's "Innovation Chasm" as described in Figure 1.

This is a concept that combines the notions of the "European Paradox" and the American 'Valley of Death. The scientific version of the European Paradox describes the state of affairs that while Europe produces outstanding academics and knowledge as witnessed by such parameters as the number of Nobel Prize winners, it tends to lag behind the US, Japan and more recently China and Republic of Korea as far as dominance of the technology market

1 Director of Research and Innovation of the University of Pretoria, Republic of South Africa, Email: dhesigen.naidoo@up.ac.za

is concerned. The "Valley of Death" in the United States of America describes a funding void for innovation and product development, even in the situation where there is substantive funding for research and where there is a developed market for technology based goods.The South African Innovation Chasm as described in the NRDS (Republic of South Africa, 2002) and Kaplan (2008) goes further and combines these two challenges with a third i.e. knowledge generated in South Africa and shared globally through such mechanisms as publications as well as information exchange is sometimes developed in products and services elsewhere in the world. These are then bought by South Africa at high prices. This is an exacerbated scenario of exporting both knowledge and hard currency.

Figure 1: Bridging the South African Innovation Chasm

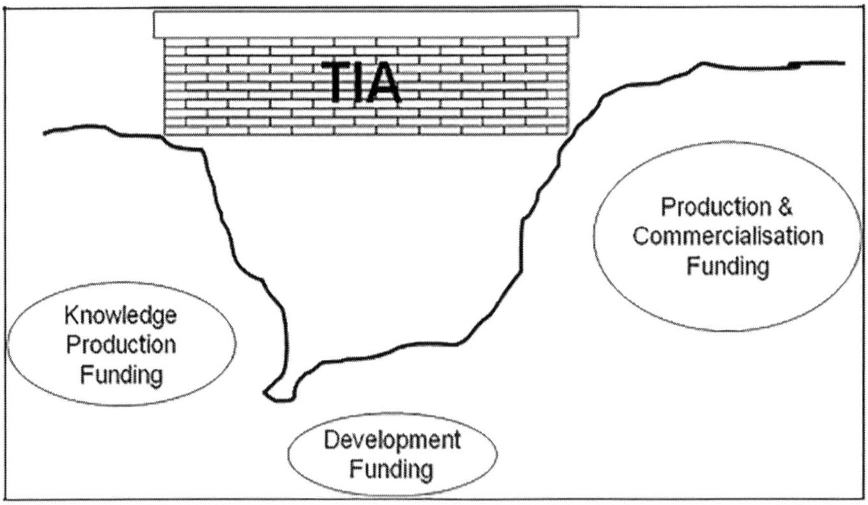

(Source: Adapted from the Draft Foundation for Technology Innovation Conceptual Framework, 2007)

The South African Innovation Chasm is composed of three distinct components:

- A funding support gap for innovation and product development.This was recognized as a market failure as the funding sources, both public and private funded either research or the commercialization of finished products, not the innovation and development of new products and services.

- A cultural gap associated with a South African dominant view that research and development of new technology based products was the privy of developed countries and the best developing countries could do was as best organize to be early adopters.
- A capacity gap particular with regard to the human capital for innovation. This would range from the product development expertise all the way through to entrepreneurship skills and the various support capacities that would be required.

The National Research and Development Strategy (Republic of South Africa, 2002) proposed the development of a public agency then called the Foundation for Technological Innovation (FTI) to address this gap. In the interim South Africa progressively set up a national Innovation Fund (IF) to begin this experiment. In time this was followed by the establishment of four Biotechnology Regional Innovation centres, the BRICS and a national support agency for plant biotechnology based product development in the form of a trust called PlantBio.Such support instruments were also set up in other sectors. Examples include the Advanced Manufacturing Technology Strategy (AMTS) and the Advanced Minerals Initiative (AMI). In parallel ***thedti*** in South Africa initiated the THRIP (Technology and Human Resources for Industry Programme), the SPII (Support Programme for Industrial Innovation) focused on small and medium enterprises and PII (Programme for Industrial Innovation) aimed at supporting large industries.

Establishing the TIA

South Africa's national system of innovation has developed a substantial repository of local knowledge.This, however, has minimal influence on the real economy currently. This is exacerbated by a number of impediments to productivity and technological innovation, including, amongst others, a lack of access to adequate financing (and particularly seed and first-stage financing); market inefficiencies; a relatively weak and uncoordinated Intellectual Property (IP) rights framework; as well as a lack of institutional coordination and alignment within the national system of innovation.These constraints together with the encouragement from the relative success of the interim support instruments have galvanized South African Government support for the development of a single public agency in the form envisaged in the concept of the FTI (Department of Science and Technology, 2007). This has since been renamed the Technology Innovation Agency or TIA.

Further support came from the results of the South African National R&D Surveys: National Survey of Research and Experimental Development for the fiscal year 2004/5 (2006) (HSRC, 2007a) as well as the South African Innovation Survey Highlights, 2007 (HSRC, 2007b) from the first National Innovation Survey conducted by the Centre for science, technology and innovation indicators (CESTII) at the HSRC. The former confirmed an increasing R&D expenditure approaching 1% of GDP.The latter indicated that the industry partners were not looking to the knowledge producing institutions like universities and research institutions for new knowledge and know how on product development and innovation.This provided further impetus to provide support to convert the knowledge generated into products for the real economy. The OECD review of the South African NSI (OECD, 2007) confirmed the need for a public support instrument to bridge the innovation chasm.

In this context, the motivation for the Technology Innovation Agency (TIA) is to develop a public institution that, together with private sector partners where appropriate, develops the capability of enhancing the country's capacity towards translating a greater proportion of local research and development (R&D) into commercial products and services.

An international benchmarking study was conducted by the DST in order to learn from successful models that could inform the development of TIA. The following institutions were examined- TEKES in Finland, VINNOVA in Sweden, the Canadian Foundation for Innovation (CFI), the Malaysian Technology Development Corporation, Innovation Norway and the Foundation for Innovation and Technology Transfer (FITT) in India.

Some of the key learning informed that since investments for bringing new technology products and services to the market require substantial amounts of resources and the corporate form of the TIA should be able to generate additional revenue for re-investment into the system through equity shareholding and the facilitation of venture capital financing, amongst other things.

The TIA was designed to build on the capacity that already existed in the system. Institutions such as the Innovation Fund and the Biotechnology Regional Innovation Centres (BRICs) have already implemented systems and processes, which will be incorporated into and further refined by the TIA in a manner that extracts synergies from existing relationships and infrastructure in order to ensure the rapid acceleration of service delivery.

Legislation and Objectives

The TIA Bill was developed and gazetted for public comment in August 2007. After a vibrant stakeholder participation process led by the Parliamentary Portfolio Committee on Science and Technology of the General Assembly and the Select Committee of the National Council of Provinces, the bill was passed as the Technology Innovation Agency Act of 2008 (Republic of South Africa, 2008).

The Act provides for the appointment of the TIA Board, Executive and staff and sets out the objects, powers and functions of the Agency, which are, amongst other things to:

I. Support the State in stimulating and intensifying technological innovation and invention in order to improve economic growth and the quality of life of all South Africans by developing and exploiting technological innovations and inventions.
II. Provide financial assistance to any person, consortium, or enterprise for the purpose of enabling that person, consortium or enterprise to develop any technological innovation or invention.
III. Draw together and integrate the management of disparate technological innovation, inventions, incubation and diffusion initiatives in South Africa.
IV. Develop the national capacity and infrastructure to protect and exploit intellectual property derived from publicly financed research.

The Objectives and Functions of the TIA

Taking into account South Africa's national context and international lessons learnt the key objectives of the TIA are to:

1. Provide the primary bridge between the formal knowledge base and the real economy;
2. Stimulate the development of technology based products and services;
3. Stimulate the development of technology based enterprises – both public and private;
4. Develop a significant technology base for the South African economy;
5. Provide an Intellectual Property protection support platform;
6. Stimulating investment – including through facilitating Venture Capital, Foreign Direct Investment (FDI) in R&D; and to,
7. Facilitate the development of Human Capital for Innovation.

The TIA's mission and strategic objectives will be achieved through the discharge of itscore function of managing, coordinating and integrating all innovation activities by way of:

- Acting as a single contact point for all innovation-related matters;
- Managing IP related to innovation;
- Enabling and motivating the private sector to participate in the innovation industry;
- Promoting the innovation industry; and
- Building capacity.
-

Figure 2: Contextualizing the TIA

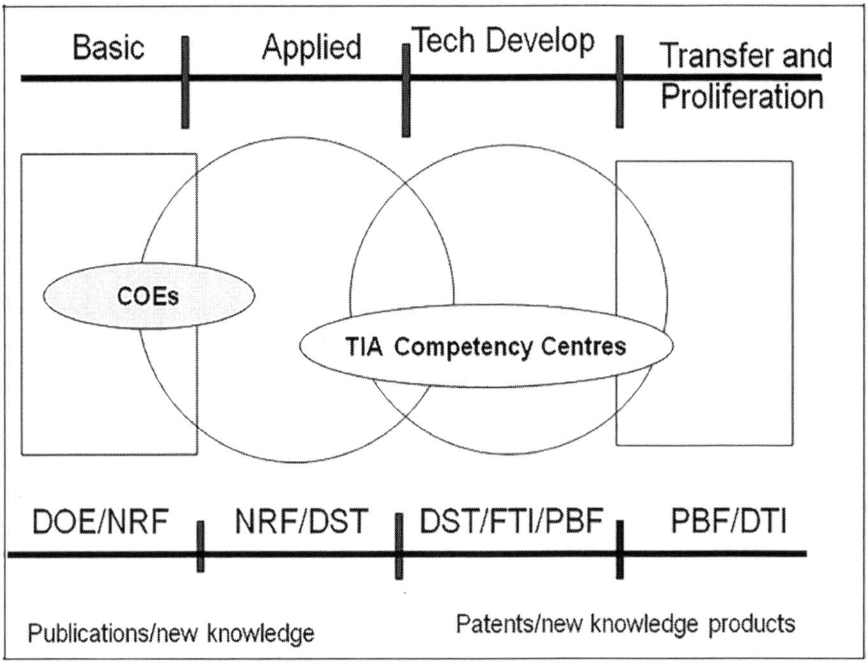

The TIA will not engage in fundamental scientific research, but will be concerned with identifying and evaluating available and new technologies. It will also provide shared R&D as well as technical business and commercialisation services for existing and emerging industries.

The TIA operational design also includes the provision of IP protection and support services, as well as Venture Capital facilitation and business process development in order to enable the development of new technology based or driven enterprises.

Another core element of the design is Human Capital Development, throughout the innovation chain. The proposed Competency Centres or 'Centres of Excellence for Innovation' will be the primary instrument of the TIA in this regard.

These structures will also serve to facilitate and consolidate linkages between national, provincial and local innovation policy and support measures. This is illustrated by Figure 2. The TIA will support the activities in the late applied research phase into the product/technology development and into the beginnings of the transfer and proliferation/commercialization phases. The Department of Education (DOE), the Department of Science and Technology (DST) and the National Research Foundation (NRF) suites of funding instruments will continue to support research and the department of trade and industry (DTI) and its related agencies will use their support instruments to support the technology transfer and commercialization activities. The Public Benefit Foundation (PBF) is envisaged as a TIA-likeagency with support instruments for the transfer of knowledge and innovations for public good.

Conclusions

South Africa's approach of creating an enabling environment towards stimulating and exploiting technological innovation is premised on a more enduring definition of sustainable, long-term economic growth through technological innovation.This is one which includes spin-off ventures and the commercialization of discoveries.This will support improvements to society and the quality of life of all South Africans.

Drawing on some international experiences and considering South Africa's own innovation development challenges and opportunities, the implications for the form, function and objectives of a TIA for the country is that of a public institution that develops a significant and commercially viable technology base for the country through:

- Stimulating the development of technology based products and services;
- Stimulating the development of technology based public and private enterprises;
- Providing an Intellectual Property (IP) support platform;
- Stimulating investment: and particularly towards higher-risk Venture Capital funding (particularly also for start-up and "first adopters");
- Providing an interface and promoting active collaboration between government, industry and academia and international FDI sources;

- Actively monitoring developments in national and international technological innovation trends with a view to accruing and providing accurate management information for decision-makers in all sectors;
- Facilitating the development of Human Capital for Innovation;
- Connecting technology entrepreneurs and enterprises with real opportunities towards greater competitiveness
- Increasing value added and finished goods exports

South Africa's experiences together with the more established experiences of other developing countries like Malaysia and India should be considered byAfrican partners who are considering developing new institutional frameworks to stimulate the development of a national knowledge economy base through protecting and harvesting locally produced and in particular indigenous knowledge through innovation, product development and commercialization as a principle element of national development strategies.

References

Department of Science and Technology (2007), 'Foundation for Technological Innovation (FTI): Conceptual Framework,' (Unpublished Draft), Pretoria: Government of South Africa.

Human Sciences Research Council (HSRC), South Africa (2007a), *National Survey of Research and Experimental Development for the fiscal year 2004/5 (2006)*, Pretoria: Government of South Africa.

Human Sciences Research Council (HSRC), South Africa (2007b), *South African Innovation Survey Highlights*, Pretoria: Government of South Africa.

Kaplan D. (2008), 'Science and Technology Policy in South Africa: Past performance and proposals for the future,' in *Science, Technology and Society*, 13(1):95-122.

OECD (2007), *Peer Review of South Africa's Innovation Policy*, Draft Report, Paris: OECD.

Republic of South Africa (2002), *The National Research and Development Strategy of South Africa*, Pretoria: Government of South Africa.

Republic of South Africa (2008), *The Technology Innovation Agency Act*, Pretoria: Government of South Africa.

Republic of South Africa, Department of Arts, Culture, Science and Technology (1996), 'Preparing for the 21st Century,' *White Paper on Science and Technology*: Pretoria: Government of South Africa.

17

Post Scriptum

Mammo Muchie & Angathevar Baskaran

The time for Africans to live in a human and naturewellbeinganchored life-world should not be delayedany more. It is the timenow to make the African future brighter rather than making predictive lamentations. The additive and multiplicative well-being for all the African people has to be systematically pursued. There is now a demographic explosion and climate change with informal and agriculture economy remaining still largely where most of the African people live. The world is also at a timein what is being described as surveillance capitalism, which is connected to the knowledge, digital, artificial intelligence, internet of things, mobile miracle, robotics, machine learning, disruptive and exponential technology stage of the fourth industrial revolution.

Africa to be innovative and renascent, there is a need to create an African Innovation System by re-framing and re-designingthe value chain from production to consumption by the inclusion of African reality, knowledge and context.

The African innovation system has to include African integration, sustainable development, capacity building for all Africans, especially the youth and build human and social capital to realise the unity and renaissance to create smart, green and well-being anchored Africa.

There is a need to develop the African innovation and development system. There is no need to continue copying and mimicking the national innovation system from western countries. Africa has not been able to unite the 55 states made by boundaries drawn during the colonial era to put on the agenda the Making of the African Innovation System that we published about in 2003.

It is critical to re-define innovation to relate to African associational values. In general, innovation has been defined with novelty and usefulness. But how have novelty and usefulness been validated? They have been validated narrowly by commerce and market that individuals through competition gain. The validation criteria for both novelty and usefulness have to be transformed. There should be an inclusion of collaborative innovative engagement, to produce and provide wellbeing, services provision, environmental protection, humanitarian criteria above the current dominant validation by merely market, commerce and economics including the current dominating e-commerce expansion. There is a need also to relate it to Africa's associational relations rather than the individualistic and egoistic commerce validating preferences that have influenced governance, leadership, institutions and systems making corruption in Africa the unending curse.

In Africa, the development also should not be measured merely by economic growth. A county may have rapid economic growth but not development that transforms, performs and reforms the livelihood of the people. Development should also be re-conceptualised beyond aid, loans and debts. A country with huge debt faces the challenge to pay debt despite whatever level of economic development it can find itself in. Development should be anchored on how the wellbeing of people and nature are promoted to create a society where no citizen begs, where no one starves and where no one is homeless and all have opportunities to learn and work, invent, innovate and create with collaboration to make everyone live a decent life.

There is a need now to build new synergy between the African innovative, renascent, integrated and sustainable development and innovation systems. Economic gain to make a profit is not sufficient. The African contextualised conceptual and theoretical framework of the innovation and development system can re-engineer African unity, renaissance and empowerment of all Africans to own rich Africa's resources with fulsome social-wellbeing and environmental protection gains. We need to synergise and not prioritize the economic or commercial variable gain by excluding the social capital, human capital, well-being, and environmental gains to reframe at the conceptual level, the African innovation and development.

Both the dominant development and innovation theories have evolved mainly dominated by economics. There is also the need to generate problem-based knowledge creation by applying all the disciplines using the unity of knowledge including the currently excluded and largely unrecognised rich African knowledge and spiritual heritage. There is a need to deal with all

Africa's specific problems and challenges by drawing from all the sciences, engineering and technologies with the African-contextualised unified conceptual framing by linking the re-designed and re-worked integrated African innovation system with tangible and measurable sustainable developmental renascent comprehensive outcomes.

Africa has suffered in the first, second and third industrial revolutions. Africa should not suffer in the current 4th and the coming 5th Industrial Revolutions by creating the African innovation, renascent, integrated, sustainable development system to make all Africans live decent lives always and ever.

Notes on Contributors

Angathevar Baskaran
Associate Professor, Department of Development Studies, Faculty of Economics and Administration, University of Malaya, Malaysia; Senior Research Associate of SARChI (Innovation & Development), Tshwane University of Technology, Pretoria, South Africa. Email: baskaran@um.edu.my & anga_bas@yahoo.co.uk

Mammo Muchie
DST/NRF SARChI Professor (Innovation & Development), Tshwane University of Technology, South Africa; Technology and Management Centre for Development (TMCD), Oxford University, UK; Associate Faculty Professor, Sussex University, UK; Adama Science and Technology University (ASTU), Ethiopia. Email: MuchieM@tut.ac.za

Steve Onyeiwu
Department of Economics, Allegheny College, Meadville, Pennsylvania 16335, USA. Email: sonyeiwu@allegheny.edu

Jan Peuckert
Department of Innovation Economics of the Berlin Institute of Technology. Email: jan.peuckert@tu-berlin.de

Jorge Gonçalves
Department of Innovation Economics of the Berlin Institute of Technology. E jorgedbg@gmail.com

Alan Ayinde Ezekiel
Department of Agricultural Economics, Ladoke Akintola University of Technology, P.M.B. 4000, Ogbomoso, Oyo State, Nigeria. Email: aaezekiel@lautech.edu.ng

Opeyemi Eyitayo Ayinde
Department of Agricultural Economics and Farm Management, University of Ilorin, Ilorin, Nigeria. Department of Agricultural Environmental, Development and Economics, Ohio State University, Columbus, Ohio, USA. Email: opeayinde@yahoo.com & opeyemiayinde@gmail.com

Matthew Olaniyi Adewumi
Department of Agricultural Economics and Farm Management, University of Ilorin, Nigeria. Email: matolade@yahoo.co.uk

Julius Ecuru
Blekinge Institute of Technology, Sweden and Makerere University, Uganda. Email: Julius.ecuru@gmail.com; Julius.ecuru@bth.se.

Lena Trojer
Professor, Blekinge Institute of Technology, Sweden. Email: lenatrojer@gmail.com.

Ziraba N. Yasin
Senior Lecturer, Makerere University, Kampala, Uganda. Email: ynziraba@tech.mak.ac.ug.

Peter O. Lating
Senior Lecturer, Makerere University, Uganda. Email: plating@tech.mak.ac.ug.

Michael Gastrow
Research Specialist, Education, Science and Skills Development Research Programme, Human Sciences Research Council, Cape Town, South Africa. Email: mgastrow@hsrc.ac.za

Ariel Gordon
Research Professor, Centro Redes and Universidad, Nacional de Quilmes, Argentina. Mansilla 2698 2° piso, C1425BDP Buenos Aires. E-mail: agordon@unq.edu.ar

Jacques Gaillard
Senior scientist at the Institut de Recherche pour le Développement (IRD), UMR 201 Development and Societies (University Paris 1 Panthéon-Sorbonne/IRD), member of the « Institut Francilien Recherche, Innovation et Société » and Labex « Sciences, Innovations, et Techniques en Société » (SITES), France. Email: jacques.gaillard@ird.fr

Anne Marie Gaillard
Consultant (Social Anthropologist). Email: anmagaill@gmail.com

Oluseye Oladayo Jegede
Department of Information and Knowledge Management, College of Business and Economics, University of Johannesburg, South Africa. Email: oluseyej@uj.ac.za, oluseyejegede@gmail.com

Geoffrey G. Gachino
Assistant Professor and Assistant Dean, College of Business Administration, University of Dubai, United Arab Emirates. Email: geoffrey.gachino@gmail.com or ggachino@ud.ac.ae

Billy Adegbola Oluwale
African Institute for Science Policy and Innovation, Obafemi Awolowo University, Ile-Ife, Nigeria. Email: adegbolaoluwale@gmail.com

Blessing Funke Ajao
Cyber Security Analyst, Willis College, 1200 St Laurent Blvd, Ottawa, ONK1K 3B8, Canada. Email: blessingfunkeajao@gmail.com

Emmanuel Makanjuola Ogunjeilua
Department of Entrepreneurship, Joseph Ayo Babalola University, Ikeji Arakeji, Nigeria. Email: makanjuola19@gmail.com

Mawuena Aggey
Research Scientist, CSIR-Institute of Industrial Research, P. O. Box LG576, Legon, Ghana. Email: aggeym@yahoo.com.

Nana K.T. Ghartey
Senior Research Fellow in Social Economics, Centre for Development Studies, University of Cape Coast, Ghana. Email: kwamtech@yahoo.com

Charles Kweku Brown
Professor in Development Studies, Centre for Development Studies, University of Cape Coast, Ghana.

Adele Botha
Meraka Institute, CSIR, PO Box 395, Pretoria, South Africa & North West Living Lab, Potchefstroom, South Africa, Email: abotha@csir.co.za.

Marlien Herselman
Meraka Institute, CSIR, PO Box 395, Pretoria, South Africa & North West Living Lab, Potchefstroom, South Africa, Email: mherselman@csir.co.za.

Ronel Smith
Meraka Institute, CSIR, PO Box 395, Pretoria, South Africa & North West Living Lab, Potchefstroom, South Africa, Email: rsmith2@csir.co.za.

Hendri Coetzee
Meraka Institute, CSIR, PO Box 395, Pretoria, South Africa & North West Living Lab, Potchefstroom, South Africa, Email: hendri@researchlogisitcs.co.za

Enwere Dike
Department of Economics, Kogi State University, Anyigba, Kogi State, Nigeria, Email: meidike@yahoo.com

Kanayo Ogujiuba
Department of Economics, Kogi State University, Anyigba, Kogi State, Nigeria.

Ibukun James Olaoye
Department of Agricultural Economics and Farm Management, University of Ilorin, Ilorin, Nigeria. Email: olaoyeibikunjames@gmail.com

Adeola Oreoluwa Oloyede
Department of Agricultural Economics and Farm Management, University of Ilorin, Ilorin, Nigeria. Email: oloyedeadeola@gmail.com

Dani W. Nabudere
(Late) Former Vice Chancellor, Marcus Garvey University, Upper Mooni, Mbale, Uganda.

Dhesigen Naidoo
Director of Research and Innovation of the University of Pretoria, Republic of South Africa, Email: dhesigen.naidoo@up.ac.za

Index

A

B

C

D

E

F

G

H

M

N

O

P

Q

R

S

T

U

V

W

Z